THE PRESIDENCY AND THE AMERICAN STATE

Miller Center Studies on the Presidency

GUIAN A. MCKEE AND
MARC J. SELVERSTONE, EDITORS

THE PRESIDENCY AND THE AMERICAN STATE

Leadership and Decision Making in the Adams, Grant, and Taft Administrations

Stephen J. Rockwell

University of Virginia Press • *Charlottesville and London*

Published in association with the University of Virginia's
Miller Center of Public Affairs

University of Virginia Press
© 2023 Stephen J. Rockwell
All rights reserved
Printed in the United States of America on acid-free paper

First published 2023

9 8 7 6 5 4 3 2 1

Library of Congress Cataloging-in-Publication Data

Names: Rockwell, Stephen J., author.
Title: The presidency and the American State : leadership and decision making in the Adams, Grant, and Taft administrations / Stephen J. Rockwell.
Description: Charlottesville : University of Virginia Press, 2023. | Series: Miller Center studies on the presidency | Includes bibliographical references and index.
Identifiers: LCCN 2023013093 (print) | LCCN 2023013094 (ebook) | ISBN 9780813950075 (hardcover) | ISBN 9780813950082 (paperback) | ISBN 9780813950099 (ebook)
Subjects: LCSH: Presidents—United States—History—Case studies. | Adams, John Quincy, 1767–1848. | Grant, Ulysses S. (Ulysses Simpson), 1822–1885. | Taft, William H. (William Howard), 1857–1930. | United States—Politics and government—19th century. | United States—Politics and government—20th century.
Classification: LCC JK511 .R636 2023 (print) | LCC JK511 (ebook) | DDC 352.230973—dc23/eng/20230613
LC record available at https://lccn.loc.gov/2023013093
LC ebook record available at https://lccn.loc.gov/2023013094

Cover art: Presidential bobbleheads courtesy of Royal Bobbles, at www.RoyalBobbles.com

To Christine

CONTENTS

Acknowledgments ix

Introduction 1

1. Choices within the State, 1776–1930: Process, Principled Innovation, and Synthesis 13

2. President John Quincy Adams and the American State in the 1820s 35

3. Presidential Decision Making and the Administrative State: Process and Procedure in the 1820s 63

4. President Grant and the American State after the Civil War 92

5. Presidential Decision Making and the Evolving State: Grant, Reconstruction, and Indian Affairs 124

6. President Taft and the 125-Year-Old American State 155

7. Taft the Builder 183

Conclusion: The Non-Development of the American Presidency and the New Scholarship of the American State 209

Bibliographical Essay: The American State and the Understudied Presidency 223

Notes 247

Index 319

ACKNOWLEDGMENTS

Many thanks are due to colleagues, friends, and family who have made this project possible. I am grateful for the support of St. Joseph's University, which awarded me a Summer Research Grant as well as a sabbatical to pursue this project. Ongoing thanks to Fordham University, Brandeis University, the Brookings Institution, and University of Michigan–Flint for supporting my work over the years. Thanks to the support and interest of my friends and colleagues at St. Joseph's, especially Ken Bauzon, who provided essential guidance when I was researching the Taft chapters. Thanks to Peter Kastor and Max Edling for including me in a project that became the edited volume *Washington's Government*, which afforded me a chance to develop my approach to how the eighteenth-century presidency relates to political science scholarship about that office. Thanks always to Sidney Milkis, Shep Melnick, and Morton Keller, my dissertation advisors from years ago, who welcomed and encouraged experiments in merging scholarship in history and political science. Thanks to Christopher Becker, who did yeoman's work researching aspects of the John Quincy Adams presidency, especially Adams's diary entries. Thanks to the anonymous reviewers of the manuscript for their insightful comments and constructive suggestions.

Nadine Zimmerli has offered insightful guidance on the text of the book and on the processes at the University of Virginia Press, and I am grateful for her patience, collegiality, judgment, and expertise. I am likewise grateful for the careful work and good judgment of J. Andrew Edwards, Clayton Butler, and everyone at the press. Grateful thanks too to Margaret Hogan for her expert work copyediting the manuscript.

Thanks always to friends and family, including my parents, Patricia and Ronald Rockwell; brothers, Ken and Dave Rockwell, and their families; Julio and Zeyda Fernandez; Carol Calogero; Jennifer and Dan Hebert; Amanda Calogero; Gina Bossiello; and Chloe. Thanks always to the Schmitt, Rorke, Vest, Weiss, Pierce, Meiner, Katz, Ninyo, Lutton, and Hauptman families.

And many thanks to my wife, Christine, for all of her love and support.

THE PRESIDENCY AND THE AMERICAN STATE

INTRODUCTION

AN ACTIVE and independent presidency led the big government of the nineteenth century. Presidents led expert administrators, promoted legislative initiatives, made consistent and significant use of executive action tools like executive orders and proclamations, exercised independent commander-in-chief authority, and utilized public rhetoric and public communication to promote policies and influence hearts and minds.

Much of what follows in this book challenges persistent conceptions of the presidency and the state in the eighteenth and nineteenth centuries. Scholars of the presidency and its relationship to administrative leadership, executive direct action, diplomacy and war-making, legislative leadership, and popular communication have highlighted the importance of these lines of analysis to ordering and improving our understanding of the office.[1] If studies of the presidency, though, fail to examine presidential activity related to matters like Indian affairs, slavery, geographic expansion, land acquisition and distribution, infrastructure development, social policy, war-making, and diplomacy, they fail to consider what the president and the federal government were doing in the late eighteenth and nineteenth centuries. Such studies offer unreliable analyses of the president's relationship to the activities of the state, and they fail to produce a reliable baseline for comparison with presidential activities in the twentieth and twenty-first centuries.

The Presidency and the American State reexamines the American presidency in light of our new understanding of American state development. The development of the administrative state and the presence of active government at the federal level began with the dawn of the republic; big government is a feature of the late eighteenth and nineteenth centuries, not a late-arriving product of the twentieth.[2] Recognition of the extensive scope and intrusive activities of the federal government and, more specifically, the administrative state, from the republic's earliest years encourages reassessment of the institutions of governance within that state.

Political scientist Jon C. Rogowski offers a broad call regarding study of the premodern presidency and its development into the twentieth century. In his study of presidential influence over the siting of post office locations from 1876 to 1896, Rogowski writes, "For all that has been written about the weaknesses of the premodern presidency, however, scholars have assembled little evidence in support of claims about congressional dominance in influencing the goings-on of the federal government."³ Summarizing the implications of his study about post office locations, Rogowski adds, "While the challenges facing the country in the wake of two world wars and the Great Depression may have indeed exalted presidential power, the evidence suggests that the divide between premodern and modern presidencies may not be as dramatic or as deep as scholarship on the presidency indicates."⁴ Rogowski is correct, as are scholars like Graham G. Dodds, Jeffrey E. Cohen, and Mel Laracey, who have pushed study of the nineteenth-century presidency deeper into the historical record and begun to supplant earlier arguments based more on assertion and assumption than on careful study of evidence.⁵

In this book, I reassess the relationship of the presidency to the American state through close examination of three presidential administrations: those of John Quincy Adams, Ulysses S. Grant, and William Howard Taft. By closely examining presidential leadership and decision making, this book casts off presumptions and unsupported received wisdom about the development of that critically important office, leading to a new baseline from which to understand the presidency and its relationship to state action.

The New Literature on the State and Administration

Literature on federal government activity in the late eighteenth and nineteenth centuries is now robust, revealing a vibrant, intrusive government in a broad variety of policy areas. John R. Van Atta, Gregory Ablavsky, and Paul Frymer have documented the detailed, shifting, and complicated federal efforts in land policy, particularly varying policies regulating distribution, which affected the lives and fortunes of millions of Americans and Native Americans. Jerry L. Mashaw has documented the administrative state's development in a number of areas, including land policy but also extending to steamboat boiler regulation and administration of Thomas Jefferson's embargo. David F. Ericson has documented the federal government's role in promoting, using, and perpetuating slavery, while Matthew Karp has documented the slave power's role in American foreign policy. Michele Landis Dauber has traced the extensive disaster relief efforts promulgated by Congress throughout the nineteenth century and argued persuasively that they served as visible and known foundations for the New Deal. In a similar vein, Larry C. Skogen has documented the development of federal programs to indemnify and benefit new settlers on the United States' frontiers. Laura Jensen has described early efforts at education and veterans' benefits in the revolutionary era, and Theda Skocpol's classic *Protecting Soldiers and Mothers* examines similar topics in the period after the Civil War.⁶

Financial and economic policy extended from Alexander Hamilton's broad efforts and Jefferson's embargo, to the collection of federal taxes at ports and harbors, to the creation of payroll deductions to pay for sailors' healthcare benefits. Federal healthcare efforts included quarantines, seaman's hospitals, and Indian vaccination efforts. Studies in the development of infrastructure reveal a network of roads, forts, bridges, canals, and coastal defenses that enjoyed direct and indirect federal support, and the scientific, exploratory, and engineering expertise that made such works possible and lasting. Western expansion combined much of this, integrating land policy, diplomatic efforts, infrastructure development, the military, postal mapping, and a system of government-run not-for-profit trading houses. Economic regulation affected the fur trade, land, steam boilers, mining, shipping, goods covered by the federal tariff, and other matters. The federal government funded scientific and technical exploration. It actively promoted religion and supported missionaries. It regulated trade in alcohol and guns; it mandated gun ownership; it produced armaments and maintained armories; it contracted with producers of weapons, powder, horses, tents, uniforms, and blankets; and it worked with middlemen to sell and ship furs and others goods. It regulated the slave trade and policed borders, it opened foreign stations, it charted trade routes on land and sea and publicized the findings to benefit American shipping and trading companies, and it maintained diplomatic efforts around the globe. The territorial system of governance and the judicial system constantly expanded and were refined, bringing federal control and adjudication, and thus the impact of federal laws, regulations, and adjudicatory authority, to new regions.[7]

Much of this important new scholarship has so far centered on policy areas. Less work has been done on how newly discovered state activity may alter our traditional understandings of the presidency, Congress, and the courts in what has often been understood as a state of courts and parties. The presidency received large grants of discretionary authority from Congress, allowing presidents, administrative experts, and their advisors to craft specific rules and guidelines for treatymaking with Native nations, land acquisition, criminal justice adjudication, economic regulation, the delivery of benefits and social services, and federal employment practices including Indian preference in the Indian service and evolving employment of enslaved laborers on federal projects. Experts within bureaucratic and administrative units supported all of this by producing reports and advice, by pressuring elected leaders to accept their recommendations, and by operating with a level of autonomy more commonly associated with twentieth-century government bureaucracies. Hamilton's reports on manufactures and the national debt, Henry Knox's reports on Indian treaties, Thomas McKenney's reports on Indian removal, and the Pacific railroad surveys are just a few examples of the impact that the administrative bureaucracy and its experts had on policy before the Civil War.

There can no longer be any doubt that the American state existed, its engines of administrative power were effective, millions of people's lives were regularly affected by those actions, and those people knew it—as evidenced by their petitions and memorials to ask for help, their petitions and memorials complaining that they were not receiving enough help, and their petitions and memorials complaining that others were receiving undue help.[8] The nineteenth century was characterized by big government, which I have defined elsewhere as the combination of national policies and programs that affect millions, the administrative capacity to design and implement such policies, and a "sense of the state," in Stephen Skowronek's classic definition: "the sense of an organization of coercive power operating beyond our immediate control and intruding into all aspects of our lives."[9]

The Presidency and the American State

The approach to these matters in *The Presidency and the American State* begins with recognition of a vibrant and intrusive nineteenth-century American state. Starting from this baseline reveals significant new understandings of the state and the presidency. If the administrative state, in particular, was fully developed in the nineteenth century in matters like expansion and Indian affairs, then the presidency would not have needed to wait until the Progressive era and the twentieth century to develop into the "modern" presidency that we see today. Looking earlier, and examining presidential leadership of long-overlooked state activity in expansion, Indian affairs, social policy, and other matters, we see that what are often considered the office's essential "modern" characteristics—executive unilateral action, legislative and administrative leadership, and popular communication—were present and active within an influential American state throughout the nineteenth century and into the early years of the twentieth. These findings offer a direct challenge to the current dominant scholarship at the intersection of American political development and presidency studies. The new scholarly understanding of the American state in the nineteenth century suggests that we can—and should—flip much of our traditional understanding of the presidency on its head. Instead of a weak state and a clerk-like presidency, we find an energetic and effective state and an active and leadership-oriented presidency.

A reevaluation of individual presidencies is an appropriate way of reexamining the institution of the presidency and its relationship to the American state. In *The Myth of the Modern Presidency*, David K. Nichols argued that the Constitution provided the foundation for the "modern" presidency so often identified by scholars and so often placed in opposition to the "traditional" presidency. In Nichols's view, what the modern president was doing was clearly both constitutional and foreseen by the Constitution's framers, especially when the exercise of presidential authority helped lead the nation to a path between "the rule of the mob or the rule of the tyrant."[10] Nichols's argument relied on familiar historical examples, like the Louisiana Purchase and Andrew Jackson's fight with the Bank of the United States, to illustrate that the exercise of executive powers throughout American history was legitimate and to anchor his main analysis of twentieth-century politics and presidential action. *The Presidency and the American State* adds further understanding of the American state and its institutions in previously overlooked historical contexts, in an effort to build up our understanding of the presidency in these years with greater recognition of its role in an active and intrusive state. By looking at individual presidents, we can see their use and utilization of executive leadership tools in the policy and communication contexts of their eras, including Indian policy, expansion, land policy, and the rest.

This book is not a deep dive into primary source, archival material. Rather, it relies heavily on the work of historians and on the work of the subjects themselves—John Quincy Adams's voluminous diaries, the papers of Ulysses S. Grant published by Southern Illinois University Press and edited by John Y. Simon and colleagues, and William Howard Taft's numerous writings and publications. As such, this is a political scientist's effort to connect and integrate political science approaches to the study of the office of the presidency with historians' collective wisdom about particular presidencies. This book demonstrates that looking for significant and regularly applied executive action and leadership from earlier presidents makes sense in a manner so far generally disregarded by political scientists, and which when presented by historians has generally been presented without explicit links to the study of the office itself.

This book is also not an exercise in counting. The effort here is not to quantify executive orders or assess the relative use of proclamations across presidencies. First, given the state of our records, such counting is fraught with difficulties. Second, counting alone shows little about the significance or impact of executive actions—and prior efforts to categorize some executive orders as "significant" and others as not have left unanswered numerous questions about such evaluations. Instead, my effort here acknowledges the difficulty of such quantitative efforts and instead seeks a broader goal: to demonstrate that executive orders, proclamations, and other executive actions taken by presidents were, in fact, important, and consistently so, affecting critical areas of policy and having impact on the course of policymaking and implementation. There were decided and demonstrable effects on the ground.

When we look for executive actions in the realm of critical nineteenth-century policies—geographic expansion, Indian affairs, economic regulation, land policy, and so on—we see early presidents behaving very much like their latter-day counterparts. The numbers may eventually demonstrate important nuances across the eras, but we must first recognize the general significance of such actions. When it comes to presidential executive action, we must stop interpreting presidential leadership and decision making in the nineteenth century as exceptional, and instead see it as the norm.

THE JOHN QUINCY ADAMS, Ulysses S. Grant, and William Howard Taft presidencies—too often overlooked or marginalized by American political development and presidency scholars—look very different when examined with an understanding of an active and influential state existing from the late eighteenth century and developing through the nineteenth. Adams is recognized here as a far more practical and effective leader than is usually thought, one who relied on the processes and protocols of governing in a well-established state in order to maintain policies and perpetuate state activity that had been functioning for three decades. Grant is seen here as an instinctive leader who perpetuated and expanded longstanding state action, even as he tried to lead the state's activity into new areas in federal education and in protecting civil rights after the Civil War. Taft emerges as a pivotal figure using the presidency to build the foundations of the American century through progressive legislation and administrative reform.

The main theme of this book is the relationship of the presidency to the American state, and the presidencies of Adams, Grant, and Taft give us insight across a broad sweep of historical time. Studying these three presidencies offers a window into the presidency and the state in the 1820s, an example of the presidency and the state after the Civil War, and an example of the presidency and the state in the Progressive era. They are useful case studies because they illustrate the wide variety of uses to which the state and presidential leadership could be put before the Progressive era and then during that era itself, which is often seen as a landmark moment in the construction of the "modern" presidency.

Moreover, each president came to the office having directly witnessed significant uses of executive authority: Adams was in Congress for the Louisiana Purchase, and he wrote James Monroe's Monroe Doctrine; Grant witnessed Abraham Lincoln's groundbreaking actions as well as the fights between Andrew Johnson and Congress over executive authority; and Taft had been an integral part of Theodore Roosevelt's precedent-shattering presidency. As presidents, Adams, Grant, and Taft offered and fought for legislative programs, managed the administrative bureaucracy and capitalized on that bureaucracy's autonomy and effectiveness, utilized public rhetoric, and used tools of executive action like signing statements, vetoes, proclamations, and executive orders. Adams, Grant, and Taft all utilized presidential powers in a manner consistent with descriptions of a "modern" presidency.

A second theme of this book is the examination of three distinctive ethics of presidential decision making available to presidents in a mature and influential state. Adams relied on procedures and processes as a guide to decision making, a decision-making ethic that underscores the advanced state of those processes and procedures at the national level by the 1820s. Grant relied on a decision-making model driven by principled innovation, one that put the large and influential—but evolving—state to use in service of his principled approaches to the wide variety of novel issues in play at the national level in the years after the end of the Civil War. Taft married these two approaches, as some of our greatest presidents have—wedding principled innovation in a changing world to the creation of new processes and procedures to guide and direct decision making in his and in later presidencies. This synthesis created much of the foundation of what would become the American century—suggesting that a broader reassessment of the Taft presidency is in order.

To be clear, I am not suggesting that these three cases illustrate a progression in presidential action from a focus on process, to one on innovation, to one on synthesis. Starting (or ending) the analysis at different points could easily show a different progression. George Washington, for example, was a synthesist, setting precedents and constructing new rules and procedures to govern the new American state's movement into an array of new policy areas. A study of Washington, John Quincy Adams, and Grant could suggest that the presidency evolved from synthesis to process to innovation. No such focus on progression in these decision-making ethics is intended here. In fact, just the opposite—every president faces a choice of how to make decisions. Even Washington might have chosen to defer more to Congress and innovate little, retreating to following whatever rules were set down for him, or he might have chosen to innovate without attention to crafting new legislation and traditions that would guide future behavior. The presidency and the state have always allowed for a choice of decision-making ethics—and even for what is true of many presidents, an opportunistic blending of decision-making approaches. Just because this book examines Adams, Grant, and Taft should not suggest that that is the only (or even *a*) developmental path for the presidency and the state.

This all leads to a final question: how much has the presidency developed over time? Development is a staple, an almost assumed dynamic, in presidency studies. How and why the presidency has developed drives much scholarship. But the relationship of the presidency and the state in the eighteenth and nineteenth centuries suggested in this book raises basic questions about that relationship in the twentieth and twenty-first. For example, the Progressive era has often been seen as the birthplace of the modern presidency. Theodore Roosevelt, in particular, is seen as moving the bully pulpit into place as a public motivator, and he is seen as utilizing administrative and executive action tools to facilitate the moral suasion and public appeals he made on behalf of his legislative agenda.

But if administrative capacity, legislative leadership, and popular communication were all staples of presidential activity for more than a century before Roosevelt ascended to the presidency, the Progressive-era presidents look very different. Without denying Roosevelt's outsized personality and his unique presidency, I argue later in the book that the Progressive-era presidency, far from being a watershed, demonstrates *continuity* in the application of presidential tools in service of state activities more than it does change. What changed in the Progressive era was the goal of state activity itself, as the liberal constitutional order of the post–Civil War United States became grafted onto the effective state apparatus that characterized the nation's first century. Roosevelt, far from being the harbinger of a new century, is, surprisingly, the last gasp of the old. It is Taft who emerges as a central figure in utilizing the presidency and the state to address the new issues and new questions of a new century, and who oversaw the building of the foundations for modern America.

In the end, reframing presidency studies in the context of a vibrant nineteenth-century American state leads to important conclusions. For state development scholars, the book enhances what we know about the scope of state activity and the mechanisms by which the state functioned. State goals were furthered through executive actions, administrative capacity, and public rhetoric, described here in three very different administrations. For presidency scholars and political scientists, the common understanding of an "imperial" presidency that developed contemporaneously with the increasing capacity of the state in the twentieth century needs to be reassessed—along both dimensions. A consequential state in the nineteenth century, driven by a variety of approaches to strong presidential leadership and decision making at the head of that state, confronts us with the surprising conclusion that the presidency has not "developed" much at all since the founding. This becomes readily apparent as one begins to examine presidential activity in those issue areas that earlier scholars in American political development and presidency studies overlooked.

Plan of the Book

I make three main arguments in this book. First, in the Adams, Grant, and Taft presidencies, presidential use of administrative leadership and executive action, legislative initiatives, and public communication were significant in a variety of policy contexts. Second, in these three presidencies, presidential action took place in complicated, unique sets of contexts, in which presidents regularly acted independently—not as the head of a unitary executive but also not as a clerk subservient to congressional or party leadership. Third, each president consistently utilized a different ethic to make decisions about how and when to deploy the power and authority of the presidency and the state. Together, these three main arguments help us to create a contextualized understanding of the presidency, incorporating institutional, political, and personal dynamics to assist us in better understanding the relationship of the presidency to the American state.

Chapter 1 examines the extent to which all three of the book's subjects were affected by, or involved in, state action throughout their lives and careers. To appreciate their eventual leadership of the state, in other words, it is instructive to examine their experiences *with* the state and to highlight the maturity and influence of that state throughout the years under study. This chapter illustrates how the state engaged in a host of actions from its earliest days, and all three of our subjects were consistent in their decision-making approaches before and after their presidencies as they engaged with various aspects of American state governance. The biographical sketches in chapter 1 help challenge any sense of a small or weak state in the nineteenth century, especially as the energy and importance of the state were perceived by Adams, Grant, and Taft themselves. This chapter helps us understand the scope of the state from the Revolution to the brink of the New Deal through the overlapping lives and careers of three subjects.

The chapters that follow examine the Adams, Grant, and Taft presidential administrations in two chapters each. The first chapter of each set demonstrates the scope and variety of presidential and state activity during the subject's administration, illustrating the use of administrative and policy leadership, executive action, and public communication. The second chapter offers close examination of presidential leadership and decision making in contexts that were particularly significant to their administrations. The goal is to reap the benefits of viewing historical presidencies as whole entities in the context of the state activity of the time, instead of breaking off pieces of those presidencies—popular communications, use of executive orders, administrative leadership—into fragmented discussions of isolated actions. This helps us uncover the relationship of the presidency to the state in fuller historical context.

To begin this analysis, chapter 2 looks at the host of diverse and important matters that came before President Adams and the American state in the 1820s, and how Adams consistently responded according to well-established procedures and longstanding practice. The very fact that Adams could rely so heavily on established processes for decision making as president suggests the effective maturation of the American state by the 1820s. Chapter 3 illustrates Adams's engagement with the American state and his allegiance to established processes when making executive decisions in three critically important issue areas. In Indian affairs, Adams worked heroically to restrain state encroachments on Native lands and defend the longstanding supremacy of the federal government's administrative capacity to manage and control westward expansion. In the context of slavery, Adams used an 1820s version of the hidden-hand presidency to undermine slavery through presidential appointments, policy and administrative action, and legal approaches. And on internal improvements, Adams's public statements about government programs and policies reveal Adams and his policy agenda at the center of American state activity.

Chapter 4 examines presidential leadership, decision making, and state activity in a kaleidoscope of issues in the 1870s. Ulysses S. Grant, his administration, and state processes confronted mistreatment of the first Black cadets at West Point, the devastating invasion of locusts in the Midwest, nascent efforts at civil service and campaign finance reform, peace-keeping diplomacy in Cuba, and war-making aggression in Korea. The state in the 1870s was invited, or intruded, virtually everywhere, and Grant's decision making was consistently inconsistent. He repeatedly responded to issues and crises on an ad-hoc basis, driven by what he believed was right at any given time and with little attention to previous procedures or future policies. Grant put the state to ad-hoc use, confounding and dividing citizens then and historians ever since.

Chapter 5 turns the focus to President Grant's approach to two central issues of his presidency. In the context of westward expansion, Grant's administration oversaw major reforms of U.S. Indian policy, land policy, and military affairs—with federal actions affecting millions of people across the continent after the Civil War. In the context of Reconstruction, Grant's commitment to the Civil War amendments, his use of the new Department of Justice, and his efforts to pacify an ongoing insurgency in the former Confederacy all speak to the scope and influence of the federal government and to the variety of matters subject to independent executive authority. These case studies demonstrate the value of reassessing the presidency in light of what we have learned recently about the scope and influence of the American state at the end of the Civil War. The state was not being created, and it was not being dismantled—it was being redirected. What was new in the Grant years was neither the scope nor the capacity of administrative and presidential power but the revolutionized landscape of rights and perceptions that coexisted with a nation in continuing upheaval and facing asymmetric resistance to its authority.

Chapters 6 and 7 address the frequently overlooked and vastly underappreciated presidency of William Howard Taft. Chapter 6 outlines Taft's efforts to synthesize rules and procedures with principled innovation throughout his presidency, including efforts to institutionalize progressive reforms, establish the president's role in national budgeting, and avoid war with Mexico. Chapter 7 spotlights President Taft and his focus on cementing into law and process progressive approaches to conservation, antitrust enforcement, corporate and individual taxation, campaign finance regulation, and international arbitration treaties. This reassessment of the Taft presidency reveals momentous, creative, and until now largely overlooked developments. Taft's efforts helped manage the increasingly crowded intersection of money and politics and built the regulatory framework for the twentieth century.

The conclusion addresses what this information means for our understanding of the "development" of the presidency and its power, arguing that the presidency, understood with a clear conception of the nineteenth-century American state, has not developed much at all since the founding. The characteristics of the "modern" presidency—executive unilateral action, legislative and administrative leadership, and popular communication—are all in evidence throughout the republic's history, in significant policy areas touching the lives of millions of people. These issue areas, critical to the American state's development, include territorial expansion, Indian affairs, land policy, and the myriad social and other policy areas addressed by the national government that have come to the forefront of state development scholarship in recent years. When we examine the activities of the American state, we see presidents behaving very much like their modern counterparts.

IN HIS landmark book, *The People's Welfare,* William J. Novak demonstrated the extent of governance taking place at state and local levels in the nineteenth century.[11] The new understanding of state development described by authors like Brian Balogh, Max M. Edling, John Van Atta, and Michele Landis Dauber mirrors at the federal level the roots of American governance identified by Novak at the state and local levels. Novak, though, also saw that a commitment to the public welfare, which for many years trumped claims to defend private right against government intrusion, began to break down in the latter part of the nineteenth century. After the Civil War, and especially during the Progressive era, the vision of active governance in pursuit of the people's welfare came into conflict with concerns about how state activity impeded on individual rights, many of which became grounded in the post–Civil War amendments. As state and local governance began to blend active governance with limits on that governance's scope, the same happened at the federal level. This is why I conclude this book with a study of the Taft presidency. Taft helped institutionalize progressive reforms like the corporation tax and campaign finance regulation even as he worked to establish limits on federal government activity, to protect individual and corporate rights against overreach. Taft's presidency is critical to understanding developments throughout the rest of the twentieth century.

We can learn much about the American state and the American presidency from assessing the development of both together. Built on, and expanding on, recent studies of American state development, my approach invites a reassessment of dominant understandings of the office of the presidency. In particular, when the full extent of the American state and presidential activity is accounted for, the Progressive era presidency evinces much less landmark "development" than is generally believed in matters like administrative leadership and executive action, legislative leadership, and popular communications.

Viewing historical presidencies with an understanding of American state development helps us to recognize the national state's broad scope in the nineteenth and early twentieth centuries. Within the structures of the American state, each of the three presidents studied here was what is generally considered a "strong" president, willing to act unilaterally, defend executive branch independence vigorously, and deploy the capacity of the state aggressively. Their reputations as weak, naive, or clumsy presidents have arisen from fundamentally misguided understandings of the nineteenth-century American state. These presidents look remarkably "modern" in their approaches to utilizing the tools of the office to lead a state and administrative apparatus that also looks modern and mature.

Rejecting what Novak called "the myth of American statelessness," and rejecting what Nichols called the myth of the modern presidency, creates a path to a new understanding of nineteenth-century American governance. A mature state in the nineteenth century, paired with a variety of approaches to strong presidential leadership and decision making on a host of issues, confronts us with the conclusion that the presidency has not "developed" much at all since the founding. The office's essential characteristics have been exercised on behalf of an influential and active state throughout our republic's history.

1

Choices within the State, 1776–1930

PROCESS, PRINCIPLED INNOVATION, AND SYNTHESIS

THE STATE and its leaders do not spring instantly into existence, yet the presidency is often studied in isolation, as though it were the only four or eight years of a president's public career. To understand the presidency and the state, it makes sense to review the interactions of our three subjects with the state prior to their presidencies. In this exercise we see how their individual lives were deeply intertwined with the development of the state. John Quincy Adams had been participating in the state's development for forty-four years when he became president in 1825. Grant had been in and out of government service to the state for many years when he became president, including serving in the military while Adams served as a member of Congress. William Howard Taft grew up during his father's time as part of Grant's presidential administration, with Taft subsequently serving as a federal judge, civilian governor in the Philippines, and secretary of war, all prior to his presidency.

The lives of John Quincy Adams, Ulysses S. Grant, and William Howard Taft developed and grew along with the American state, with each individual playing central roles in the state's activities and exercising decision-making approaches to the application of state power that would characterize each as president. Adams relied on the procedures, protocols, and rules already extant in the American state by the last decades of the eighteenth century, and he remained loyal to the state's rules and procedures in his early political efforts, as one of the new nation's most important diplomats, and in his legendary post-presidential fight against the gag rule in Congress. Grant innovated according to personal principle in his time in the private sector and in the state's military apparatus, he applied the same approach to the tricky question of his public responsibilities under the new and controversial Tenure of Office Act after the Civil War, and he operated in a similar manner in his few post-presidential years. Taft was always a synthesist, marrying principle and procedure as a federal judge and while designing new civil governance mechanisms in the Philippines, and again after his presidency while serving as chief justice of the U.S. Supreme Court.

Examining the pre- and post-presidency experiences of these three men offers an unbroken look at how individuals interacted with the state, and how the complexity and obtrusiveness of the state, from its inception, made possible a variety of leadership and decision-making options. From the first decades of the republic, a leader could rely on established procedures and rules as guides to behavior, another could innovate based on principle in pursuit of novel results, and a third could marry principle and procedure to synthesize lasting reforms into the state and its communities. These brief biographical sketches show the subjects' decision-making ethics in action before and after their presidencies, and they illustrate the broad scope and influence of the state itself in these years.

The Lifelong Procedurist

John Quincy Adams was at the center of American governance throughout his career. For our purposes, it is significant that much of his work was solidly within established norms and traditions. The simple fact that there *were* established norms and procedures for mezzo-level officials in American governance in the late eighteenth and nineteenth centuries speaks subtly to the early extent of American state building. Although he negotiated agreements as a diplomat and later as secretary of state that increased American geographical holdings, and while he fought the gag rule in the House of Representatives, among other important efforts, Adams rarely broke new ground in the scope and influence of governance. There was little new about signing treaties with foreign nations, acquiring land and negotiating boundaries, or enforcing procedural rules in Congress.

This is, of course, not meant in any way to denigrate Adams's lasting achievements and his contributions to the nation. It is merely to highlight the integrity with which Adams's decision-making ethic began and remained that of what I call the procedurist. He was not motivated by the pursuit of broad principles as much as the principled innovator, and he did not build new mechanisms to take governance into new issue areas or address old ones in demonstrably innovative ways. He was—before, during, and after his presidency—a stickler. What he contributed, he usually contributed through application of traditional protocols and established procedures. Sometimes these rules and procedures were applied to new *topics,* such as a different piece of land or a new procedural question, but Adams generally used established methods to tackle new issues.

ADAMS'S EARLY career in Congress was brief, but it reflected his commitments to procedure and process. Elected first to the Massachusetts state senate in 1802, Adams was selected by the state legislature in 1803 to serve as one of Massachusetts's two U.S. senators. In the U.S. Senate, Adams helped revise the articles of war and the Senate's rules, helped acquire books for the Library of Congress, helped write legislation for the Louisiana Territory and the District of Columbia, and pushed for a national road system connecting Atlantic ports with the Ohio River Valley.[1] During the Jefferson administration, then-Federalist Adams supported the Republican Thomas Jefferson's Louisiana Purchase. The purchase obtained rights from France by which the United States would eventually purchase or obtain through conquest vast lands in the South and West, at a cost estimated at around $2.6 billion.[2]

The purchase set off decades of sweeping federal government activity, including federal dominance in the acquisition of land through the treaty system and a series of trade and intercourse acts, and the expansion of federal regulatory and judicial authority into western areas. A dedicated nationalist committed to territorial expansion from his earliest years, Adams supported a transaction that promised national growth geographically as well as expansion in the authority of the national government to manage and control the continent. The purchase's transfer of acquisition rights from France to the United States was in keeping with protocol at the time; France had only recently reobtained those rights from Spain. Adams interpreted the agreement with France as a treaty not requiring further legislation; the Senate approved Adams's motion, rendering all other questions and potential actions, like a constitutional amendment, moot. Adams then voted *against* giving Jefferson the power to tax the residents of Louisiana or to appoint territorial officials, arguing that such authority would deprive the territory's inhabitants of the right to self-determination.[3]

Adams crossed party lines again to support the embargo of 1807–9, which rested on congressional acts that delegated vast discretionary authority to President Jefferson. The goal was to stop all transport of goods from U.S. ports to foreign destinations, a "massive attempt at economic regulation" aimed at preventing U.S. ships and assets from getting caught up in the conflict between France and Britain.[4] Adams even helped write the legislation, and he was the only Federalist to vote in favor.[5] Much like his support of the Louisiana Purchase, Adams's willingness to use the national government's legal and administrative authority in support of national goals remained consistent, even though the policy infringed directly on his home region's maritime economy.[6] Jerry Mashaw has documented just how extensive and intrusive were federal operations implementing the embargo.[7]

These actions, together with Adams's refusal to support the effort to impeach U.S. Supreme Court Associate Justice Samuel Chase, have often been used to illustrate Adams's independent streak.[8] They also suggest his early commitment to procedure. The Louisiana Purchase, while controversial from the standpoint of presidential power, was an unexceptional national act, consistent with international relations and acquisitional protocol. The Chase impeachment aimed at undercutting the institutional independence of the judiciary, a core element of the separation of powers system and critically important to the regular, procedural functioning of the three main institutions of constitutional governance. The embargo was procedurally sound, even if politically controversial and thereafter widely reviled. Adams's support of expansive presidential powers, an independent judiciary, and federal interventions in foreign policy and domestic development were all consistent throughout his career, before, during, and after his presidency. If one imagines decisions made on the basis of established procedure and protocol, all three decisions by Adams make sense.

THROUGH MUCH of his diplomatic career, Adams was a skilled envoy, protecting and extending the United States' place as a new player in world politics and diplomacy. President John Adams appointed John Quincy to be minister to Prussia in 1797. John Quincy negotiated a 1799 peace treaty with Prussia that protected the rights of neutrals, a focus of Adams's diplomacy throughout his career.[9] As minister to Russia from 1809 to 1814, Adams prevailed on the czar to free American ships and seamen held in Russian ports, enlisted the czar to intervene with the Danish government to free others, and worked to open Russian waters to free trade with the United States.[10] Adams also served at the negotiations for the Treaty of Ghent, which reestablished peace after the War of 1812, joining a negotiating team that included Henry Clay and Albert Gallatin.[11] The treaty returned the United States and Britain to the status quo antebellum, a significant victory for a United States that had seen British forces invade Washington and burn the White House. The treaty established an arbitration process for handling disagreements peacefully in the future.[12] "I consider the day on which I signed it," Adams later wrote, "as the happiest of my life because it was the day on which I had my share in restoring peace to the world."[13]

In 1815, at the age of forty-seven, Adams became minister to Great Britain, the highest American diplomatic post of the era. There, with Clay and Gallatin, Adams negotiated the Anglo-American Commercial Convention of 1815, which stood as a template for U.S. trade agreements for decades. In the final negotiations, Adams displayed his commitment to correct procedure. When the negotiators gathered to sign their respective copies of the treaty, both nations' copies of the treaty listed Great Britain first and the United States second in their texts and provisions—an affront to Adams's efforts to secure to the United States an equal and respected position in global diplomacy, but, perhaps more importantly to Adams personally, a breach of diplomatic protocol. Clay and Gallatin were ready to let the matter pass, but Adams insisted that the U.S. copy be redrafted, listing the United States first.[14]

In this post, Adams also negotiated an important agreement involving naval disarmament on the Great Lakes, at the time a center of tension and risk between western possessions of the United States and British Canada. The Rush-Bagot Agreement of 1817 reduced the U.S. and British presence on the lakes to just that required to handle customs duties: "a landmark voluntary agreement for reciprocal naval disarmament that would become the longest-lasting and most successful agreement of its kind in the world," according to biographer Harlow Giles Unger.[15] All of this work helped pacify and normalize U.S.-British relations, which over the previous thirty years had generated two bloody wars and decades of on-the-brink tension.

ADAMS REACHED the peak of his skills as President James Monroe's secretary of state. At the heart of a great career lie eight years in which Adams helped develop the United States along some of its most critical dimensions, with two achievements in particular defining Adams's tenure. The first was the Transcontinental Treaty of 1819, also known as the Adams-Onís Treaty. Now lost to history in the public mind and overshadowed by the attention given to Andrew Jackson's military forays, threats, and executions in Florida, the Adams-Onís Treaty obtained Florida from Spain and ensured American access to the Gulf of Mexico all the way to New Orleans. The treaty secured vast territories west of New Orleans into Louisiana and Texas, it set the boundary with Mexico, and it established the United States' claim to the Oregon territory.[16] Historian William Earl Weeks, in fact, sees the Northwest border aspect of this treaty as the most significant part, as it opened the United States to the West and even to Asia.[17] Historian Lester Harris called the treaty "the greatest diplomatic victory won by any single individual in the history of the United States of America."[18] Adams himself called the Transcontinental Treaty "the most important of my life . . . an event of magnitude in the history of this Union."[19] Such treaties, of course, were far from self-executing: just as the Louisiana Purchase set off decades of negotiations, purchases, and administrative activity, the Adams-Onís Treaty resulted in years of federally led adjudication of Spanish land-grant claims as well as ongoing efforts to obtain, through purchase, negotiation, or conflict, lands held by Native Americans in Florida, along the Gulf Coast, and in the Northwest.[20]

Illustrating the early state's extensive reach, Secretary of State Adams also negotiated one of the world's first international environmental agreements. As European and Russian seal hunters collided in the Bering Strait, Adams negotiated an agreement to protect seal enclaves for future growth and limit the amount and extent of seal hunting in the entire region.[21] Adams negotiated an important fisheries agreement with Britain securing for American fishermen access to the great cod fields of the North Atlantic—and providing procedures and regulations for handling future disputes.[22] An 1818 agreement secured the restoration of U.S. fishing rights along the Canadian coast and allowed the Russian czar to mediate the issue of compensation to Americans for enslaved people taken during the War of 1812 by the British.[23] The agreement fixed the U.S.-Canada border from the Great Lakes through the Rockies, creating a foundation for the eventual U.S. northern border all the way to the Pacific Ocean.[24] In addition, Adams worked to limit the actions of pirates, and he worked to grow the Asia trade in China through activity along the Columbia River, continuing close ties between the government and John Jacob Astor's global trading operations.[25] Lastly, Secretary Adams's negotiations with Latin American nations in the early 1820s helped develop and sharpen his views on the region, which were then codified in the Monroe Doctrine.[26]

The Monroe Doctrine of 1823 was Adams's greatest contribution as secretary of state, declaring the United States' intent to exclude European powers and their monarchical forms of governance from South America and the Western Hemisphere. It was no small declaration to cast the young nation's umbrella of influence and protection over Central and South America, and in this example we see Adams temporarily break from his procedurist foundations and serve as a builder, a synthesizer of principle and procedure.[27] And Adams knew when to say no. He shrewdly rejected a proposal from England that Britain and the United States *jointly* guarantee the independence of nations in South America. Adams correctly discerned that despite the prospect of a mutually beneficial alliance with a great power, a mutual statement would tie the United States too closely to Britain, and in a potentially subordinate status. He insisted, successfully, that the United States issue its own, independent statement and set itself up as the guarantor of the independence of those southern nations.

Before Adams ascended to the presidency, he had secured a reputation as a tough negotiator, a man willing to defend the use of force, and an advocate of strong executive authority. Adams's foreign policymaking as secretary of state succeeded through careful, calculated, and muscular attention to national interest, power, unification, and independence.[28] Adams effectively used the threat to Spain posed by Andrew Jackson's incursions into Florida to push treaty negotiations forward in the American interest.[29] He was the only member of President Monroe's cabinet to support Jackson's incursion into Florida, and he supported the use of force against privateers and interlopers in the cays and inlets around Amelia Island and Galveston.[30] Adams also built a tough-as-nails reputation for closing the deal. He refused even a few strands of face-saving solace to Spanish envoy Luis de Onís at the end of the Transcontinental Treaty negotiations, in a rare instance of Adams pushing beyond established protocols, insisting that boundaries be drawn along the southern and western borders of rivers, rather than in the middle, as was customary, and by refusing to allow that West Florida had not been part of the Louisiana Purchase.[31] After Onís secured a friendly conciliation from President Monroe at the very end of the negotiations, Adams prevailed on Monroe to retract the nicety and revert to Adams's slam-dunk win.[32]

Illustrating the early state's extensive scope and influence domestically, Secretary of State Adams also supervised the 1820 U.S. Census, arranged for the publication of legislation, and oversaw the Patent Office. He reorganized the State Department's filing system with a scheme that remained in use for almost a century.[33] He defended the interests of free Black seamen in southern seaports, who were being imprisoned under state laws. In a key instance, Adams convinced authorities in South Carolina to suspend enforcement of their Negro Seamen's Act. In another example of how federal action visibly and directly engaged the public, though, vigilante groups formed to oppose Adams's efforts and the efforts of federal courts, allowing South Carolinians to continue to enforce exclusion laws through "private" efforts.[34]

Lastly, Adams wrote a ridiculously comprehensive survey of weights and measures, domestically and internationally, after Congress asked the secretary's office for a report on the feasibility of trying to standardize the nation's weights and measures. Adams linked the benefits and development of standardized weights and measures to the benefits and development of civil society, including the idea that "the proper province of law, in relation to weights and measures, is, not to create, but to regulate."[35] Even though Adams's report promoted the benefits of the metric system, Adams the procedurist quickly eschewed fighting to build that system into the United States, noting that such would be an effectively impossible endeavor.

AFTER HIS PRESIDENCY, Adams's commitment to procedure as a guide to state action continued. Adams was the driving force behind regularizing the lasting work of that great American conglomeration of museums and artifacts, the Smithsonian Institution. James Smithson, a British gentleman who died in 1829, bequeathed to the United States more than $500,000 to be used to support "an establishment for the increase and diffusion of knowledge among men." Adams wanted the funds to support original scientific research, relying on the terms of Smithson's gift to make his case against others who preferred the creation of a national university, who wanted the funds to establish children's schools, or who wanted the money to anchor education at a naval academy. In a years-long fight over the bequest, Adams utilized congressional rules to help protect the funds from being frittered away on minor or short-lived projects and won the core fight over the bequest—it would not be used for schools to merely disseminate information. Instead, the resources would be used to support original research, together with intellectual projects and a museum. Perhaps most significant, Adams's management of the bequest ensured that the principal sum would be established as a long-term endowment and not be spent—thus the Smithsonian continues today. Importantly, Adams returned again and again to the *words* of Smithson's bequest, arguing the process-based point that it was not Congress's right to appropriate the resources in any manner other than as Smithson had directed.[36]

What many scholars see as Adams's greatest career achievement lies in his opposition to the "gag rule" in the House of Representatives, perhaps the most notable example of Adams's lifelong commitment to procedure. The gag rule, through a series of iterations, required that petitions, memorials, and resolutions regarding slavery be automatically tabled, with no further action taken. The measures blocked one of the most popular and time-honored mechanisms for active political engagement.[37] In his diary for December 1837, in just one of many gag rule–related entries, Adams wrote, "When my name was called I answered I held the resolution to be a Violation of the Constitution of the right of petition of my constituents and of the people of the United States, and of my right to freedom of Speech as a member of this House."[38]

Adams's fight against the gag rule has inspired almost as much writing as his presidency. Adams saw the gag rule as an attack on core First Amendment protections of free speech and the right of petition. His opposition to slavery was important, certainly, but we should not mistake Adams's actions. This was no quixotic fight against slavery, no one-man show aimed at abolition. Rather, Adams seemed much more incensed at the violation of procedural fairness that the gag rule symbolized. Fighting for the right of the people to petition for redress, and for the right of members to speak freely in Congress, it was almost a fortuitous accident for Adams that the procedural fight involved a particular issue about which he was also passionate.

This was a core aspect of Adams's approach to public duties: process mattered immensely. He succeeded again and again in enshrining processes in the many treaties and agreements he signed, anticipating that future disputes could be managed and mediated peacefully and effectively through fair, predictable, and mutually acceptable process. Similarly, the process of introducing petitions from the public, of moving them through Congress and committees, and of doing so without constraint on the discussion and debate of congressional members, to Adams created a mechanism that worked to protect liberties and ensure good government. The gag rule violated the core of that free process of deliberation.

The fight over the gag rule endured for eight years before Adams finally won.[39] He knew it would be a long battle, and his tendency to envision the long-term nature of governance and consider future generations was on prominent display. To thwart the gag rule, Adams applied endlessly creative ways of discussing slavery in Congress that were procedurally sound—the more the gag was tightened, the more he found ways to slip his voice through. Adams used a magician's trunk full of procedural feints, parliamentary sleight of hand, and rule interpretations to needle supporters of the gag rule, using logic, humor, irony, and common sense.[40] Eventually, Adams prevailed, and the museum at the U.S. Capitol displays a beautiful ivory cane given to Adams by abolitionist supporters, inscribed with the words "Right of Petition Triumphant." But note the words—Adams's odyssey should never be confused with a fight to end slavery. While that was part of what Adams was doing, his true motivation and his animating dynamic was the right to petition and the pique he felt at misapplication of established rules in the House.[41]

ADAMS'S MOST famous moment arguing for principle similarly obscures his first commitment to established rules and procedure. In the early summer of 1839, fifty-three men, women, and children previously kidnapped in Africa were forced aboard the slave ship *Amistad* in Cuba. They managed to take control of the ship a few nights later, and they ordered the crew to sail to Africa. The crew sailed the ship but not to Africa—in August, the ship rested off of Montauk Point, Long Island, where it was confronted by officers from a federal revenue cutter. Eventually, the ship was towed to New London, Connecticut. The Africans were charged in a U.S. district court with piracy and murder.

The Africans asserted that they were free—and that the deaths that resulted were the effects of their legitimate right to free themselves from captivity. The legal case was complicated and politically volatile. The administration of President Martin Van Buren opposed setting the captives free, believing such action would alienate pro-slavery constituencies ahead of the 1840 elections.[42] Shippers wanted the Africans punished for interfering with the slave trade. U.S. government agents wanted the rewards that came from salvaging property, and the Spanish government demanded that the Africans be returned to Spanish control. Abolitionists and antislavery forces wanted the people freed and returned to their lives.

Adams's involvement followed actions taken by the Africans' initial supporters, including longtime abolitionist Lewis Tappan. Tappan and others knew that having Adams on board the legal team would boost both the prominence of the case and the chances that the Supreme Court justices would rule sympathetically to the Africans' interests. Adams expressed some reluctance due to his age and infirmities.[43] He was seventy-three years old when he agreed to argue on behalf of the African captives before the U.S. Supreme Court, in an era when the average life expectancy was around forty.[44] Adams threw himself into the work, making procedural motions and arguments. At one point, he accused the Van Buren administration of falsifying submissions to the Court, arguing that the administration had willfully mistranslated Spanish-language documents. Adams called for and got a congressional committee to investigate; the committee adopted Adams's report but refused to censure the administration. Throughout the case, ex-president Adams would be critical of the Van Buren administration's positions.[45]

In the main event, Adams made an impassioned appeal to the Supreme Court. Arguing that courts were the keepers of justice, Adams highlighted the gap between human-made law sanctioning slavery and natural law expressed in the high principles of the Declaration of Independence. Adams's argument before the Court thus pushed far past the legal implications of a dizzying array of treaties and practices, to touch on principle: the unconscionable nature of human slavery. Adams opened his case discussing the fundamental freedoms and rights of human beings.

Intriguingly, though, Adams's efforts on behalf of the *Amistad*'s Africans were more deeply founded in examining and applying complicated provisions of international treaties that Adams himself had negotiated earlier in his career. He was able to point to specific provisions, clear language, and antislavery applications in the Adams-Onís Treaty, the Treaty of Ghent, and other agreements that he had helped write. A goal of those negotiations had always been to provide the basis for fair and open process as means for state entities (like courts) to resolve disputes peacefully and with justice. In the *Amistad* case, a key dispute turned on interpretation of passages from article 10 of the Treaty of Ghent, which had aimed at halting the African slave trade. Other issues relied on interpretation of Pinckney's Treaty of 1795, which Adams had updated in negotiations years later. In an example of Adams's sense of humor, he mocked Spain's effort to include the *Amistad*'s people as merchandise due to be returned to Spain. The language of the treaty required the return of merchandise to be "restored *entire* to the true proprietor." Adams used that language to dismiss the idea that the passage could possibly refer to people: "A stipulation to restore human beings *entire*," he wrote, "might suit two nations of cannibals, but would be absurd, and worse than absurd, between civilized and Christian nations."[46]

Adams's summation runs to almost eighty pages when printed; only the first few pages are about higher principles. The remainder, the vast majority of Adams's argument, focused on treaties, laws, interpretations, letters, arguments, evidence, passports, malfeasance, and impropriety, indicting President Van Buren and many others for misreading their duties, misunderstanding the laws, misapplying their authorities. Adams's conclusion explicitly anchored his argument in law and procedure, *not* in higher principles like human liberty:

I have avoided, purposely avoided, and this Court will do justice to the motive for which I have avoided, a recurrence to those first principles of liberty which might well have been invoked in the argument of this cause. I have shown that Ruiz and Montes, the only parties in interest here, for whose sole benefit this suit is carried on by the Government, were acting at the time in a way that is forbidden by the laws of Great Britain, of Spain, and of the United States, and that the mere signature of the Governor General of Cuba ought not to prevail over the ample evidence in the case that these Negroes were free and had a right to assert their liberty. I have shown that the papers in question are absolutely null and insufficient as passports for persons, and still more invalid to convey or prove a title to property.[47]

The Court ruled in favor of the Africans, and the surviving men and women returned, free, to Africa. Importantly, the majority opinion by Justice Joseph Story relied not on an argument about natural liberty or other higher-order values but rather on a careful assessment of the status of the Africans under a variety of laws and treaties. It was a legal and procedural decision, just as Adams's main argument was a legal and procedural one.

THE STATE was already in full operation on its citizens (and others) by the time Adams became president, and Adams's actions alone would have affected shippers, traders, sailors, fishermen, free and enslaved persons, Indigenous Americans, people with claims against the United States or other nations, and a host of others (and their families). It is perhaps Adams's experience, his work in diplomacy, and the attractive principles behind his fights against the gag rule and for the *Amistad* survivors that drive the sense of lost promise that inhabits so much writing about Adams as president. Yet we should not mistake Adams for an idealist. The *Amistad* and gag rule cases especially demonstrate that Adams's most fundamental commitments were to rules and procedures, aspects of a mature state within which one *could* appeal successfully—sometimes *more* successfully—to established procedures than to vaguely defined values. Adams appealed to already extant understandings of national power (the Louisiana Purchase), administrative authority (the embargo), international relations (treaties), congressional procedure governing interactions with the populace (the right of petition), and judicial commitment to the rule of laws established by Congress and signed by the president (the *Amistad*). He was well aware of the principles involved, of course, but he was most animated, and most effective, when those principles were supported by procedural rules and existing laws that were seen as fair, inclusive, and binding on all.

As president, John Quincy Adams was guided most often by similar fealty to the state's well-established procedures, rules, and protocols as guides to state actions that had direct effects on millions of people. Adams's presidential decision-making ethic reflected the commitment to procedure that drove his decision making throughout a life of public service. Mature states and procedurists complement each other without much friction.

The Principled Innovator

As John Quincy Adams was fighting the gag rule in Congress and defending the rights of the Africans captured with the *Amistad,* Ulysses S. Grant was growing up in the nation's Middle West, graduating from West Point, and serving in the U.S. Army in Mexico and on the West Coast. Born among the abolitionists of southern Ohio, raised in the charged racial contexts of Ohio and St. Louis, and later working as a young man in business and public service among the Indigenous communities of the Pacific Coast, Grant's early life overlapped the closing chapters of Adams's.

Grant's experience was like that of many people—the raising of a family, a search for business success, time in and out of the military. He entered West Point in 1839 at the age of seventeen, graduating in 1843 and reporting south of St. Louis to Jefferson Barracks. As Congressman Adams voted against the annexation of Texas and opposed President James Polk's war with Mexico, Grant fought in that war and participated in the U.S. occupation of Mexico City—while at the same time nurturing a secret engagement to Julia Dent, the sister of a West Point classmate. Married in 1848, Ulysses and Julia moved around—together to Detroit, together to Sacketts Harbor in New York, and then Ulysses alone to the West Coast in 1852, as the pregnant Julia returned to the Midwest.

On the West Coast, Grant participated in the nation's expansionist efforts, its support of private development, and its coordinated infrastructure programs, helping to outfit Captain George McClellan's railroad survey across the mountains. Grant resigned from the army in 1854 to be near his wife and children. After a stay in St. Louis, in 1860 the family moved to Galena, Illinois, where Grant's two brothers set him up with a job in the family store. Galena had been a center of government activity during the John Quincy Adams administration, as the government worked to control the region and its Native populations, and it then became a center of federally regulated mining on public lands. The Grants' store was in a city that had seen the army issue thousands of permits and license fifty-two smelters long before Grant even arrived.[48]

Grant had a dry sense of humor, an above-politics aloofness that served him well throughout his life, and an unwillingness to brag or introduce his war record in conversation.[49] He held deep-seated beliefs but did not flaunt them. He seems never to have harbored any doubts about the wrongness of slavery, for example, yet he never seems to have made a big deal of it. There were stands but quiet ones: Grant freed a slave he received as a wedding present from his father-in-law, and he refused to put his wife's family's enslaved people to work in his own fields; instead, he hired free Blacks and paid them above-average wages.[50] And there were innovations: he disobeyed orders and left camp in the army in Monterey, Mexico, in 1846, in order to join the fighting; he tried to pick up extra money in what historian Joan Waugh gently calls "extracurricular activities" and "moneymaking schemes" during his service, such as trying to sell ice to San Franciscans, growing and harvesting crops for sale, and operating a boardinghouse. According to Waugh, two of Grant's lifelong traits were "impetuousness and impecuniousness."[51] All of this made Grant a principled innovator—making his own way according to principles personally defined, with an effort to blaze a path rather than follow one. Grant refused to be a slave owner, and he was unhappy and not very successful as a storekeeper, entrepreneur, or farmer. He just moved on from all these possibilities without making a big fuss about any of them.

Back in the army after the 1861 attack on Fort Sumter, Grant was appointed a colonel and then a brigadier general. His time in the military helped develop his understanding of how creativity and innovation were necessary parts of success. In Mexico he had served as a quartermaster, and he had run logistics while heading his own commands during the Civil War. His memoirs are full of understanding about the role of administration and organization in winning wars, and even his detractors applaud his attention to the creative logistical and organizational adjustments necessary for successful military campaigns. In the Civil War, Grant fought a number of important battles in the western theater, establishing a reputation as a skillful tactician and an aggressive leader, even as the Army of the Potomac underperformed in the East. "Unconditional Surrender" Grant could not have provided a more stark contrast to the hesitant General George McClellan. As McClellan gathered troops, information, and horses, proving repeatedly reluctant to use them to attack, Grant struck at his opponents again and again, adapting to whatever circumstances he found and whatever advantages he had.

Grant's papers offer many illustrations of a man reaching his own conclusions about what was "right."[52] At one point Grant sympathetically allowed citizens to take their belongings and various foodstuffs from a warehouse he was about to burn down, and he showed a persistent concern for rights of property during wartime. Grant claimed credit for setting up the first innovations in what eventually became the Freedmen's Bureau.[53] At other points, Grant was judgmental about what he saw as the *wrong* course to take. He offered a careful constitutional analysis demonstrating that Texas had no right to secede, for example, and he condemned the Confederate media for misleading southerners with fake news that created an inflated sense of southern victories and presented the Union as on the verge of collapse. Grant wrote that such misrepresentations raised false hopes and made the eventual process of coming to grips with defeat much more difficult.[54]

Grant's signature victory came at Vicksburg, Mississippi. Taking Vicksburg, Grant knew, would give the Union control of the Mississippi River and split the Confederacy in two, sundering Texas, Arkansas, Louisiana, and the Confederacy-aligned Native nations of the Indian Territory from the states of the Old South. Following a months-long siege, Grant forced the surrender of Vicksburg on July 4, 1863—at almost exactly the same moment Union forces were repelling Robert E. Lee's disastrously ill-advised offensive at Gettysburg. The two massive Union victories turned the tide of the war.

At Appomattox, Grant's keen handling of Lee's surrender again illustrated his ability to innovate according to principle. Grant chose to impose no embarrassments, and he let Lee's troops head home with their arms and respect intact, even allowing troops to take their horses home to enable them to put in crops—all of which helped cement a legacy that would benefit Grant for decades, even in the South. Many of Grant's decisions at Appomattox appear to have been unplanned—just the instincts of a seasoned commander of strong character and insightful analysis.[55] Even on the terms of surrender, Grant acted on instinct, in the moment with General Lee. In his *Memoirs*, Grant wrote of the surrender terms: "When I put my pen to the paper I did not know the first word that I should make use of in writing the terms. I only knew what was in my mind, and I wished to express it clearly, so that there could be no mistaking it."[56] One has a hard time imagining John Quincy Adams making it up as he went along, without a painstaking analysis of prior peace treaties and accepted protocols. Grant had evolved in his writing and character, too: biographer Ronald C. White notes that at Appomattox, "he thought and wrote in a way wholly unlike the surrenders demanded of Simon Bolivar Buckner at Fort Donelson and John Pemberton at Vicksburg. Having gained a reputation as a hard-war warrior, at Appomattox he offered a magnanimous peace."[57]

The subject of intense and ongoing controversy even today, Grant's career as a military leader is variously ascribed to his humanity and genius, to his inhumanity and coldness, to the numerical and industrial advantages of the North, to the centrifugal forces of the South. His military career—rarely by the book, often driven by tactical adjustments in pursuit of principles like victory, respect, and dignity—creates unending arguments over his choices, his motivations, and his success. Debate follows the principled innovator.

BY THE CLOSE of the Civil War, Grant's preparation for high civilian office was extensive. His early life gave him an understanding of ordinary life in the nation's Midwest, and of a variety of business and transportation contexts along the Pacific Coast. He had enjoyed a terrific look at the vastness and diversity of the growing nation, from Ohio to California and Washington State, and from Minnesota to Mexico. He served in the military from the bottom up, with stops as quartermaster, battle tactician, negotiator, and strategist. He learned a political shrewdness as he moved up the ladder and dealt with striving underlings, competitive colleagues, intrigue, and ambition. He learned the politicians when he got to Washington, and he understood the connections between mastering politics and military effectiveness.[58] By the war's end, Grant knew everyone, had worked with everyone, and had won the war.

Grant remained prominent after the war. As general in command, Grant was a key player during the Tenure of Office Act fracas between Congress and President Andrew Johnson. With Republicans fearful that President Johnson would dismiss Secretary of War Edwin Stanton and others in an effort to control the course of Reconstruction, Congress passed an act requiring that appointed officials who had been confirmed by the Senate could not be removed by the president without Senate approval. The new law, passed over Johnson's veto, upended the longstanding tradition by which the president was at liberty to dismiss any of his cabinet appointments without Congress's involvement, an authority recognized for decades as essential to the effective and efficient operation of the executive branch. The act eventually became a centerpiece of impeachment proceedings against Johnson.

At the heart of the matter was Johnson's effort to dismiss Stanton and put Grant, or later someone else, in his place. As Stanton had been appointed by Lincoln, it was unclear whether or not he was covered by the act. Johnson suspended Stanton while the Senate was out of session, in accordance with the law, replacing him with Grant. The Senate, when it returned, would then evaluate the dismissal and either confirm it or return Stanton to office. The crux of the dispute became what Grant had promised, or not promised, to do in the event that the Senate reinstated Stanton. The law suggested that a reinstated official would resume office, and anyone refusing to vacate the office or otherwise interfering would be subject to a fine and jail time for breaking the law. The situation, in brief, placed new procedural rules in direct conflict with established tradition governing the president's removal authority.

The development of the case was complicated and controversial, and the cause may have been an honest misunderstanding between Johnson and Grant.[59] When Stanton was indeed reinstated by the Senate, Grant vacated the secretary's office and Stanton returned immediately as secretary of war. Johnson felt betrayed by Grant, who he believed had reneged on a pledge to the president to either resign the office and allow Johnson to appoint a replacement before Stanton could resume his duties, or stay and force a test case in the courts regarding the constitutionality of the Tenure of Office Act.

Grant, for his part, seems to have believed that he conveyed clearly to Johnson his intention to leave the office if Congress reinstated Stanton. Grant believed he had done this clearly, carefully, and responsibly. Important for our purposes is the controversy itself. At the time, and among historians ever since, there is a sense that Grant's positions and statements were unreliable and shifting. Much of this is because Grant made decisions based less on laws and rules and more on what he assessed to be correct. As Grant wrote to Johnson on the Tenure of Office Act, dismissing legal interpretations and resting interpretation on more prosaic (and inevitably controversial) foundations: "The meaning of the law may be explained away by an astute lawyer but common sense and the views of loyal people will give it the effect intended by its framers."[60] It is hard to imagine John Quincy Adams so readily dismissing an argument over the meaning of the law, determined by experts *in* the law, and turning instead to "common sense" and intended effects.

Grant was an honest and principled man but with shifting goals and priorities. He assessed and reassessed his position and his duty and his plans at every opportunity, and he believed that others shared, or *should* have shared, common-sense understandings of complicated issues. It is entirely conceivable, then, that Johnson misunderstood, or that Grant changed his mind, or that Grant betrayed Johnson in order to try to protect the army, or any of several other possible explanations. Similar uncertainty surrounds Grant's brief career in business and politics after he left office.[61] The principled innovator left himself open to such disagreement and invited controversy by the nature of his decision-making ethic.

The Enduring Synthesist

Grant's most significant post-presidential achievement was the writing of his memoirs, still among the best examples of its genre.[62] As Grant struggled to complete the *Memoirs* before his death from throat cancer in 1885, William Howard Taft was graduating from Yale and Yale Law School and serving as an assistant prosecutor and local collector of revenue in Hamlin County, Ohio. Taft's engagement with the American state defined his early career, his presidency, and his post-presidency. Before his presidency, Taft served as a judge on the Ohio Superior Court, as a federal judge, as solicitor general (arguing eighteen cases before the Supreme Court), and as civilian administrator of the Philippines. He was President Theodore Roosevelt's secretary of war and right-hand man, traveling to Cuba, Central America, the Philippines, and Asia to resolve crises, manage construction of the Panama Canal, and promote American interests. After the White House, Taft advocated for international arbitration treaties, world courts, and the League of Nations to promote peace. He served as chief justice of the U.S. Supreme Court, leading a modernizing overhaul of the entire federal judiciary. He was involved in landmark decisions on executive powers and Major League Baseball's antitrust exemption.

Taft's life illustrates the consistency with which he applied a synthesist's decision-making ethic, building new rules and procedures to ensure that innovative understandings of governing principles endured. Reviews of Taft's opinions as a judge reveal a balanced and fair approach to the competing claims of corporations and labor, one of the main issues of the day. Taft wrote important rulings on antitrust, labor, and corporate conduct—all cutting-edge fields in the 1890s. Biographer Jonathan Lurie calls Taft a "progressive conservative" even as a federal circuit judge, "reconciling changing industrial conditions with long-held expectations of due process, precisely the goals of the Progressive Era."[63] Biographer Herbert S. Duffy found Taft's major opinions as a federal judge balanced, and he credited late nineteenth-century Judge Taft with striking "the first blow" for the Sherman Antitrust Act, paving the way for the early twentieth-century antitrust actions of the Roosevelt and Taft presidential administrations.[64] Taft "saved the Sherman Act" as a circuit court judge, and he invented the formula for expansion of the Commerce Clause in his *Addyston Pipe* opinion.[65]

Sandwiched between his stints as state judge and federal circuit judge, Taft spent two years as President Benjamin Harrison's solicitor general. Taft argued eighteen cases before the U.S. Supreme Court, winning sixteen.[66] He "contradicted numerous traditions" in the office, refusing to allow stale process to interfere with new demands, even comparing the justices of the Supreme Court to tombstones and calling them "a lot of mummies."[67]

PRESIDENT WILLIAM McKINLEY appointed Taft to head the Second Philippine Commission in 1900, and Taft worked to redirect the United States' presence in the Philippines toward civilian measures: establishing civil governance, protecting and promoting federalism and localism, building schools, nurturing political leaders. These efforts overlapped with the end of a bloody and brutal war, compared by many writers to the American experience in Vietnam.[68] While Philippine independence would be a controversial issue in American and Filipino politics for the next forty years, the Taft era came to rest on a commitment to civil process; the rule of law; and compromise, cooperation, and organized contest among differing viewpoints.

The functions of the Taft Commission, as it came to be called, included exporting a version of American regime values. Taft was to build a government in the Philippines marked by separated powers and institutions, dividing responsibilities among executive, legislative, and judicial departments. He was to appoint officials for the judicial, educational, and civil service systems; organize a federal-style system of interrelated municipal and provincial governments; and gather revenues through taxes, customs, and imposts in order to appropriate the funds back into public expenditures. In a word, the commission would be nation-building from the ground up, on a grand scale.[69] Taft put to use in the Philippines a natural ability to build coalitions, promote civil service, and develop educational, communications, and infrastructure projects.

After wresting control from the military, Taft delegated powers, shared decision making, and decentralized authority to build support across the islands.[70] Early on, he promoted specialization among the commissioners, assigning to each a section of the task at hand: to Dean Conant Worcester, municipal corporations, forestry, agriculture, and public health; to Bernard Moses, schools and taxation; to Luke Edward Wright, policing, the criminal code, franchises, and public improvements. Henry Clay Ide was given banking, currency, and registration laws, and also responsibility for drafting a new code of civil procedure for the courts. Among the early legislative acts of the commission were bills touching on forestry, mining, statistics, and government bureaus.[71]

First among the early acts of the commission was Taft's bill for a civil service in the Philippines, a notable and revealing example of how Taft understood the foundations of public administration. His dedication to process is revealed in this bill, which established a merit system and competitive examinations for promotion. Every member of Filipino government was covered, top to bottom, and the bill created a procedure for administrative oversight centered on a Civil Service Board. Taft wrote the bill in a manner that would make it adaptable to future circumstances, recognizing that laws must not be too fine or too constraining.[72]

An extraordinary extent and variety of issues arose while Taft was civilian governor. The commission's initiatives included creating a Department of Public Instruction, including eighteen divisional superintendents and numerous local school boards; establishing common schools in every community; and directing curriculum. Six hundred teachers were brought in from the United States.[73] A Constabulary Bill, an act for a postal service, a forestry service act, and an act creating a board of health were all passed in July 1901. The commission's achievements included a code of civil procedure, with provision for civil courts and protections of the core principle of habeas corpus.[74] Two hundred forty-eight laws were passed in the commission's first year.[75] Taft's character as a builder was on display in his tenure in the Philippines, as he cemented together a set of principles of governance with carefully crafted rules and institutional structures designed to stand the test of time and replace the ad-hoc decrees and innovations of the foregoing U.S. military command.

Evaluating imperialist efforts is always dicey, and there is no escaping the ethnocentrism and paternalism at the heart of the American effort. It mirrors in many ways the self-serving "civilizing" and educational efforts visited on Indigenous Americans throughout the nineteenth and twentieth centuries, efforts that did grave damage to Native cultures and communities. Still, and despite the difficult and tragic circumstances of the war and occupation, Taft's years earned him the lasting devotion of many Filipinos.[76] In part, this was due to Taft's dedication to securing peaceful and respectful relations across the races. Dances and other social events characterized William and Nellie Taft's social leadership, with Taft insisting on "a truly integrated political and social framework."[77] Historian Cathleen D. Cahill, in fact, writes that the Philippine Civil Service Commission was the only government bureau that compared favorably with the Indian service in terms of encouraging the hiring of married women and maintaining racial diversity.[78] No color line was drawn at official or unofficial events, and Taft argued that, while "the ladies of the army ... regard the Filipino ladies and men as 'niggers' and as not fit to be associated with, we propose ... to banish this idea from their mind."[79] In social issues as well as administrative development, Taft merged principle and consistent process to build enduring traditions and protocols.

TAFT RETURNED to the United States in 1904 to become President Roosevelt's secretary of war. As secretary, Taft led negotiations on an agreement to break the logjam of efforts to obstruct the construction of the Panama Canal. Taft's agreement did not erase all of the controversies over the canal, but it did smooth the progress. Popular programs, such as PBS's *American Experience* video biography of Theodore Roosevelt, suggest that Roosevelt built the canal almost "by force of his will alone." In fact, worried that the canal was not progressing, Roosevelt sent Taft to Panama to get the project back on track. Working with managers, engineers, and workers from many backgrounds, and facing tremendous physical and political dangers, Taft managed to get things in order and running relatively smoothly.[80] Stanley D. Solvick, in an essay that warns against seeing Taft's pre-presidential experience solely through the lens of his career as a judge, emphasized how the Panama situation exemplified Taft's attention to concrete detail and demonstrable achievement. "Taft's belief in a life of service," Solvick wrote, "[had] a precise meaning: the accomplishment of definite and limited tasks in the public interest. 'I am anxious to point to things done' was a sentiment that Taft expressed with plaintive frequency during his presidency."[81]

Taft returned to the Philippines in 1905, stopping in Japan to quiet concerns there that Roosevelt was favoring Russia in negotiations then taking place, and Taft traveled to the Philippines again in 1907.[82] Taft's trip to Russia in 1907, returning through Asia, was an important influence on Taft's approach to Asia as president.[83] In another, more tense, situation, Secretary Taft wound up assuming temporary control of the government of Cuba in 1906. An insurrection against President Estrada Palma had created disturbances in Havana, and Taft, having been sent to support the government in power, believed that the situation was about to explode. He assumed control of the government and ordered a landing by U.S. marines to maintain order and disarm rebels.[84] Throughout these assignments, Taft's efforts consistently synthesized established rules and traditions with principled innovations, building in those areas mechanisms for progress and stability that were integrally related to Taft's vision of American regime values.

William Howard Taft's post-presidency is among the greatest in American history. He rejected the idea of resuming a private law practice after he left the presidency, since he would be working in front of judges he had appointed: "Six of the nine Supreme Court Justices bear my commission," he said, "and forty-five per cent of the Federal judiciary have been appointed by me. That is the reason why I could not practice law as an advocate." Instead, he was elected unanimously as the president of the American Bar Association in 1913. He taught at Yale College and its law school for eight years, and coached a freshman debate team.[85] He served as chair of the Lincoln Memorial Commission, involved in details down to the selection of the type of marble to be used. He served as co-chair of the National War Labor Board in 1918 and 1919, staving off strikes during World War I by building compromises between management interests and workers. After the war, he advocated tirelessly for the League of Nations, and he became an advocate for women's suffrage.[86]

President William Harding nominated Taft to be chief justice of the U.S. Supreme Court in June 1921; the Senate confirmed him the same day.[87] Taft remained a true synthesist, articulating and achieving reforms in the federal judiciary that helped define the judiciary's role and processes for the next century and more. Notably, in Alpheus Thomas Mason's study of Taft as chief justice, so little is about Taft's opinions and so much is about his political and administrative leadership of the federal judiciary.[88]

Taft's most visible contribution is the Supreme Court building. Taft spearheaded the move for a new building, an idea that split many Court watchers and even the justices themselves. As president Taft had recognized the need for an independent branch of government to have an independent building and not to be stuck in the bowels of the Capitol, as the Court had been for a century. Taft, in other words, recognized the importance of turf. But it was a radical change: moving such a staid and respected institution to a new building, upsetting the justices' traditional habits, threatening the tradition that serves as the reservoir of the Court's public support—all of this generated opposition to the move.[89]

As chief justice, Taft also led reform of the Court's procedures and reorganization of the lower courts. He led a movement to initiate national conferences of federal judges. He raised an idea for a roving band of federal judges to alleviate docket backlogs. He exerted unmatched and novel influence on Court nominations, especially during the Warren G. Harding administration, in a manner usually not thought prudent for the chief justice. He secured from Congress the 1922 Judicial Conferences Act, allowing the Court to work with lower courts to reduce and manage appeals. He secured the Court's profoundly important right to choose which cases it hears by lobbying successfully for the Judges Bill of 1925. His efforts to reform and standardize innovative judicial procedures in the interests of new issues facing the courts reached fruition with Congress in 1934 and 1938, after his death.[90]

As chief justice, Taft led an active Court, one that overturned a heady amount of legislation. The Taft Court offered landmark rulings allowing wiretaps and searches of automobiles, upholding local zoning laws against claims of property rights advocates, upholding Major League Baseball's antitrust exemption, permitting sterilization of undesirable citizens, expanding executive powers, protecting Black voting rights, beginning the incorporation of the Bill of Rights, and offering a mixed set of results on regulation by state or federal authorities.[91] At the same time, Taft led a purposeful effort to decide cases and reduce the number of dissents that the justices wrote. Taft emphasized the role of the Court and the virtues of clear decisions over the personal preferences and peccadilloes of the justices, suppressing dissents and making the Court's operations efficient through characteristic good humor, teamwork, and leadership.[92] The changes Taft wrought in the functioning of the Supreme Court are considered great advances by scholars of the judiciary, who see them as preparing the Court for the twentieth century and contributing to its ability to balance the constitutional powers of the executive and legislative branches of government into the twenty-first century.[93]

A few short pages here hardly convey the weight of Taft's impact after he exited the White House. Much of what he accomplished is so familiar, like the Lincoln Memorial and the Supreme Court building, that we see the results every day without considering that someone had to lead the *building* of them.

Conclusion

There has always been a cottage industry in trying to predict the behavior of would-be presidents. The lives and presidencies of John Quincy Adams, Ulysses S. Grant, and William Howard Taft suggest that when a consistent decision-making ethic can be identified in a candidate's background, that ethic may be expected to carry over and inform that person's presidency. Adams was a consistent procedurist before he became president, working within established laws and approaches to promote and direct state activity. Grant innovated in the private and public sectors prior to his presidency, developing new approaches to his quartermaster's duties, diving into new business endeavors, adapting nimbly to battlefield circumstances, and charting his own course through the Tenure of Office Act controversy, all the while maintaining allegiance to what he thought right. The pre-presidential Taft synthesized principled innovations with the construction of enduring rules and procedures, particularly as a judge, as solicitor general, and in the Philippines. All three applied the same ethics to their post-presidential lives and careers. As presidents, enmeshed in the operations of the American state, their decision-making ethics became reliable predictors of their presidential approaches to the complex and difficult questions that politics and active governance present. Adams, Grant, and Taft would bring those decision-making ethics to bear on the vast opportunities for presidential leadership and administrative management afforded by the scope and activities of the American state.

2

President John Quincy Adams and the American State in the 1820s

THE FIRST thirty or forty pages of volume 8 of Charles Francis Adams's printed edition of John Quincy Adams's diary, covering the first six months of 1828, provide a brief, eye-opening introduction to the scope of state activity and presidential decision making in the John Quincy Adams era. In these pages, President Adams was called upon to resolve longstanding disputes over command of the U.S. military; to lead treatymaking with Winnebago, Creek, Cherokee, Choctaw, and Seneca leaders from places as far-flung and diverse as New York, Mississippi, Florida, Michigan, Indiana, and Arkansas; to plan the Pacific expedition with Secretary of the Navy Samuel Southard; to respond to New England insurers who requested better naval protection for commercial ships in the Mediterranean; to work with Secretary of the Treasury Richard Rush to fill in details and resolve contradictions of social policy and benefits programs left ambiguous in congressional acts; to interpret conflicts of interest in the position of attorney general at a time when that office still allowed its occupant to practice law privately; to oversee the construction of a diverse, ongoing array of internal improvements, ranging from harbor development to canal construction and the building of fortifications; to sign off on a million-dollar investment by the United States in stock offerings of the fledgling Chesapeake & Ohio Canal, just authorized by Congress after years of lobbying; to retool his cabinet just months before the 1828 election; and to protect himself from dangerous horses and would-be assassins.[1]

It was a whirlwind of activity, indicating in a few pages the broad range and widespread impact of presidential decision making. The American state was already broadly engaged, and Adams both led the administrative bureaucracy and made a host of complicated decisions on long-term policy issues and sudden, immediate events.

Adams relied on established rules and procedures as the essential mechanism guiding his decision making. Some decisions were relatively straightforward applications of longstanding approaches or deeply set guidelines and procedures; others required more creativity, albeit with a baseline approach that applied established principles and procedures as much as possible to new issues and questions. Adams worked within a host of issue areas and made numerous decisions that, collectively, make readily apparent the scope of the state and the impact of national administration. The very fact that President Adams could rely on extensive, established procedures and guidelines to help him make decisions on matters that directly affected thousands of people indicates the rapid maturation of the American state by the 1820s and the central role played by the president.

Reassessing John Quincy Adams's Presidency

In 1882, before a century of boisterous and telegenic presidents in the mode of Theodore Roosevelt, historian John T. Morse Jr. gave John Quincy Adams a much more sympathetic assessment than authors have in recent years. "So far as the rule of Mr. Adams was marked by any distinguishing characteristic," Morse wrote, "it was by a care for the material welfare of the people. More commercial treaties were negotiated during his Administration than in the thirty-six years preceding his inauguration. He was a strenuous advocate of internal improvements, and happily the condition of the national finances enabled the Government to embark in enterprises of this kind."[2] Morse was correct—Adams's efforts to empower the American public through improvement projects and social initiatives, to expand the country's territory while carefully binding that territory together, and to empower and protect the people through trade agreements and effective defense all redounded to the president's credit.

A "country prosperous and at peace" by the time of the 1828 election suggests a remarkable dissonance between history and presidential assessment. Scholars have long judged Adams by his 1828 reelection defeat, but biographer Fred Kaplan points out that Democrats and the Andrew Jackson team were forced by Adams's policy successes to focus "almost exclusively on personalities and vague generalities" in the campaign.[3] Adams himself was satisfied, too. Despite the many works about Adams that allege his depression and sense of failure at not being reelected—many written with a romantic sense of lost promise surrounding America's most well-prepared president—Adams's diary provides strong evidence that his abiding faith in the long term, his tremendous patience, and his knowledge of what he had achieved as president sustained him. "The sum of my political life sets in the deepest gloom," he wrote in December 1828, "but that of my country shines unclouded." In January 1829, he wrote, "The prosperous condition of the country takes from the load of public care all its pain, and almost all its weariness."[4]

In fact, John Quincy Adams's vision set the course for succeeding years. The historian Lynn Hudson Parsons acknowledges that "nearly everything [Adams] advocated eventually came to pass"—often through local improvement projects with Jacksonian Democrats on board.[5] Indeed, the Jacksonians used internal improvements and other projects to build their own support leading into the 1828 elections: federally supported local projects in Charleston and Savannah; the Chesapeake & Ohio Canal; the extension of the National Road; new canals including one in the Great Dismal Swamp, the Cleveland & Akron, and the Louisville & Portland; and in 1828, construction of the first passenger railway, the Baltimore & Ohio Railroad.[6] Jackson himself would throw the weight of the federal government, its army, and its administrators into Indian removal and western defense, massive projects requiring the forced relocation of tens of thousands of people, the expenditure of millions of federal dollars, and the nationalization of vast expanses of western lands.[7] Jackson proved a big-government president, and the Democrats a big-government party. The years after Adams left office, too often told as a retreat to limited government and localism, in fact maintained and expanded on Adams's vision.

Federal spending on internal improvements and other Adams initiatives actually *increased* under Jackson.[8] West Point engineers helped railroad development and made civil improvements. The Pacific Expedition, one of Adams's most important initiatives, would be mounted in 1838, two years after Jackson signed the bill authorizing the United States Exploring Expedition. The effort was called the "first National Expedition" and enjoyed up to $300,000 in initial funding.[9] The long legacy of the effort included advances in government publishing, fixing many of the problems associated with publishing the journals of the Lewis and Clark expedition, and the U.S. Botanic Garden, grown from the seeds and live plants brought back by the expedition and its leader, Charles Wilkes. Adams's idea for a naval observatory reached fruition in the 1840s, again under the Democrats; his push for a naval academy was realized in 1845. Expeditions by Henry Schoolcraft, mineral lands surveying by David Dale Owen, and army-led scientific exploration add to the list of Adamsonian efforts given formal life in the years of Andrew Jackson and Martin Van Buren.[10] Marlana Portolano writes that "by the time of Adams's death in his seat in Congress in 1849 [sic], every one of the scientific institutions or programs, proposed unsuccessfully during his presidency, were established by succeeding administrations."[11] So much built in the 1830s and 1840s by the Jacksonians, despite their antigovernment rhetoric, rested on the foundation of Adams's presidency. As Adams anticipated, "The cause will no doubt survive me, and, if the Union is destined to continue, will no doubt ultimately triumph."[12]

Adams's effectiveness as president is important to recognize. Adams may have had trouble exciting people, especially later historians, about his vision, but in the long run much of his appeal to order, process, law, and tradition effectively bridged the gap from the founding generation to the next. Adams's presidency is a lynchpin of the United States before the Civil War, as he protected the processes that governed westward expansion, laid the foundation for fighting slavery through administrative and procedural maneuvers, and married traditional values and understandings of the federal government's appropriate scope to a set of procedures and specific policy proposals aimed at actively improving the people's welfare. The words he wrote to his father, when John Adams had been defeated in the 1800 election by Thomas Jefferson, as easily apply to the legacy of President John Quincy Adams: "In your retirement you will have not only the consolation . . . that you have discharged all the duties of a virtuous citizen, but the genuine pleasure of reflecting that by the wisdom and firmness of your administration you left . . . [the] country in safe and honorable peace."[13] Adams, whose entire life operated within state activity at the national and international levels, was the center of the intersection of the presidency and the state during his administration.

The President and Domestic Affairs

The idea of active national government had been established long before the start of Adams's presidency. Decades before Adams took office, the national government was involved in managing key sectors of the national economy like land, furs, and trade; it was a key player in the development of infrastructure like canals, harbors, and the National Road; and it had developed social initiatives in areas as diverse as marine hospitals, vaccination programs, education, and veterans' benefits. Once we recognize the scope of federal governance in the eighteenth and nineteenth centuries, and its connection to active governance to promote the people's welfare, it becomes inescapably apparent that Adams and his presidential decision making touched on a host of areas.

Adams was clear about his conception of government's relationship to the public and the nation, and this understanding of early nineteenth-century American political history suggests how solidly in the mainstream were Adams's plans for the future.[14] Historian William Earl Weeks writes that Adams

> believed that government, as the instrument of the people (and of God), had a moral obligation to assist desirable enterprises that profit-minded entrepreneurs would not undertake; that it had a literal obligation to "establish justice," "provide for the common defense," "promote the general welfare," and otherwise ensure that the promises of the preamble of the Constitution were kept. The subsidization of education, the promotion of a favorable business climate, and even the planning of cities were to Adams all legitimate activities of government.[15]

Certainly some politicians of the day decried Adams's big plans and used the rhetoric of small government against him, but in no way should that suggest to us that they believed it or governed accordingly. It was small-government advocate Thomas Jefferson who initiated the Louisiana Purchase and the embargo of 1807, who signed off on the National Road and West Point. Andrew Jackson, despite his antigovernment rhetoric, used the army to move American Indians west and grabbed authority over lands and policies across the continent. Presidents of all persuasions supported national universities and plans to have the national government repatriate Africans, run vaccination programs against smallpox, administer land title reconciliation commissions, offer indemnities and payments to territorial settlers to compensate them for alleged attacks by Indigenous peoples and to deter retaliation, and develop a national postal communications system.

Internal improvement, of course, occupied a central place in the Adams agenda. In the next chapter, we will see how Adams defended and perpetuated the government's role in such endeavors through public rhetoric appealing to long-established institutional processes and constitutional understandings. In the details, though, we see how President Adams applied order and process to the American System, which envisioned a nation tied together through canals and roadways, coordinated to develop western areas, improve trade, encourage settlement, and consciously bind together East and West—a nation built and unified through government money and management. Adams believed, as did Henry Clay and many others, that the best way to ensure a peaceful future for inhabitants of the continent was to make sure that they all saw themselves as members of the same national community.[16]

By the time he was elected president, John Quincy Adams had supported national involvement in infrastructure and economic improvements for decades. He claimed credit as the visionary of the American System by pointing out that he had supported Albert Gallatin's report recommending nationally coordinated improvements back in 1808.[17] In 1822, Adams had written that "the first *duty* of a nation, [is] that of bettering its own condition by internal improvement."[18] In his address at the groundbreaking for the Chesapeake & Ohio Canal, Adams located national connectivity and improvement as the third major stage of national development, after the Declaration of Independence and unification under the Constitution. He saw improvement as a moral duty, and one that the federal government had an obligation to promote. By the end of his term, the Chesapeake & Ohio Canal, the Washington–New Orleans Road, and a canal from northern Vermont to the Connecticut River were all nearing completion. Under Adams, the National Road was extended from Wheeling, West Virginia, to Zanesville, Ohio; a road from Detroit went west fifty miles; and a road from Maumee to Detroit was underway. The next three years saw surveys completed for a wide variety of specific projects, including extension of the National Road east to Washington, DC and west to

St. Louis, and construction of numerous other road, canal, harbor, and waterway improvement projects around the country. Thirty piers were authorized between 1826 and 1828.[19]

Adams employed a procedurized, small-bid contract mechanism to manage the government's role in planning and building projects, and scholars have emphasized the blend of public and private partnerships and national and local focus in designing and building the projects.[20] The executive branch led in key aspects, including the work of experts at the War Department in pushing Congress to pass what became the landmark 1824 General Survey Act, which authorized the president to assign military engineers to civilian projects "of national importance."[21] In 1826, Simon Bernard and Joseph Totten, at the head of the board established by the 1824 act to operationalize President Monroe's distinction between national improvement projects and local ones, "helped Congress piece together the first omnibus river and harbor act." Adams, for his part, offered "eager support" to the Board of Engineers of Internal Improvements.[22]

Executive leadership also led initiatives in military road construction in Michigan, Florida, and Arkansas.[23] Roads were built using new macadam technology and local materials, and technical assistance on the ground reinforced formal government planning reports. Creative financial aid initiatives assisted government-led construction, such as using grants of public lands in the West and government subscriptions to corporate stock issues in the East. Rights of way were granted to spark development, with Congress and the executive working in collaboration. According to Treasury Secretary Richard Rush, the government spent $14 million on such efforts between 1824 and 1828. More money was appropriated for improvement projects during Adams's term than in all previous presidential terms combined.[24]

In one illustrative example, President Adams worked with Congress and state representatives in integrated land, internal improvement, and Indian affairs policies in Indiana.[25] Here, with a federal treaty specifying regulations for road building in Indian country, Congress debated provisions and appropriated funds, and state officials jockeyed for influence over decisions about locating the road, surveying details, and implementation issues—they jockeyed among themselves and with Secretary of War James Barbour, General Land Office officials, the Indian agent in the region, and Potawatomi leaders. The president, top administrators, and field agents worked with congressional, state, local, and tribal leaders to work out complex details for siting, engineering, and other dynamics in this and many similar situations.[26] Adams was fully engaged in such efforts.

As one might expect in such circumstances—and as is the case in modern infrastructure debates—politics played a more significant role than engineering and technical approaches to internal improvement initiatives.[27] In this we see another example of executive branch leadership as well as the ability of executive branch officials—both in the capital and in the field—to lead others in crafting and implementing decisions. The critical criteria that projects should be "of national importance" to receive federal aid led railroads and other entities to press their arguments for worthiness based on national defense and other relevant considerations, often including facilitating Indian removal.[28] Railroads used the defense applications of their roads to lobby the president and the War Department, Congress and congressional delegations, and state politicians to secure federal aid.[29]

Robert G. Angevine, for example, describes how politics were involved with federal support of the Baltimore & Ohio Railroad, the first to gain assistance from the War Department under the 1824 General Survey Act. The railroad sent three of its most influential directors to meet with the Adams administration, with Adams referring them to Secretary of War Barbour. Barbour—as he corresponded with allies in Maryland about Adams's reelection effort—dispatched three engineering brigades to survey the road; by July 1828, twelve army engineers worked for the Baltimore & Ohio Railroad itself. Angevine concludes, "The true measure of a railroad's importance in the eyes of the War Department was the political clout of its supporters, not its national or military utility." Politics advanced the request for help from the administration, as the regional influence of the railroad's advocates dovetailed with Adams's reelection needs.[30]

Improvement efforts, including "harbor development, stream-bed clearance, canal and road construction," proved to be the most popular and successful domestic programs of the Adams administration.[31] Not only did the administration move successfully on these projects, but many were approved by opposition Democrats in Congress and many projects were continued by subsequent congresses and by the Jackson administration long after Adams had left office. In the heat of the 1828 election campaign, in fact, Adams and a hostile Congress worked together to pass into law numerous improvement projects, a solid record of achievement grinding along beneath the more familiar rhetoric and rancor of that particular contest. Congress passed the Chesapeake & Ohio Canal bill in the middle of the 1828 campaign, along with a bill appropriating $200,000 and giving the president discretionary authority to have built a breakwater at the mouth of Delaware Bay. "The whole work will probably cost five or six millions," Adams wrote approvingly, before sneering at the political attacks leveled at broadly popular government activity: "This discretionary power and control over public money singularly contrasts with the report of the [congressional] Retrenchment Committee, containing near one hundred and fifty pages of invective upon every Department of the Government, except the Post Office, for extravagance and waste of public money."[32]

Beyond the importance of politics, these projects also demonstrate the deep expertise developed within the executive branch by the 1820s.[33] Over the years, Adams wrote of government improving navigation by surveying the Connecticut River above Hartford; congressional appropriation for preservation of islands in Boston Harbor; changes to the use of scientific devices, with the surveyor of the port of New York proposing to make experiments "to ascertain the comparative merits of hydrometers"; removal of obstructions from the Mississippi and Ohio Rivers and construction of dry-docks at Charlestown, Massachusetts, and Gosport, Virginia; erection of warehouses in cities to store important merchandise; and proposals for contracts for supplying oil to all U.S. lighthouses. A senator from Mississippi and a representative from Alabama called on Adams "to urge the appointment of engineers for a survey in which their States have a special interest."[34] The U.S. Army built roads for defense and to encourage settlement, like the critical military road from Detroit to Fort Dearborn (Chicago) built in 1825.[35]

Internal improvement projects were popular, funded, and dispersed throughout the country—not by fiat but through institutional collaboration, discussion among competing interests, and regularized process and procedure. The works were important and popular in themselves, but they also spurred new settlement and population expansion. With government money and projects came workers and industry to western areas; with workers and industry came commercial supporters like carting companies, food suppliers, blacksmith shops—and eventually families and new settlers. Even slow and delayed development spurred settlement.[36]

All of this activity never reached the level of centralized planning envisioned in the 1808 Gallatin report, but it does represent the effective leveraging of national resources for coordinated projects that benefited the nation and its communities. President Adams's efforts and those of executive branch administrators helped lead to massive construction and engineering projects developed with a healthy blend of local, national, technical, and political influence. Adams himself did not seem disappointed at the progress made in the numerous and popular projects continuing or begun on his watch. The annual report of the secretary of war in November 1828, for example, worked up by Secretary of War Peter Porter and submitted by Adams to Congress, touted the work being done on military roads as well as the extensive support given by army engineers and other federal officials to civilian projects.[37]

FOR ADAMS, the state's obligation to empower the nation and its inhabitants did not stop at the construction of roads and canals. He added initiatives in scientific development, education, bankruptcy legislation, and management of the public debt. He pushed for a naval academy, a national university, and geographical and astronomical exploration.[38] Adams signed bills for the relief of Revolutionary War veterans, and as president he took advantage of his opportunity to interpret ambiguous legislation and determine by executive action the scope of the class of beneficiaries. In his diary, Adams noted the frustration of his secretary of the treasury, Richard Rush, when it came to this program: "Mr. Rush brought me the Act for the benefit of the surviving officers of the Revolutionary War, passed at the recent session of Congress, the execution of which is devolved, much to his annoyance, upon him instead of the Secretary of War." Adams described the law: "The Act provides for officers to whom half-pay for life was promised by resolution of Congress of 21st October, 1780, which extended to officers who should continue in service to the end of the war."[39]

Adams then continued, noting ambiguities in the legislation: "One question was, whether it would apply to officers who entered the service after the passage of the resolution. The other question was, whether the Act included the officers in the Medical Department who were not named in the resolution of 21st October, 1780, but for whom a similar provision was made by resolution of 17th January, 1781." Adams did not duck the quandary left by Congress: "I told Mr. Rush," he wrote, "that if it was a penal statute I should not consider it as embracing either of these descriptions of officers, but, as it was beneficent and remedial, I thought that it should be construed to include them both."[40] Thus Adams as president made a key decision that expanded the population of beneficiaries in Congress's program, and he expressed the logic of beneficence that supported his decision.

President Adams likewise gave impetus to one of the greatest forgotten initiatives of the nineteenth century: government exploration of the Pacific Ocean. Scientific exploration supported by the federal government was nothing new, of course—the government had supported such efforts for decades, most notably in the expeditions of Lewis and Clark. Adams conceived of a plan to send ships around South America's Cape Horn and up through the Pacific Ocean to the Bering Strait, exploring and investigating along the way. Critically important for America's seafaring expansion, when the idea reached fruition under Jackson and Van Buren and set sail in 1838, 6 ships and 350 men charted waters and islands, looked for coaling stations, contacted Native populations, and recorded fishing and whaling sites and movements.[41]

It was a massively successful effort to bring together information that would benefit American shipping and industry. The fruits of the exploration would be felt long afterward, as Matthew Maury and others coordinated the information through naval observatories and government publications. President Adams laid the foundation for one of the nation's most significant and successful efforts in scientific, commercial, and cultural exploration. On land, army topographical engineers helped build roads and public works, map travel and trade routes, locate wells and water, and generally aid the United States in a managed takeover of the continent.[42] Mountain men and private whalers would not have been able to map the land and sea in the same manner, with the same efficiency, and with the same public benefits as government workers did for decades in the nineteenth century. Under Adams, the work expanded into some of its greatest achievements.

Few of these represented new ideas, and Adams did not extend the application of governmental authority into new areas of policy. Adams concentrated on executing existing ideas and either cementing in place or expanding government's role in issues and policies where it already existed. There were no revolutionary expansions of government scope or procedure under Adams—just incremental advances respectful of institutional collaboration and established processes. The National Road began under Jefferson in 1806, pension legislation had passed in 1818, debtor relief legislation in 1821. Assistance for Revolutionary War veterans went back to the war itself. Science historian A. Hunter Dupree noted that, from the founding generation, "universities and learned societies were in fact internal improvements."[43] Adams's commitment to the people's welfare drove his efforts to expand infrastructure, extend social policy benefits, and initiate new exploration, all the while driving a significant acceleration in economic growth.[44]

Adams was not always successful. His effort to pass bankruptcy legislation was modeled on his father's measure, which had been repealed under Jefferson. Aimed at commercial bankruptcies, the new provision aimed to add agricultural interests to already-protected groups of merchants and traders—an effort to increase Adams's support in the West and in farming areas. The measure succumbed to a mix of politics, sectional differences, and "partisan obstructionism."[45] Adams also failed in women's education. Emma Willard, the leader of a female seminary in Troy, New York, visited President Adams in August 1826, with the idea that Adams could prevail upon Congress to support an institution for educating women. Adams wrote in his diary,

> Mrs. Willard is a sensible and spirited woman, and I told her that the purpose of improving female education had my approbation and hearty good wishes; and with regard to any assistance from Congress, I was sorry she must expect nothing more. Congress, I was convinced, would now do nothing. They will do nothing for education of boys, excepting to make soldiers. They will not endow a university. I hoped this disposition would change, but, while it continues, any application to Congress for female education must be fruitless.[46]

Notable, of course, when assessing the role of the presidency, is that Willard considered the president an appropriate person to help her sway Congress through application from the president. It was the context, not the constraints of the office, that deterred Adams in this case.

Adams did prevail, though, on administration measures to reduce the public debt. Adams and Treasury Secretary Rush protected their efforts to refinance the public debt and secure the Bank of the United States as a resource for national development and investment.[47] Adams also worked to maintain a system of land sales that would keep funds coming to the federal government, especially once the public debt was retired. This effort cut against the interests of many westerners, who sought cheaper land available more quickly.[48]

IN THESE and a host of other matters Adams regularly appealed to laws and rules as guides to decision making, even in novel cases. He also applied decision-making and executive leadership techniques that are often the subject of current advice for leaders in public administration. Adams utilized collegial decision making, he absented himself from meetings in order to allow the cabinet to discuss matters with candor, and he sometimes advocated for full disclosure in communications with Congress.[49]

One typical example of Adams's approach to complicated questions involved the commandant of the Marine Corps, Archibald Henderson, and his appointment of Captain J. L. Kuhn as paymaster. Kuhn had held the post for several years but had recently brought charges against Henderson. A Court of Enquiry exonerated Henderson, who then sought to remove Kuhn from his office. Henderson wrote to Secretary of the Navy Samuel Southard about the matter, with Southard indicating a belief that the president had the right of appointing the paymaster, not the commandant.

Adams wrote in his diary, "The question depends upon the construction of three or four Acts of Congress, which Mr. Southard thinks have been incorrectly construed, but upon two of which, at least, my opinion inclines to the old construction, and upon the other I am not entirely without doubt." Adams requested a consultation with the cabinet "before we undertake to introduce a practice entirely new and opposite to that which has been long established and considered as legal." A subsequent cabinet discussion examined the series of relevant laws and differing interpretations, as well as consequences of various decisions that Adams might make. "It was finally determined," Adams wrote, "that the Secretary of the Navy should inform Colonel Henderson verbally that it is thought best no change of the appointment should be made before the session of Congress, and that then some measure should be adopted to remove all ambiguity from the law [governing appointment of staff officers of the Marine Corps]."[50] Adams had created a practical workaround consistent with his conclusion that the laws were ambiguous: no change would be made until Congress had a chance to respond by clarifying the laws regulating the appointment process.

In another example, Adams was confronted with West Point entrance exams, including a physical examination, that suddenly required applicants to appear naked before the examiner. Adams wrote,

> One of the regulations directs that no candidate for admission shall be received who is deformed, or diseased infectiously, or disqualified by it for military service. In execution of this rule, candidates for admission this year were, for the first time, required to undergo the inspection of a surgeon naked. Three of them—a son of Mr. Clay, a son of Mr. Reed, the late Senator from Mississippi, and Anderson [whose father brought the matter to Adams's attention]—refused to submit to this examination, and were not admitted.

Adams was confronted by Anderson's father, who "was extremely indignant at this act of oppression, as he considers it. He seemed unwilling to admit the possibility that I should not be as angry at this measure as he was, and could hardly endure the comparative coolness with which I considered it." Adams fell back on systematic analysis, writing, "I told him that I felt some repugnancy to this mode of ascertaining the fact of their bodily soundness, and some surprise at its being thus suddenly introduced, but that before making up my judgment upon it I must recur to the old principle, 'Audi alteram partem' [Listen to the other side]." Adams decided the case in keeping with traditional approaches: "As to the regulation excluding from admission persons infected with contagious disease, I recommended that hereafter it should be executed without an exposure of absolute nakedness."[51]

There are other, quicker moments where Adams appealed to established procedures and understandings as a basis for decision making. His diary is full of passages like this:

> Mr. Brent brought me a draft of a proclamation declaring a suspension of the discriminating duties upon vessels and their cargoes belonging to the subjects of his holiness the Pope. But he had erroneously copied the former proclamations, founded on the Act of 3d March, 1815, which is repealed. I told him it must be founded on the Act of 7th January, 1824; read to him the fourth section of the Act, and directed that the proclamation should follow it, as far as possible, word for word.[52]

In October 1826, Adams invoked traditional protocol to dispense with another request: "Mr. Rind came to solicit my subscription to a newspaper which he proposed to start at Georgetown; and Mr. Meyer for a scientific periodical publication in this city. By a long-established rule, the President never puts his name to subscriptions, and I refer all such applicants, who are numerous, to my son."[53] This suggests a careful understanding of the role of the president's name and reputation in matters interesting to the public.

The American state was sufficiently established to allow a president to rely on laws, rules, and administrative guidelines as polestars for presidential decision making. The scope of decisions that confronted the president in the 1820s was wide, affecting thousands of individuals in their interactions with various offices and programs of the government.[54] From making policy by interpreting ambiguous statutory guidelines, to negotiating details of improvement projects, to overseeing administration at West Point—and to being solicited for help in passing education legislation and in applying favors by proclamation regarding shipping duties—presidential action and the intrusiveness of the administrative state are readily visible.

President Adams and Indian Affairs

The Adams administration inherited and furthered a variety of government programs for territorial expansion, including the Indian treaty system, federal dominance in land acquisition, and federal government control of diplomacy. Since the earliest days of the republic, a stable system of U.S.-Indian relations had rested on federal treaties that recognized Native nations as political sovereigns, set geographical boundaries, and established protocols for trade, criminal justice, education, and other policies. Within the treaty system, a series of national trade and intercourse laws regulated commerce, licensing, and other interactions between American Indians and traders, developers, new settlers, and others. The United States provided aid to Native nations in the form of farming implements, education benefits, and vocational training—often as payment for lands ceded by Native communities. An administrative system indemnified white settlers against losses from conflict with American Indians and paid claims to whites whose holdings had been damaged. Nonprofit government trading houses and a network of Indian agents regulated the fur trade and secured a federal presence in areas of increasing interactions between U.S. and Native interests. All in all, what existed by the 1820s was a sophisticated system of interconnected national policies, developed with great care at the federal level because of the tremendous significance national and state leaders attached to Indian affairs and national expansion. Designing and implementing these policies relied on executive direct action, as well as interactions with Congress, in an issue area that often straddled the line between foreign and domestic policy.

This entire network of policies relied on national supremacy—the cornerstone idea that the national government, not the states, controlled the course and direction of land exchanges, trade relations, and Indian affairs. Again rooted in the early republic, state leaders themselves had surrendered many of their interests to the organization and supervision of the national government, recognizing that state-by-state trade agreements with various tribes, and state-by-state peace agreements, were inefficient and often counterproductive. It was in every state's interest, as well as the nation's, to avoid conflict with Native nations. Leaders believed that any such conflict might metastasize into a larger war, which in turn could encourage British, French, or Spanish forces to renew fighting in North America and threaten the success of the American experiment. Indian affairs were a significant issue throughout the nineteenth century, fraught with risk and carefully managed by national officials.

Adams not only grew up with this worldview in expansion and Indian affairs—he had helped build it. Adams's career as a diplomat, international negotiator, and policy architect make him a crucial figure in American history, a designer and a defender of foundational foreign and domestic policies. Adams's work before moving into the presidency not only prepared him for that office; it meant that he entered the office with deep knowledge and experience of existing policies and procedures. He was steeped in law, policy, and protocol. He understood not only the geopolitical ramifications of international policy and negotiation but also the reasons why things were done the way they were done. To Adams, upholding treaties and agreements was far more important than immediate political expediency—a nation of laws must abide by those laws. By the time he was president, Adams was administering a set of policies and programs that, at a series of very critical junctures, he had helped build. Adams's world valued treaties and diplomacy, and it placed the national government in a dominant position regarding continental expansion and relations with still-powerful American Indian nations.

Adams's Indian policies were based on a commitment to regular order and transparent administrative processes. The Adams administration's treaties with Native nations worked to protect U.S. interests, as treaties had since the Washington administration. One of the most significant was a treaty with the Osage and Kansa nations in 1825. Adams delegated to the field service authority given to him by Congress to make the deal, which secured tribal consent for the marking of a road between Missouri and New Mexico. In turn, this agreement resulted in the landmark 1825 agreement at Council Bluffs that opened a protected Santa Fe Trail for commerce, communication, and transportation. The treaty guaranteed that the protected area would include "a reasonable distance on either side [of the road], so that travellers thereon may, at any time, leave the marked tract, for the purpose of finding subsistence and proper camping places."[55] The Corps of Topographical Engineers would work on improving the road for years afterward, as thousands of Americans traversed it for adventure and economic gain.

Other treaties to protect trade and traders were signed with Native nations along the Missouri River in 1825. As Congress resisted pressure from fur-trading companies to build a fort and protect the area through military force, Adams's diplomatic commissioners, General Henry Atkinson and Indian agent Benjamin O'Fallon, signed nine treaties with Poncas, Oglalas, Cheyennes, Mandans, and others along the river in the summer of 1825. These were traditional treaties of trade and friendship, not treaties aimed at land cessions or at reestablishing peace after conflict. The treaties acknowledged the tribes' existence as political sovereigns, they pledged friendship, and they committed the tribes to U.S. supremacy and its right to regulate trade. The United States agreed to expand its oversight of the fur trade and continue to license authorized traders, and the treaties outlined familiar processes for dealing with injuries, thefts, and other common problems. More treaties were signed in the fall with Otos, Pawnees, and Omahas.[56]

Historian Francis Paul Prucha concludes, "These treaties were a straightforward use of the treatymaking power to regularize relations with frontier tribes, to bring them formally into the political orbit of the United States, and thus force them to cut ties with the British and turn their trade to American, not British, traders." Close to thirty treaties focused on commercial relations and friendship were proclaimed in Adams's four years as president.[57] President Adams also negotiated an end to violent conflict with the Winnebagoes and pardoned influential leaders.[58] He signed an aggressive guarantee to the Cherokees in Arkansas respecting their lands. And he worked to maintain peace and establish conflict-mediation procedures in Florida using negotiation, diplomacy, and purposeful interpretation of treaty language to ease tensions that, under Andrew Jackson's leadership, would fester and then explode into the vicious Second Seminole War.[59]

Adams also defended transparency and the United States' longstanding commitment to process in treatymaking. He refused to proclaim a corrupted treaty, for example, made with the Senecas west of New York State. The Seneca had, since 1810, refused to sell remaining lands, especially the critically important lands of the Buffalo Creek Reservation. The Ogden Land Company was a New York–based effort that tried for years to get the Seneca to sell. In 1826, the company secured the signatures of Seneca leaders, including Red Jacket, on an agreement selling vast tracts of Native lands. Present at the negotiations was Oliver Forward, appointed by Adams to represent the federal government at a negotiation sanctioned by Congress. When the agreement was to go before the Senate for ratification, however, a variety of complications arose. Most importantly, Red Jacket and other Seneca leaders appealed to the president directly, claiming that they had been tricked and coerced into the sale, that they had been threatened with forced removal if they did not sell, and that the vast majority of their people opposed the sale.

Adams refused to cave to pressure to put the presidency's authority behind the treaty, and he effectively resisted the pressure brought by the extraordinary experience and political weight of the forces attempting to drive the treaty through to ratification. Not only Forward but the Ogden Company's agents, local politicians, and Seneca leaders allied behind a leader named Young King argued for the validity of the treaty. Within the administration, Indian affairs head Thomas McKenney, Vice President John C. Calhoun, and Secretary of War Peter Porter—a powerful New York player and a force in the dispossession of American Indians in the New York area—all leaned toward validating the agreement. Adams stood against his top administrative experts and some of the strongest players in New York—and he did so on the verge of a presidential election in which New York's support was widely seen as crucial. In the event, Adams would lose New York to the ticket of Andrew Jackson and New York's Martin Van Buren, an upstate force of the first water. Adams refused to surrender his position, though, instead ordering an investigation and refusing to resubmit the treaty to the Senate. He wanted to know how the process had taken place, because an unfair process or violations of established procedures would render the treaty unacceptable. The treaty was neither ratified by the Senate nor proclaimed by the president.[60]

Committed to established processes but also steeped in the contradictions of U.S. history, Adams struggled with the conflicted history of U.S.-Indian relations as it continued to play out in new ways. His response to the Cherokees' effort to write a constitution, for example, reflected how his commitment to existing relationships struggled when confronted with creative developments and the rapid pace of state-administered territorial expansion. "The Cherokees in Georgia have now been making a written Constitution," Adams wrote in his diary in January 1828, "but this imperium in imperio is impracticable, and in the instances of the New York Indians removed to Green Bay, and of the Cherokees removed to the Territory of Arkansas, we have scarcely given them time to build their wigwams before we are called upon by our own people to drive them out again." Adams appealed to the U.S. Constitution and to Congress in trying to find a resolution to the issues posed by the Cherokees' new constitution, writing, "I thought that the Indians could not by any formation of a Constitution change the character of their relations to the United States, or establish an independent civilized government within the Territories of the Union."[61] Like the Florida situation discussed above, and the Creek situation discussed in detail in the next chapter, Adams's efforts to manage practical issues in the Cherokee context while respecting treaties and laws would explode into violence and forced removal under Jackson and Van Buren.

In the West, Adams confronted a situation made by his predecessors. Cherokees in Arkansas possessed a strip of land under U.S. protection, but white settlers had discovered that the land was excellent—"and they are swarming thither like bees," Adams wrote. "They are covering it with unlicensed settlements, and the people of the territory are loudly claiming that the land should be offered for sale."[62] Adams issued a strong, explicit statement in the Arkansas case, establishing a clear goal: "It being the anxious desire of the Government of the United States to secure to the Cherokee nation of Indians . . . a *permanent* home, and which shall, under the most solemn guarantee of the United States, be, and remain, theirs forever—a home that shall never, in all future time, be embarrassed by having extended around it the lines, or placed over it the jurisdiction of a Territory or State, nor be pressed upon by the extension, in any way, of any of the limits of any existing Territory or State."[63] Adams indicated that his "own opinion is that the most benevolent course towards them [the Cherokee] would be to give them the rights and subject them to the duties of citizens, as a part of our own people," but he stated that "even this the people of the States within which they are situated will not permit." Adams recognized that American policy was paradoxical and inconsistent, promising at once to extinguish Native title in favor of whites while simultaneously guaranteeing that Native nations "should hold their lands forever." Adams identified the deeper issue: "This collision between the just and reasonable demands of our own people and the pledge seemingly given to the Indians is very embarrassing, and it is scarcely imaginable that within so recent a period the President and Secretary of War [James Monroe and John Calhoun, in 1820 and 1821] should have assumed so unwarranted an authority and have given so inconsiderate a pledge." Adams searched desperately for a valid construction of the written promise that would protect Cherokee interests but also allow white settlement.[64]

The details of the Adams administration's approach to Lovely's Purchase, as the tract at issue was called, exemplify much about the presidency and the state in these years. The tract itself had been purchased by a government subagent without formal authorization to make the purchase. As Cherokees and white settlers competed for the land and expanded settlements, a diverse variety of interests pressured the president, Congress, and the courts. Adams took the lead in negotiations at the federal level, eventually breaking an impasse that saw McKenney, Calhoun, and the Cherokees on one side and Secretary of War Barbour, members of Congress, and Arkansas state representatives on the other. Adams sided with McKenney, Calhoun, and the Cherokees, in the process ordering the suspension of a land survey that had been explicitly authorized by Congress. Adams exerted direct pressure to reach a settlement that, in the end, made many of the participants opponents of government action but which worked to manage competing interests and help secure good land to the Cherokees surrounded by clear, protectable boundaries.[65]

As for the presidency, Adams regularly became directly involved in treaty negotiations with Native nations and related negotiations with state representatives and members of Congress, all of whom were keen to shape the process and protect their interests. Adams often met with Native delegations when they arrived in Washington, then let Barbour, McKenney, and others (sometimes chosen in response to particular circumstances, like Michigan territorial governor Lewis Cass) carry out the detailed negotiations. Adams remained in the background, regularly informed of the negotiations and often weighing in to resolve sticking points and make critical decisions. Adams's cabinet members also negotiated carefully with key U.S. senators like Thomas Hart Benton to shape the treaties before or after they were submitted for the Senate's consent, and with House members regarding necessary appropriations and other legislative matters.[66]

All of these actions continued established processes and national supremacy in Indian affairs, including the central role of presidential leadership at the intersection of national expansion and national values, manifested in concrete policy decisions. Importantly, Adams would never yield on the question of forced removal or on the sanctity of the nation's agreements, as we will see in detail in the next chapter. Adams broke little new ground as he applied longstanding executive powers, protected existing national commitments, and led the administration of Indian affairs, all the while remaining loyal to established state processes.

The President, Defense, and Foreign Affairs

President Adams also worked to manage and oversee a variety of defense and foreign affairs initiatives. As in domestic affairs, most of Adams's actions were not novel—instead, they expanded preexisting approaches and addressed new events through the application of established processes.

Adams considered foreign policy, especially the promotion of U.S. trading interests, as a primary focus of his administration. By the 1820s, the president was firmly established as the nation's chief international promoter of American trade and business interests. Even George Washington advocated international trade agreements, of course, despite his Farewell Address's warning against entangling alliances, and so again Adams was breaking little new ground. Economic nationalism drove Adams, as it had driven many of his colleagues: he dedicated his administration to increasing shipping, increasing cargoes, and expanding and multiplying markets.[67] Adams still prioritized procedures and rules, though. He promoted commercial access, reciprocity, and freedom of the seas, including protections for neutral shipping and global sea lanes open to all nations, all outlined and guaranteed by treaties or international agreements.

The Adams administration settled numerous individual claims; completed nine general commercial treaties; preserved and extended agreements with major players in Europe like England, France, and the Netherlands; began work (completed under Jackson) with Austria, Turkey, and Mexico; and signed important if short-lived agreements with nations in South and Central America.[68] The commercial treaties included Denmark in 1826, the Hanseatic League and Scandinavian countries in 1827, and Prussia and Austria in 1828.[69] Adams concluded a convention with Great Britain in 1826 over enslaved people taken by Britain during the Revolutionary War, an issue that had been passed forward since the Treaty of Ghent.[70] In 1827, Gallatin signed an extension of the 1815 commercial convention with Britain, originally negotiated by Adams. Mary W. M. Hargreaves sees a treaty signed with the federation of Central America as "the showpiece of the administration's goals in international commercial relationships and as a model for its negotiators in drawing up subsequent arrangements." Many of these agreements included provisions establishing protocols and processes to cover future disputes and claims.[71]

Adams also stepped up U.S. involvement in those treaties with Native nations that aimed at defense more than friendship and trade. Francis Paul Prucha's comprehensive study *American Indian Treaties* outlines how Adams's administration focused on crafting peace agreements among competing tribes. The landmark Treaty of Prairie du Chien in 1825, and two later treaties in 1826 and 1827, for example, delineated formal boundaries among the Chippewa, Menominee, Sac and Fox, and Winnebago. More than a thousand American Indians gathered with federal commissioners to sign the treaty.[72] Adams even dealt personally with leaders of nations from New York that had been displaced into the Old Northwest and were running into tensions with Native peoples already inhabiting the area. He addressed conflict between Winnebagoes and encroaching lead miners in Wisconsin in 1825, bringing Winnebago leaders to Washington after some violent outbreaks to negotiate a cession of the mineral lands at issue.[73] Prucha also discusses an 1828–29 removal by the U.S. Army of white intruders encroaching on Winnebago lands, coming at the behest of the Adams administration. The military managed to defuse the conflict and establish "a complete cordon of forts from Green Bay to the Mississippi River," protecting the Indian trade and pacifying relations with nearby nations.[74]

The Adams administration secured an agreement with the Choctaw Nation in 1825 that smoothed the way for implementation of the controversial Treaty of Doak's Stand, signed five years earlier.[75] In another case, a treaty signed with removed Cherokees in 1828, the Adams administration set a pattern for intertribal treatymaking and the articulation of boundaries that became a model for the next generation of Plains treaties.[76] Treaties of the Adams era typically included provisions for presents and annuities, promotion of U.S. initiatives in farming and housing, resources for education, and payments by the United States of claims against the tribes levied by U.S. citizens.[77] None of this was groundbreaking—such efforts expanded and extended practices, principles, and processes that were by the 1820s familiar and well-accepted—but it again demonstrates the scope and influence of the state and the importance of presidential leadership and administrative decision making.

Adams even sought to protect religious freedom, for Americans and for others, through the administration's agreements. The 1826 agreement with Mexico guaranteed freedom of religious exercise for Americans in Mexico. Adams had even more success in protecting Americans' religious exercise in his efforts with Latin American nations.[78]

Adams failed at times in foreign policy, too, and Central America was the key player in one of Adams's most noted policy failures. Importantly for this study, this "failure" is directly tied to Adams's commitment to procedure—and in the case of the 1826 Panama Congress, to his belief that interbranch collaboration could be the right procedure to follow, even if it was not necessarily the only path or even the most likely to succeed. The Panama Congress was an effort by Adams to send American representatives to a conference in Panama being attended by representatives of Mexico and Central American nations. Adams believed it would be a good opportunity to build ties with those nations, expand commitments to the Monroe Doctrine, and promote American values like religious freedom. The failure of the effort is often blamed on Adams's decision to involve Congress in selecting the delegates, rather than selecting them through simple presidential appointment.

Yet the story surrounding the Panama Congress offers insights into the use of presidential tools. Adams unilaterally accepted the invitation to send delegates in an exercise of executive power, and he saw it as completely within the president's authority to do so. He then engaged the Senate in the process of nominating and confirming delegates to the Congress, and the House in relation to appropriating funds for the mission.[79] Adams clearly understood the significance of public opinion to effective diplomacy, and he publicly pressed his hopes for the Panama Congress, including the opportunity to promote religious liberty, by including it in the proposals he outlined in his First Annual Message and then by issuing a special message to Congress on the matter in late 1825.[80] Adams's efforts were so prominent and proactive that they were singled out by Senator Hugh L. White of Tennessee, who warned that the moves reflected a dangerous assumption of power by the president.[81]

Sniping at the administration within the House and Senate delayed the appointments and doomed the U.S. mission. Appropriations lagged, American divisiveness alienated Latin American leaders, and the American delegates did not arrive until well after the conference was to have taken place.[82] Adams's detractors focus on the failure of a popular effort brought down by political partisanship that Adams seemed to invite.[83] Yet Adams chose to involve Congress because the conference would be concerned with the future fate of Cuba and of slavery in the Southern Hemisphere, and delegates would be discussing matters involving other neighbor nations like Mexico and Colombia. These issues involved sectional and political interests within the United States, and Adams believed that the president should not make these important decisions unilaterally.[84] Instead, he chose an open yet contentious process of selecting the delegates and defining their mission that involved a broad array of representatives and interests. Relying on such processes resulted in successful efforts in many of the contexts discussed above; it led to a failure of Adams's hopes for the Panama Congress, even as it maintained the decision-making and leadership integrity of the Adams administration.

SOME OF the administrative responsibilities of the Adams presidency crossed lines between what might be considered foreign and domestic policy. Many events in Indian affairs blended elements of foreign affairs, like treatymaking and diplomacy, with aspects considered by some to be more strictly domestic affairs, like land acquisition and distribution and the extension of judicial jurisdictions. Other matters also saw foreign and domestic matters overlap. Adams worked diligently to administer government procedures aimed at settling indemnity claims, including claims arising from depredations to American shipping, some of which went back decades. Adams supervised a process of cleaning up longstanding and divisive issues with foreign nations such as France, Russia, Sweden, Holland, Denmark, and Brazil.[85] Important to remember are the shippers, investors, captains, lawyers, and business owners waiting to have these claims retired, and using that process as the basis for decisions about future commercial efforts.

Closer to home, Adams's work as president included managing national government programs aimed at *domestic* indemnity claims: relieving settlers of the risk and damages they sustained as they moved into new geographic areas. Such programs encouraged settlers to strike out to new places and helped protect the investment necessary to do so. Some of the programs, for example, paid claims to westerners who lost improvements or crops to American Indians—a federal program constructed by the United States to encourage settlement and to pacify and regularize these interactions—thus trying to deter people from taking justice and vengeance into their own hands. Believing that payouts could quiet the urge for vendettas and violence, the Adams administration facilitated the processing of claims—even as Congress and the Adams administration's Indian Office refused to pay claims that were unsubstantiated or that were submitted by people who had suffered losses after unlawfully entering Native lands.[86] Adams supervised claims from Georgia about destruction or theft by Creeks of new settlers' property, claims from Florida stemming from Jackson's Seminole campaign, and land claims from Florida to Arkansas Territory centered on Spanish land grants. He did not invent these programs—they were up and running before he entered office, and would continue under Jackson and others long after Adams left.[87] But Adams's administrative skill, and the consistent application of established procedures by his administration, led to steady resolution of claims.

Finally, Adams's work included continuation of construction for a national system of naval and coastal defenses begun in 1816, led by Simon Bernard. These defenses eventually stretched from Maine to Florida, and included Fort Knox in Maine, fortifications among the Harbor Islands off of Boston, Fort McHenry in Baltimore, and fortifications in and around St. Augustine, Florida. These efforts sought to deter European powers from considering attacks on major cities like Boston or making forays via navigable rivers like the Penobscot in Maine. A map of these fortifications shows a carefully designed and prepared plan to protect the entire East Coast.[88] The projects brought jobs and the economic resources of the nation to local areas. They challenged architects and military leaders, they sparked improvements in engineering and construction, and they served many purposes over their long lives. The forts in the Harbor Islands of Massachusetts later served as prisoner-of-war camps during the Civil War and then as muster and training stations during World War I and World War II. Fort Sumter, part of the system and with a prominent place in American history, began under Adams in 1827 and 1828.[89]

As in domestic affairs, Adams's efforts in foreign affairs, trade, treaties, policy on the high seas, claims settlement, and so on were dominated by appeals to rules and procedures to organize and manage common and novel situations. Adams created little that was revolutionary and new; instead, he used or adapted existing procedures, protocols, and traditions. For Adams, this was the best way to ensure fairness in dealing with earlier occurrences, and stability and predictability moving forward.

Administrative Leadership

All of this was done by a president with a lifetime of public service experience leading a sophisticated executive branch apparatus. Adams, who as secretary of state had reorganized the State Department in the Monroe administration, knew his way around the bureaucratic reorganization and modernization efforts that characterized the early republic. Reform of the State Department remained ongoing into Adams's presidency, and he recommended a reorganization plan in his First Annual Message.[90] Other reform efforts during Adams's presidency targeted Treasury, the U.S. Navy, and the War Department.[91] Adams knew that bureaucratic agencies needed to adapt to new circumstances in order to provide the best services possible to the American people, and he understood how to run operations, having spent years working as a diplomat in other administrations.

Adams's leadership of the bureaucracy reflected his ethic as president: commitment to procedure, rules, and established practice. This allowed Adams to maintain continuity among his officeholders, which he valued as conducive to good administration and accountability, and it allowed him to delegate authority and decision making to subordinates who understood their responsibility to uphold those same rules and processes and to restrain from freelancing. Adams's leadership made it clear to public servants that following rules and procedures would protect administrators against outside charges and removal from office for reasons other than those directly associated with their job performance.

Adams outlined his views on the benefits of continuity in office throughout his diary. He criticized, for example, Treasury Secretary William Crawford's patronage effort, built on an 1820 bill that required reappointment to office after four years. Concerned that the bill's purpose was to make all government appointments dependent on Crawford and the Senate, Adams argued that the bill was unconstitutional. Adams highlighted the need for continuity and wrote that "efforts had been made by some of the Senators to obtain different nominations, and to introduce a principle of change or rotation in office at the expiration of these commissions; which would make the Government a perpetual and unintermitting scramble for office. A more pernicious expedient could scarcely be devised." He continued, "I determined to renominate every person against whom there was no complaint which would have warranted his removal, and renominated every person nominated by Mr. Monroe, and upon whose nomination the Senate had declined acting. Mr. Monroe always acted on this principle of renomination."[92] Adams held over much of Monroe's administration.[93]

With a lifetime of experience in public office and executive departments, Adams delegated authority and expected subordinates to follow the rules. When they did, they would be protected; Adams dismissed federal officers only when he had convincing evidence of unfitness for duty or of actual misdeeds.[94] Presidential scholar Mary Hargreaves likens Adams's leadership style to that of a modern board chairman—"available for consultation, but delegating operational responsibility."[95] He assembled a team of experts and led them in the directions he charted. Cabinet meetings were held weekly, and Adams met frequently with his secretaries. He consulted on, and set, general policies, then delegated to his experts the details of policy design and implementation, returning as necessary to resolve sticking points or make critical choices. Adams gave Henry Clay primary responsibility for drafting diplomatic notes and instructions, he gave Samuel Southard the lead in navy reorganization, and he gave John McLean more authority as postmaster than Monroe had allowed.

Adams trusted his appointees and the field officers at these departments to do their jobs. He had seen this in action his entire career—he had thrived on the discretion he enjoyed to pursue the nation's objectives as a diplomat abroad, and he had witnessed how hamstrung Spain's envoy Luis de Onís became without clear authority to act on his own judgment.[96] Adams understood and valued discretionary authority, and he generally erred far toward the side of allowing federal agents too much, rather than too little, leeway to pursue their public objectives.[97]

ADAMS VALUED tried and true processes for interbranch respect and collaboration. As we will see in more detail in the next chapter, he regularly involved state officials and members of Congress in discussions over how to resolve disputes in Indian affairs, he refused to circumvent or ignore the parts of the governing system that made slavery legal, and he worked hard to persuade Congress and the public to support internal improvements, infrastructure projects, and scientific progress. He understood that congressional acts had more force, more legitimacy, and more staying power than unilateral executive actions in everything from shipping controversies to exploration missions and the use of the Smithson bequest.[98]

Adams repeatedly demonstrated respect for judicial process as well. Having made an early reputation for independence when he refused to support the politically driven impeachment of Samuel Chase, Adams continued to value the procedural importance of an independent judiciary when he was president. Visitors, for example, once asked Adams for an order to stay a prosecution. Adams responded by appealing to "the principle that the Executive should not arrest the arm of the law; and I observed that as to the veracity of the witnesses the Court and the jury before whom they would testify would have far better means of scrutinizing that than I could." He upheld sharp and severe penalties for compromising the security of the mail and refused to release people from jail merely because they were horribly sick.[99] Adams's approach thus extended to a well-considered understanding of the president's relationship to the administrative bureaucracy and to the other constitutional branches of government at the federal level.

Throughout his presidency, though, Adams protected executive prerogative and independence, constantly evaluating congressional actions in light of their potential impact on presidential powers. Adams never surrendered his prerogatives as president to ensure that treaties were upheld and that the national government, especially the presidency, continued to play a strong and leading role in Indian affairs and other policy areas. He defended executive prerogatives in military appointments against encroachment by the Senate.[100] He unilaterally broadened his options in the long and ugly fight between Edward Gaines and Winfield Scott for the highest command post in the army, eventually opening the competition to other candidates and selecting General Alexander Macomb as the winner.[101] He utilized executive action tools and pardoned Winnebago leaders who had been sentenced to hang following violence between encroaching white lead miners, Winnebagoes, and others in and around the Galena region of Illinois and Wisconsin, as noted above.[102] Adams defended the president's authority to negotiate treaties before submitting them to the Senate, and he often resisted congressional requests for documents, seeing them as "new and unprecedented" tactics to delay and harass the execution of business by the president. Part of the delay in the Panama Conference negotiations, in fact, was Adams's stubborn response to an inquiry from the Senate as to whether or not they might publish communications between the executive and the Senate regarding nominations for the conference. Adams insisted that communications in such matters were confidential.[103]

In another example, Adams believed that the Constitution's grant of authority to Congress to declare war had been a mistake. In the context of seizing Florida's Amelia Island to stop the illegal introduction of enslaved people to the United States, and also of negotiations with Spain over Florida, Secretary of State Adams argued that the involvement of Congress in decisions of war encouraged secret laws and provisions—and he defended executive secrecy as entirely legitimate.[104] As a former president, Adams continued to support executive action. In the House he voted in favor of the 1833 Force Bill, granting President Jackson authority to use the military against nullifiers and to enforce revenue and tariff laws. Adams terrified slave interests in the North and the South by expressing the belief that the president and the commander of the army had authority to order the universal emancipation of enslaved people.[105] Adams was also not above manipulating news media on behalf of the administration's objectives.[106]

With numerous demands for action and decision making placed on the president, Adams vigorously applied the prerogative inherent in the constitutional presidency to promote his goals. At the end of his administration, for example, Secretary of War Peter Porter's annual report to Congress recommended collecting all American Indians in an Indian Territory in the West, and

Adams reinforced the recommendation in his annual message in December 1828. In the message, Adams also criticized civilization and education funding for Indians. He believed that Indians were most likely to remove or be assimilated, and in his final message to Congress he recommended that Congress take up the issue. "This state of things requires that a remedy should be provided," Adams wrote, "a remedy which, while it shall do justice to those unfortunate children of nature, may secure to the members of our confederation their rights of sovereignty and of soil."[107] The legislative initiatives outlined publicly by Porter and Adams were introduced to Congress in January 1829 but not passed by Congress in the brief session that preceded Adams's leaving office.[108]

Adams acted independently when the situation allowed. We should not confuse an approach built on established processes with a narrowly constrained one—Adams did not believe the presidency was under the thumb of other institutions or that it could not act independently, on its own authority. He was just careful to identify such opportunities, articulate the circumstances, and refrain from acting independently when such action was clearly constrained by the Constitution, by law, or by procedure. Adams and Secretary of the Navy Southard, for example, pressed ahead with extensive preparations for the Pacific Expedition despite weak official support, the House having approved some of the basic outlines of the endeavor and the Senate not having approved them at all. Adams and Southard used contingency funds for the navy to begin preparations, with Adams pushing the measures because he felt that if the expedition were not underway before the succeeding session of Congress, they would lose the chance.[109]

In other cases lacking explicit congressional authorization, President Adams also acted—even felt *obligated* to act. In considering an 1826 act appropriating funds to remove Creeks to west of the Mississippi River, for example, Adams confronted the question of whether the Creek agency—which had not been reauthorized by Congress—could still function. "The two years having expired, the question is, whether, by the last Act of appropriation, the agency can be continued and the moneys applied to defray the expenses of removal of other parties of the Creeks," Adams wrote. "I had no doubt that the new appropriation was an implied extension of the time, and shall understand the law accordingly."[110] In Florida, the Adams administration managed a series of tense events, checking aggressive whites and working to build ties with an increasingly organized array of Florida Natives. Adams, for example, by executive proclamation increased reserved land in Florida to try to help Seminoles avoid starvation.[111] His diary is full of creative workarounds, involving everything from purchasing an enslaved person in order to free him, to finding ways to care for an aging government employee, to finding funds for surveying lands involved in Indian treaties.[112]

Adams's creation of a live oak farm in Florida provides a final example illustrating the multifaceted nature of the presidency in action in the 1820s. Having become interested in trees and botany, and enamored of the benefits of patient botanical study and vegetative growth, Adams issued an executive order to fund a plantation of live oaks in Florida—what biographer Fred Kaplan ranks as "the earliest instance of a government-sponsored agricultural station."[113] In Kaplan's telling, trees were part of the national wealth, used for ships and homes, furniture and firewood—justifying for Adams the federal government's sponsorship of lumber farms and reforestation.[114]

Presented almost as an odd bit of trivia by Kaplan, the live oak farm was actually an important endeavor and provides, in one example, evidence of all five characteristics usually associated with the "modern" presidency. The importance of the input of government officials on the issue of conservation and national security stemmed back to the 1790s, as administrative officials pushed for congressional efforts to ensure adequate resources of timber for warships. The 1799 Naval-Timber Purchase Act followed testimony to Congress from Joshua Humphreys, who had been appointed naval constructor in 1794 and is often called "the father of the U.S. Navy." Secretary of War James McHenry testified on the same topic in 1797, and Navy Secretary Benjamin Stoddert followed up in 1798, all pushing Congress toward the eventual 1799 law. The 1817 Naval-Timber Reserve Act delegated expansive authority to the president, and President James Monroe and his agents surveyed and reserved lands in 1820.[115] This suggests that similar actions and presidential-congressional collaboration might be uncovered in this issue in presidencies predating Adams's. The involvement of these and other administrative experts demonstrates just how far back the nation's public service expertise in conservation goes, and how influential administrators were in guiding congressional action.

The live oak farm itself resulted from executive direct action. Of course, the live oak farm tapped into the president's commander-in-chief and war-making responsibilities, as Adams recognized the central role of the live oaks in the construction of warships. Beyond that, much of the activity to create and staff the plantation was driven by President Adams and Navy Secretary Southard, who took independent action months before notifying Congress, and who then led congressional activity and directed Congress's attention, provided details for congressional investigations, and exceeded statutory authority in developing and running the farm.[116] Adams's direct orders to establish and run the farm are clear instances of presidential direct action, as Kaplan correctly notes. The Adams-Southard team, which exceeded their strict authority to prepare for the Pacific Expedition, worked beyond their legal authority here as well. In their later condemnation of the station, the Jackson administration highlighted what they saw as Adams's and Southard's violation of the limits placed on the president's authority by Congress in the 1817 act.[117]

Once begun, Southard requested authority from Congress to resolve contentious Spanish land grants; clear titles, often through legal process; and purchase lands. He and Adams engaged in the very kind of back-and-forth communication among the president, his administrators, and Congress that characterizes any president promoting a legislative agenda. Southard's report to Congress in 1827 recommended four specific measures and resulted in the 1827 Timber Trespass Act.[118] This is exactly the kind of presidential advancement of a legislative agenda that is often considered a defining trait of only the "modern" presidency.

Finally, President Adams consciously sought to draw public attention to the importance of his conservation efforts by directing materials to Congress and by describing his efforts in his final annual message. Adams "recognized the ultimate necessity of awakening the American people to the urgency of preserving and restoring the nation's forests," historian William R. Adams wrote, quoting the president as writing to his son Charles, "My purpose is as far as may be in my power to draw the attention of my countrymen to it."[119] The story of the Florida live oak station, long forgotten, illustrates in one tiny case the role of administrative expertise and leadership, bureaucratic autonomy, executive direct action, the promotion of presidential legislative agendas, and presidential public communication in support of the president's goals.

Adams summed up his approach to the independence of the presidency in 1826, writing in his diary, "I added that I found no article or clause in the Constitution of the United States delegating the right or the power to define, limit, or declare what are or are not the constitutional powers of the president."[120] This is how Adams saw the presidency, and this is how he governed—not from weakness but from strength; not from subordinate status but from independence; not from personal desire but from constitutional authority. Adams's commitments to procedure and practice did not undercut executive authority—if anything, they strengthened the president's hand. Taken together, the record of Adams's leadership as president demonstrates surprising effectiveness, strength, and acumen at the head of the influential, active, and intrusive American state of the 1820s.

3

Presidential Decision Making and the Administrative State

PROCESS AND PROCEDURE IN THE 1820s

JOHN QUINCY ADAMS's decision-making ethic prioritized the application of established procedures over all other values. Colloquially, he might be called a stickler—in an effort to stay within the law and ensure fairness, Adams applied rules and procedural guidelines strictly in order to address thorny issues. He developed this ethic long before his presidency, and it stayed with him long after. In this chapter, I examine Adams's decision making at the intersection of the presidency and the state in three critical examples: the federal-state standoff with Georgia over access to Creek Nation lands, the difficult leadership dilemmas facing an antislavery president in an age of legalized and constitutionally protected slavery, and the fight to continue the nation's tradition of federally directed internal improvements against increasing challenges. In each case, Adams appealed to established rules and guidelines to defend initiatives, find policy approaches, and render decisions.

In his approach to process and procedure, Adams hewed closely to what many modern students of administrative ethics recommend as a systematic approach to an environment characterized by diverse rules and guidelines, a process of interpreting values and policy goals inside of established decision-making frameworks. Works by authors like Terry L. Cooper emphasize the benefits to fairness, representation, and collaboration that come from abiding by established procedures, or adapting those procedures carefully to the novel situations that constantly arise in public policy.[1] Such an approach also aims to minimize the impact of an individual's personal desires or policy positions in a nation of disagreement and differences of opinion: careful procedures are often designed to be inclusive and respectful of diverse opinions and stakeholder interests.

The fact that established procedures, administrative paths to action, and opportunities for public leadership existed in the 1820s illustrates the advanced maturation of the American state and the very "modern" approaches to the presidency taken by President Adams. For Adams, his personal beliefs were sometimes at odds with what established rules and guidelines demanded—putting him in the classic position of an administrator or even an elected leader whose opinions and values run counter to the way the law is structured or to what the law mandates. Sworn to uphold the Constitution and faithfully execute the laws, John Quincy Adams modulated the effect of his own policy preferences and beliefs by prioritizing administrative procedure within the state.

President Adams and the Almost Civil War of the 1820s

Just a few years before U.S. troops under President Andrew Jackson shackled and forcibly removed thousands of Native Americans from their houses and lands, President John Quincy Adams defended Native interests against aggressive encroachment by white intruders. Under Adams's leadership, the national government upheld U.S. treaties and laws and the U.S. Army stood opposed to state and local forces.

Adams's use of federal power to ensure federal preeminence in Indian affairs and expansion policy is an important and largely overlooked example of a president upholding the rule of law and constitutional prescriptions against powerful engines of localism and racism. Adams's interactions with Georgia, Alabama, and the Creek and Cherokee Nations echoed the assertive executive actions of George Washington during the Whiskey Rebellion and foreshadowed Dwight Eisenhower at Little Rock. Adams understood that the Constitution mandates protection of certain principles and policies, in particular the status of national treaties and the principle of national supremacy over the states. Adams's protection of U.S.-Indian land boundaries guaranteed by federal treaty against encroachment by southerners aligned with Georgia and Alabama was high-stakes politics, teetering dangerously close to civil war in the 1820s. Just one generation removed from the initial compact that gave birth to the United States, civil conflict between states and the national government in the 1820s could have spelled the end of the union, with a profound impact on continental history. Adams's decision making exemplifies the ability of a president in the 1820s to apply executive action, established laws, and accepted processes to defuse a tense, rapidly developing situation.

THE CHALLENGE TO FEDERAL SUPREMACY IN INDIAN AFFAIRS

During the Adams presidency, energetic forces labored to alter the established framework of relations between the United States and Native nations. Southern politicians in particular saw the federal boundaries established with nations like the Creeks and Cherokees as obstacles to growth and expansion. Native lands blocked the extension of cotton and cattle culture, provided hope and refuge for enslaved people trying to escape slavery, and blocked exploitation of gold and other resources. American Indians themselves existed as competitors in the slave trade, competitors in economic areas like cotton and agriculture, and competitors to the dominance of white civilization. State officials pressured presidents and other federal officials to break treaties or negotiate new ones; to remove the Creeks, Cherokees, and other southern nations; to seize their holdings; and to open their lands for exploitation and new settlement.

Adams, too, believed that Indians should be either removed or assimilated, and throughout his career he complained about a few hundred "savages" here and there controlling large amounts of territory.[2] His field agents worked to pressure and cajole Native leaders to sign removal treaties and head west. He seemed to see Natives as unable to become "civilized" and as obstacles to the continental expansion of the union.[3] And yet Adams fought during his presidency to stave off changes in the federal relationship with Native nations and with the states.[4] The period of Indian affairs with which Americans today are most familiar—Indian removal, especially the Cherokees' hellish Trail of Tears—came *after* the Adams administration. Andrew Jackson and Congress worked together in the 1830s to change radically the direction and the principles of federal Indian policy, moving quickly toward forced relocation and what would today be called ethnic cleansing.[5] The national government remained critical to this movement, as the Jackson administration managed removal, administered western reservations, and retained executive control of western lands. The change in direction and tone, though, was dramatic: the Jackson years launched decades of relocations and concentrations of American Indians on dismal reservations of land, greatly expanding executive and federal power to remove and relocate Native peoples throughout the continent by force.

Adams's baseline principles in Indian affairs exemplify how the national state and its rules could constrain and guide the behavior of public officials in the 1820s. The Constitution and regime values can be effectively placed above personal belief. While Adams's personal views tilted toward pressure on Natives to remove or assimilate, as president Adams believed that he was not free to abrogate treaties, violate agreements, or otherwise undercut the foundational principles of decades of public policymaking. Adams subordinated his own prejudices and worked to uphold the nation's commitment to its laws and agreements. His commitment was to the legal sanctity of Indian treaties, and he saw no way in which the United States could abrogate those treaties unilaterally to serve its own interests. Moreover, Adams took seriously U.S. commitments enshrined in those treaties to protect Indians, to police boundaries established by treaty, and to maintain the critical and leading federal position in Indian affairs. He also categorically refused to use direct force to remove Indians.[6] These public obligations led Adams to eschew his personal expectations and instead rely on established rules and procedures to manage the conflict raised when the Georgia state government began to push into Indian country in violation of federal treaty commitments.

Georgia, the United States, and the Creek Nation

Conflict developed over many years, built on two major agreements. In 1802, Georgia had ceded to the United States its claim to western lands in exchange for a promise that the national government would quiet Indian title to the lands. By the 1820s, Georgia leaders were growing increasingly frustrated that the Natives were still there. Then, in 1825, a mixed-heritage Creek leader named William McIntosh ceded all Creek lands in Georgia and Alabama to the United States by the Treaty of Indian Springs. The United States agreed to pay $400,000 for the land.[7]

The 1825 treaty, though, was a fraud. McIntosh did not represent the Creek Nation—he was merely a willing individual with a small following who had been bribed by U.S. and Georgia officials into signing off on the land cession. After the deal became public, McIntosh was executed under Creek law mandating the death penalty for any member selling the nation's lands.[8] The U.S. Senate ratified the treaty in the very last days of the Monroe administration, and new president Adams proclaimed the treaty in one of his first presidential acts—with little awareness of the corrupt machinations behind the treaty or of the widespread opposition to it within the Creek Nation.[9] An old agreement and a fraudulent new treaty thus set the stage for a conflict that would threaten civil war.

At first, Adams and Governor William Troup of Georgia seemed to believe that the McIntosh killing portended an uprising among the Creeks which threatened nearby white populations. Adams initially expected that he might have to send the U.S. military to the area to protect Georgians, and he considered calling the adjourned Congress back into special session.[10] But when Adams was informed that the McIntosh killing was an internal Creek matter and that Governor Troup was at odds with federal agents operating in the region, Adams started to recognize the deception behind the treaty. Adams's secretary of war, James Barbour, ordered the area's military commander, Edward P. Gaines, to protect American citizens, restore peace after McIntosh's killing, and reunite the divided Creek Nation. Gaines also investigated the background to the treaty and sent his conclusions about the fraud to Governor Troup on July 10, 1825. He had his findings published in the *Georgia Patriot*, suggesting one way the Adams administration communicated directly with the public about a key issue.[11]

As convincing information about the frauds behind the Treaty of Indian Springs began to reach Adams, the president faced a difficult choice. Should he renegotiate the treaty? If renegotiation failed, could he try to undo a ratified treaty? Or should he just accept the flawed treaty as a done deal, despite the Creeks' opposition? Adams's personal beliefs ran toward pushing the southern Indians to remove west, but he also understood that a blatantly corrupt treaty put the nation's reputation and its responsibilities at risk. Adams quickly began to take action to rectify the situation through a new negotiation with legitimate leaders of the Creek Nation.[12] Meanwhile, Georgia moved forward under the provisions of the ratified Treaty of Indian Springs. That agreement set dates by which the Creeks would have to remove, and it set dates after which the Georgia state government could begin to survey the ceded Creek lands to prepare them for sale and encourage white settlement. Georgia capitalized on the unsettled state of things, speeding up its surveys of lands prior to the dates allowed even by the flawed treaty.

Adams faced an immediate critical choice. He could allow Georgia to move forward, expecting the Creeks to remove from the area and Georgia eventually to take over the lands—a result that Adams seems to have believed inevitable. But even if inevitable, that path followed the flawed treaty and also sanctioned Georgia's violation of even the flawed agreement, undercutting national supremacy in Indian relations and posing the risk that other states would begin to whittle away at the provisions of federal treaties—eroding the entire framework that had been built to manage Indian affairs and oversee the nation's expansion across the continent. Adams issued a strong warning to Troup in May 1825 to postpone the surveying of Creek lands. In June, Adams wrote in his diary, "I proposed that Governor Troup should be answered that the U.S. will not be responsible for any consequences of a survey of Indian Territory attempted by Georgia now.... Corresponding orders should also be given to Gaines; and also that he should keep near the spot all the disposable force."[13]

Following extended cabinet discussions in July 1825, Adams wrote that "Mr. Barbour is to prepare a letter to Governor Troup, giving him notice that the Government of the United States will not permit the [early] survey to be made."[14] Adams sent a message to Governor Troup clearly specifying his expectation that the early survey would be "abandoned by Georgia, til it can be done consistently with the provisions of the treaty."[15] Adams described the delicate touch such a letter demanded:

> The object was to instruct General Gaines, if necessary, to prevent by force the survey of the Creek lands by the order of the Governor of Georgia, and to give him notice of this. Governor Barbour's draft used the term "forbid," and called upon Troup to yield obedience. I suggested the use of milder terms, as, "not permit," and "acquiescence;" but, the positive order to Gaines being given in the instructions to him to furnish Troup a copy of them, it was concluded to be the proper course.[16]

Barbour notified Troup that the U.S. military was authorized to block Georgia entry into Creek lands: "I am directed by the president to state distinctly to your excellency that, for the present, he will not permit such entry or survey to be made."[17]

Troup wrote to say he would not make the survey. For the time being, Adams, relying on the letter of the flawed treaty, had prevailed.[18] But the matter was becoming a public crisis. The *Nashville Republican* worried in September that a civil war might be looming and suggested that the crisis was more important than the Whiskey Rebellion of 1794 had been. Andrew Jackson alluded to the issue's seriousness in a newspaper article about General Gaines, and nonregional and even international newspapers covered the story.[19] Word even got to one of the nation's delegates to the Panama Congress, at that moment traveling from Cartagena to Bogotá. Richard Clough Anderson wrote in his diary on December 5, 1825: "A hot morning. This day the Congress of the US. meets. They will no doubt find subjects to keep them together until May—altho I know none likely to produce much heat except the contest with Georgia about the Creek lands & Creek Indians."[20]

WHILE ENGAGED in brinksmanship with Troup and Georgia, Adams was working a different channel with the Creeks. Trying to keep his options open and find a path to a peaceful resolution—which might also serve Adams's goal in legally and agreeably getting the Creeks to cede their lands and move west—Adams oversaw negotiations with the Creeks. The president's representatives met with Creek leaders, telling them that Congress was unlikely to abrogate the Treaty of Indian Springs unless a new treaty had been signed that could immediately replace it. This path would be consistent with established procedures, meaning simply the replacement of an old treaty (for whatever reason) with a new one, and not portending the precedent of abrogating a treaty made under questionable circumstances—a criterion that might call into question most, if not all, U.S. treaties with Native nations. Ideally, the Creeks would agree to a new treaty and the procedural problems would evaporate.

Adams and his advisors, assisted by officials from the Cherokee Nation, eventually badgered the Creeks into submitting to Georgia's demands for the boundary line. A modified treaty, the Treaty of Washington, was signed on January 26, 1826; it replaced the Treaty of Indian Springs, which was declared in the new treaty's first article "null and void."[21] Georgia did not get all it desired, with 192,000 acres of Creek land still unceded, but the Creeks gave up far more than they wanted.[22]

This is when the situation got even more dangerous: Governor Troup failed to respect the new treaty. On the day that the original Treaty of Indian Springs authorized surveyors to enter the Creek lands, September 1, 1826, Georgia did just that—Troup sent men in to stake out lands for sale by the state.[23] On January 29, 1827, Secretary of War Barbour told the Georgians that Adams would "employ, if necessary, all the means under his control to maintain the faith of the nation by carrying the treaty into effect" and preventing early surveying. The next day, U.S. Attorney Richard Habersham was ordered to obtain arrest warrants for the surveyors.[24] Adams and Troup were edging toward a battle in the woods of the Creek Nation, between the U.S. Army and the Georgia militia.

Tensions tightened further in March 1827. A letter from Troup arrived in Washington, "setting the authority of the United States at defiance," Adams wrote, and "accompanied with an order for rescuing the surveyors who may be arrested, for indicting the officers of the United States who may arrest them, and for two divisions of the militia of the State to be in readiness to resist hostile invasion."[25] Troup was threatening civil war.

Process, Law, and the Constitution

Adams's decisions in the Georgia-Creek case offer a window into his commitment to process, law, and constitutional principles. This is particularly well illustrated here because Adams personally envisioned a result very similar to what Georgia wanted: a cession of all Creek lands and removal of the Creeks to the West.[26] But whereas Georgia's leaders were willing to discard the constraints imposed by national treaties and an established system of national policy, Adams refused to subordinate policy and process to his personal expectations or to expediency.

The discussions of the Creek-Georgia conflict within the Adams administration touched on fundamental principles of law and policymaking. Adams wrote of a cabinet meeting on the issue in December 1825 at which the members discussed Indians, the Constitution, and the future in the context of what to do about Georgia's intransigence and treachery. Henry Clay discoursed on the unlikely prospect of American Indians ever becoming civilized members of the broader community: "It was not in their nature," Adams reported Clay arguing. "They were not an improvable breed, and their disappearance from the human family will be no great loss to the world." Clay stated that Indians were rapidly disappearing and would be gone completely in fifty years. Much of Clay's statement was in response to a suggestion of Barbour's, "a plan for incorporating the Indians within the States of the Union—ceasing to make treaties with them at all, but considering them as altogether subject to our laws."[27]

Adams's cabinet, then, clearly considered broader policy innovations within its discussion of the Creek-Georgia conflict. Notable, though, was Adams's position. Adams, in fact, leaned toward Clay's view: "Governor Barbour was somewhat shocked at these [Clay's] opinions, *for which I fear there is too much foundation.*" Adams, though, relied not on his own opinions but instead worked his way to the legal underpinnings. "But the question was what should be done now," he wrote, after implying that Clay's view might prevail in the long run. In response to Barbour's proposal for incorporating Natives under state law and ending the practice of treatymaking, Adams offered this pointed response: "I asked him if he did not think there would be made question of the constitutional power of Congress to change so essentially the character of our relations with the Indian tribes."[28] Adams, although inclined toward either the assimilation of Natives or their eventual disappearance, remained governed in his public decision making by established practice, law, and constitutional foundations.

The very next day, Adams drove this point home even more forcefully. Here, the context related to political peacemaking and expediency. Barbour brought to Adams a draft of a communication to be made to the Georgians regarding the conflict with the Creeks. Barbour reported that Georgia senator Thomas Cobb "had been with him this morning in a state of very high excitement, and had threatened that unless we should concede this point [in Georgia's favor], Georgia would necessarily be driven to support General Jackson," presumably in the next presidential election. Barbour used Clay's argument and asked, if Indians were headed to an inevitable destruction anyway, "what need was there for us to quarrel with our friends for their sakes, and why should we not yield to Georgia at once?"[29]

Adams's response captures his commitment to process as his guide to decision making, and his refusal to subordinate that principle to electoral expediency: "I said I had considered Mr. Clay's observations yesterday as expressing an opinion of results founded upon the operation of general causes, but not as an object to which we ought purposely to contribute; that we ought not yield to Georgia, because we could not do so without gross injustice. And that as to Georgia's being driven to support General Jackson, I felt little concern or care for that."[30]

A cabinet meeting in January 1827 further demonstrated Adams's commitment to procedure. Adams laid out the central issue: "The Creek Indians have arrested the surveyors from Georgia. Governor Troup has ordered out a troop of horse to protect the surveyors and force the survey. Question discussed, what is to be done?"[31] Adams's review of the discussion moved from a foundation in the law, to the question of expediency, and then to the question of actual action moving forward. Adams demonstrated a keen awareness of his options and of the possible effects of his actions—what Terry Cooper calls "projecting probable consequences" in his argument for a systematic approach to ethical decision making in public affairs.[32] Adams began with the law, with the "Act of Congress of 30th March, 1802, consulted." He then related his analysis:

> Section 5 [of the Act of 1802] forbids surveying. Section 16 authorizes the military force of the U.S. to apprehend any person trespassing upon the Indian lands and convey him to the civil authority in one of the next three adjoining districts. Section 17 authorizes the seizure and trial of trespassers found within any judicial district of the U.S. It was proposed to order troops to the spot to apprehend the surveyors and bring them in for trial, by authority of Section 16. I have no doubt of the right, but much of the expediency, of so doing.[33]

Adams had numerous options open to him, from doing nothing to continued negotiation with Georgia, the use of federal forces to remove the surveyors, apprehending and trying the surveyors in federal court, or of course using the military to remove the Creeks or at least support the survey. Allegiance to process does not necessarily provide only one path of action—given the complexities of governance and the varieties of state power, even in the 1820s, many alternatives presented themselves as justified even under established guidelines and practice. Adams clearly believed that apprehending the surveyors and trying them was the most righteous and legally supported course, but he was also aware that that was not necessarily a workable approach: "The Georgia surveyors act by authority and order of the State. To send troops against them *must* end in acts of violence."[34]

Thus, Adams began to look for other alternatives that would be valid interpretations of the law. "The Act of 1802 was not made for the case," he wrote next, and he was correct—the law was really aimed at individual trespassers, not teams of public surveyors operating under authority of a state government.[35] So the law as written did not necessarily apply strictly to the case at hand. This was a rationalization, perhaps, but one that got Adams out of the bind of being responsible for sending troops against the surveyors, and presumably against the Georgia militia—an option that almost certainly would have led to violence and would not necessarily have resolved the issue. It might also have led to civil war and dissolution of the union.

Adams reverted to process. "Before coming to a conflict of arms I should choose to refer the whole subject to Congress," Adams wrote. "Governor Barbour proposed sending a confidential agent to warn the Georgians against proceeding." These steps were taken, and Adams gained time, continuing to move forward through negotiating channels with the Georgians and the Creeks. After discussion of whether, and how, to deliver a communication to Congress, Adams decided to deliver the message and then maintain silence.[36] Using language referring to the prospect of civil war, Adams asserted in his message to Congress that Georgia was in "direct violation of the supreme law of this land, set forth in a treaty." "Entertaining no doubt that in the present case the resort to [military force or civil process], or to both, was within the discretion of the Executive authority," Adams noted that he had so far chosen to pursue only civil process. Adams made the endgame clear, however:

> In the present instance it is my duty to say that if the legislative and executive authorities of the State of Georgia should persevere in acts of encroachment upon the territories secured by a solemn treaty to the Indians, and the laws of the Union remain unaltered, a superadded obligation even higher than that of human authority will compel the Executive of the United States to enforce the laws and fulfill the duties of the nation by all the force committed for that purpose to his charge.

Adams ended the message by asking Congress to determine whether any further legislation might be necessary or expedient "to meet the emergency which these transactions may produce."[37]

Adams thus managed to bring Congress and its representatives into the discussions, soliciting their viewpoints and their institutional power to see if a new law was needed to address the issue. Throughout the crisis the Adams administration was in contact with congressional and state representatives as it dealt with an important issue that straddled the line between foreign and domestic policy. The House and the Senate responded with ambiguity, offering little to help Adams resolve the conflict.

Adams's message to Congress, he knew, was profoundly significant. It is difficult for us now to understand the concern Adams had at the time—a time of generational change, and of increasingly direct conflict between southern state governments and the federal government for supremacy, law, and constitutional principle. Adams and his cabinet, and the Georgians, really did see this issue as potentially destructive of the bonds of union. "This is the most momentous message I have ever sent to Congress," Adams wrote in his diary.[38] Adams knew that the United States had a long history of removing unauthorized whites from Indian lands and controlling access into Indian country, but Georgia's aggressiveness had created a new twist—the likelihood that such action in 1827 would lead to armed conflict between national and state forces.[39]

IN FEBRUARY 1827, Adams was still searching for answers to the Creek-Georgia crisis. He examined the laws, the journals of Congress, speeches of George Washington, the history of U.S.-Indian affairs, even the origin and growth of the army—all to better understand Indian affairs in the context of the situation. He came down even more firmly in his defense of national supremacy—research strengthened his resolve:

> In the controversy with Georgia, the powers of the General Government and those of the Government of Georgia are in conflict, and it is indispensable to know the whole history of our Indian relations of peace and war, to understand the ground upon which we stand. It was debatable ground far more under the [Articles of] Confederation than now, but Georgia and some other States are disposed to revert to the State claims under the Confederation.[40]

The Creeks eventually signed a new treaty with the United States at Fort Mitchell on November 15, 1827, ceding the remainder of their territory.[41] But while scholars have sometimes focused on Adams's securing a result that still failed to protect Creek interests, the president had stood up to Georgia through diplomacy and a credible threat of force against Georgia's surveyors and militia.[42] By so doing, Adams reinforced national control and the sanctity of treaties at a time when the South and other areas were becoming increasingly aggressive about forcing Native Americans to remove. Adams reestablished national dominance in Indian affairs and refined a traditional treaty practice by which the United States could argue that cessions made under great pressure were still legal and had followed legitimate and established process. Congress, for its part, was very willing to be *re*active—it engaged the issue after Adams had submitted the January 1827 treaty, and again after Adams submitted the November 1827 treaty, with key senators, committees, and the full Senate debating consent to the treaties and with the House debating the proper level of appropriations. Legislation followed, appropriating funds for settling Creek claims and for supporting delegations of Creeks to travel to the West to inspect new lands.[43] Despite Troup's public complaints that Adams was exceeding the president's powers, Congress did not constrain or limit the president's activities or authority.[44]

Adams had refused to walk away from the nation's treaty commitments and, by positioning U.S. troops against Georgians in the heart of the South, he refused to subordinate national supremacy to the aggressive bigotry and radical federalism of Georgia's leaders. Adams protected national supremacy and the place of nation-to-nation treaties in Indian affairs and in westward expansion—dynamics that were cornerstones of the United States' effective continental expansion through the rest of the nineteenth century. The Indian Removal Act, signed into law by President Jackson in May 1830, explicitly guaranteed the nation's ongoing commitment to earlier treaties, just as the end of formal treatymaking in 1871 would guarantee continued observance of existing treaties.

Adams, Slavery, and the Hidden-Hand Presidency in the 1820s

Public servants face some of their most challenging decisions when their own moral judgments on critically important issues run counter to law. In the matter of slavery, John Quincy Adams's personal predilections differed from what was required by law and by what he saw as the demands imposed by the Constitution and regime values. When considered in context of Adams's preference for decision making according to established rules and processes, his lifelong abhorrence of slavery banged directly against a constitution and national state that accepted slavery, even protected it, by law and by custom. The complex nature of the American administrative state, though, provided Adams with a variety of below-the-headline options that would not require the kind of fiery rhetoric often demanded by partisans and searched for by historians.

Adams personally deplored slavery, but his commitment to procedure and to the law constrained his outward approach to ending the peculiar institution—leading some historians and biographers to present him as a hypocrite or even a coward for apparently doing so little to fight against slavery.[45] Indeed, Adams's options were narrow. Adams needed to uphold the Constitution and faithfully execute the laws, and both legalized and perpetuated slavery. President Adams maneuvered within the interstices of slavery policy as well as he could, attacking through well-established procedural action what he did not feel empowered to fight more openly or directly on the basis of moral principle. In the context of slavery, Adams pursued a suite of hidden-hand executive actions designed to undercut the institution and whittle away at its foundations with an eye on long-term success.

ADAMS AND SLAVERY

Adams opposed slavery as early as his youth. Traveling to St. Petersburg with Francis Dana in 1781, the fourteen-year-old Adams wrote to his father about the "abject slavery" of farmers in Poland. "They are bought and sold like so many beasts, and are sometimes even chang'd for dogs or horses. Their masters have even the right of life and death over them, and if they kill one of them they are only obliged to pay a trifling fine."[46] In 1820, Adams excoriated slavery under the Constitution: "It perverts human reason ... to maintain that slavery is sanctioned by the Christian religion, that slaves are happy and contented in their condition.... The bargain between freedom and slavery contained in the Constitution of the United States is morally and politically vicious, inconsistent with the principles upon which alone our Revolution can be justified."[47] In private notes during his post-presidency congressional tenure, Adams admitted to being an abolitionist.[48] Later in life, Adams's personal abhorrence of slavery continued, as he refused to attend the ceremony marking completion of the Bunker Hill Monument, commemorating a battle that Adams had watched as a child. Adams was incensed that this memorial to the fight for liberty would witness the insulting attendance of President John Tyler and a cabinet of "slave-drivers."[49]

Adams, though, recognized the collision between slavery and American founding principles. He long believed that the foundational principles of the Declaration of Independence, that all men are created equal, had been incorporated into the new nation through the Constitution.[50] Thus, the Constitution's provisions protecting and sanctioning slavery were at odds with other regime values of equality and freedom. Adams also expressed the idea that insurrection would give the national government, particularly Congress or the president as commander in chief, legitimate authority to free enslaved people. The two positions anticipated Lincoln's Emancipation Proclamation and his rhetorical incorporation of the Declaration into the post–Civil War understanding of the American union.[51] For Adams, then, careful consideration of the Constitution's provisions, the regime's values, and the conflicting practices in American law and policy since the founding created some space for public action against slavery. The laws must be faithfully executed, but competing values created some room for interpretation of just *how* they should be executed.

As a policy issue, slavery is too often considered to have presented all-or-nothing choices. It can seem like a big-picture policy necessitating wholesale change, or a civil war, to do away with it. But it need not have been so, and we make a mistake to look in the American system of government only for dramatic opportunities to implement overhauling change. States and localities had made progress in abolishing slavery by the early decades of the nineteenth century, using a variety of methods and means and timetables. The federal government had also taken measures. It banned the importation of enslaved men, women, and children and used the navy to interdict slavers on the high seas. Its treaties with other nations took cognizance of the issue, even in the hornets' nest of the slave power's leverage in the Senate to modify or reject agreements.[52] Yet the Constitution still protected personal property interests in enslaved people, and it built slavery into its system of legislative representation.

Presidents had at their disposal a wide variety of incremental options, even in the early nineteenth century. George Washington had many of the same options available to him as Adams had, and it does Washington little credit that he put his majestic stature behind none of them. Washington was presented with opportunities to purchase land and move his enslaved laborers there as tenant farmers; with plans to send freed persons back to Africa;

and with proposals for gradual manumission, much as New York passed in the 1790s.[53] Washington toyed with the idea of freeing his enslaved people before taking the oath as president, to set a precedent that American presidents would not be slaveholders.[54] And when we recognize the administrative opportunities stemming from federal interactions with slavery in already maturing federal agencies like the Post Office, the General Land Office, the War Department and Indian Office, and the military and its scientific and exploratory divisions—with all of that available, it is clear that presidents had many tools available to them beyond merely making public statements or taking symbolic acts.[55] Washington opted to do none of these things, to support none of the trial policies, to make no symbolic acts, to use none of the administrative tools available to him to fight slavery. In fact, to the extent that Washington pulled on administrative levers, he did so to protect his personal interests in his enslaved people.[56] We second-guess Washington at our peril, but it is disappointing that the only effort he seems to have made was to free his enslaved workers only after he and his wife were comfortably dead.

President John Quincy Adams understood that he operated in a system of conflicting values within which the legality of slavery, the illegality of the slave trade and importation of enslaved people to the United States, and the lack of consensus within the American population regarding slavery in general left public officials room to maneuver. Adams also understood that the constitutional system is best suited for, even designed for, incremental and slow procedural change on those issues that create fundamental divisions among the American populace. Adams did speak out against slavery, although not to the extent of making antislavery a central point in his public pronouncements. Given the times and given the laws, Adams's reluctance to say more, or to push harder, is, like Washington's, understandable if not exactly heroic. A bolder effort might have sparked opposition and conflict, perhaps creating a counterproductive, blowback reaction. And that blowback might have affected even more than just the slavery context—responsible for faithfully executing the laws, presidents tread near a cliff when they condemn those laws. As long as slavery was indeed legal, sanctioned by the Congress and the Constitution and significant portions of the American public, President Adams would go only so far in speeches. He would choose to speak subtly but act nimbly.

Behind the speeches, Adams worked the levers of the administrative state, and always within the law. Adams recognized that he had options available to him as president that lived within the gaps and grey areas of a conflicted set of regime values and constitutional provisions. Today, we are accustomed to looking for executive action, particularly through the administrative bureaucracy, and we find much presidential activity that is below headline material.

Appointments to key posts and policymaking through agencies and departments are all familiar and legitimate ways by which presidents influence policy without the bold strokes of large policy proposals or congressional action. The nineteenth century has too long been considered devoid of administrative action and executive maneuvering on policy. But what we now call the administrative state—the array of semi-autonomous bureaucratic agencies that design and administer public policies, usually associated with the New Deal—was a characteristic feature from the earliest days of the republic. Adams leveraged the scope and influence of the War Department, the State Department, and the Post Office, and he capitalized on opportunities afforded him through judicial process, domestic policy initiatives, and executive action to fight slavery behind the headlines. If we take seriously the idea of presidential action in the grey areas left by the Constitution—what Jerry Mashaw calls the administrative Constitution—we see President John Quincy Adams acting energetically near one of the era's most dangerous terminals.[57]

Adams's strategy and the maturation of the American state here are illuminated by comparing them to a modern classic of presidential action, Fred I. Greenstein's revelatory study of President Dwight Eisenhower's "hidden-hand" leadership. While much of Adams's leadership and Eisenhower's differ in technique and, of course, context, what Greenstein identified as "unique" in Eisenhower applies to Adams in the context of slavery. Greenstein recognized that the basic dilemma at the heart of the constitutional presidency is that "the American president is asked to perform two roles that in most democracies are assigned to separate individuals. He must serve both as chief of state and as the nation's highest political executive." Of Eisenhower, Greenstein wrote, "The unique characteristic of Eisenhower's approach to presidential leadership was his self-conscious use of political strategies that enabled him to carry out both presidential roles without allowing one to undermine the other." Greenstein's presentation of Eisenhower's leadership style includes selective practice of delegation as well as hidden-hand leadership: "A president who seeks influence and cultivates a reputation for not intervening in day-to-day policy-making will necessarily hide his hand more often than one who seeks recognition as an effective political operator."[58]

This helps explain why so many scholars have overlooked Adams's successful efforts in a variety of contexts. These approaches make sense only in a government complex enough to allow behind-the-scenes maneuvering, and in contexts in which presidential leadership is a public activity. Greenstein even identified the hidden-hand leadership style as one commensurate with "the rise of big government," and throughout his book Eisenhower's ability to capitalize on the complexity of the modern state and its overlapping responsibilities is evident.[59] Traditionally, our understanding of the relationship of the presidency to the state precluded looking for such a strategy in the nineteenth century. Yet recent heightened awareness of state activity related to Indian affairs, expansion, and a host of other matters in the nineteenth century encourages us to look for hidden-hand leadership even in the 1820s. This is where we find Adams, the consummate insider, working to end slavery. He was not a bystander, and he was not a hypocrite to wait to go fully public against slavery in his post-presidential congressional career. President Adams nimbly exploited the complexity and maturity of the American administrative state to allow him to pursue political ends even as he remained, and appeared, the chief of state.

Diplomacy and the Navy versus the Slave Trade

John Quincy Adams pushed hard to combat slavery through administrative procedures, internationally and domestically. Internationally, Adams focused on stemming the international slave trade—what he called "that abominable traffic."[60] Adams targeted the slave trade through the U.S. Navy, international agreements, and diplomacy—all legitimate processes open to presidential leadership.

Adams worked with Samuel Southard to use the navy against the slave trade. He appointed Southard to head the Navy Department, and worked with him in many policy areas, from blocking privateers and protecting fishing fleets to enforcing international treaties and devising plans for a naval academy. Southard directed a reorganization of the navy, Adams deployed it to enforce laws that he believed could be used to ameliorate some of the slave trade's evils, and he publicly highlighted the West India Squadron's successes in his First Annual Message. The navy stopped and seized slavers along the coast of Africa in the 1820s, although under Adams the navy's efforts were neither well-supported nor well-funded by Congress.[61] Still, the fact of having laws on the books, ships on the sea, and ongoing efforts to negotiate enforcement agreements with more committed nations like Great Britain kept the issue afloat, maintained awareness among pirates and slavers, and worked toward incremental measures.

Adams also utilized the navy and other offices in a series of little-known, complicated circumstances involving slave ships taken as prizes, wrecked in U.S. waters, or landed on U.S. territory. In cases that foreshadowed the *Amistad* case, and which share many of the same characteristics, Adams consistently sought to uphold the law but pressed cases to defend individual freedom when he could. In particular, having been involved in the disastrous case of the *Antelope* when he was secretary of state—a case in which the Supreme Court randomly divided Africans who had taken over their slave ship but wrecked off the coast of the United States, setting some free and sending others back into captivity—Adams sought to use new laws to return Africans to their home continent. Ever attentive to rules and procedures, Adams asked Congress to clarify *exactly* what the president could do with illegally imported enslaved people.[62]

Adams shaped his understanding of international agreements in order to bring together his antislavery goals and a fair, defensible interpretation of the rules under which presidents acted. As secretary of state, Adams had negotiated an agreement with Great Britain that would have allowed each nation to interdict ships of the other on the high seas to stop piracy—newly redefined to include slavery. The Senate removed key parts of the agreement, however, rendering it unacceptable to Britain, and as president Adams was unable to revive it.[63]

This example illustrates Adams's approach to thorny issues of public ethics and the responsibility to faithfully execute the laws and uphold the Constitution. Adams had a significant change of heart on the idea of opening American shipping to British inspection. Devoted to law and process first, even beyond his own personal feelings against slavery, Adams knew that there was little he could do as secretary of state or as president unless his antislavery actions could be understood as legal and appropriate. Initially, he believed that allowing the British to search American ships for captive persons being transported was a violation of the rights of neutrals on the high seas. But then Adams hit on the idea of considering enslaved people as contraband—searching for contraband was legal and accepted practice. If enslaved people were contraband, then there was nothing to stop British ships from helping interdict illegal slaving. That turn of legal interpretation drove Adams's effort at getting a workable antislaving agreement with Britain, even if it proved too much for the U.S. Senate. As Adams explained in his diary, "The object is to capture *pirates;* and, without any distrust of our own Executive officers, we may give our aid and accept that of another for the more effectual execution of a law common to both."[64]

The case highlights Adams's commitment to higher principles of constitutional governance. Adams knew that his actions were constrained by law and by the Constitution. But once he hit upon sound constitutional logic to get him where he wanted to go, he seized on it. This kind of approach will strike some as self-serving, and they may be right. But not every argument can be bent and twisted to fit a constitutional logic, and the process itself helps refine arguments and evaluate their strength. The act of shaping logic and circumstances, of comparing them to constitutional prescriptions and proscriptions, is in itself a worthwhile activity. For a devotee of procedure like Adams, it forces a comparison of *ends* with the standards and processes by which we have agreed to govern and be governed. Until Adams could make his end consistent with the Constitution and the laws, he seemed to feel himself powerless—and he opposed the idea of British officials boarding American ships. Once he found a viable way to reconcile his personal and moral goals with the standards of the Constitution, consistent with the laws—knowing full well that there would rarely be universal agreement on the reconciling—Adams satisfied himself that his path was within established procedures and limits, and he took action.

Finally, as president Adams tried to use diplomacy as a way of advancing an antislavery approach. The Panama Congress, discussed in the previous chapter, was something that southern representatives opposed so strongly in Congress because they thought Adams was going to use it to push an antislavery agenda. The prospect of Black diplomats from Haiti sitting down with white American ministers in Panama was too much for southern members of Congress, many of whom saw Adams as dedicated to emancipation.[65]

These southern politicians may have been on to something: Adams did have a habit of using the president's power of appointment to further the fight against slavery. For example, Adams appointed Federalist Rufus King as minister to Great Britain. King had tried to ban slavery in the Land Ordinance of 1785, had argued for banning slave imports as far back as the Constitutional Convention, was a member of the African Colonization Society, and opposed extending slavery to federal territories. King had even suggested that proceeds from federal land sales be used to support education and perhaps to fund the emancipation and exportation of enslaved people.[66] Adams's appointment of King as minister to Britain, in which capacity he served in 1825–26, was a significant move. Given the importance at the time of the Slave Trade Convention, amid negotiations for right of search and cooperation in fighting slavery as piracy, Adams made a conscious choice to appoint someone who shared his approach in a high-profile way. Adams's description of his conversation with King, who had looked toward retirement, emphasizes how Adams viewed the appointment's significance.[67] The choice of who to appoint to attend foreign conferences or hold diplomatic offices was clearly within the president's legitimate authority, and so Adams could work to erode slavery's hold and still remain well within established procedures and protocols.

Internal Improvements and the Post Office versus Slavery

President Adams worked against slavery domestically as well. Adams's options in domestic policy were more limited than those he enjoyed in international diplomacy, where piracy and the importation of enslaved people into the United States were clearly illegal. Domestically, however, slavery was broadly protected and even expanded by federal laws and procedures. Adams needed to fight carefully, with his eye on the long-range future effects of actions he could take.

Adams attacked slavery via the central focus of his presidency—internal improvements. The historian Richard R. John writes that Adams "assumed that his domestic agenda would strengthen the power of the central government relative to that of the states, rendering the eventual abolition of slavery far more likely."[68] Adams hoped that the economic development of non-slaveholding regions under the course of improvement would tip the balance of power against the slaveholding regions and their political influence. Adams's support for internal improvements thus reflected in part his hope that the extension of roads and canals, and the flood of national money and wealth that accompanied those developments, would break down the localism and prejudice of southern and slave regions. In 1830, Adams wrote in his diary, "I have cherished the principle and the system of internal improvement, under a conviction that it was for this nation the only path to increasing comforts and well-being, to honor, to glory, and finally to the general improvement of the condition of mankind." After reviewing the enduring, widespread support for the improvements program, even from John Calhoun and from Andrew Jackson during the 1828 election, Adams explained the growing opposition and political flip-flops they engendered: "The slaveholders of the South have since discovered that it will operate against their interest."[69]

Adams also used the mails as a means of extending federal authority into new regions. For example, Adams hoped to utilize the public contracts and jobs that accompanied construction of major post roads to diminish the relative influence of regional slaveholding interests in the West and South.[70] Adams believed that expanded federal spending and supervision could slowly but effectively whittle away at the localism and prejudice that helped sustain slavery. In fact, Adams's commitment to procedure helps explain in two ways a common criticism of the Adams presidency: his continued employment of the disloyal postmaster general John McLean. McLean was seen by many at the time as deeply disloyal to Adams, favoring instead Andrew Jackson and the interests of the Democratic Party. Adams's confidantes urged him to dismiss McLean and replace him with an Adams ally—which would not only bolster Adams's support in the Post Office but allow a new, loyal postmaster to fill patronage jobs across the country with Adams supporters.

Adams's refusal to dismiss McLean has long been seen by Adams's critics as a glaring example of his political naïveté, which led to widespread disaffection among his supporters and helped the Jacksonians stretch their influence to burgeoning areas in the South and West.[71] Adams, though, held onto McLean for two reasons. First, Adams consistently refused to relieve a government officer of his post unless presented with clear evidence of corruption, malfeasance, or maladministration. Keeping McLean was consistent with his view of proper administrative procedure for removal from government office—and for Adams, adherence to procedure and practice were more highly valued goals than partisan loyalty or reelection. Second, he believed that McLean was doing a terrific job of expanding the Post Office's efficiency and reach, which helped Adams whittle away at the slave power in a manner that did not violate the law or undercut the Constitution.

In May 1827, for example, Adams defended his choice to maintain McLean in office: "As he is an able and efficient officer, I have made every allowance for the peculiarity of his situation, and have not believed him willfully treacherous." In November 1827, under sharper questioning from Barbour, Adams offered this defense:

> This officer [McLean], who came into that place in 1823, has given great satisfaction in the administration of it. For three or four years before, it had been a burden upon the Treasury, requiring annual appropriations of nearly a hundred thousand dollars a year. Its condition since then has been constantly improving, and this year the receipts exceed the expenditure more than a hundred thousand dollars. The accommodations to the public, and the facilities in the transportation of the mail, have at the same time been multiplying in like proportion.[72]

McLean's innovations accelerated when Adams succeeded James Monroe as president, as Adams delegated increasing authority to McLean to appoint lower officials and to innovate with the use of stagecoaches, the hiring of private contractors, and the development of strong public-private partnerships.[73] This resulted in a 41 percent increase in number of post offices; a 30 percent extension in miles of post roads from 1823 to 1828, especially into the West; improvements in deliveries and reliability; and the introduction of express mail. McLean instituted new and effective accountability measures, and utilized the media to promote the postal service's activities.[74] For most of his presidency, Adams's working relationship with McLean seemed fine, and McLean's salary was elevated to cabinet level in 1827.[75] In October 1827, as Clay relayed rumors to Adams about McLean's duplicity, Adams wrote that McLean had "improved the condition of the Post Office Department since he has been at its head, and is perhaps the most efficient officer that has ever been in that place."[76]

Only in 1828 did Adams in his diary begin to be sharply critical of McLean, but even then the criticism was tempered by Adams's appreciation of the fine public service McLean had rendered.[77] And even after Andrew Jackson's election in 1828, Adams penned a final defense of McLean. Adams wrote in his diary that McLean had been made a justice of the Supreme Court by Jackson precisely because McLean refused to let Jackson commandeer the Post

Office's patronage. "McLean is made a judge of the Supreme Court to set him aside," Adams wrote. "He declined serving as the broom to sweep the post offices."[78] Arbitrary dismissals were virtually unknown at the time, and stability was an important staple of the Post Office's success.[79]

As long as McLean was running and expanding an effective national postal network, Adams continued him in office. Given the significant relationship of the Post Office to national supremacy and to Adams's efforts to undermine the slave power, his choice to keep McLean makes a great deal of sense. Adams's efforts here offer earlier suggestions in line with Jon Rogowski's study of the Post Office and presidential power in the period from 1876 to 1896, in which the president's relationship with the administrative bureaucracy provided a strong counterweight to power long assumed to have been centered in Congress.[80] Adams's retention of McLean also calls to mind Greenstein's discussion of the role of delegation in *The Hidden-Hand Presidency*: "A particularly important presidential personnel-management quality, judging from the several presidencies in which the president employed advisors who reinforced his own weaknesses or shortcomings, is the capacity to choose subordinates who compensate for one's own weaknesses."[81] To the extent that McLean's patronage skills, and his ability to combine political patronage with state-building administrative development and improvement, filled in one of Adams's most notable weaknesses, the Adams-McLean tandem makes sense. It furthered Adams's political goals in pursuing antislavery measures without sparking direct blowback, it was consistent with Adams's apolitical administrative leadership principles, and it shrewdly delegated in a manner that compensated for Adams's difficulties, in the slavery context, of being seen as both chief of state and chief political executive.

ADAMS'S COMMITMENT to expanding the reach of the Post Office, his attacks on the international slave trade, his appointments and retentions of key administrative leaders, and the deeper effects of internal improvements were all parts of his effort to fight slavery legally and constitutionally. Adams extended the federal government's reach and significance through administration and procedural action consistent with the laws, rather than by making speeches questioning the legitimacy of those laws.

In each of these areas, Adams carefully operated within his authority and within the accepted scope of well-established procedures for executive action. Adams did take action against slavery and against the slave trade as president. While these actions often fail to satisfy righteous observers today, and failed to mollify abolitionists at the time, they were concrete actions by a president who understood long-term battles and who was committed to a respect for law and process. Adams remained unwilling to undermine the law or the

Constitution, or to circumvent procedure, to pursue what he felt was right. He was very willing, though, to do everything he thought he could as president, legally and constitutionally, within the American state.

Internal Improvements and Public Rhetoric

Adams recognized, promoted, and defended what we now think of as a big part of big government. His ideas about government and internal improvements reflected the dominant ideas of his era, and beyond a legislative agenda including such measures, Adams articulated an approach to active governance at the national level in an effort to make federal action and its benefits safe for future generations.[82] In mounting an energetic defense against rhetorical challenges to the actions of the national government, Adams appealed to long-established processes and understandings about the proper scope of federal authority. Adams communicated publicly and forcefully to defend what he believed was sanctioned by American history, the Constitution, and the laws: internal improvements and government action in pursuit of the people's welfare.

Adams's arguments for his national policy agenda were aimed at influencing the populace on big ideas. Adams articulated an argument defending and promoting what already was—a government network of policies and programs that would protect and empower the nation and its inhabitants.[83] In his landmark book *The People's Welfare,* historian William J. Novak traces the extensive nineteenth-century history of governance and regulation at the state and local levels: a century that welcomed and saw as noncontroversial a host of local regulations designed to maximize the health, safety, development, and productivity of ordinary people.[84] The federal government, too, had for decades managed expansion, dominated the trade in land, regulated the trade in furs, and run a variety of economic and social regulatory initiatives through federal departments and field officers in the interests of the populace and the welfare of the nation.

President John Quincy Adams challenged the demagoguery of those arguing for scaling back the national government's scope and powers. "It was an article of faith to him," historian William Earl Weeks writes, "that effective leadership depended on the president's having a moral vision of the nation's future."[85] Adams saw his moral vision of active governance as squarely located within the constitutional procedures and processes that had characterized the nation's first decades.

THE INAUGURAL ADDRESS AND THE FIRST ANNUAL MESSAGE

Adams's Inaugural Address and his First Annual Message articulated an explicit understanding of the Constitution and the nation's regime values and laid out an aggressive policy agenda. Historians have often seen Adams's pronouncements as idealistic, out of touch, and pie in the sky. They have written that Adams was ahead of his time, apart from the public, a focus of ridicule and laughter—a visionary, but not an effective presidential leader.[86] But Adams was not ahead of his time. Adams was celebrating the past and creating the future, building on decades of big government and big ideas long understood to be consistent with the national government's authority.

The Inaugural Address, delivered in March 1825, candidly laid out Adams's governing principles and centered Adams within the cozy confines of the nation's values. Adams began by stating the foundation of his approach to the presidency, specifically invoking his "countrymen" as audience despite the delivery of the speech to Congress:

> In unfolding to my countrymen the principles by which I shall be governed in the fulfillment of those duties my first resort will be to that Constitution which I shall swear to the best of my ability to preserve, protect, and defend. That revered instrument enumerates the powers and prescribes the duties of the executive magistrate, and in its first words declares the purposes to which these and the whole action of government instituted by it should be invariably and sacredly devoted—to form a more perfect union, establish justice, insure domestic tranquility, provide for the common defense, promote the general welfare, and secure the blessings of liberty to the people of this Union in their successive generations.[87]

Adams not only appealed to the document, he borrowed its language extensively and directly to remind his audience of his own primary duty to the Constitution and its enumeration of the basic general principles for which government is designed. A little later, after a review of the growth and development of the nation's first decades, Adams returned to the importance of the document itself: "Such is the unexaggerated picture of our condition under a Constitution founded upon the republican principle of equal rights." Adams here invoked the egalitarian ideal of the Declaration of Independence. Later, Adams returned again to basic principles: "Our political creed is, without a dissenting voice that can be heard, that the will of the people is the source and the happiness of the people the end of all legitimate government upon earth.... The policy of our country is peace and the ark of our salvation union."

Adams thus based his vision of the presidency as preserving, protecting, and defending the Constitution, the values of which were agreed upon by all and which could be explicitly reviewed as general operating principles. Commitments to the future, to equality, to peace, and to happiness were all explicit.

ADAMS PRESENTED himself as taking up the torch of the revolutionary generation. Because of the watershed status often assigned to Andrew Jackson's presidency, there is a tendency sometimes to see John Quincy Adams as a representative of the founding era. But Adams was a child during the Revolution. His father had been a driving force behind independence, and Adams's predecessor as president, James Monroe, had fought as a young man in the war. John Quincy Adams, on the other hand, belonged to the next generation—he was a vanguard, not an endpoint. "Since the adoption of this social compact," Adams said of the Constitution and its founders, "one of these generations has passed away.... We now receive it as a precious inheritance from those to whom we are indebted for its establishment, doubly bound by the examples which they have left us and by the blessings which we have enjoyed as the fruits of their labors to transmit the same unimpaired to the succeeding generation." The cause of Adams's generation, and the government's responsibility, was to carry the founders' achievements forward, preserving them intact for future generations. "Standing at this point of time, looking back to that generation which has gone by and forward to that which is advancing, we may at once indulge in grateful exultation and in cheering hope." The consistent use of "we" and "our" perpetuated the connection to a general audience—an address fashioned for all.

Much of what followed was a litany of what the national government had achieved by the hand of the founding generation, with more than a little flavor of government action and orderly procedure:

> In the compass of thirty-six years since this great national covenant was instituted a body of laws enacted under its authority and in conformity with its provisions has unfolded its powers and carried into practical operation its effective energies. Subordinate departments have distributed the executive functions in their various relations to foreign affairs, to the revenue and expenditure, and to the military force of the Union by land and sea. A coordinate department of the judiciary has expounded the Constitution and the laws, settling in harmonious coincidence with the legislative will numerous weighty questions of construction which the imperfection of human language had rendered unavoidable.... A population of four millions has multiplied to twelve. A territory bounded by the Mississippi has been extended from sea to sea. New states have been admitted to the Union in numbers nearly equal to those of the first confederation. Treaties of peace, amity, and commerce have been concluded with the principal dominions of the earth.

All of this had been accomplished with liberty and law marching hand in hand, Adams said, and he highlighted the organizing and ordering roles of practice and procedure in his mentions of "laws enacted under [the Constitution's] authority and in conformity with its provisions," "subordinate departments" distributing executive functions, and the "harmonious" collaboration of the Congress and judiciary to settle matters of construction left ambiguous by the Constitution's text. The image one gets is of a well-functioning machine, built not on personal whims and unexpected actions but instead resting on collaboration and orderly procedure. Returning to the language of the Constitution itself, Adams concluded that "union, justice, tranquility, the common defense, the general welfare, and the blessings of liberty—all have been promoted by the government under which we have lived."

In other words, none of this was new—government had helped build what Adams's audience in 1825 enjoyed. Adams followed with an even more specific litany of what had been allowed and accomplished during the recent presidency of James Monroe:

> Sixty millions of the public debt have been discharged; provision has been made for the comfort and relief of the aged and indigent among the surviving warriors of the Revolution; ... the Floridas have been peaceably acquired, and our boundary has been extended to the Pacific Ocean; ... progress has been made in the defense of the country by fortifications and the increase of the navy, toward the effectual suppression of the African traffic in slaves; in alluring the aboriginal hunters of our land to the cultivation of the soil and of the mind, in exploring the interior regions of the Union, and in preparing by scientific researches and surveys for the further application of our national resources to the internal improvement of our country.

The conclusion of the Inaugural Address was Adams's discourse on the future. Having established the guiding principles of the Constitution, the revolutionary generation's great accomplishments, and the continuing improvements and energetic orderliness of the Monroe administration, Adams tried to deliver a knockout punch to the argument that all of this could suddenly be, in 1825, unconstitutional. Adams married the themes of government activity and its obligations to future generations in his most compelling passages, as he articulated the argument for internal improvements not only as constitutional, not only as common, but in fact as duties of the government: "To the topic of internal improvement ... I recur with peculiar satisfaction. It is that from which I am convinced that the unborn millions of our posterity who are in future ages to people this continent will derive their most fervent gratitude to the founder of the Union; that in which the beneficent action of its government will be most deeply felt and acknowledged."

Adams then positioned his plans for improvement and government action inside of the longstanding tradition of government activity he had traced. Adams was trying *not* to appear revolutionary, not to appear to be suggesting anything novel or untested. Internal improvements, rather, had been the basis and foundation of American growth and success, sanctioned by the preceding generation and built under their supervision and leadership:

> Nearly twenty years have passed since the construction of the first national road was commenced. The authority for its construction was then unquestioned. To how many thousands of our countrymen has it proved a benefit? To what single individual has it ever proved an injury? Repeated, liberal, and candid discussions in the legislature have conciliated the sentiments and approximated the opinions of enlightened minds upon the question of constitutional power. I cannot but hope that by the same process of friendly, patient, and persevering deliberation all constitutional objections will ultimately be removed. The extent and limitations of the powers of the general government in relation to this transcendently important interest will be settled and acknowledged to the common satisfaction of all, and every speculative scruple will be solved by practical public blessing.

What Adams envisioned for the country was not radical, not new—it was in keeping with the basic principles and purposes of the Constitution, the nation's values, and its history. Moreover, Adams had great faith in the way that the *process* would safely reconcile differing opinions: "I cannot but hope that by the same process of friendly, patient, and persevering deliberation all constitutional objections will ultimately be removed." Adams had appealed to the familiar in his recitation of the founding generation's accomplishments, including the mechanisms and processes by which such great achievements had been made possible. He appealed to those processes of deliberation and to those traditional understandings of the federal government's scope and authority under the Constitution in his call for continued action.

ADAMS RETURNED to these themes in his First Annual Message nine months later, which concluded with a bold appeal to Congress to accept its responsibilities for pursuing the general welfare through government action. The First Annual Message staked out a plan of internal improvements, national development, and government support for science and education. Almost all of Adams's cabinet members urged him not to deliver it, but Adams took a longer view: "I concurred entirely in the opinion that no projects absolutely impracticable ought to be recommended; but I would look to a practicability of a longer range than a simple session of Congress.... The plant may come late, though the seed be sown early."[88]

Following a report in the annual message on the status of the nation and of various initiatives of his term in office so far—including statements of the progress being made in internal improvements sanctioned by Congress—Adams introduced a more aspirational message. The substance of that message mirrors the concept of *salus populi* traced by Novak in the activities of state and local governments. Adams proclaimed,

> The great object of the institution of civil government is the improvement of the condition of those who are parties to the social compact, and no government, in what ever form constituted, can accomplish the lawful ends of its institution but in proportion as it improves the condition of those over whom it is established. Roads and canals, by multiplying and facilitating the communications and intercourse between distant regions and multitudes of men, are among the most important means of improvement. But moral, political, intellectual improvement are duties assigned by the Author of Our Existence to social no less than to individual man.
>
> For the fulfillment of those duties governments are invested with power, and to the attainment of the end—the progressive improvement of the condition of the governed—the exercise of delegated powers is a duty as sacred and indispensable as the usurpation of powers not granted is criminal and odious.[89]

Adams invoked Washington's proposals for a national military academy, which had been realized by Jefferson's administration at West Point, but he also invoked Washington's proposal for a national university, which remained undone. He appealed to Congress to support scientific research, particularly in exploration of the earth, sea, and heavens. He appealed for development of the executive and judicial branches to match the development of Congress; he appealed for progress on copyright and patent protection, and he called for a naval academy to complement the work of West Point.

Adams closed his message by invoking again the basic foundational language of the nation's values and its founding document in an effort to center his proposals solidly within established traditions, understandings, and processes. And he placed *inaction* as *outside* those established understandings:

> But if the power to exercise exclusive legislation in all cases whatsoever over the District of Columbia; if the power to lay and collect taxes, duties, imposts, and excises, to pay the debts and provide for the common defense and general welfare of the United States; if the power to regulate commerce with

foreign nations and among the several States and with the Indian tribes, to fix the standard of weights and measures, to establish post offices and post roads, to declare war, to raise and support armies, to provide and maintain a navy, to dispose of and make all needful rules and regulations respecting the territory or other property belonging to the United States, and to make all laws which shall be necessary and proper for carrying these powers into execution—if these powers and others enumerated in the Constitution may be effectively brought into action by laws promoting the improvement of agriculture, commerce, and manufactures, the cultivation and encouragement of the mechanic and the elegant arts, the advancement of literature, and the progress of the sciences, ornamental and profound, *to refrain from exercising them for the benefit of the people themselves would be to hide in the earth the talent committed to our charge—would be treachery to the most sacred of trusts.* [emphasis added]

Not to act would be treachery; not to act would "doom ourselves to perpetual inferiority." Not to act was to abrogate the nation's history and its understanding of the way things had been done—not to act would be radical change. For Adams, improvement of the nation's infrastructure and of the people's welfare was a sacred trust, an essential power of government, and in no way radical. For someone like Adams, relying on established understandings of state action and anticipating its ongoing salutary effects on the general population, *not to act* would be outside the norms of practice and procedure and would violate government's ethical and moral responsibility. In his most visionary statement, John Quincy Adams still appealed to established procedural norms to anchor his understanding of the state's role.

What scholars have often missed is the mainstream nature of Adams's public rhetoric and its location at the very center of state action. In other words, if we look at Adams's words from an understanding that the state had done little before the 1820s and had had little noticeable impact on people's lives, Adams's statements look idealistic and aspirational—as they have to so many of Adams's biographers and students of his presidency. And as a result, Adams's statements also do not look like serious contributions to a public discussion of policy and politics. But by recognizing state action from the 1790s to the 1820s—three decades of infrastructure development, indemnification programs, seamen's hospitals, international diplomacy, military action, economic policy, trade regulation, land acquisition, Indian affairs, and so on—with that new understanding of the scope of the American state as a baseline, Adams's comments appear in a more accurate, and more understandable, context. Adams's public rhetoric discussed politics, it discussed policy, and it did so in detail—marking past government achievements and arguing strenuously in defense of specific current policy initiatives. To argue that Adams did not "talk politics" or use moral suasion in public rhetoric fashioned for all misunderstands the politics and issues of the nineteenth century.

Conclusion

In Adams's single term, we see several important dynamics at the intersection of the presidency and the state. For the president, we see the use of public rhetoric and moral suasion to support policy initiatives; we see the use of a hidden-hand style of leadership to weaken slavery; and we see the deployment of a range of executive action tools, including commander-in-chief authority, unilateral action, administrative and legislative leadership, and even public communication to fend off aggressive action by Georgia aimed at undercutting federal supremacy. In terms of the national state, we see a complex, mature, and effective administrative state, affecting millions of people directly and intrusively, as President Adams relied on public administrators and on established processes to address major issues.

4

President Grant and the American State after the Civil War

THE STATE remained active and presidential leadership remained important in the years after the Civil War. Ulysses S. Grant served as president in a time of great change, when the American state began to be redirected toward new ends. Looking at the Grant presidency, we see executive action and a fully mature administrative state in a condition of evolution. The state that John Quincy Adams had engaged with as president was being redirected, deployed in new and different ways. Hidden-hand antislavery efforts became headline-grabbing actions against recalcitrant rebels and regions. Indian affairs continued longstanding administrative processes but picked up new goals and redirected others as national expansion moved westward, engaging new settlers, new Native nations, new topographies, and new issues. And many other policy areas—environmental crises, social issues, race and gender issues, monetary policy, infrastructure development, diplomacy and international affairs, defense and the military, administrative management—continued to be the focus of national activity and presidential leadership directly affecting the lives of millions of people.

The extensive scope and influence of the state offered the nineteenth-century president a wide variety of options for leadership and decision making. As president, Grant was far less concerned than Adams had been about procedure, rules, or established practice. Confident in his sense of values, Grant deployed state authority quickly and decisively—even if his decisiveness was frequently subject to equally decisive fast reversals. President Grant was what I call a "principled innovator." His principles drove his presidential initiatives and his leadership of the administrative bureaucracy. He governed with tactics that shifted as circumstances shifted, with innovative approaches to rapidly changing situations. He sought to reform and to create in order to advance broad principles, often aiming to realize immediate goals in particular circumstances.

Executive decisions followed Grant's evaluation of how best to get where he wanted to go, sometimes innovating and occasionally demonstrating allegiance to traditional procedures or careful analysis of laws and past practice. Rarely, though, did Grant have at his fingertips a deep understanding of what policies and procedures had been followed in the past. Many of Grant's decisions bucked tradition, aimed at fast resolution, and lacked sustained effort to establish lasting legislation. Grant preferred to work for the future through executive action and administrative programs. The continuing existence of an extensive state apparatus, together with a president who had no prior experience in elected office, enabled this particular marriage of presidential leadership and state action.

This chapter examines Grant's leadership in domestic and foreign affairs, as well as his leadership of the administrative bureaucracy, to illustrate some of the uses to which the continuing state was put after the Civil War and to illustrate Grant's approach to exercising executive power within that state. Contrary to assertions of a weak state returned to localism, of clerk-like presidents dominated by courts and parties, and seen-but-not-heard presidents refusing to talk politics or use official messages to make recommendations to Congress, Grant's two terms illustrate an active and intrusive national state very much influenced by presidential efforts.[1] President Grant approached a diverse constellation of issues with creative and ad-hoc applications of executive authority and action; leadership of the executive branch; efforts to work with Congress, including by the recommendation of specific measures; and the use of presidential communications aimed at broad public audiences. Grant followed no simple playbook, instead choosing and re-choosing from the variety of tools available to him as president and applying diverse tactics and executive actions within rapidly evolving policy and political environments.

The President, the Public, and the State after the Civil War

President Grant's annual messages are remarkably similar to what we now know as the president's State of the Union Address. Like presidents today, Grant offered data and patriotic messages about America's values and greatness. But also like presidents today, the vast majority of his annual messages were long and detailed, offering some general and some specific discussions of the issues of the day. In these messages one begins to see the vast, continuing, and evolving scope of the national state after the Civil War.

Grant offered numerous recommendations for specific legislation in his annual messages, using language like "I suggest," "I would ask for," and "I recommend legislation to." In his First Annual Message, he made seventeen such proposals and addressed at least twenty-three separate issues in detail, offering explanations, rationales, and information. In his Seventh Annual Message, in 1875, he made twenty-nine specific calls for legislation and referred to even more proposed legislation appearing in four separate reports from administrative departments that would be submitted directly to Congress or had been already. He offered detailed discussion of at least fifteen separate issues. Considerable continuity in topics and approach mark the annual messages, illustrating the ongoing nature of governance and administrative management across Grant's two terms.[2]

The topics covered in these addresses ranged broadly and offer a window into the scope of state activities in the Grant years. In his First Annual Message Grant recommended legislation, repeal of legislation, congressional action, or postponement of congressional action on a host of topics:

- "enact a law authorizing the governor of Georgia" to take action to rectify that state's legislature's actions in refusing to seat elected members who were Black
- a promise to propose plans regarding commerce in the wake of the war's disruptions
- specific recommendations regarding gold and specie ("I earnestly recommend to you, then, such legislation as will insure a gradual return to specie payments and put an immediate stop to fluctuations in the value of currency.... To secure the latter, I see but one way, and that is to authorize the Treasury to redeem its own paper, at a fixed price, whenever presented, and to withhold from circulation all currency so redeemed until sold again for gold")
- two proposals regarding taxes and tariffs
- five recommendations directly affecting the Treasury Department's business and administrative operations
- legislation related to intercontinental communications cables
- "such legislation as will forever preclude the enslavement of the Chinese upon our soil under the name of coolies," and legislation aimed at preventing American shipping from "engaging in the transportation of coolies"
- the repeal of the Tenure of Office Acts
- a proposal for revenue-producing legislation that would protect seal fisheries on both coasts
- recommendations regarding the War Department's operations, including for the sale of obsolete arsenals and lands
- a reminder of the need to prepare for the 1870 census
- a recommendation for "favorable consideration [of] the claims of the Agricultural Bureau for liberal appropriations"
- a recommendation for increasing the salaries of Supreme Court justices[3]

This list suggests the scope only of Grant's specific recommendations to Congress. It does not address the depth of information presented in the message, particularly the president's extended explanations of situations involving

American Indians and U.S. expansion, Cuba and Spain, the *Alabama* claims stemming from Britain's involvement in outfitting ships during the Civil War, veterans' pensions, the census, immigration and naturalization issues, and government administration, among many others. Later addresses contained ongoing discussion of many of these matters while adding new issues that arose: military conflict in Korea (Second Annual Message); the Ku Klux Klan, a youth exchange program with China and Japan, plans for uniting the telegraph system with the postal system, and Mormons and polygamy in Utah (Third); river and harbor improvements, politics and partisanship involving the Department of Justice, and a recommendation for the planting of forests (Fourth); election reform, the line-item veto, exploration of the Amazon, and bankruptcy reform (Fifth); judicial reform (Sixth); Black Hills gold and the grasshopper scourges (Seventh); and relations with Hawai'i and preservation of the collections from the centennial celebration (Eighth).[4]

Grant also identified and explained numerous executive actions taken independently, either by him as president or by administrative units within the executive branch. In his First Annual Message, these included

- instructions to the U.S. minister to Colombia to obtain authority for the United States to assess the practicability of an interoceanic canal
- the sending of a commissioner and secretary to Peru regarding the adjustment of claims ("No appropriation having been made by Congress for this purpose, it is now asked that one be made covering the past and future expenses of the commission")
- the State Department's consideration of transit rights for Americans and Europeans across Nicaragua
- the president's direct action regarding Spanish gunboats being prepared in New York for use in the war between Peru and Spain
- withdrawal of the U.S. representative in Paraguay due to dangerous wartime conditions there
- detailed and extensive executive action regarding the *Alabama* claims
- finalization of claims against the United States by the Hudson's Bay and Puget Sound Agricultural Company, resulting in an award of $650,000 ("an appropriation by Congress to meet this sum is asked")
- executive action related to transatlantic communications cables
- direction to diplomatic and consular officials "to scrutinize carefully" claims for protection from people posing as U.S. citizens
- presidential leadership related to Indian affairs[5]

In further acknowledgment of the scope and range of the American state—and hinting at the seriousness with which Grant took the president's responsibility to suggest specific measures to Congress—Grant ended his first message by noting, "There are many subjects not alluded to in this message which might with propriety be introduced, but I abstain, believing that your patriotism and statesmanship will suggest the topics and the legislation most conducive to the interests of the whole people."[6] In other words: you have other things to do as well, but the foregoing represent those items about which the president's involvement and leadership is underscored.

In that first message, Grant addressed matters that were partisan hotspots, like race and free education; he discussed matters that were of widespread political interest, like pensions for veterans and their families; he wrote of matters important to thousands of Americans, like protections for merchant seamen—often using language designed to appeal to a broader audience than just Congress. On Cuba, for example, Grant wrote, "For more than a year a valuable province of Spain, and a near neighbor of ours, in whom all our people can not but feel a deep interest, has been struggling for independence and freedom." On pensions, he wrote of his request for an appropriation of $30 million, "Public opinion has given an emphatic sanction to these measures of Congress, and it will be conceded that no part of our public burden is more cheerfully borne than that which is imposed by this branch of the service." He invoked the importance of "public feeling" among Americans—"a sensitive people"—to explain his temporary disengagement from wartime claims negotiations with Britain.[7] Grant's words carried weight on contentious issues, and they were eagerly anticipated and discussed domestically and abroad.[8]

The addresses were both "public" and "popular," with Grant and his advisors working carefully to assess content, tone, and expected audience reaction. Every message received discussion among the cabinet, and outside interests were frequently offered the opportunity to comment on content and draft language. And even as there was general agreement among cabinet members that the annual messages should not bear too much detail and should maintain a tone of unanimity in the country and not partisanship, the grey areas around those goals—what would be acceptable and what might go too far or undercut the general etiquette surrounding the messages—was the subject of ongoing debate about details, wording, and so on. A good example of this is the debate between Secretary of State Hamilton Fish and Secretary of the Interior Zachariah Chandler regarding Grant's Eighth Annual Message, specifically involving how Grant's message should approach the issue of Democrat-led violence, upheaval, and fraud in the South during the 1876 election.[9]

Grant went "over the heads" of Congress on some matters, highlighting links between public opinion and his positions that the Congress would be wise to respect. Grant wrote in his Fifth Annual Message, for example, "The Secretary of the Interior renews his recommendation for a census to be taken in 1875, to which subject the attention of Congress is invited. The original suggestion in that behalf has met with the general approval of the country." Later in the same address, Grant wrote of improvements in Washington, DC: "I recommend a liberal policy toward the District of Columbia, and that the Government should bear its just share of the expense of these improvements. Every citizen visiting the capital feels a pride in its growing beauty, and that he too is part owner in the investments made here." Finally, Grant wrote, "I would suggest to Congress the propriety of promoting the establishment in this District of an institution of learning, or university of the highest class, by the donation of lands. There is no place better suited for such an institution than the national capital. There is no other place in which every citizen is so directly interested."[10] All three statements directly tied the president's recommended action to public opinion, casting the public as uniformly in favor of the measure and offering that support as a reason for Congress to take action. Historian Kenneth R. Bowling, in fact, gives Grant credit for establishing the word "capital" in the public mind (replacing "seat of government" and "federal city") when referring to Washington, DC, as the president used his comments and policies to build the city into a world-class center of governmental leadership.[11]

In the Sixth Annual Message, Grant appealed directly to the public. Following extended discussion of armed conflicts and ongoing racism in Louisiana and Arkansas, Grant addressed the partisan and politically charged issue of "executive interference with the affairs of a State." He wrote,

> I invite the attention, not of Congress, but of the people of the United States, to the causes and effects of these unhappy questions. Is there not a disposition on one side to magnify wrongs and outrages, and on the other side to belittle them or justify them? If public opinion could be directed to a correct survey of what is and to rebuking wrong and aiding the proper authorities in punishing it, a better state of feeling would be inculcated, and the sooner we would have that peace which would leave the States free indeed to regulate their own domestic affairs....
>
> Let there be fairness in the discussion of Southern questions, the advocates of both or all political parties giving honest, truthful reports of occurrences, condemning the wrong and upholding the right, and soon all will be well. Under existing conditions the negro votes the Republican ticket because he knows his friends are of that party. Many a good citizen votes the opposite, not because he agrees with the great principles of state which separate parties,

but because, generally, he is opposed to negro rule. This is a most delusive cry. Treat the negro as a citizen and a voter, as he is and must remain, and soon parties will be divided, not on the color line, but on principle. Then we shall have no complaint of sectional interference.[12]

Grant ended his Seventh Annual Message by recapping five "questions which I deem of vital importance which may be legislated upon and settled at this session."[13] He concluded with another direct appeal to the public's support for his agenda: "Believing that these views will commend themselves to the great majority of the right-thinking and patriotic citizens of the United States, I submit the rest to Congress." These passages from Grant's messages were issue-based, they addressed issues concerning party and partisanship, and they were "fashioned for all." They were public and popular presidential communications that directly engaged controversial issues, and the public responded directly to them.[14]

While Grant did not relish making public speeches, make them he did. A speech that Grant made in December 1870 to firefighters gathered outside the White House, for example, galvanized the movement to keep the nation's capital in DC by stating a clear position and effectively threatening a veto over congressional efforts to move the capital without a constitutional edict or a congressional supermajority. When Senator John Logan, Horace Greeley, and others agitated for relocating the national capital to the West, they gave a variety of reasons, among which were the progress of the nation to the West, the need to recognize new western interests, and the symbolism after the Civil War of moving the capital from George Washington's slave city closer to the home of the great emancipator, Abraham Lincoln. Grant, though, helped stymie the movement by appealing, in repeated annual messages and at least one influential public speech, to the goal of a world-class capital city in Washington, DC, that would make all the nation's citizens proud and serve as a symbol of national unity.[15]

Grant's speech sparked public debate in newspapers and letters to the president, and perhaps more importantly, it effectively ended the relocation movement when it led to new congressional appropriations for building constructions in the winter of 1870–71. Those appropriations, coming immediately on the heels of Grant's rhetorical efforts, guaranteed the presence of the federal government in DC for years to come. Grant supported the creation in 1871 of DC's territorial government, he appointed Alexander Shepherd to oversee the public works program, and he pressed Congress repeatedly and publicly to support the program with adequate appropriations.[16] As Bowling writes of the long-lasting effects of Grant's work to fashion DC into a national capital: "Long after abandoning Reconstruction in the South, Republicans pressed forward with the reconstruction of Washington so that the city physically, constitutionally, and symbolically reflected the supremacy of the federal government over the states."[17]

Overall, Grant addressed numerous controversial policy topics and discussed partisan matters in public speeches and official communications. These examples suggest the need for a more thorough assessment of speeches by Grant and other nineteenth-century presidents. In *The Rhetorical Presidency*, for example, Jeffrey K. Tulis listed Grant as having offered twenty-five public speeches during his two terms, with those speeches qualifying for only three out of nine "purposes" defined by Tulis: greetings, speech associated with a ceremony, and reassurance by presence ("seeing and being seen").[18] Yet just those speeches included in the *Papers of Ulysses S. Grant* could easily be interpreted as including the other purposes that Tulis did not connect to Grant's speeches: "patriotic exhortation," "attempts to establish peace and harmony among the regions or sections of the nation," articulation of general policy direction of an administration, defense of war policy or action (especially seen in speeches to Native American delegations, an audience that Tulis marginalized), identification of the president's position as partisan, and attack or defenses of specific legislative proposals.[19]

There is argument to be had in the interpretations: some of Grant's comments on current issues—on banning sectarian education, for example, or on equal rights—might not have been directly tied to a specific piece of legislation or name a particular political party or organization, but certainly at the time it would have been clear to audience members that Grant was touching on matters that divided the public and the parties, and that were related to specific legislation and constitutional amendments. These examples make it clear that the president and the state were both active, engaged, and visible forces in the issues of the 1870s, and they make clear the president's use of formal messages as well as public speeches to address specific issues, including issues that were contentious and upon which the parties had distinct differences.

President Grant and Leadership in Domestic Affairs

Public communication was only one tactic that Grant deployed to push his agenda and lead the American state. As president, Grant eschewed established tactics and gave what he considered common-sense commands to get where he wanted to go. If he changed his mind, he reversed course. A discussion in his *Memoirs* explained his approach as a military leader, but the passage also captures his approach to the presidency. Of the time when he commanded a regiment in Mexico during the U.S.-Mexico War, Grant wrote, "I had never looked at a copy of tactics from the time of my graduation. . . .

I found no trouble in giving commands that would take my regiment where I wanted it to go and carry it round all obstacles. I do not believe that the officers of the regiment ever discovered that I had never studied the tactics that I used."[20]

Grant and the Inflation Bill Veto

One of the best windows into Grant's style of presidential leadership after the Civil War occurred with his veto of the "Inflation Bill," which illustrates Grant's independent decision making as president, his use of the veto, and the deployment of public communication, all at the conjunction of interbranch relations. From the outset of his presidency, Grant took decisive and controversial action on economic policy. He signed the first act Congress passed in 1869, arguing for the Public Credit Act and helping to push it through Congress.[21] Grant and Treasury Secretary George Boutwell teamed up to smash the effort by Jay Gould and Jay Fisk to corner the gold market in the fall of 1869.[22] Grant and Boutwell intervened to balance monetary policy again right before the 1872 election.[23] Administration policy was shrewd and decisive, even if characterized by a case-by-case approach to a series of crises and emergencies.

With the Panic of 1873, Americans across the country again demanded action from the federal government. Major firms were failing; the Chesapeake & Ohio and fifty-five other railroads went into default; railroad defaults pummeled the iron industry, which in turn affected coal and petroleum companies.[24] Congress, after four months of detailed policy analysis and compromise decisions influenced by panicked constituents, succumbed to calls for retroactively allowing millions of greenback dollars back into circulation while at the same time establishing a precedent for addressing future credit and money crunches by releasing more paper money—risking rampant inflation in the pursuit of getting more money circulating. Congress passed the bill after intense lobbying and aggressive deal-making by forces on all sides of the money issue. The inflation bill provided for a $46 million increase in circulating currency, to a total of $400 million. Hard money conservatives saw it as an "entering wedge" that would begin a period of paper issues and risk lasting inflation.[25]

In short, the inflation bill would have expanded access to paper money at a time of monetary crisis, satisfying those arguing for debt relief but worrying those, like Grant, who were publicly committed to returning to hard money after the chaos of the Civil War. Congress and the parties were key players in drafting the bill, but the outcome would rely on the president, and on a particular individual assessment of merits and principle. Even as the House and Senate worked on the issue, Grant intervened with a public memorandum specifying hard-money details necessary for getting presidential approval for the bill. Republican monetary expansionists saw this intervention as "unwarranted and unprecedented."[26]

Once the bill had been finalized, Grant drafted what he referred to as an "unusual, and almost unprecedented" message to accompany a signature on the bill—but he also drafted a veto of the bill.[27] Grant acknowledged that a full public debate and careful analysis by Congress had led to a compromise bill satisfactory to many parties. He understood that presidents traditionally vetoed bills based on concerns about their constitutionality, and there was little doubt about the inflation bill's constitutionality. In such a case, established procedure would have likely led to Grant's signing the bill and defending the action by appealing to past practice and basic separation of powers relationships.

Nevertheless, Grant found himself wanting to issue a veto. He argued his way to this conclusion by replacing the traditional standard of decision, the president's usual role in signing a procedurally sound and constitutional measure, with what Grant saw as higher-order principles. Grant wrote that signing the bill would violate the principle of integrity, since he and many members of Congress had for years publicly stated their opposition to such a measure. He wrote, "The theory [of the proposed measure] in my belief is a departure from true principles of finance, national interest, national obligations to creditors, Congressional promises, party pledges—both political parties—and of personal views and promises made by me, in every Annual Message sent to Congress, and in each inaugural address." He also argued to his cabinet that "the good faith of the nation" required him to veto the measure.[28] Grant vetoed the bill, basing his decision on a unique evaluation of tactics, goals, and competing higher-order principles.[29]

In taking such action and crafting messages for both signature and veto, Grant not only used the executive tool of the veto to influence policy outcomes, he utilized the president's communications options to explain himself directly in a manner accessible to the public. Even though the messages were formally directed at Congress, it is clear that Grant recognized the interest of a wider public audience, just as he did in his annual messages. Grant's messages on the inflation bill—his veto and also his draft of a message to accompany his signature on the bill—both explain the background of the case and the logic of his decision in understandable terms reminiscent of Franklin Roosevelt's fireside chat explaining the bank holiday in 1933. The determining factor in Grant's presentation was integrity—and he brought into the decision the integrity not just of himself as president but of himself as candidate and also of members of Congress and his party. Grant was making an explanation and argument to the public, and one that referred directly to prior public communications made by members of the party and government. The messages on the inflation bill are exactly what we think of when we think of public communication from a president. The messages are content-laden and also independent. Grant's decision was his as president, not dictated by party and not determined by Congress. It was an action by the president on a national issue affecting millions of people's lives.

Grant and Executive Action

Grant's approach to presidential decision making sprang from the idea that the president can and should innovate, and Grant's actions leave no doubt that he saw the presidency as an office of unilateral action and leadership. He issued multiple vetoes, and he was the first president to request the line-item veto. He acted to impound congressional appropriations. He vetoed a bill that would have reduced the president's annual salary from $50,000 to $25,000; he defended himself against a congressional inquiry into his absences from the capital, invoking the Constitution and regime values; he dismissed an executive branch administrator for making unauthorized communications with Congress. He issued a signing statement when he signed the Rivers and Harbors Bill into law, generating condemnation that foreshadowed current controversies about signing statements, and he vetoed a bill to pave Pennsylvania Avenue using contractor labor because the bill omitted dates and other details Grant felt were required for the successful completion of the job.[30] He negotiated a workaround with Congress on the Tenure of Office Act, rendering it moot for his presidency.[31] He defended executive power in foreign affairs against encroachments by the House of Representatives. In 1874, Grant pardoned three Buffalo men convicted of registering Susan B. Anthony and other women to vote.[32] He repeatedly encouraged and promoted government assistance to the historic 1876 Centennial Exposition in Philadelphia.[33] Grant issued a general clemency order in 1876, which worried some who believed that leniency might be perceived as weakness.[34] He worked to remove the stain of his own Civil War order removing Jews from his military district in 1862 by appointing Jews to federal office.[35]

Grant issued 217 executive orders, according to the American Presidency Project. Many of Grant's executive orders dealt with appointments to command positions in the military, deaths of notable public figures like Edwin Stanton and Franklin Pierce, and matters related to the Centennial Exhibition. Others addressed more critical issues, including one in 1869 establishing the Board of Indian Commissioners and setting up its rules, orders in 1871 mandating recounts of the 1870 census in New York City and Philadelphia, and several in 1872 and following years regarding civil service protections. He issued orders forbidding federal appointees from running for state offices unless they first resigned from their federal posts and others that ended military districts in areas brought back into the Union. Orders in 1875 banned breech-loading rifle sales in Alaska (and provided enforcement mechanisms) and set out rules for civil engineer James Eads's interests as related to federal projects for harbor and river improvements. An intriguing order in 1876 banned specific types of ammunition in Indian country.[36]

The American Presidency Project also counts fifty-four proclamations issued by Grant on a variety of issues.[37] Some were ceremonial, such as Thanksgiving Day orders. Some were more momentous, including a number related to new state constitutions for former Confederate states and on critical issues like suspending habeas corpus; establishing law and order and sanctioning elected officials in South Carolina, Louisiana, Mississippi, and Arkansas; implementing the 1875 convention with Hawai'i; and enforcing the Fourteenth Amendment. Numerous proclamations were "warn orders," some involving Canada and the conflict between France and Prussia in 1870. When issuing proclamations related to the 1871 Enforcement Act, Grant offered explanations of his decision and authority to act and implored the public to act appropriately. When issuing his proclamation to order the disbanding of white rifle clubs prior to the 1876 elections, he offered a careful argument for executive power and prerogative.[38]

Grant also used proclamations to direct more mundane but still salient issues like federal workers' pay and hours, in a back and forth involving Congress and administrative units. Workers had been guaranteed an eight-hour workday in an 1868 bill passed by Congress and signed into law by President Andrew Johnson. The law, however, did not protect salaried workers from prorated pay reductions if their hours were reduced. Johnson's attorney general—and then Grant's—specified that the law addressed only hours, not wages, offering no help to workers. In response, Grant signed a proclamation in 1869 protecting workers' wages from cuts stemming from reduced hours.[39] When it became clear that the proclamation was being ignored in some parts, Grant issued a second proclamation in 1872, in an effort to ensure compliance and sparking Congress to include workers' back pay in an appropriations bill.[40] Grant regularly created effective workarounds to shape and adjust responses to existing rules and guidelines, arguing that "it is preposterous to suppose that the people of one generation can lay down the best and only rules of government for all who are to come after them, and under unforeseen contingencies.... We could not and ought not to be rigidly bound by the rules laid down under circumstances so different for emergencies so utterly unanticipated."[41]

Finally, Grant used the president's opportunities for judicial appointments to push his governing agenda. He appointed William Strong and Joseph P. Bradley to the Supreme Court, in part to overturn *Hepburn v. Griswold*, the U.S. Supreme Court's 1870 decision that had effectively ruled unconstitutional the 1862 Legal Tender Act, which treated U.S. paper notes as legal tender.[42]

Bradley and Strong tipped the balance of the Court the other way in 1871's *Legal Tender* cases, which reversed *Hepburn* and sanctioned the paper notes in question. Grant appointed an array of judges to the new postwar circuit courts who pressed the administration's aggressive approach to the new rights and new national obligations set out in the Civil War amendments, as detailed in the next chapter. Even more directly, Grant used his appointment power in 1870 to place James B. McKean as chief justice for Utah to enforce the Morrill Anti-Bigamy Act of 1862. When McKean confronted strong opposition from what he called a "theocratic state" in Utah, it was Grant who recommended legislation to address the issue in his December 1873 annual message to Congress. Congress passed the Poland Act in 1874, abolishing the offices of the Utah territorial marshal and attorney, empowering federal officials, and clarifying the jurisdiction of the federal courts in the territory.[43] Grant regularly used the appointment power to appoint men who were dedicated to particular propositions that Grant favored.

Grant and Legislation

Grant worked actively with Congress to push for specific legislation and congressional action. The Public Credit Act, mentioned above, benefited from presidential support; so did the Fifteenth Amendment, discussed in more detail in the next chapter, and a bill that Grant signed into law in March 1875 prohibiting the importation of women to be used as prostitutes, a policy he had promoted repeatedly in public addresses.[44] Grant supported federal liquor taxes, a position that affected his support in western North Carolina. The combination of revenue authority and federal interference created a clear "sense of the state" in the region. Federal liquor taxation "emerged as a major issue in mountain politics during the 1870s," according to historian Bruce E. Stewart, and Grant's involvement on the side of the revenuers (together with 1873's Whiskey Ring bribery scandal, advantaging bribe-givers while leaving many moonshiners still under the thumb of the federal revenue service) was used to diminish Republican support in the region.[45]

The Grant administration also actively worked toward what became the Timber Culture Act, which sought to build on the model of the Homestead Act by granting land to people who planted trees on the frontier. The belief was that trees could be an important resource in the arid West, and that trees might even bring rain to agricultural regions. The public demanded federal action to increase rain on the Plains, and the leading option was to amend or update the Homestead Act in a way that would offer more land to people who would plant and nurture trees. Action moved through Congress in the late 1860s and early 1870s. Similar efforts passed at state levels, and the Grant administration provided support from government experts and reports from the Department of

Agriculture, General Land Office, and U.S. Geological and Geographical Survey. Experts at the Smithsonian, outside scientists, railroad interests, and promoters of western settlement all jumped on board. Grant was "much impressed with the idea of forestation on the plains," and so when Grant mentioned the idea in his Fourth Annual Message it was not a throwaway line—it was the president weighing in, supporting a well-developed specific approach to legislating on an issue that captured the attention of millions of Americans inside and outside of government. Congress passed the Timber Culture Act in March 1873.[46]

Grant advocated for civil service reform in his Second Annual Message. A divided Congress could not come to agreement on legislation, but it did pass a bill granting the president broad authority for making rules and regulations to implement civil service measures.[47] Grant appointed a high-profile team of reformers to a body that became known as the Civil Service Commission, including the leader of the reform movement, George William Curtis, and Joseph Medill, owner of the Chicago *Tribune*. The commission proved effective and promulgated rules and designed competitive examinations through 1872, which had salutary effects on administration at the time and moving forward.[48] The effort eventually ran aground due to divisions within the Republican Party, and the House refused to appropriate more money to Grant's commission. When the resources for implementing civil service reforms dried up, Grant acquiesced, leaving it to Congress to come back to the reforms in later administrations.[49]

Some legislative actions that had Grant's influence behind them were temporary and emergency measures, such as the Ku Klux Bill and Congress's delegation to Grant of the authority to suspend habeas corpus. Grant asked for much of this, and Congress gave it to him, but for limited duration and applicable to limited geographic regions and specific contexts. Other pieces of landmark legislation that passed during Grant's presidency, such as the 1872 General Mining Act, the 1872 Yellowstone Park Act, the 1872 Arnell Act requiring equal pay for women in the federal government, the 1876 Anti-Assessment Act, and the 1877 Desert Land Act, appear to have little of Grant's imprint on them, although further research may prove otherwise. At the very least, such legislation signed into law suggests again the considerable, ongoing scope of the national state in the 1870s.[50]

Grant and Presidential Responses to Crises of the Day

Executive action applications of state authority under Grant addressed a variety of issues, including matters touching on racial discrimination, gender equity, and the environment. Grant's reactions were often immediate, involving a kaleidoscope of executive actions and unpredictable efforts at administrative development.

Grant's executive actions on race and gender equity put on stark display Grant's ad-hoc approach to applying executive power to new issues. One good example is the case of James Webster Smith. Smith, the first Black cadet at West Point, and Henry O. Flipper, the first Black graduate, both arrived during Grant's first term. Both endured hazing, abuse, and loneliness at West Point, and Smith in particular felt the brunt of opposition from white cadets. Smith was subjected to numerous controversies with other cadets and subject to two court-martial proceedings. O. O. Howard, former head of the Freedmen's Bureau and considered knowledgeable and sympathetic, was selected to be presiding officer in Smith's critical second court-martial. The court-martial's outcome was a sentence of dismissal for Smith from the academy. Secretary of War Walter Belknap, acting for the president, shaved the sentence to a reduction in standing of one academic year, essentially meaning that Smith would repeat his freshman year. Belknap's official announcement of the sentence explained,

> The proceedings, findings and sentence are approved, but in view of all the circumstances surrounding this case and believing that the ends of public justice will be better subserved and the policy of the Government—of which the presence of this cadet in the Military Academy is a signal illustration—better maintained by a commutation of the sentence than by its rigid enforcement, the President is pleased to mitigate it by substituting, for dismissal from the service of the United States, reduction in his academic standing one year.[51]

Grant's intervention was situational, undercutting rules, a court-martial's finding, and established procedure in order to serve higher goals of justice and fairness in a new and unique situation.[52] There was little effort on Grant's part, though, to build new procedures or protections for Black cadets at West Point. Smith, continually harassed, was eventually found deficient in the areas of natural and experimental physics and was dismissed.[53] Flipper, who graduated from West Point in June 1877, benefited more from Smith's advice to refrain from any "forward conduct" than from any institutional reform built by the Grant administration.[54]

President Grant used his influence to innovate in cases involving race in other ways. He hosted an interracial inaugural ball in 1873, with dancing.[55] He was the first president to receive a prominent Black public official at the White House, when he hosted Lieutenant Governor Oscar J. Dunn of Louisiana in April 1869.[56] The earliest known Black letter carrier was appointed in June 1869, and the earliest Black postal inspector was appointed in 1870. Grant appointed the earliest known and longest serving Black woman to serve as a postmaster: Anna Dumas, appointed as Covington, Louisiana's postmaster in 1872.[57] Grant appointed Black people to other federal posts as well, including the first Black chief of mission in U.S. history, Ebenezer Don Carlos Bassett, and the first Black minister and consul general to Liberia, James Milton Turner.[58]

Grant seems to have acted in the interests of gender equity as well. Grant is credited with intervening on behalf of Belva Lockwood, who in the spring of 1879 became the first woman admitted to practice law before the U.S. Supreme Court and who a year later became the first woman to argue a case before the Court. A few years earlier, after studying law at National University Law School, of which President Grant was titular president, Lockwood and another female student were denied their diplomas even after attending classes and lectures. Lockwood wrote twice to Grant, once patiently laying out her request for Grant's intervention, and then later the same day with "a note, short and alarmingly rude," demanding her diploma. Grant did not answer the letters, but two weeks later Lockwood received her diploma.[59]

OTHER IMMEDIATE crises subject to executive action included presidentially directed disaster relief for people suffering from locust swarms on the Plains. Rocky Mountain locust swarms devastated the Great Plains in 1874-75, midway through Grant's second term. Private relief efforts fell short, state relief efforts bogged down, and citizens on the Plains were starving, in dire need of food and clothing as the locusts destroyed crops and anything else in their path. Federal military officials investigated and documented the circumstances, and General Edward O. C. Ord, commander of the Department of the Platte, advocated for immediate federal assistance. Ord argued to the commissary general of subsistence that hundreds of Americans would die if relief were not granted immediately out of federal military stores. Ord was refused, and Secretary of War Belknap upheld the refusal.

As the issue attracted national attention in November 1874, though, Belknap presented part of Ord's plan to Grant. Despite the lack of a clear precedent for executive action—Congress and state governments had often led such ad-hoc relief efforts, and the locusts were a familiar scourge—Grant authorized the distribution of surplus army clothing to the disaster-stricken residents of the Plains. During the winter, more than 16,000 coats, 20,000 pairs of shoes and boots, and 8,400 blankets were given away by the federal government to Americans in need. Congress would follow these actions by passing a relief bill in February 1875, appropriating $150,000 for food relief to the affected areas.[60]

Experts working within the Grant administration then provided the impetus for a lasting legislative response. C. V. Riley and Cyrus Thomas offered data and analysis of migration patterns for the U.S. Geological Survey's 1875 annual report, summarized in a popular article by another contributor,

A. S. Packard Jr., who praised the contributions of the U.S. Signal Bureau and local observers. Packard wrote, "The government has provided a well-organized core of meteorological observers, and we submit that a number of competent entomologists should take the field, under government auspices.... A commission of entomologists should be appointed to make a thorough detailed study for several successive seasons of the habits of the locusts in the Territories mentioned."[61] Packard offered specific cost-benefit breakdowns for the damages caused by the locusts and the savings that might be had from a coordinated state-federal response.

These executive actions led directly to legislation, as Congress passed an act formally creating the U.S. Entomological Commission in March 1877, operationalizing Packard's specific suggestion "that the recommendations made at the recent meeting of Western governors at Omaha, that an appropriation be made by Congress, and a commission be attached to the existing United States Geological and Geographical Survey of the Territories, is the most feasible and economical method of securing the speediest and best results."[62] The commission would be led by Riley, Thomas, and others with long experience studying and responding to the swarms.[63] The enduring effects of these efforts—"the work by the government for the people against insects"—were documented by H. T. Fernald, writing in 1928: "Seventy-five years ago such a thing as economic entomology was almost unknown. We have been obliged to learn by experience what insect pests really mean to a country and then how to control them. Once begun, though, progress has been rapid."[64] Grant's efforts were fast and decisive in 1874, administrative efforts improved long-term study and administrative capacity, and legislative action followed.

Grant supported other immediate efforts to relieve suffering: he signed a bill in 1874 to aid victims of Mississippi River flooding, he successfully urged Congress to appropriate money for a telegraph line in Texas to help protect U.S. settlers from conflicts with Mexicans and Native Americans, and he successfully urged Congress to appropriate emergency funds to meet a crisis at the Red Cloud Agency in 1876.[65] Early civil service reform efforts, support for the Signal Corps, and the creation of the Entomological Commission exemplify the ways in which presidential leadership in the 1870s facilitated the ongoing development of data collection and analysis within the executive branch.

Grant's final crisis saw him overseeing the investigations and bipartisan compromises that followed the immediate aftermath of the bitterly contested 1876 presidential election. Grant even had Rutherford B. Hayes take the oath of office almost immediately after Congress had finalized their Electoral College vote—Grant apparently did not want to give opponents of the final decision the extra day they would have had to mount a protest or organize any actions, and so he took the unusual action.[66]

Taken together, all of these examples suggest a pattern characterized by immediate reaction to events. Grant's approach to the inflation bill, civil rights, civil service reform, and even locust swarms all suggest principled decision making and immediate adjustments to meet new issues. Some then witnessed the slow creation of programs and administrative capacity, like the entomologists. Others passed without apparent efforts to build for the long-term: Grant did not institute new procedures at West Point to protect the next James Webster Smith, and he did not propose new rules for the law school to protect the next Belva Lockwood. He did not work to produce any institutional mechanism for dealing with contested elections in the future, or to create a regular approach to issuing vetoes. Together, though, Grant's actions represent a steady stream of presidential interventions, deploying the power of the state through executive action tools like executive orders, proclamations, vetoes, and administrative leadership in matters ranging from disaster relief and monetary policy to social issue leadership and institutional administration.

Grant and Leadership of the Administrative State

Grant's leadership and presidential actions fostered an organizational culture within his administration that mirrored his approach, emphasizing innovation and the creative use of discretionary authority. The extent of bureaucratic specialization and activity in the Grant years is striking, evidenced by the government's responses to fighting insects, planting trees, collecting liquor taxes, extending postal and communications networks, and conducting diplomacy, along with its activities in other matters. Each policy area featured the activities of longtime practitioners and extensive networks of experts addressing issues. This was not new—John Quincy Adams engaged with a similar array of experts in Indian affairs, naval expeditions and construction, postal development, military and exploration units, and diplomats—but by Grant's time the number of different offices and units, and the landscape for which they were responsible, had grown. Grant's appointees—at the cabinet level, within administrative units, and even to the judiciary—reflected his approach to decision making and energized a vibrant national state after the war.[67]

Grant famously made his first cabinet appointments on his own, without asking for advice.[68] For many at the time and for many historians since, this was an example of Grant's narrow experience, personal loyalty, and naïveté about government.[69] For others though—even at the time—it was an effort to break the hold of entrenched power at the highest levels.[70] Reformers landed throughout the Grant administration. Grant's treasury secretary, George Boutwell, had experience as commissioner of internal revenue during the Civil War, but he had also been instrumental in passage of the Fifteenth

Amendment protecting the right to vote.[71] A proponent of Black suffrage as early as 1865, Boutwell (after returning to Congress) would be the only prominent Republican in the debates over the 1875 civil rights bill to defend school integration as a means to defeat discrimination.[72] At Treasury, Boutwell advanced the government's abilities and expertise, and the department began assuming some aspects of a central bank.[73]

John Creswell at the Post Office also proved effective, increasing routes and personnel, lowering costs, rewriting and standardizing rules and regulations, revising postal treaties, and even introducing the penny postcard. He fought the franking system and also Western Union's telegraph monopoly.[74] The effective and reform-oriented Marshall Jewell served as postmaster general during Grant's second term.[75] Henry Wilson of Massachusetts became Grant's second-term vice president; Wilson was a standard bearer for universal suffrage, the leader in Congress of the movement to pass the Fifteenth Amendment, and an ally in promoting Ely Parker's Indian affairs reforms in Congress.[76] Elihu Washburne, appointed minister to France in 1869, offered valorous service to Americans, Germans, and French citizens during the German siege of Paris in 1870, while Alphonso Taft—William Howard Taft's father and a longtime opponent of slavery—served Grant briefly as secretary of war and then as attorney general at the end of Grant's second term.[77] Grant placed, and protected, the complex fighter and nation-builder William Tecumseh Sherman at high posts in the army, delegating to Sherman vast discretion in the policing and settlement of the West.[78]

Grant also had the new Department of Justice, created by Congress in 1870 to handle the increasing amount of litigation involving the United States after the Civil War. Grant had the opportunity to shape that agency through appointments and the setting of priorities, and he took charge immediately. Attorney General Amos Akerman became one of the strongest forces for reform, using the Civil War amendments and legislation passed by Congress as the foundation for aggressive federal protection of civil rights, especially among newly freed people in the South. Akerman knew that the potential promise of the new powers brought into being by the Civil War amendments needed to be exercised immediately, lest the chance be lost. Akerman directed the nation's legal strategy, but he also directed significant organizational development in the new Department of Justice. Akerman used his tools broadly, even using Congress's Enforcement Acts to try to protect Chinese immigrants in San Francisco.[79]

The most important of Grant's appointments turned out to be Hamilton Fish, named secretary of state after numerous attempts to nominate others had failed. Fish was not an inside-the-system power broker, but he and Grant made a steady, pragmatic, and effective diplomatic team. Perhaps the most crucial of Grant's cabinet members, Fish was genial and gentlemanly, with a line of realistic cynicism that grounded his views of politics, people, and public affairs. Grant and Fish brought productive reforms to the State Department, especially the diplomatic service. Grant's foreign policy relied heavily on his advisors and delegates: Fish and his diplomatic team did much of the legwork on the *Alabama* claims, for example, and Fish was closely involved in drafting the foreign affairs sections of Grant's annual messages.[80]

Other key Grant appointees pushed innovative reforms at lower levels of the administration. Benjamin Bristow, who had been appointed district attorney for Louisville in 1866, led heroic judicial battles against the Ku Klux Klan in Kentucky. Bristow's results improved once Grant became president, when Bristow enjoyed greater support from the White House and when his cases could be appealed to federal circuit courts stocked with Grant's reform-oriented judicial appointments. Bristow had been stymied under Andrew Johnson, both by the absence of sympathetic courts and also by a lack of support from Johnson's conservative and cautious attorney general. But once Grant appointed E. Rockwood Hoar as his first attorney general, and followed him with Akerman, Bristow's efforts (and those of other federal officials working local cases) began to bear fruit. Grant appointed Bristow the nation's first solicitor general in 1870, and Bristow became treasury secretary in the second term, a post in which he excelled.[81]

At the Office of Indian Affairs, Grant appointed Ely Parker to shake up an Indian service that Grant believed was entrenched and corrupt. Parker's roots stretched back to matters that had occupied John Quincy Adams. As we have seen, one of President Adams's first decisions had blocked a corrupt treaty with the Seneca of New York and encouraged a full investigation of the process that led to the fraudulent deal. In the years immediately following, however—especially under Presidents Jackson and Van Buren—the federal government and the Ogden Land Company had continued their efforts to obtain Seneca land near Buffalo. Parker began his public career as an interpreter in the 1840s, just two years after the corrupt Treaty of Buffalo Creek condemned many Senecas to removal, and he became a leader in the Seneca resistance movement. Parker developed a deep understanding of U.S.-Indian relations and extensive knowledge of U.S. policy and administrative practice.[82] Later, Parker served as a civil engineer for the Treasury Department and then as General Grant's aide, standing by his side at Appomattox; after the Civil War, Parker served as U.S. treaty negotiator to southern tribes that had allied with the Confederacy, including the Cherokees. He remained active in the Andrew Johnson administration, conducting reviews and submitting recommendations to Grant and to Secretary of War Edwin Stanton. Parker understood the significance of treaty terms and, like Adams, was willing to use the military against non-Indians to uphold such agreements. Parker took the president's general goal of peace, discussed in greater detail in the next chapter, and designed structural reforms within the government bureaucracy.[83]

Innovations at the Interior Department went beyond Indian affairs. It was under Grant that the United States began to administer its new territory in Alaska. William Seward's efforts here were agreed to in 1867 and 1868 before Grant came to office, but the initial administrative efforts in Alaska itself were taken under Grant. When Congress denied Interior Secretary Columbus Delano's request for legislative approval and appropriations for a new agent in Alaska, Delano—consistent with the administrative culture described here—went ahead and appointed a special agent anyway, on his own authority. And below Delano, the Office of Indian Affairs led the effort to enact legislation providing government services in the Alaska territory, demonstrating again the initiative and relevance of administrators in the executive branch.[84]

Grant's innovation-oriented leadership ethic worked its way down through other units of the post–Civil War administrative state. Grant put his own military experience to use as president, recognizing the ways in which science, exploration, and even weather impact on military movements, trade, and the well-being of the citizenry. He supported navigational research into the Isthmian Canal beginning in 1869, ordering the Bureau of Navigation to explore possible routes and appointing an Interoceanic Commission to evaluate the findings. Grant's appointees to the commission were experts in the field—he appointed the chief of the navy's Bureau of Navigation, of course, and also the chief engineers of the army and superintendent of the Coast Survey. The explorers and scientists in the field completed their work in five years, and science historian A. Hunter Dupree concluded that "for the first time the United States had sufficient reliable data on which to base a canal policy."[85]

Grant also contributed his influence to promote irrigation efforts in California, the study of steam boiler explosions, healthcare, and the relationship of the use of telegraph lines between private companies and government services.[86] On the last, just as an example of the institutional interplay common to the Grant years, Congress supported the Signal Corps by passing a law promising punishment for private actors interfering with the corps' activities, while Grant issued a note calling for government operatives to stop using the threat of government lawsuits to, in Grant's language, "Black Mail" private companies into particular behavior.[87]

Grant had long been involved in the operations of the Signal Corps, some of the earliest efforts of which sought to provide storm warnings through a chain of observation stations in the Great Lakes and Atlantic seaboard regions.[88] Grant had recommended the influential Albert Myer's promotion in 1867, and the Signal Corps in the 1870s became a source not just of weather reports but also of government surveillance of Indian affairs and labor issues. The Signal Corps helped organize international cooperation on weather and data sharing beginning in 1871, as it began its path toward becoming a national weather bureau. The office gained permanent status in the War Department in 1875 and later cooperated with the new Entomological Commission discussed above.[89] The Signal Corps is a good example of how broadly influential, and administratively innovative, the Grant team could be, and Grant's precise role in its development merits further study. Other examples of state development in these years abound: western surveys progressed under Grant, including what came to be known as the U.S. Geological Survey and government support for the explorations of John Wesley Powell. The office of what we know now as the Surgeon General was established in 1871, as Supervising Surgeon in the Marine Hospital Service.

Much of this activity took place in an era of scandal frames, and it is unfortunate that corruption charges dominate the Grant administration's reputation. Science and exploration became politicized, and Parker's ignominious exit from the Bureau of Indian Affairs is particularly instructive.[90] Parker was forced out of office under a cloud of charges about mismanagement, even though the case that entangled Parker was typical in Indian affairs. What Parker had done was to respond to a looming crisis in Indian country that threatened the starvation of hundreds of people, by contracting with a private firm to move goods and food to the West. Parker made the deal quickly, and in violation of the rules under which he and his office operated. It was the kind of deal that field agents, especially, made all the time. As historian C. Joseph Genetin-Pilawa convincingly describes, Parker was targeted precisely *because* his reforms, which Grant had embraced, aimed at fundamentally changing the nation's Indian policy and its administrative system. The people targeting Parker represented the status quo. In the context of the era, the charges against Parker looked to many as though he was just another corrupt Grant crony. The appearance of the charges was enough to doom Parker's career at the Indian Office, despite the understandable and even sympathetic context of Parker's decision—principled innovation at the mezzo level of the administrative bureaucracy.[91]

The attorney general's office also became a center of criticism, perhaps predictably given the vehemence of opposition to reunification efforts after the war. As cases multiplied, so did spending, along with charges of corruption, partisanship, and maladministration. Legal scholar Robert J. Kaczorowski's study of the Department of Justice in these years at times reads like a parallel tale to that of Parker at the Indian office, as Grant administration reforms threatened established interests and generated broad charges. Akerman was dismissed in December 1871, and historian William S. McFeely has argued that the cause was that Akerman's commitment to equality worried interests in both the North and South. Grant appointed George Williams as the new attorney general; Williams continued the effort to enforce civil rights, courageously pursuing civil rights cases after Akerman's departure.[92]

Many of Grant's appointments traveled a similar arc: a choice by Grant of a reformer, often an aggressive outsider, followed by charges of maladministration or corruption brought by the entrenched interests that Grant and the appointee were fighting. These stories often ended with Grant backtracking, sacrificing the appointee by either forcing a resignation or issuing a dismissal. Parker's successor, for example, E. P. Smith, and then Interior Secretary Columbus Delano, also became caught up in charges of corruption sparked by their reform efforts, and both were brought down by the same Board of Indian Commissioners that did so much damage to Parker. Interior Secretary Jacob Cox would be forced to resign when his reforms challenged entrenched power in Congress. Eventually Interior would fall to Zachariah Chandler, who, despite his support for patronage and spoils, continued the reform work at the department.[93]

The contested legacies of so many of Grant's appointees mirror that of Grant himself. Appointed often for their dedication to reform, for their creativity and willingness to innovate, Grant's team—George Boutwell, Ely Parker, Benjamin Bristow, and Elihu Washburne among them—did not always enjoy the safe harbor of procedural loyalty. Instead, they acted and they innovated, often in response to particular situations and often with immediate, responsive initiatives. Yet Grant's administrators were vulnerable. In an era of scandal frames and divisive politics, with aggressive congressional investigations and sharply, violently contested elections, with a president who changed his mind decisively and was willing to cut himself loose from problematic subordinates—all of these factors endangered the principled innovator's like-minded appointees. Without a clear allegiance to established rules to fall back on, cabinet officials, mezzo-level administrators, and field operatives easily became mired in believable charges of corrupt politics and malfeasance. The list of Grant's appointees and even regional military commanders who were challenged and forced out or transferred in his eight years as president is long. Encouraged to act on their convictions and principles, they attracted the calumny of both political and partisan enemies as well as the slings and arrows of anyone, then or now, who held or holds different views or different values, goals, and principles.

Presidential Leadership in International Affairs

Grant's use of executive authority in international affairs was likewise instinctive and situational. Some of his efforts utilized presidential powers in innovative ways to strive for lasting changes, even as he generally pursued traditional American state goals in foreign affairs: promoting geographical expansion, promoting and protecting individual freedom, and protecting American citizens and commercial interests. Grant's application of presidential action is evident in a variety of contexts, including four major ones: the *Alabama* claims, the *Virginius* incident, Grant's approach to the Ten Years' War in Cuba, and Grant's attempt to annex Santo Domingo. These examples and several others illustrate the complex interconnectedness of state policy in the 1870s, as well as the variety of tools utilized by the president to control the policymaking environment in matters affecting millions of people.

The *Alabama* Claims, the *Virginius*, the Ten Years' War, and Santo Domingo

The Treaty of Washington represents one of the Grant administration's most successful and lasting contributions, as the Grant administration drove efforts to institutionalize international arbitration agreements as a way of resolving problems through predictable process. Biographer Louis A. Coolidge ranked the Treaty of Washington as President Grant's greatest achievement. Historian John Bassett Moore called it "the greatest treaty of actual and immediate arbitration the world had ever seen," and recently historians Tom Bingham and Jay Sexton have concurred.[94]

The matter at hand for Grant was persistent American insult at Britain's allowing ships that raided Union interests along the U.S. coast during the Civil War to be fitted out in British ports. These ships caused great losses to the Union, driving other commercial ships out of action and encouraging the Confederacy to think of Britain as an ally. The monetary losses were eventually settled at more than $15 million, but an early version of an agreement was rejected overwhelmingly by the U.S. Senate because it did not adequately account for the symbolic injury done to the United States by the British actions.[95]

Grant delegated responsibility to Fish and personnel at the State Department to negotiate settlement of what became known as the *Alabama* claims, named for one of the ships involved. Grant utilized his appointment powers to influence and redirect the negotiations, replacing John Lothrop Motley, an ally of influential Senator Charles Sumner (who opposed Grant on annexing Santo Domingo), with Robert Schenck.[96] The Treaty of Washington that emerged from the negotiations secured an arbitration panel, which in a few short months reached a conclusion satisfactory to both the United States and Britain—a peaceful resolution to a thorny issue and the foundation of the use of arbitration panels to resolve international disputes. (John Quincy Adams's son Charles Francis Adams played a key role in the arbitration process at Geneva.⁹⁷) Not only did the United States sign a treaty that established a multinational arbitration panel to review and settle the claims, but the *principle* of so doing was what really attracted Grant's biographer Coolidge: "Thus Grant must have the credit for establishing the principle of arbitration in international disputes; for this was brought about by reason of the firmness with which he held to the validity of American demands."⁹⁸

With symbolism reflecting the Treaty of Washington's significance, the Senate approved the treaty on Queen Victoria's birthday, ratifications were exchanged on Bunker Hill Day, and Grant proclaimed the treaty in full effect on the Fourth of July 1871. It was an innovative and lasting effort, the result of skillful application of executive tools including administrative delegation, appointment powers, interbranch relations, and public communication, as Grant offered regular updates on the matter in his annual messages.

As THE *Alabama* negotiations played out slowly over Grant's two terms, the 1873 incident of the *Virginius* saw Grant nimbly avoid war with Spain while bucking public calls for action and defending the rights of Americans. The *Virginius* case is all but forgotten now, receiving almost no coverage in recent works on the Grant administration, but it enjoys extensive discussion and plaudits in older works.⁹⁹ The focused intensity of this crisis stands in contrast to the patient work done to resolve the *Alabama* claims, but the interaction of the two issues offers a window into the complex interconnectedness of governance in the 1870s. The two issues also highlight the significant role of diplomats and bureaucrats in designing and administering American state policy.

The *Virginius* case involved a ship flying the American flag that had been taken by a Spanish ship off the coast of Spanish-controlled Cuba in 1873. The ship was American-built and had been involved previously in aiding the Cuban insurrection against Spanish rule by landing military parties. Brought by the Spanish ship to Santo Domingo, Cuba, the passengers and crew of the *Virginius* were tried by court-martial. Fifty-three were executed, among them eight U.S. citizens. Outrage exploded in the United States, and Grant was pressured to take swift and stern action to avenge the killed Americans. Grant, though, pursued a process of diplomatic investigation to find out the truth of the matter—he fended off popular calls for vindicating American rights through force while working with Spanish authorities, through Secretary of State Fish and his diplomatic team, to find out more about the *Virginius*. Grant simultaneously *prepared* to use force, and he made public statements that restitution and adequate apology would necessarily have to be forthcoming from Spain should the ship turn out to have been a legitimate American vessel.¹⁰⁰

In the end, the *Virginius* was found to have been flying American colors illegally. While the administration defended the goal of protecting ships flying the American flag, regardless of whether such identification was fraudulent or not, the administration also recognized that the *Virginius*'s identification had been gained through fraud and that this was a significant factor in assessing the incident. Grant had avoided an open invitation to a crowd-pleasing war, patiently allowing a careful and thorough investigation to get to the facts of the case.

The executive branch also worked diligently to outflank Congress and maintain control of the crisis response. Part of this related to the administration's ongoing efforts to resolve the *Alabama* claims, because a full-throated defense of the *Virginius*'s involvement in the Cuban insurrection would have been based on the rights of a neutral nation to allow the outfitting of ships in its harbors—the very same activity that the administration condemned on the part of Britain in the *Alabama* cases. So Grant and Fish needed to be careful—to find out the real story in the specific incident, react appropriately to defend American citizens and interests, and simultaneously protect their negotiating position in relation to the larger international issue. Grant's December 1873 message on the *Virginius* laid the groundwork for peaceful resolution, preempting Congress before that body could convene and take action itself.[101]

THE *VIRGINIUS* incident, along with the *Alabama* claims resolution, illustrate the Grant team's careful approach to claims relating to control over ships and the practice of attributing nationality that was rooted in increasingly popular notions of international law.[102] The Grant administration's policy toward Cuba and Spain in the Ten Years' War likewise illustrates the Grant team's commitment to international law and its openness to innovation in the application of American power. The Cuba situation riveted public attention nationwide, and Fish and Grant worked diligently to maintain control of Cuba policy, outflanking members of Congress and managing members of the public who wanted faster and more decisive action.[103] Grant and Fish used a variety of executive and administrative actions, supported by delicate engagement with Congress and other nations. Moreover, Grant and his team utilized carefully crafted public messaging to secure popular and governmental support and tamp down opposition on a protracted but significant national issue that captured popular attention.

The problem for the administration was that the rebellion against Spanish rule in Cuba, which lasted for years, never reached the point where the rebels controlled significant territory, controlled ports, or established a governing entity that could reliably be looked on as a competitor or alternative to Spanish rule on the island. Cuban activists often thought they had met the threshold, and it seems clear that Grant and others wanted them to meet the threshold—so that Grant could back the rebellion and its calls for justice and an end to slavery.[104] But they never got there. The question facing Grant throughout his presidency was how, and to what extent, he might support the rebellion, maintain normal relations with Spain, and abide by international norms for recognition of independents or belligerents—all of which were fresh issues in the minds of American leaders who had faced similar questions for four years during its own Civil War. The larger Cuba issue was thus tangled up again with issues still playing out in the *Alabama* claims and in contexts including that of the *Virginius,* the outfitting of privateers and filibusters, and the holdings of enslaved men, women, and children in Cuba by American citizens.

Grant worked with Congress, regularly including updates about Cuba in his annual messages, offering a special message on America's neutrality in June 1870, and receiving open-ended authorization from Congress to recognize the independence of Cuba "whenever in his opinion a republican form of government shall have been in fact established."[105] At the same time, the major thrust of the Grant team's work was to preempt Congress and prevent that body from taking the lead, or making assertive decisions, regarding Cuba's status. The House of Representatives, for example, at one point passed a resolution calling on Grant to recognize belligerent rights in Cuba.[106] But Grant carefully considered his prerogative as president to decide whether to recognize the rebels. Grant's address to Congress in 1870 announced a new effort and also headed off any potential attempt by Congress to grant belligerent rights to Cuba, just as Grant's 1873 message preempted a congressional response to the *Virginius.* This cleared the administration of the threat that Congress would act, and set the government on the course of expanding and adapting international law as a way to address the issue instead of relying on sympathies and prejudices.[107]

The Grant team's management of events and messaging led up to Grant's critically important 1875 Annual Message. Fish outflanked Congress in the institutional dialogue, making sure that members of Congress did not get out in front of the president's position or issue any resolutions boxing the president in or directing the course of events. Fish prepared U.S. ministers in foreign posts to act as soon as Grant's 1875 address had been given. The American public, Congress, and foreign leaders waited on Grant's speech to signal the U.S. position. Spain intentionally acted just before the speech, indicating the significance Spanish leaders attached to the president's words as determinative of U.S. policy.[108]

Grant's annual message "announced a striking foreign-policy initiative," in Sexton's words, calling for engagement by European powers with Spain to nudge Spain to resolve the issues in Cuba. It was a novel application of the Monroe Doctrine, aiming to invite European powers into the debate over an island ninety miles off the U.S. coast but also aiming to keep those interests at arm's length, restricting them from playing anything other than a contributing role centered in European capitals. The Grant team thus innovated broadly, as Fish engineered an increasingly engaged foreign policy on the part of the United States. The successful resolution of the *Alabama* claims and the *Virginius* situation, together with Grant's willingness to mediate the Franco-Prussian conflict in 1870, drew Fish and Grant further toward multilateral approaches resting on international law. Grant and Fish explicitly invoked John Quincy Adams to help center their actions within a tradition of American cooperation with foreign powers.[109]

The Grant administration's actions were nimble, designed and implemented within the executive branch, and clearly communicated to Congress and the public through presidential messages. Jay Sexton concludes that while the multilateral policy was not a grand success on the world stage or in Cuba, it met its goals domestically: the "home-effect" worked, keeping control and decision making in the executive and effectively outflanking efforts rooted in Congress.

ONE OF Grant's most memorable foreign policy initiatives was an effort to annex Santo Domingo, as the Dominican Republic was commonly known. Grant reasoned that annexation would help freed people, giving them a place to go if they sought to leave the United States. Grant also believed that having Santo Domingo within the American economic system would help freed people sell their labor in the South for higher wages. Ultimately, the effort failed, but Grant invested sustained attention and applied presidential influence in innovative ways.[110]

Grant's public argument for annexation looked to the future of the United States and its citizens, and he explicitly invoked government's obligations to protect and empower the American people. Yet while some of the goals were by this time traditional ones, such as furthering the Monroe Doctrine, others had more controversial pedigrees, such as asserting national control over international sea-trade routes. The acquisition of Santo Domingo, Grant announced,

> is an adherence to the "Monroe Doctrine"; it is a measure of national protection; it is asserting our just claim to a controlling influence over the great Commercial traffic soon to flow from West to East by the way of the Isthmus

of Darien; it is to build up our Merchant Marine; it is to furnish new markets for the products of our farms, shops and manufactories; it is to make slavery insupportable in Cuba and Porto Rico, at once, and ultimately so in Brazil; it is to settle the unhappy condition of Cuba, and end an exterminating conflict; it is to provide honest means of paying our honest debts, without overtaxing the people; it is to furnish our citizens with the necessaries of everyday life at cheaper rates than ever before; and it is in fine a rapid stride towards that greatness which the intelligence, industry and enterprise of the Citizens of the United States entitle this country to assume among nations.[111]

Grant worked hard to secure annexation. He initially sent his trusted aide Orville Babcock to Santo Domingo to negotiate a treaty. Later, acknowledging that such an initiative was outside of established protocols, Grant offered to have the treaty re-signed through more official channels to ensure its legitimacy. He exerted unusual direct pressure on U.S. senators to try to gain their support.[112] Grant added a threat of blacklisting opponents of annexation from patronage positions in the administration, and he tried to bargain for support in the Senate by removing Attorney General Hoar.[113] He accepted an investigatory commission set up to look into the matter, and he implored a member to look carefully into prevalent corruption rumors that Grant had financial interests in Santo Domingo which would be rewarded with annexation. He used his annual messages as a bully pulpit to recommend the measure, first while the Senate was focused on the project and later in an effort to restart negotiations.[114] He appeared at the Capitol, sent a message to the Senate in May 1870, submitted a special commissioners' report to Congress in April 1871 with comments, extended the ratification period for the treaty, and consistently offered clear and thorough public explanations of the logic and purpose of annexation, in line with the quotation above. He returned to the debate in his Second Annual Message, reflecting the tremendous popular interest and participation in debating the question.[115] His last words in his Eighth Annual Message were essentially an I-told-you-so, arguing that the nation would have been better off if it had annexed Santo Domingo as he had said.[116]

The effort failed, ultimately, although Grant did not take losing lightly—he maneuvered to have Charles Sumner removed from the Senate Foreign Relations Committee after Sumner led the charge to defeat annexation and, as noted above, he withdrew Sumner's ally John Lothrop Motley from his post in England as payback for blocking annexation and to turn the *Alabama* negotiations toward their new goal. All in all, Grant's tactics were active and innovative, and they adapted to shifting circumstances over several years as he pressed the case. Yet he refused to try to annex Santo Domingo by executive action, and when the Senate continued to balk, Grant accepted defeat.[117] The effort failed, but not because of an absence of effort or creativity on the president's part.

Exerting Influence, Extraditing Criminals, Fighting in Korea, Signing Treaties

A host of other examples demonstrate the important role of the president in international affairs in an era too often thought of as dominated by Congress, characterized by a weak or ineffectual presidency, narrowed by American isolation, and sputtered by a small or ineffective state. Grant exercised presidential authority in foreign affairs that was often driven by his own goals and values more than by appeal to established rules and commitments.

Grant intervened on behalf of Jews in Russia and Romania, for example, departing from traditional noninterference in Russian affairs to respond to requests by B'nai B'rith and Jewish groups to help resettlement of Jews in Russia. Grant's pressure was innovative in 1869 and again in 1872, in the first instance by bringing pressure on Russia and in the second by trying to get Russia to pressure Romania. Grant in these cases was more aggressive than Fish or diplomats onsite, and Grant tied his innovations explicitly to human rights principles. Historian Ronald J. Jensen calls Grant's intervention "a bold, unprecedented act." Grant's use of diplomatic pressure, his administration's efforts to gather evidence and then supplement early reports with more thorough and detailed information, and his use of the nomination power to appoint a consul to Romania who would prioritize human rights over the consulate's traditional attention to commercial matters all speak to Grant's use of executive tools to influence affairs in other nations. Although those efforts did little to influence Russia and Romania, they did much to advance awareness in the United States and demonstrate the links between the presidency and Jewish interest groups.[118]

Moreover, Grant conducted successful negotiations with Spain to free enslaved people in Puerto Rico, and made efforts to do the same in Cuba.[119] He acted aggressively to ward off a Cuban filibuster, secured the extradition of convicted New York machine politician Boss Tweed from Cuba, and engineered the arrest of indicted smuggler and former customs inspector Charles L. Lawrence in Ireland.[120] Grant examined extradition policies with Spain and Britain, and effectively ended an extradition treaty with Great Britain after England refused to honor its terms.[121] The administration settled boundary disputes with Great Britain and claims with the American republics, signing numerous trade agreements and treaties and resolving numerous claims and other issues, many of which were listed by Grant in his annual messages.[122] Grant and Fish worked diligently to resolve matters involving the border with Canada and the matter of access to fisheries. In policy issues stretching back to agreements worked out by John Quincy Adams, the Grant administration managed to stave off conflict with Britain and even Canada, resolving key issues as part of the Treaty of Washington settlement.[123]

Some of Grant's other efforts were more controversial. Grant oversaw an early foray into Korea, for example, aimed at expanding U.S. influence and trade in the manner of the openings to Japan and China. Misunderstandings and American field officers' actions led to vicious fighting and hundreds of deaths in one of the largest and most violent deployments of U.S. forces overseas in the second half of the nineteenth century. Five heavily armed warships and more than 1,200 sailors and marines eventually confronted Korean forces in battle in 1871, delaying a peaceful opening of Korea for more than ten years, according to historian Gordon H. Chang.[124] In another case, Grant signed a treaty with Hawai'i in 1875, providing that Hawaiian territory would not be disposed of to a third power.[125] In both situations, and consistent with U.S. foreign policy since the earliest days of the republic, complicated results followed presidential leadership based on ethnocentrism, perceived superiority, and the goal of expanding trade.

What we see here is a president inhabiting a very familiar role as the nation's chief foreign affairs officer—establishing the basis for diplomatic interactions, promoting expansion and fostering defense, managing international crises, overseeing risky trade and military initiatives, shaping public opinion on a host of matters, and effectively competing with Congress for lead authority over the nation's foreign policies.

The numerous contexts and specific cases that arose during Grant's two terms belie the idea of quiet presidencies and congressional dominance after the Civil War. The matters here that have received the most scrutiny from historians and other scholars—the Treaty of Washington, the *Virginius* incident, and annexation of Santo Domingo—clearly demonstrate the president's use of executive tools, persuasion, pressure, delegation, and leadership. Grant's tactics were creative, as in the Santo Domingo and Russia cases, and some of his results were novel, as in the Treaty of Washington. Grant never seems to have agonized over such actions in the way that John Quincy Adams did, though, and Grant did not invoke and scour laws and treaties to understand the United States' role and commitments. Grant's approach to presidential leadership and decision making thus reflects a different ethic than Adams's, but presidential use of available executive tools to lead Congress and the public in foreign policy decision making raised few eyebrows.

Conclusion

Grant's leadership of the state is easily the most controversial of the three presidents examined in this book. He relied on his own sense of values, even as he proved malleable, shaped and reshaped by organized interests. He was willing to change his mind on policies and appointments, and he was often mercurial to the point of exasperating advisors like Secretary of State Fish. He waffled on Cuba, whiffed on protecting Black cadets at West Point, dug in and then backed off on Santo Domingo. He supported the appointment of reformers, only to abandon them when they came under fire from Congress. He planned to sign, then ultimately vetoed, the inflation bill.

This record suggests both a positive and a negative spin. On the positive side, it suggests a willingness to adjust and adapt as circumstances evolve—situations on the ground change, politics change, the forces in play at any moment for a public representative change, and public opinion must be respected. Grant was ready to alter his applications of executive power as circumstances shifted, putting the state to a series of uses through application of a variety of executive action tools. On the negative side, though, such changes may indicate that Grant lacked a set of stable principles by which to decide how to use state power. Grant's reversal on the inflation bill, for example, was maddening to interests that wanted to see the bill signed. Adams maintained firm principles on many issues, including Indian affairs (the sanctity of treaties and laws), slavery (legal but abhorrent), and personnel matters (no dismissals for partisan reasons, only for cause); Grant's administrative principles and personnel practices wavered, and he was persuadable depending on circumstances and politics, producing both advantageous and detrimental effects throughout the bureaucracy. Grant was at the middle of a collision-inducing intersection of the presidency and the American state.

5

Presidential Decision Making and the Evolving State

GRANT, RECONSTRUCTION, AND INDIAN AFFAIRS

Ulysses S. Grant's years in the presidency did not signal a retreat to localism or the instability of a weak state. The previous chapter illustrates a broad variety of matters in which national state activity and presidential actions mattered. The state acted, intruded, evolved, and succeeded in many new and many continuing missions and tasks.

The legacy of Reconstruction is contentious and its success disputed, but it received critical attention from the Grant administration. The focus of the state in matters related to Reconstruction evolved, as Grant used the executive tools at his disposal to help develop the state's role as protector of individual and group rights. The military drawdown in the former Confederate states led first to a blend of federal military and civilian efforts to secure the Civil War's gains, and later to primarily civilian and judicial efforts as support for military efforts receded.

In the other critical issue of the era, westward expansion and Indian affairs, we see the continuation and extension of the state—longstanding administrative measures combined with new initiatives, new techniques, new areas of state activity, and new mixtures of civilian and military authority. In Indian affairs we see the resilience of the American state, the relentless focus of the president on the matter of continental expansion, and a similarly contentious and unsettled legacy.

Reconstruction policy and postwar Indian policy were both efforts to pursue principled policy goals and shift hearts and minds, on one hand, and to develop more effective, efficient, and controllable national administrative structures, on the other. This chapter offers an overview of these two giant, controversial, and intrusive areas of state activity that affected millions of people, and it highlights the ways that President Grant applied a variety of executive tools to further principled innovations in policy and administration. In the contested legacies of Grant's Reconstruction and his Peace Policy we see the risk and endemic controversy of the principled innovator as president.

President Grant, the Administrative State, and Reconstruction

Grant's use of state capabilities was on display in his approach to the myriad concerns that arose during Reconstruction. Grant zigged and zagged, trying new approaches, shifting tactics, putting out fires, deploying and redeploying state capacity as he struggled to pacify and reconcile a still-fractured nation. Grant utilized executive orders and proclamations, public communication, and administrative leadership, particularly through the appointment of people who shared his goals and whom he trusted, in situations in which ordinary process and even traditional values had been overthrown. In the end, the president's efforts proved vulnerable to an increasingly determined Congress and a more disciplined Supreme Court. What follows is a necessarily brief and impressionistic overview, but the eight years of Grant's terms as they relate to Reconstruction demonstrate the relevance of the presidency and its ability to influence and even direct novel applications of state power after the Civil War.

Zigzagging toward Peace

To address post–Civil War fragmentation, resistance, violence, and confusion, Grant publicized a simple goal when he ran for president in 1868: "Let us have peace." As one reads through eight years of orders and decisions regarding affairs in the South, and despite the changes in personalities and events taking place in state after state and county after county, one discerns peace as Grant's basic guiding principle. Grant was not suddenly a pacifist, nor did he seek peace in all cases or at any cost.[1] Grant deployed troops when he thought it was warranted, and when he was able to do so, in Reconstruction and in Indian affairs. Grant's efforts in several key areas of Reconstruction, though, reflect his application of situational tactics and case-by-case creativity in pursuit of an overriding principle. This can be seen in President Grant's efforts to enforce equal protection under the Fourteenth Amendment, expand the right to vote under the Fifteenth Amendment, and respond to calls for military action from across the South and West.

The Grant administration generally supported Black property holding, access to contracts and wage labor, and the prospect of improved economic conditions. It promoted Blacks' ability to testify at trial and sit on juries, and it pushed for improved and expanded education for freed people just as it pushed for education among American Indians. Grant promoted equality in his First Inaugural Address, and he petitioned forcefully in his Second Inaugural Address for what became the Civil Rights Act of 1875, which made racial discrimination illegal in juries and places of public transportation, accommodation, or entertainment.[2] Grant anchored policy directions in the Fourteenth Amendment's prohibition against states' depriving any person of life, liberty, or property without due process of law, or denying any person the equal protection of the laws.

At the same time, administration and policy were haphazard. Different initiatives took precedence at different times and in different places, which is why it is so difficult to generalize about government's social policy efforts during Reconstruction. Grant did not seek to design much that would survive in the way of programs or even formal rules and procedures; he did little to put the tools of the presidency to work for long-term legislative initiatives. This resulted in part from the unstable context of myriad southern and western environments and in part from Grant's situational approach to governing and innovation.

Grant believed that the right people would develop the right policies in a wide variety of situations, and he relied on his appointments and the organizational culture discussed in the previous chapter to drive much on-the-ground decision making. The biggest initiative of the era with the most long-term staying power was the new Department of Justice, placed under the existing Office of the Attorney General. Grant appointed aggressive, dedicated people like Amos Akerman and Benjamin Bristow to administer the new department. But Grant had little to do with creating the agency, and he did little work to guide its early activities—preferring instead to set broad goals and appoint administrative leaders of like mind. He did not promote uniformity in process, even as he strove to unify a sense of mission toward defending the principles enshrined in the Fourteenth Amendment, and ultimately what he saw as peace. Grant repeated his personnel-focused approach in his efforts to influence the judiciary. He appointed men dedicated to vigorous protection of civil rights to the new circuit court system created by Congress in 1869.[3] He appointed Joseph Bradley and William Strong, early advocates for nationalizing civil rights enforcement consistent with the spirit of the Civil War amendments, to the Supreme Court. Grant believed that carefully selected appointees and case-by-case adjudication would lead the government toward peace.

Notably, President Grant actively and publicly supported passage of the Fifteenth Amendment, prohibiting denial of the right to vote based on race, color, or previous condition of servitude. Newspapers in 1868 and early 1869 widely reported Grant's support for the amendment before he was inaugurated, and Grant promoted the amendment's ratification in his First Inaugural Address. Grant's actions went beyond rhetorical support. As president, he pressured Nebraska governor David Butler to call a special session of that state's legislature in 1870 to secure ratification of the amendment, and Grant's support directly influenced Nevada's ratification a month later. In addition, his pressure on Congress to seat Black legislators from Georgia, who had been turned out by Democratic resistance, paved the way for Georgia's ratification of the amendment and its subsequent readmission to the Union.[4] The statement Grant issued upon certifying the Fifteenth Amendment in March 1870 made a very public plea for education as a force that empowers everyone.[5] After ratification, administration officials worked to secure electoral reforms and access to the ballot for Republicans and freed people in the South.

And yet, again, Grant's support and actions were focused on big-picture endgames; his tactics varied, zigging and zagging based on situations. Even his basic support for Black voting rights flipped and flopped. Grant did not always favor "Negro suffrage," as it was often called at the time, and he suggested after his presidency that the government might have made some mistakes, in part because by giving the suffrage "we have given the old slaveholders forty votes in the Electoral College. They keep those votes, but disfranchise the negroes. That is one of the gravest mistakes in the policy of reconstruction."[6] In his memoirs, Grant suggested that the effort had gone too far too fast, but that President Andrew Johnson's overreach had driven this outcome—Congress's actions had become "an absolute necessity," and Grant had adapted to circumstances and become pro-suffrage around the same time.[7]

This is not to condemn Grant. Whereas President John Quincy Adams inherited a relatively stable set of issues, laws, and approaches, Grant was thrown into a new mix of controversies that lacked long-established procedures and protocols. But as we will see with William Howard Taft beginning in the next chapter, the alternative open to a president in such a situation is a commitment to creative innovation that simultaneously builds new and lasting procedures and protocols. Taft synthesized principles and processes for the long term; Grant responded to immediate situations with ad-hoc fixes.

PRESIDENT GRANT applied the same approach to the military questions that came up, and to the ways in which military and civilian administrative options presented themselves in a variety of different contexts. To promote implementation of the Civil War amendments' goals, and to pursue peace, his administration tried to blend targeted applications of force, utilizing the limited military resources available, with organized civil jurisdiction.

Situations where reactionary elements sought through violence or other means to intimidate voters, grab public office, or otherwise influence the course of Reconstruction were stunningly unpredictable. It was next to impossible to know how best to respond, since aggressive action sometimes won the day, scaring reactionary elements into quitting the field, while at other times aggressive action backfired, sparking greater animosity and greater violence as intransigent forces dug in their heels and multiplied their efforts. But softer moves carried the same unpredictability—sometimes cooperation and restraint seemed to work, quieting disruptions and leading to negotiated compromise. At other times, cooperation looked more like appeasement, and reactionary forces gained strength and moxie from what appeared to be federal weakness or lack of commitment. L. Cass Carpenter, collector of internal revenue in South Carolina, for example, wrote to Grant in 1876 that "many of the leading spirits of this movement [against freed people] are men who were charged with Ku Kluxing in 1870 &. 1871, and are more bitter today, than they were then, simply because they think the government will not punish them now, any more than it did then. The leniency and clemency of the national government have been mistaken for cowardice, and the longer they live, the bolder and more outspoken they grow."[8] As historian William L. Barney put it, "Republican efforts at conciliation were interpreted as a sign of cowardly weakness, and harsher coercive measures were seen as confirmation of the unconstitutional tyranny that Republicans were trying to force on the South."[9]

It is in part because Grant often refused to send troops when asked—and because he responded, at times, with troops only after severe violence—that Grant's leadership remains controversial among scholars of the era. Could faster deployments have saved lives? Could a firmer hand have kept the forces of reaction in check? Did he respond too inconsistently, answering a call for troops here but not there? This leads to deeper questions: How should a president respond when two parties claim victory in state or city elections? Or when the judiciary in a state supports one candidacy and the state's legislature another? How does a party leader respond, while trying to build the party in hostile territory, when the party's leaders themselves split over whether to support new voting rights for freed people or whether to restore voting rights to former Confederates? During his presidency, again and again, a brief note from Grant taking (or refusing to take) some action followed multitudinous, conflicting communications Grant had received on the matter, with dire predictions of varied outcomes to varied options coming to him from state and federal political and administrative officials.[10]

Grant tried to delegate, to let local officials and federal officers in the field make decisions and reach agreements. He worked to establish a bias toward local discretion, for example, for deciding how and when to deploy troops. A typical passage from Secretary of State Hamilton Fish's diary illustrates this proclivity, after Attorney General Akerman brought up a request from the acting governor of Georgia related to the prospect of federal troop support: "The President thinks (as anyone would suppose) that he has nothing to do with a speculative case of the kind. It is for the State to settle."[11] Grant worked with governors to decide when and how to deploy federal troops, and eventually he came to rely on formal requests for troops from state governors as a way of making clear that requests from subordinate state officials or military authorities would not normally be honored. Grant was trying to establish a chain of command that would make a process clear to all involved, and that would empower law and order and decision making at state levels.

And yet it has always been difficult to discern a consistent application of the principle. Sometimes Grant sent troops: to New Orleans in 1874 to restore Governor William Kellogg to power, to Mississippi in 1875 after riots in Vicksburg. Sometimes he issued orders, as when he issued a proclamation aimed at dispersing white rifle clubs in 1876, which proved effective.[12] At other times, Grant used political pressure to secure local deals or promote national goals: in Georgia in 1869 and 1870, securing legislative seats for elected Black representatives and Georgia's ratification of the Fifteenth Amendment; in Arkansas during the "Brooks-Baxter War," which saw competing factions fight for years in the courts and the streets, and in which Grant's formal support for Elisha Baxter helped restore Baxter to power and end the matter; in Mississippi, as Justice Department officials forged a shaky compromise among competing factions. Sometimes he refused to exert pressure, as in Texas in 1873–74: Grant refused to support sitting Republican governor E. J. Davis when the Texas Supreme Court ruled his election unconstitutional.[13] Grant's inaction handed the governorship to Democratic challenger Richard Coke, returning the Democrats to power in Texas. And sometimes Grant focused on judicial process, as in Kentucky and the Carolinas in the fight against the Klan and other groups in 1870 and 1871.

Each of these cases, and numerous others, have been the subject of careful study and debate by Grant's contemporaries and by later analysts. The fact of the ongoing debate suggests the absence of a clear, discernible process or decision-making principle, aside from the overarching meta-goal of securing peace: Grant called them as he saw them, and applied the tools of the presidency and the power of the state as he saw fit. Sometimes the resulting actions were effective; sometimes not.

The President and Congress

Grant's efforts—principled, ad hoc, and reactive—and his applications of state power—situational, sometimes aggressive, sometimes deferential—eventually proved vulnerable to actions taken by Congress and decisions rendered by the courts.

At the start of Reconstruction and then again in the Grant years, U.S. troops provided parallel governments in the South—contenders for authority with state and local jurisdictions that, in the absence of peace, remained superior to those authorities. Military tribunals, military judgments, and military approaches to governance held sway at times. Grant favored a muscular response to affairs in the South, toward more troops, broader deployments, and clearer authority. The wisdom of this approach is reinforced by historian

Gregory P. Downs's recent findings that troops were integral to the effective deployment of federal authority and decision making: the mere presence of troops helped Union officials secure the war's gains. As troops were consolidated in major southern cities over time, though, isolated areas descended into violence and lawbreaking. As troop numbers declined and forces left even cities, the fact that it might take a handful of troops a few days even to *get* to a trouble-spot meant that localized defiance grew with impunity. It seems that Grant's preference for more troops had been correct.[14]

But along with facing the uncertainty about what reactions military activity would provoke in any specific circumstance, Grant also faced the fact that the Constitution gives to Congress the authority to raise troops and the authority to raise money to pay them. Grant's focus on the goals of peace and the principles of the Civil War amendments worked in tandem with his commitment to the separation of powers system, limiting him in ways that more aggressive presidents have ignored. Believing the presidency constrained in its authority and respecting the role to be played by Congress under the Constitution, Grant put forth no theories of a unitary executive; he did not reject congressionally mandated demobilizations. Instead, each time he was blocked by Congress, Grant tacked in a different direction. If he could go no farther down one path of action, blocked by Congress's legitimate authority under the Constitution, he would search for a different path.

Prospects for military occupation had diminished rapidly under Johnson, for example, as Congress sought to disengage from continued violence. Troops were demobilized after the war, funds cut and redirected, units moved to the West. The withdrawals continued under President Grant. As Republican and then Democratic Congresses demobilized troops, cut spending on the military, and restricted the president's ability to deploy forces, they closed off many of Grant's options.

As he was gradually deprived of his ability to use the military as much as he wanted, Grant leaned increasingly toward civilian enforcement. He relied heavily on a series of enforcement acts that put teeth into the president's ability to protect the principles of the Civil War amendments. Congress passed the first on May 31, 1870, to protect against discrimination in elections. One section aimed directly at the Ku Klux Klan, and another authorized the president to use military force "to aid in the execution of judicial process." Other provisions applied to enforcing the Fourteenth Amendment. A second Enforcement Act passed on February 28, 1871, aimed at protecting voter registration and the right to vote, primarily in northern cities. A third act, often called the Ku Klux Klan Act, aimed at enforcing provisions of the Fourteenth Amendment.[15]

President Grant's willingness to work with Congress is apparent in these efforts. In addresses and special messages he laid out for Congress the problems in the South, and he highlighted ambiguities in the laws that were diluting the president's ability to address the problems. Grant pressed Congress for special legislation to clear up the confusion regarding his authority, calling Congress into special session and issuing a written request outlining the seriousness of the situation. Congress responded to Grant's leadership and passed the third act on April 20, 1871, authorizing the president to suspend habeas corpus until the end of the next succeeding session of Congress.[16] Grant utilized the law effectively to battle the Klan in South Carolina, suspending habeas corpus in nine counties in October 1871. Hundreds of arrests were made by federal troops, and around two thousand Klan members fled the area. U.S. Attorney G. Wiley Wells brought seven hundred indictments in Mississippi, and hundreds more were brought in North Carolina beginning in 1871.[17]

Several historians have recognized that Grant dealt aggressively with Klan violence, "using all the instruments at his disposal," and that Grant sought to reconcile the country by moving hearts and minds through executive action.[18] Grant issued important public messages to Congress in the mid-1870s decrying violence in Louisiana, Mississippi, and South Carolina.[19] Grant's appeal for equality and justice in his 1873 Annual Message gave a boost to Charles Sumner's efforts on behalf of civil rights and racial equality, resulting in the Civil Rights Act of 1875.[20] In short, Grant was using whatever executive tools he could to bring about his desired end. He issued orders and proclamations, made public speeches and sent formal message to Congress, spoke behind the scenes, floated ideas, recommended legislation, made shrewd appointments, and led administration. Grant pursued a comprehensive approach to a principled goal, with some innovative ideas and some traditional tactics, all the time adjusting to rapid changes on the ground.

Grant's multifaceted efforts included administration of government attorneys. Grant's first attorney general, E. Rockwood Hoar, was a respected antipatronage advocate who worked to professionalize and organize the government's legal efforts. Hoar's reputation influenced reformers in Congress who were creating the new Department of Justice, and historian Jed Handelsman Shugerman argues that the department was established less to be an advocate for civil rights and more to organize and professionalize the government's attorneys. Critical to the Department of Justice Act were prohibitions on hiring outside counsel for government cases and the continuation of Tenure of Office Act protections for U.S. Attorneys, solicitors, and other officials. The goals were financial retrenchment and the insulation of U.S. Attorneys and others from patronage and political influence—an effort to create a professional bureau, removed from political pressure, with increased bureaucratic autonomy and expertise.[21]

Much as we saw in the previous chapter in the contexts of the U.S. Entomological Commission, the Signal Corps, and other offices, the reformers surrounding the creation of the Department of Justice had deep experience; they were part of burgeoning movements to professionalize the legal profession in the 1860s and 1870s. Grant oversaw a new agency in which his attorney general was able to set standards and directions for pushing civil rights cases, especially once Grant retained Akerman as attorney general and Bristow as solicitor general. But the agency itself stood for more than a civil rights focus—it represented a new application of ongoing government reform in the nineteenth century, consolidating government efforts, prohibiting outside counsel, and removing overlap and consolidating attorneys from other government departments, in a reform effort that sought to depoliticize the federal government's approach to its lawsuits. So, while the Grant team's utilization of the Department of Justice was partly about smashing the Klan and protecting civil rights, the broader story is about how the department's creation and early development furthered the nation's commitment to administrative expertise and professionalism centered at the national level.[22]

The effort worked, reducing violence, crippling the Klan, and restoring what Eric Foner called "acquiescence in the rule of law."[23] As the 1872 presidential election approached, the Ku Klux Klan had been demolished. The administration began constructing agreements throughout the South to reduce further the levels of violence and protect the sanctity of polling places and the right to vote, in exchange for easing the pressure of federal enforcement efforts. The 1872 election was, as a result, the most peaceful and fair election in the United States for many years before and after. Grant enjoyed victory in the election, with the largest winning margin in the popular vote in any presidential election between Andrew Jackson's first election in 1828 and Theodore Roosevelt's election in 1904.[24]

By March 1873, Grant's Justice Department had helped turn a terrible situation around. Congressionally authorized powers and the federal government's administrative apparatus were instrumental in Grant's successful effort to dismantle the Klan.

BUT THE ground shifted. Reactionary elements in the South interpreted the administration's southern agreements as signaling a retreat by the executive from aggressive federal enforcement, creating space for renewed resistance. Congress for its part had consistently signaled a wavering commitment to Reconstruction, and the evidence of military demobilization and the consolidation of ever-smaller detachments suggested that federal resolve overall might be weakening.

The administration's focus shifted to civil process, but pursuing peace and federal dominance through judicial process at lower levels in the federal court system was not an easy task. Federal prosecutors faced off against local populations who deplored their efforts and fought back with violence. Republicans, freed people, prosecutors, and judges were beaten and hanged, shot, drowned, and murdered. Friendly local juries refused to convict, even in the face of overwhelming evidence. A general conspiracy worked against the federal efforts, putting at risk the careers and lives of those associated with the Grant administration's work, or with the work of Republican forces in state and local areas. Courthouse after courthouse, town after town, and rural area after rural area became controlled by reactionary forces. Prosecutions took a long time. And while the Grant administration's efforts crushed the Klan in Kentucky and the Carolinas and secured convictions of hundreds of people, many efforts were defeated by local populations, prejudice, and violence.[25]

Grant's administration struggled to pay for all of the prosecutors, investigations, paperwork, court reporters, and others necessary for such a large undertaking with the limited funds allocated by Congress.[26] And given the attention to partisanship and scandal in the era, with Democrats and even Republicans raising concerns about the Grant administration's fairness, every prosecution ran the risk of confirming the impression that the new Department of Justice and the new federal judges were not meting out impartial justice according to law but instead were targeting beliefs and intimidating opposition party members for electoral advantage.[27]

The President and the Supreme Court

Grant and Congress had gone back and forth regarding aggressive enforcement and progressive development in the South. Congress's initial efforts had stalled because of Andrew Johnson; renewed vigor followed Ulysses Grant's election, but the demobilization of the military weakened the federal presence. The Enforcement Acts ramped up Grant's powers for a time, and the successes of Grant's enforcement of those acts, especially against the Ku Klux Klan, brought a peaceful election in 1872 and four more years for Grant, by now increasingly popular throughout the country. Yet Congress continued to shrink the military, and its legislators balked at supporting large-scale social reform through administrative agencies like the Freedmen's Bureau or the Justice Department.

The president's enforcement of the laws and the Civil War amendments ultimately came to rely on the federal judiciary. The investigations, arrests, and prosecutions brought by attorneys at Grant's Department of Justice took a leading role in trying to defuse southern opposition to civil rights, but federal judges sat in judgment of southerners' actions. These judges would determine how the reformed Constitution and its new amendments, and the innovative new authorities granted by Congress to the president and his agencies, were to be interpreted.[28] If federal judges accepted the administration's interpretation of the Civil War amendments, with the national government as the appropriate protector of those interpretations, the effort to enforce the war's gains might succeed. If, on the other hand, the courts failed to back up these efforts, the whole enterprise might collapse.

At the crux of the matter was a conflict over constitutional interpretation, which created a critical split among the nation's judges. Federal trial judges, usually very close to their local communities in the South, tended to be swayed by that localism—their interpretations protected community values, which in most cases meant protecting the established white power structure and responding to its demands. Federal judges at the district level were locals, with local prejudices; witnesses, defense attorneys, and others were tightly networked and effective at limiting the impact of federal prosecutions and in making those prosecutions as costly and taxing as possible.[29] Most of the district judges had not been appointed by Grant, and so reform had a difficult time taking hold. Reform would not come from the federal district courts.

The clash arrived at the level of the new federal circuit court system created by Congress in 1869. Grant had appointed all of the new circuit court judges, and he consistently appointed men who shared his vision of a new Constitution, informed by the spirit of the Civil War amendments and backed up by the power and authority of the national government to enforce those laws and principles. A vast divide emerged between district court judges' rulings and the rulings issued by the new circuit court judges, as the levels of the federal judiciary clashed over the meaning of federalism, race, and Reconstruction.[30]

The U.S. Supreme Court was called on to reconcile the differences, or to choose a winner. As the Ku Klux Klan prosecutions went forward and things were running effectively in the South, the Supreme Court heard oral arguments in the *Slaughterhouse Cases* in February 1872 and issued a decision in *Blyew v. United States* in April of the same year. In these and subsequent cases, the Supreme Court narrowed the scope and application of the amendments and the series of Enforcement Acts, rendering them all but ineffective. Grant's efforts collapsed; after 1873, he would lack both the funds and the legal basis for continued action.[31] Following Grant's conciliatory moves in 1872, Congress's withdrawal of support for the Justice Department, and the Court's decisions in *Blyew* and *Slaughterhouse*, the South saw a federal government that appeared to be in retreat from civil rights enforcement. In 1874, with federal troops in the South down to four thousand, violence exploded. The Grant administration and Congress tried to respond, but the South put together a widespread and massive series of resistance actions. The administration surrendered its efforts in May 1875, as new Attorney General Edwards Pierrepont pulled the plug on future arrests and prosecutor efforts.[32]

The Supreme Court dealt further blows to Grant's efforts in two more devastating decisions. *Reese v. United States* involved an electoral official in Kentucky who had refused to register a Black citizen's vote in a municipal election. The official was charged with violating two sections of the 1870 Enforcement Act designed to implement the principles of the Fifteenth Amendment. In a ruling that narrowly construed the Enforcement Act's application, the Court found that the Constitution conferred on no individual a right to vote; instead, that right was derived from the states, and as such states—not the federal government—could decide which voters were qualified to vote and also how and when voting would be allowed. Grant put everything the administration had into the effort to convince the justices that the Fifteenth Amendment conferred a right to vote that should be protected. Attorney General George Williams argued the case before the Court in January 1875, and Williams gave the case extra support including hiring a special prosecutor—future Supreme Court justice, and lone *Plessy v. Ferguson* dissenter, John Marshall Harlan. Still, the administration lost.[33]

Finally, in 1876 the Supreme Court decided *United States v. Cruikshank*. Whites had massacred more than one hundred Blacks in a courthouse in Colfax, Louisiana, setting fire to the building and shooting those who ran out to escape the flames. The United States brought a civil rights action against the perpetrators, under the 1870 Enforcement Act, which prohibited two or more people from trying to deprive citizens of their constitutional rights—in this case, the right to assemble and the right to bear arms. In the final act of a brutal and twisting case, the Court overturned the government's only three convictions, arguing that the Fourteenth Amendment only protected Blacks against action by states—since the perpetrators were private actors, the Enforcement Act did not apply. State and local officials, not the federal government, had jurisdiction. *Cruikshank* represented another significant narrowing of the applicability of the Civil War amendments and the Enforcement Acts designed to give them teeth.[34]

Chief Justice Morrison Waite delivered the decisions in *Reese* and *Cruikshank* on March 27, 1876, bringing a final curtain down on Grant's efforts to protect the Union's victories in the Civil War and move toward a progressive future.[35] Having struggled with Congress to secure the principles of the Civil War amendments, Grant's enforcement strategy was gutted by these rulings. In the fall of 1876, John Bagwell of Plainfield, New Jersey, wrote to Grant opining that the Hamburg Massacre in South Carolina in July of that year was the "first fruit" of the Court's declaring the Enforcement Act unconstitutional.[36]

Lieutenant General Phil Sheridan complained of too few troops and the Court's rulings in September 1876, writing,

> It is my belief that this small force of cavalry—and it is all that can well be sent—would not, by its influence nor by any positions it might occupy, secure fair voting throughout the state [of Louisiana]. It has been my belief that since the Congresses of 1874 and 1875 weakened, and the [Supreme Court's] decision on the Grant Parish [Colfax courthouse] massacre took place, it is extremely doubtful if any fair election can be held in Louisiana.[37]

The Court would eventually rule most of 1871's Ku Klux Klan Act unconstitutional in 1883 in *United States v. Harris,* and it ruled the 1875 Civil Rights Act unconstitutional in the same year in the *Civil Rights Cases.* One legal scholar sees the Court's decisions as an intentional act: "The Supreme Court's handling of the Fourteenth, and, apparently, the Fifteenth Amendments suggests that its decisions were a calculated effort to reverse the constitutionally centralizing thrust of the Civil War and Reconstruction."[38] The Court had effectively rolled back efforts made in the Grant years to secure the gains of the Civil War.

Reconstruction and the Complexity of State and Presidential Action in the Grant Years

Several lessons about the presidency and the state can be gleaned from even this brief overview of Grant and Reconstruction.

The first lesson is about the importance of presidential leadership. Hasty study of Reconstruction often passes too quickly through eight years of hard-won progress amid the storm of southern opposition: an ongoing and fluid postwar conflict that Grant fought despite a divided party, a balky Congress, and a reactionary Supreme Court. In the end, Grant's Reconstruction exemplified an informed approach to counterterrorism. Grant worked diligently to tamp down the level of anger and volatility, to cool down rhetoric and response, as a means of fighting terrorism politically—he emphasized peace to pacify hearts and minds, and he deployed tactics that maximized peacefulness and minimized violence when he could, as first steps toward an enduring reunification.[39] When biographer Louis A. Coolidge summed up Grant's achievements as "the restoration of a semblance of order in the South," it may sound unimpressive—but considered against what came before and after, it is noteworthy.[40] Grant deployed the range of tools available to an American president, adapting to ever-changing circumstances and appealing to citizens and officials as opportunities arose. The president as principled innovator can be an effective leader.

Second, though, there is a lesson here about the limits of the presidency in a system of separated institutions. In some ways, the interpretation that the Supreme Court had the final say supports the notion of a state of courts and parties. Grant was unable to marshal his party to continue the fight for civil rights, and the Supreme Court effectively resolved the stalemate that had emerged between Congress and the presidency. Decades of Jim Crow, convict gangs, segregation, torture, and terrorism followed. The executive's resources and administrative capacity were effective when supported—but when those resources were diminished and its capacity sabotaged, the state's purposes as defined by the president failed. Party splits over the 1875 civil rights bill and the annexation of Santo Domingo, among other matters, indicate presidential limitations and the continuing salience of party dynamics. Congress stymied Grant's efforts on numerous occasions. The Court became a tie breaker, as we have seen at other times in American history when powerful branches collided—think Watergate. Importantly, though, it was not the "courts" that broke the stalemate—it was the Supreme Court. The courts, meaning the federal courts, divided—the circuit courts supporting the new national vision of the president and the administrative bureaucracy, the district courts supporting, in effect, the localized and wearying vision of Congress.

The third lesson is a reminder that Reconstruction, as the work of government officials and regular citizens, proved a success in many ways. In the face of violence, fragmentation, and dogged opposition, in a system designed for institutional conflict and simultaneous respect and deference, the years of the Grant administration witnessed tremendous advances—what historian Douglas R. Egerton has recently called "America's most progressive era."[41] Much of the early progress emerged from the work of the Freedmen's Bureau, but even after Andrew Johnson killed the bureau, Black Americans made sustained advances through the Grant years. Schools opened, teachers were hired, children learned. Black churches organized and expanded. Hospitals were built and staffed. Black landholding increased. The ability to sign labor agreements and make contracts increased. Blacks owned businesses, ran newspapers, served on juries, testified at trials.[42]

Moreover, Black Americans held public office at the federal, state, and local levels. Black voters helped put them there by participating at high levels. Eighteen Black politicians served as lieutenant governor, treasurer, secretary of state, or superintendent of education at the state level during Reconstruction; sixteen sat in the U.S. Congress. The numbers increased for a time, with more than six hundred Blacks, most of them former enslaved people, serving in state legislatures. Blacks moved deeply into local offices too. Foner notes that without Reconstruction, "it is difficult to imagine the establishment of a framework of legal rights enshrined in the Constitution that, while flagrantly violated after 1877, created a vehicle for future federal intervention in Southern affairs."[43] These advances are too often overlooked, either from an overawareness of the Jim Crow years that followed or a hyperactive focus on the Johnson impeachment that preceded them.

The fourth lesson is that the eventual retreat from Reconstruction does not signal a reversion to localism. These were new tasks taken on by the state, in many ways, with new and refined administrative structures like the Justice Department. To retreat from them after the Grant years does not demonstrate state weakness—it represents a choice about how, and whether, to deploy state power. Grant and the federal government were effective in pursuing Reconstruction, and could have been more effective. It was not endemic and unfixable administrative weakness that ended the effort, or some mythical commitment to localism, but political choices. And the movement for justice, equality, and civil rights did not end there, as the state and its officials continued to argue about the proper balance between individual rights and state power, a topic I pick up in the conclusion.

The retreat from Reconstruction should not serve as the only basis for evaluating the scope and influence of state activity after the Civil War. The state continued to run programs and intrude on people's lives in other areas, as we saw in the previous chapter and as the next section on the West demonstrates. State activity and executive action continued, even expanded, in numerous contexts, including westward settlement and Indian affairs. Even if one sees in Reconstruction a weak presidency and a failure of the state, it would be a mistake to allow that one issue area to serve as the sole basis for drawing conclusions about state activity and presidential action after the Civil War. As noted above, Reconstruction was in some ways a failure to graft onto the American state a new set of purposes—that effort slowly engendered new opposition that would help define the state's actions moving forward, as William Taft and then Franklin Roosevelt and others worked to calibrate balances between state action and defenses of individual and group rights. But the slow churn in this area of state activity should never obscure ongoing and even expanding state activity in other realms, which illustrates the continuity of state action and presidential leadership. The American state and the president exhibited far more continuity after the Civil War with pre–Civil War America than a study of Reconstruction and civil rights alone might suggest.

The real story here is about a fight over the *use* of the state, a fight driven at least in part by the *effectiveness* of an intrusive military and a civilian Department of Justice, both of which demonstrated the capacity to affect matters on the ground until deprived of necessary resources and political will. The state continued its attention to disaster relief, fiscal policy, administrative reform, and international diplomacy, among a host of other matters. And it would maintain its longstanding attention on the West, intruding on the lives of millions of people in ways both familiar and novel.

President Grant, the Administrative State, and Indian Policy

Consideration of Indian affairs, more than any other issue area, demonstrates the continuation and expansion of the American state after the Civil War. In Indian affairs and related matters of westward expansion, we see the state's intrusive actions and we see leadership by an active president driving policy reform. Court and congressional action took cues from executive action, following presidential messages, supporting presidential initiatives, and sanctioning administrative actions—a far cry from a state of courts and parties reconciling disputes and serving as the drivers of policy action, and anything but a retreat to localism. President Grant and his team worked with Congress to expand executive power, administrative discretion, and a sense of the state for tens of thousands of Native Americans and American citizens.

From Adams to Grant in Indian Affairs

Between the presidencies of John Quincy Adams and Ulysses S. Grant lie forty years of tragedy in Indian affairs, much of it sparked by strong executive leadership and supporting actions by Congress. The Indian Removal Act of 1830, pressed hard by the Andrew Jackson administration as soon as Jackson gained office, accelerated the tortured passage of more than 100,000 Native Americans from their houses and farms in the Southeast to contested lands west of the Mississippi River. Removal also targeted Natives in the Old Northwest, affecting communities in Ohio, Indiana, Illinois, Michigan, and New York. The United States moved tribes from the East into the middle of an already occupied West, where Plains tribes saw the newcomers as threats to their own lands and ways of life. Eastern tribes struggled to acquire a measure of safety and security in their new homes, having heard the same propaganda as whites had regarding the ferocity and barbarity of the Plains tribes. Tribes in the Pacific Northwest and along the West Coast, those along the lengthening southwestern border of the United States, and even those in the northern Plains suffered greater and greater encroachment from migrants along the Santa Fe and Oregon Trails, from expansion into California, and from railroad survey parties like that outfitted by Captain Ulysses Grant in the early 1850s. Treaty followed treaty, removal followed removal, as dozens of communities were forced by state actors and private interests to relocate to regions isolated from the main lines of migration and white settlement, and away from the main areas of fertile fields, stocked rivers, and temperate weather.

Reports of corruption and poor administration stalked the new federal reservations in the 1850s and 1860s. Reformers and reporters complained that millions of dollars in goods and services obligated to Native nations by treaties and other agreements were being siphoned off and stolen by Indian rings involving private actors and government agents. Thieves and con men targeted Native lands, and railroad and other developers were believed to be complicit in stealing land and resources from Natives and the broader public.[44] American Indian nations fractured over the best course and the best future for their communities and their families.[45] And there was still violence. During the Civil War, some tribes had aligned with the Confederacy; many had sent soldiers into the Confederate forces; and some, especially in the West, battled over issues hardly related to the Civil War at all. These years saw the 1862 U.S.-Dakota War, sparked by callous denial of food and supplies to Dakotas along the Minnesota River in southwest Minnesota, which ended with the largest mass hanging in U.S. history, at Mankato, Minnesota, in 1863. These years witnessed the 1864 Sand Creek Massacre of more than 150 Arapahoes and Cheyennes by state and local militia forces, and the 1863–64 Long Walk of the Navajo (Dine)—a forced march of 350 miles through blizzards to a desolate reservation at Bosque Redondo, facilitated by Kit Carson and his volunteers, who killed sheep, poisoned wells, and burned crops and orchards on the Navajos' traditional lands.[46]

Mission Change in Indian Affairs: President Grant's Peace Policy

Grant's desire for reform of Indian policy was clear and expected; the details of what he wanted to see, exactly, were not. The Peace Policy was a mixed bag of measures addressing different aspects of the nation's Indian policy, put together on the fly and constantly adjusted, in keeping with the management style of the Grant administration.[47] Like Reconstruction, the Peace Policy had multiple goals—it aimed at a shift in the nation's principles regarding Indian affairs but also at improving administrative efficiency, cost savings, and clarity in management.

The public focus of Grant's Indian policy was peace, a major change after years of government efforts devoted to forced removals and resettlements, and after the complicated battles and alliances of the Civil War years. In an atmosphere of corruption charges and mistrust of civilian administrators in Indian affairs, and together with the recent success of the Union Army and the violence constantly reported in the West, Grant's goal of peace was a courageous and controversial choice. By the end of Grant's two terms, only some of it still aligned with established procedures or traditional protocols, and almost everything had been challenged and debated, driven by the president's openness to reform. Grant would zigzag his way through supporting and opposing a variety of new initiatives aimed at reforming and pacifying Indian affairs.

Even before he was inaugurated, Grant was thinking about moving Indian policy in new directions. As early as 1867, Grant had asked Ely Parker "to develop a reform agenda for the BIA," in the words of historian C. Joseph Genetin-Pilawa.[48] As president-elect, Grant toured the West and met with Quaker reformers advocating for changes in the nation's Indian policy.[49] In a dramatic move, Grant appointed Parker, a Seneca, as commissioner of Indian affairs. Parker emphasized Grant's support for reform in February 1869, in a letter to Quaker reformer Benjamin Hallowell, before Grant had been sworn in. "General Grant, the President elect," Parker wrote, asking for names of recommended Indian agents, is

> desirous of inaugurating some policy to protect the Indians in their just rights and enforce integrity in the administration of their affairs, as well as to improve their general condition. . . . Any attempt which may or can be made by your society for the improvement, education, and civilization of the Indians under such agencies will receive from him, as President, all the encouragement and protection which the laws of the United States will warrant him in giving.[50]

The message of an open door for reform ideas had been sent.

Parker responded to Grant's 1867 inquiry about a reform agenda with a suggestion for a ten-member commission composed of both whites and Natives.[51] Numerous precedents provided models for Indian reform, from the U.S. Christian Commission during the Civil War to the Freedmen's Bureau, the Indian Peace Commission, and formal government-missionary collaborations going back to 1819's Civilization Fund and even earlier.[52] This reminds us of the nation's long history of creating ad-hoc advisory boards and commissions to work on varying aspects of policy review, reorganization, and reform. It is partially for this reason that Grant's role in pursuing the creation of a Board of Indian Commissioners to facilitate policy reform is sometimes overplayed. Officials, reformers, journalists, and activists had been working for years toward reform. Grant's openness to the idea cleared a path and helped set the conditions for action, but he was not the prime mover.[53]

At the same time, Grant's role can too easily be *under*valued. The president was a central and independent force in the creation of the board and in the rules that would guide its activities. Grant highlighted the significance of Indian affairs in his First Inaugural Address and supported the concept of an independent citizens' board, and Congress created the board in 1869. Grant then appointed its members.[54] To flesh out implementation of the law, Grant issued an executive order in 1869 setting the guidelines for the board's functioning.[55] "A commission of citizens having been appointed under the authority of law to co-operate with the administrative departments in the management of Indian affairs," Grant wrote, "the following regulations will till further directions. [sic] control the action of said commission, and of the Bureau of Indian Affairs in matters coming under their joint supervision." Grant proceeded to state that the commission would "make its own organization, and employ its own clerical assistants," keeping track of expenses. He authorized the commission to have access to Indian Office records, to inspect agencies, to attend purchases of goods and payments of annuities, to attend "consultations or councils with the Indians," and to "advise Superintendents and Agents in the performance of their duties." Grant established lines of authority for the commission to make reports, register complaints, track expenditures, keep records, and submit plans and budgets for policy recommendations. He "enjoined" "all the officers of the government connected with the Indian Service" to cooperate respectfully and to offer full access to records.[56]

The back and forth between the administration and Congress in drafting the law, and the president's independent purposes in the construction of the precise text of the executive order, are revealed in communications among interested players.[57] William Welsh, the board's first chair, for example, resigned from the board almost immediately over disagreements about the control of resources and the level of independence and influence the board would have in relation to the Interior Department's officials.[58] The law passed by Congress suggested that the board would share decision making with Interior, perhaps even on an equal footing, but Grant's order made it clear that the board's suggestions would be subordinate to decisions made by regular government officers.[59] Interior Secretary Jacob Cox wrote to Welsh, explaining that he had insisted on certain requirements for the legislation as it moved through Congress, namely "that it should be left entirely discretionary with the President as to whether *any* direct supervision & control of the public moneys should be vested in the Commission," and that any such authority the president might grant "must not be independent of this Department which would remain responsible necessarily for the general conduct of Indian affairs."[60] These decisions would encourage conflicts among the board, Interior Department, and Parker, and public criticism by the board and challenges within Congress would lead to the exit of Parker and Cox from the government. The board's members resigned en masse in 1874, angry at being marginalized by the Grant administration's officials. This dustup indicates the independence of the administration and the autonomy of Interior and the Indian Office, even as it suggests the ongoing power of the board and of Congress to inflict direct damage on administration officials and hinder executive branch policymaking.[61]

Beyond matters involving the board, Parker designed the details of the administration's approach. Parker and Grant went back a long way, having met before the war when Parker was a civil engineer for the Treasury Department building customs houses. Parker had long been involved at the intersection of government policy and Native governance, as outlined in the previous chapter.[62] He was a bureaucrat and technician, and his long experience in government made him more inside-bureaucrat than outside-activist. Parker worked to improve the overall quality of the Indian Office's activities by clarifying and standardizing administrative practices in the interests of efficiency, oversight, and effectiveness.[63] In 1873, Congress created the position of inspector and authorized Grant to appoint up to five inspectors who would report to the commissioner of Indian affairs, gradually replacing regionally oriented superintendents.[64]

These efforts were as much about administrative systematization as about the policy goals involved. As such, Parker's initiatives rammed against entrenched interests in Congress and among the members of the Board of Indian Commissioners.[65] There is an important parallel with the creation of the Department of Justice here. Both are often viewed in terms of their principled goals, the Department of Justice in its efforts to protect the rights of freed people and the Peace Policy–era Indian Office in its role as change agent in Indian affairs. But developments at both agencies also involved streamlining and improving accountability, efficiency, and management—they aimed at better delivery of state services that impacted directly on people's lives and communities.

IN THE Peace Policy's signature innovation, social policies and aid would be administered on reservations by personnel selected by religious organizations and the new Board of Indian Commissioners.[66] This process also exemplifies the Grant administration's contentious back and forth with Congress in these years. Grant initially wanted military personnel to run the reservations, but Congress prohibited that in order to defend patronage interests in so many lucrative and influential government positions. In another example of the president's independence, though, Grant—unwilling to cede the field and patronage benefits to Congress—reacted by allowing the board to select reservation agents, furthering Grant's reform mission by outflanking Congress, placing religious personnel at reservations, and trying to starve Indian rings of their benefactors in Congress.[67] The development of this main pillar of the Peace Policy was thus more of an ad-hoc tactical response to events than it was a carefully worked out reform plan.[68]

Another major initiative of the Peace Policy era aimed to clarify lines of authority between the civilian side of Indian affairs and the military, thereby addressing the longstanding confusion brought on by overlapping authority shared blurrily by the Interior Department's Indian Office and the War Department.[69] Civilian and military officers in the government had worked closely together since the earliest days of U.S. Indian policy, but overlaps and confusion meant competing lines of authority and confused responsibilities in the field. During a series of shifts in design, Grant and Parker worked to establish the idea that the dividing line between civilian and military leadership would be the boundary lines of the reservations.[70] Grant and Parker tried to enshrine a distinction between "hostile" and "nonhostile" Indians, a distinction that would be defined by reservation boundaries. Inside the reservation, religious leaders and civilian agents would manage populations, encourage farming and education, and try to lead Natives from many different cultures and with many different histories to embrace a U.S.-imposed way of life. Outside the reservation boundary, though, Natives would be considered hostile—and be under the hair-triggered eye of the military. This sharp line was innovative and clear, easily understood and acted on. Grant popularized the distinction in his annual messages. The approach broke with core understandings in Indian affairs administration, though, which had, since the dawn of the republic, placed civilian administrators in positions superior to the military, with the military tasked with backing up civilian objectives when requested.

Reform and Innovation: Culture, Land, and Education

In addition to innovations in personnel selection and clarifications about the importance of reservation boundaries, a variety of other executive-led innovations aimed at improving Indian affairs and promoting peaceful relations and a peaceful future. Grant's administration sought reform through cultural change, especially efforts to alter the customs of Native life and reorient federal land and education policies. These efforts are often categorized together as initiatives in "civilization." All have been controversial since their inception. Grant's executive actions broke new ground in pursuit of broad values, leaving a legacy that has been applauded by his proponents and condemned by his detractors.

Grant pushed his vision early and prominently in public rhetoric. In his brief First Inaugural Address, he touched on only a few issues—but he gave Indian affairs a place, following discussions of the recent war, the economy, and foreign affairs. "The proper treatment of the original occupants of this land—the Indians—is one deserving of careful study," Grant stated. "I will favor any course toward them which tends to their civilization and ultimate citizenship."[71] Grant's openness to innovation and "any course" that would help are clear; as in other issue areas, the tactical means could be found out. He returned to the subject in his Second Inaugural Address, giving Indigenous peoples extra attention at the close of a long list of items on which Grant pledged to focus in his second term:

> And, by a humane course, to bring the aborigines of the country under the benign influences of education and civilization. It is either this or war of extermination: wars of extermination, engaged in by people pursuing commerce and all industrial pursuits, are expensive even against the weakest people, and are demoralizing and wicked. Our superiority of strength and advantages of civilization should make us lenient toward the Indian. The wrong inflicted upon him should be taken into account and the balance placed to his credit. The moral view of the question should be considered and the question asked, Cannot the Indian be made a useful and productive member of society by proper teaching and treatment? If the effort is made in good faith, we will stand better before the civilized nations of the earth and in our own consciences for having made it.[72]

Anchored in an ethnocentric effort to educate and "civilize" Native peoples, Grant's message and his guiding values were clear: peace over war, education and support over neglect, mediation over retribution. These were big ideas pushing for big change, with presidential rhetoric about important issues aimed squarely at Congress and the public.

The Grant administration's initiatives were not new, exactly—federal policy had long provided some resources for education and "civilization," for example, and land allotments had begun years before Grant was elected—but contextualized next to the Peace Policy's high-profile administrative reforms, Grant's efforts inflated their prominence and contributed to the gradual expansion of efforts aimed at changing the lifeways of tens of thousands of Indigenous people. Grant, Parker, and the reformers of the Board of Indian Commissioners supported efforts to help Native individuals hold and maintain property through individual allotments, and also to break off tribal lands for use by non-Natives. Grant and Parker also believed deeply in the promise of education, and the administration supported trial-and-error efforts to expand the government's role, including support for reservation boarding and day schools. The legacy of such efforts remains controversial today, as well-meaning initiatives, complex support and opposition, some successes, and lasting trauma resulted from what became disastrous full-scale allotment, assimilation, and boarding-school policies in the 1880s and 1890s.

Policymaking by Executive Action

Just before he became president, and despite his interest in policy reform, Grant had advocated for military increases in the West and for an aggressive policy to "squelch the Indians."[73] He was a proponent of "transfer," or moving responsibility for Indian policy and its administration from the Interior Department back to its original home in the War Department.[74] Transfer policy enjoyed considerable traction throughout the 1860s and 1870s, and the government in Washington could have shifted its military to the West as it removed troops from the South.

After supporting the idea of transferring Indian affairs to the War Department, though, Grant came to reject options that might invite militarism as the way to organize the West.[75] Transfer was not seen by Grant and Parker as a way to encourage military action but instead as a way to improve administrative outcomes that would encourage peace. Grant hoped to protect Natives from aggressive white settlers and squatters while at the same time encouraging settlement and expansion. Transfer represented faith in bureaucracy more than it did militarism: the War Department was seen as the best-supported, most effective government agency, and of course it was one which Grant understood and within which he had had tremendous success and commanded great respect. Grant and Parker wanted Indian affairs in the War Department because of its management potential.[76]

In his first few months as president, Grant ordered a halt to the army's large offensive actions on the Plains and on the West Coast and increased his resistance to "transfer."[77] Grant's early emphasis on the Peace Policy helped derail efforts to move Indian affairs to the military's direct control, as Grant supplanted his support for transfer with support for innovations inside the Interior Department.[78]

OTHER MATTERS involving the military witnessed similar efforts by Grant to find the right tactics to get him to his overall goals. In the matter of intentionally destroying the buffalo on the Plains, for example, Grant's executive actions, while influential, again zigged and zagged. The army helped traveling shooting parties and private traders, called "hidemen," destroy millions of buffalo after the Civil War. Many of the participants, including military leaders like William Tecumseh Sherman and Phil Sheridan, explicitly connected the destruction of the buffalo—the source of so much food, resources, and meaning in Native cultures—with the destruction of the Indian. In the same years of the late 1860s and 1870s, though, activists, animal rights supporters, and even members of the military condemned the killing, criticizing the slaughters and even pushing legislation at state and federal levels to protect buffalo. Grant suggested at times that he would protect the buffalo, and historian David D. Smits, while indicating the limits of Grant's protective efforts, at the same time writes that the slaughter slowed considerably in the early years of the Peace Policy due to

Grant's shift in approach in Indian affairs.[79] But Grant wavered—he pocket-vetoed an 1875 bill that aimed at ending the slaughter of buffalo on the Great Plains, he seems to have done little if anything in some cases to prevent the army's support for the killings, and he failed to follow through on specific promises to protect buffalo from slaughter.

In the Black Hills, Grant used executive actions to zigzag through upholding treaty commitments, withdrawing from those same commitments, and influencing public messaging with an impact that has lasted for a century and a half. The 1868 Fort Laramie Treaty, signed at a peak of Native strength against the United States, established boundaries for the Great Sioux Reservation and commitments by the United States to respect those boundaries. As white prospectors, miners, and would-be settlers looked to encroach on the Black Hills in search of gold, officials and field officers in the Interior and War Departments staunchly defended the treaties and the boundaries. Grant made it clear that the borders would be protected while the government sought to renegotiate the 1868 treaty and purchase the Black Hills. Grant ordered publication of the government's position and its promise to uphold the treaty and expel trespassers.[80] Grant further ordered Sherman to issue orders to continue to keep trespassers out of the Black Hills country until the treaty commission finished its work.[81]

The military, with thousands of troops and many officers and soldiers dedicated either to Indian rights, to treaty provisions, or simply to following orders, stood ready to defend the borders and assist Natives in policing their land boundaries.[82] Prospecting parties were detained by the military, their weapons confiscated and their wagons, provisions, ammunition, and other property destroyed by U.S. soldiers. Such conflicts sparked vehement public denunciations of government oppression and illegal behavior.[83] The unsettled nature of prospecting, government restrictions, new agreements with Native nations, and the promise of opening the territory impacted on the lives of thousands of people and received steady, breathless attention in the media and among citizens and Natives. A sense of the state infused the region's diverse populations as well as interested parties in other parts of the country.[84] Yet as government expeditions and the news media popularized the idea that the Black Hills were full of gold, and as court rulings in the region limited the legal application of the administration's exclusion policy, enforcement became crippled and the army "relaxed" its policy in the summer of 1875.[85]

The military was conflicted, with its chief officials willing to defend the treaty line as long as their orders were to do so. President Grant's leadership thus proved crucial. When Grant supported the terms of the 1868 treaty, so did the military and so did the public messaging. In some ways this echoed

John Quincy Adams's efforts with Georgia, as both presidents initially supported existing agreements as they worked to secure new treaties, and both presidents deployed the military to defend boundaries and uphold treaty provisions. In a key respect, though, Grant's effort was directly at odds with that of Adams. Grant gradually allowed the existing treaty to be broadly violated as he worked to negotiate new agreements. As Grant wavered and weakened his position, the military followed his lead. Sheridan wrote to Brigadier General Alfred Terry of Grant's revised approach in November 1875, following a meeting of Grant and his top decision makers:

> The President decided that while the orders heretofore issued forbidding the occupation of the Black Hills country, by miners, should not be rescinded, still no further resistance by the military should be made to the miners going in; it being his belief that such resistance only increased their desire and complicated the troubles. Will you therefore quietly cause the troops in your Department to assume such attitude as will meet the views of the President in this respect?[86]

The president's role in both cases was critical. Unlike Adams, though, Grant bent toward expediency rather than the sanctity of the law.[87] Both examples demonstrate the significant role of the president in administrative leadership and in matters of major import to U.S. citizens and noncitizens.

Having earlier communicated the administration's position to the public through newspapers and military orders, Grant rationalized his eventual actions to American citizens and others in his annual messages. In his Eighth Annual Message, Grant offered a detailed explanation of policy choices and announced that his Indian policy "has been humane and has substantially ended Indian hostilities in the whole land except in a portion of Nebraska, and Dakota, Wyoming, and Montana Territories—the Black Hills region and approaches thereto." He argued that "hostilities there have grown out of the avarice of the white man, who has violated our treaty stipulations in his search for gold." Raising the question of "why the Government has not enforced obedience to the terms of the treaty prohibiting the occupation of the Black Hills region by whites," Grant said that troops did remove whites at first, but once gold was discovered it became impossible—because "an effort to remove the miners would only result in the desertion of the bulk of the troops that might be sent there." Grant closed by defending a new treaty, pending before Congress, that would remove "all difficulty in this matter."[88] That public messaging, misleading as to the military's abilities and loyalty, and as to his own responsibilities, has dominated interpretations of the issue's history for a century and half.[89]

There were other matters affected by executive action, minor in the grand scheme of things but of life-and-death significance to their participants. Grant, for example, was directly involved in deciding whether to use his pardon power to mitigate punishments in the wake of the Modoc War.[90] In another case, Grant apparently used the attention given to his office to secure a claim by a woman named Fanny Kelly against the Lakotas, to be paid by the United States. Kelly argued that she had helped deter attacks on U.S. forces while she was a captive of the Lakotas, and she filed a claim for suffering and lost property. The claims had been adjusted by the Indian Office and by Congress, and payments had lagged. Grant invited Kelly to meet with him and assured her that her claims had been filed properly. Historian Larry C. Skogen writes, "Such notoriety compelled the lawmakers to compensate Kelly, and it accounts for the fact that she was one of the few claimants in the post–Civil War era to whom Congress provided indemnities."[91]

And in yet another local crisis, federal, tribal, and local officials were in conflict during what was called the "Goingsnake" affair between federal marshals and Cherokee officials threatening to arrest each other. As complicated matters developed, Grant called for a normalization of relations with the Cherokee Nation and engineered the dropping of cross-cutting charges. Grant sent to Congress a twenty-page report prepared by the acting secretary of the interior about the matter, in response to a Senate inquiry. Grant explicitly and successfully recommended the creation of a judicial district in Indian Territory, "as a measure which will afford the most immediate remedy for the existing troubles."[92] Subsequently, the U.S. district attorney, Western District, Arkansas, on October 21, 1873, wrote to Indian agent John Jones: "I was directed by the Attorney General of the United States to dismiss the case of *U.S. v. Zeke Proctor* and others for murder at Goingsnake District, but was further directed that if the authorities of the Cherokee Nation should attempt to prosecute any of the Marshals' party to indict again Proctor and his party."[93] The Grant administration—with Grant's direct involvement—had mitigated the crisis, successfully pressed Congress to expand the federal judiciary, and then used the chain of command through the civilian bureaucracy to achieve a lasting resolution.[94]

Ending New Treaties, Continuing Old Ones, and Multiplying Executive Orders

Congress formally ended treatymaking with Indian nations in 1871; Grant was an influential proponent of the change. Congressional debate of the matter relied at times on Grant's public pronouncements of the Peace Policy's success to argue that treaties were no longer an appropriate means for the United States to interact with Indian nations.[95] Institutional battles for control of resources sped reform as well. The change had many advocates and "was largely finalized by peripheral events" more than by Grant's leadership, however, suggesting (as with religious organizations' selection of reservation personnel) that the president was important but not alone in realizing reform.[96]

At the same time as it forbade new treaties, though, Congress explicitly continued in force all existing treaties and all existing national commitments, a debate in which Grant and administration experts played key roles. Protection of existing treaties in 1871 resulted in part from sophisticated and effective lobbying by Native delegations, with particular focus on Congress and on Grant's appointees on the Board of Indian Commissioners. The administration's work in defense of existing treaties helped perpetuate significant protections and rights for Native nations.[97]

The end of treatymaking, and the continuance of existing treaties, led to diverse outcomes—some of which limited the presidential role in Indian affairs and the disposition of lands, some of which continued the executive's traditional role, and some of which expanded the president's role significantly. Historian Francis Paul Prucha broke the "substitutes" for treaties into three broad categories: executive agreements (sometimes called "articles of convention"), statutes, and executive orders.[98]

Executive agreements that replaced treaties were often conducted by Interior Department officials under explicit but general authority delegated by Congress. Executive branch officials would negotiate an agreement in the field, very much as they always had, with the additional involvement of some agreements negotiated by the new inspectors.[99] A bill would then be drafted, including the agreement and implementation recommendations, which would be sent directly to Congress or to Congress via the president. Congress would debate the provisions, often resulting in extended delays as local politics and lobbying slowed the process. The final result in some cases was a failure to ratify at all, but in others a statute would enact the agreement or the agreement would be enacted within an appropriations bill. Overall, this suggests continuity in the way that agreements were made in the field. At the same time, though, Congress grafted new ways of affecting people's lives in the field onto traditional state practices. Rather than *substituting* for what the executive branch had always done, Congress in effect *added* an increased role for itself.[100]

Direct statutes without executive agreements stood in as a second replacement for prohibited new treaties, and Congress by law moved Native populations around, provided for allotments or changes in landholdings, provided for civilization initiatives, and so on.[101] Other laws passed by Congress included an 1871 pro-allotment law, laws in 1874 and 1875 detailing work requirements for American Indians receiving government benefits, and in 1875 limits on freedoms of chiefs and headmen and rules promoting individual homesteads and landholding by Natives who severed their tribal ties. Grant aided and supported these laws, despite the contradictions with the Peace Policy; his actual role and the degree of pressure he brought to bear is obscure though.[102] Prucha concluded with regard to executive agreements and statutes that "Congress was *both* continuing the treaty system by means of negotiated agreements *and* dealing with the Indians by direct legislation as it did with white citizens of the United States."[103]

The third category of substitutes for treatymaking proved the most consequential. The 1871 end to treatymaking radically expanded presidential powers as presidents "increased tremendously" the use of executive orders, especially in the context of establishing reservations and defining the status of lands. In other words, as executive orders became the primary method of establishing Indian reservations, the processes of reserving lands and making changes to land status—as well as developments in population and settlement, economic development, military action, and so on—sat squarely with the president. Even this was not wholly new, as presidents had long exercised both independent and delegated authority to affect land status, with Congress and the courts regularly deferring to and accepting such authority. Acts of Congress had presumed since at least 1830 that the president possessed such authority, and the courts had concurred. President Franklin Pierce created the first executive order reservation in 1855, and executive orders kept the presidency at the center of U.S.-Indian relations from 1855 to 1919.[104] The president could establish reservations, alter their borders, and issue orders patenting individual allotments through treaty and other provisions by executive action that directly affected the lives of thousands of Natives and non-Natives.[105]

Grant was the first to begin to exploit such broadened executive powers to pursue goals in Indian policy after Congress ended treatymaking. He and presidents after 1871 issued dozens of orders reserving land, unreserving land, and affecting other aspects of policy. Grant established a reservation of almost three million acres by executive order for the Chiricahua in December 1872.[106] By Grant's executive order, in 1873 and 1874 the Blackfeet gave up "some of their best lands and accepted a reservation.... These agreements opened up the Sun, Judith, and upper Musselshell River basins to the penetration of stockmen. They also meant sadness and loss for the Blackfeet," wrote historians Michael P. Malone and Richard B. Roeder. The Blackfeet and other tribes, though, still hunted buffalo, thanks to executive action in 1875.[107] Also in 1875, Grant issued three important executive orders affecting the Sioux.[108]

By executive order, Grant protected the land base for the Kumeyaay of southern California, enlarged the lands reserved for Makah and Quinault in the Pacific Northwest, and in 1876 established the Hoopa Valley Reservation.[109] He signed orders reserving or protecting lands in other cases, deployed the military to remove unauthorized squatters from Native lands, and troops were deployed to protect Pawnee timber resources from theft by whites.[110] Grant also blocked unfair treaties from going into effect.[111]

The changes in the specifics of the orders, endemic to not only Grant but also later presidents, indicate the ongoing and active role of the president in matters affecting thousands of people directly, and even drawing letters and petitions to the presidency recommending various actions. For example, Grant established a reservation for the Mescalero Apache Tribe by executive order in 1873, following guidance from the commissioner of Indian affairs. The next year, though, Grant cancelled that order and issued a new one with redrawn reservation boundaries; following that, Grant and later presidents issued executive order adjustments in 1875, 1882, 1883, and 1910.[112]

In the Northwest in 1873, Grant ordered that Chief Joseph and the Nez Perce could have a reservation in the Wallowa Valley, but pressure from whites and from state and federal politicians energized a review in the Indian Office. Grant followed with executive orders in 1875 and 1877 rescinding the decision and mandating that the Nez Perce move to the Lapwai Reservation in Idaho.[113] Grant signed executive orders setting aside land for Mission Indians in California, then rescinded them when whites opposed the reservations and Native populations refused to relocate. Dozens of other executive orders were issued and then modified, often returning all or some lands to the public domain at the behest of Native and white Americans alike.[114] Executive orders in these years were diverse in terminology, purposes, and administrative details, very much in keeping with the localized specificity of most Indian affairs administration, with many executive orders being seen as equivalent to treaties.[115]

Political scientist and Native sovereignty expert David E. Wilkins concludes, "Although the legal title of executive order reservations was debated for some years, it was one of the most important means many Indian tribes had of gaining some measure of recognized title. All of the twenty-one reservations in Arizona were created by executive order, except for the core part of the Navajo reservation, which was established by treaty in 1868."[116] Twenty-three million acres of public domain would be set aside by executive order between 1871 and 1919, when Congress forbade further use of executive orders to establish or alter reservations.[117] The role of the president and of the state intersected at the apex of westward expansion policy. As we learn more and more about the scope and influence of the administrative state in the nineteenth century, we learn more and more about the regular and influential use of independent executive power.

Conclusion

The Peace Policy remains controversial today, as Grant's proponents portray a well-intentioned and largely successful effort to improve the conditions facing American Indians and reorient U.S. policy away from aggressive militarism, and his detractors see an ethnocentric series of arbitrary, short-term decisions that failed to result in significant improvement or even increased peace.[118] All, however, see an active president driving policy reforms affecting exactly *how* the state would intrude upon the lives of millions of people.

It is not the goal of this book to offer an evaluation of the effects of executive action, and of policy generally, but rather to highlight the importance of state actions. Such actions directly affected the lives of thousands of Natives and would-be new settlers, and dozens of organized interests: construction companies, saloon keepers, railroad engineers, blacksmiths.[119] Many of them opposed the Peace Policy from the beginning and followed its development through breathless news media accounts; many others contacted Grant directly to praise his decisions.[120] Grant worked to change hearts and minds, to change the spirit of the nation's Indian policy—through policy reforms, rhetoric, and framing. His refrain of peace led members of Congress, reformers, and the general public to reconsider what they knew of the West and its Native inhabitants. Christian reformers were energized, and writers and other observers like Harriet Beecher Stowe and Lydia Marie Child took time to engage the topic. Helen Hunt Jackson published her classic, *A Century of Dishonor*, in 1881, encouraged by the era's spirit of reform.

Grant summed up his approach in his Fifth Annual Message in December 1873: "With the encroachment of civilization upon the Indian reservations and hunting grounds, disturbances have taken place between the Indians and whites during the past year, and probably will continue to do so until each race appreciates that the other has rights which must be respected."[121] Grant's statements could anchor hours of heated discussion today about the legacy of U.S. Indian policy and westward expansion, but at bottom of that discussion would be a powerful and intrusive state, characterized by influential executive leadership.

The most enduring legacy of the Grant administration is controversy. Grant's leadership helped unify the nation and secure peace, but it left millions of freed people, Republicans, and Native Americans at the mercy of their opponents or their too-well-intentioned friends. Grant pursued peace in the South, trying every policy and action he could think of to reunify the nation and protect new civil rights—even as the constraints imposed by an increasingly reluctant Congress and an increasingly opposed Supreme Court slowly strangled his efforts. He pursued peace in Indian affairs through evolving reform efforts and direct, consequential executive action advocating education, administrative improvements, and reserved lands, but deciding on the fly when those measures would give way to force. It is not surprising that Grant's major successes, his major failures, and the foundations of his eternally contested legacy lie in those areas in which his zigzagging support for principled innovations most decisively influenced state intrusions into millions of people's lives.

6

President Taft and the 125-Year-Old American State

WILLIAM HOWARD TAFT's presidency illustrates the continuing importance of innovative executive action in the deployment of the American state. Taft came to the presidency with extensive governmental and administrative experience, having served as a federal judge, solicitor general, U.S. civilian governor of the Philippines, and secretary of war. By the Progressive era, the American state had been robust, intrusive, and effective, run by long-tenured policymakers and administrative experts, for more than a century. It had pushed westward by treaty and by war, uniting the continent, and by Taft's presidency the "closing of the West" was twenty years in the past. Government programs supported veterans, widows, sailors, and Native Americans, and regulation had addressed finance, the fur trade, steamboat boilers, railroads, economic combinations and monopolies, and matters of race and gender. Commissions and boards had supplemented the work of numerous federal departments since the earliest days of the republic, staffed with expert administrators experienced in a variety of detailed and complicated fields.

Together, the presidency and the state busied themselves adapting national governance to the new rights and protections of the Civil War amendments and the Progressive era, even as they sought to perpetuate the state's traditional role in organizing and managing society. Through active presidential leadership of state functions, President Taft led the charge to calibrate the new blend of governance for the coming American century. Taft was a creative, innovative president, dedicated to the rule of law, transparent process, and the Constitution but also driven by a vision of active government—furthering the federal government's responsibility to protect and empower American citizens and noncitizens.

Taft was what I call a synthesist, marrying the creativity and principled innovation of someone like Ulysses S. Grant with the commitment to lasting process and procedure of someone like John Quincy Adams. Taft pursued principled goals, and he innovated, but he built the foundations of enduring programs and initiatives through executive action and new law. Taft was a builder, achieving demonstrable successes and establishing lasting programs for the future. This chapter begins by examining the misleading myth of Taft as a constrained, conservative president, and then reviews his use of executive action, public communication, and interbranch cooperation to achieve landmark results on a host of issues in executive branch administration, domestic policy, and international affairs.

The Taft Myth

If Grant is the most easily recognized active president among this book's three cases, Taft is the most obscured. Taft is still best known in presidency scholarship for his advocacy of a restrained presidency, even though historians and other scholars have been trying to debunk and dissolve the Taft myth for seventy years or more.[1] He famously articulated a vision of the presidency and its powers in context with Congress and the rest of the constitutional system, and the following quotation appears, as if by publishing mandate, in books on presidential power:

> The true view of the Executive functions is, as I conceive it, that the President can exercise no power which cannot be fairly and reasonably traced to some specific grant of power or justly implied and included within such express grant as proper and necessary to its exercise. Such specific grant must be either in the Federal Constitution or in an act of Congress passed in pursuance thereof. There is no undefined residuum of power which he can exercise because it seems to him in the public interest.[2]

By chronology and by philosophy, Taft is often presented as the last gasp of the nineteenth-century presidency. The quotation above is usually set against Theodore Roosevelt's aggressive exercise of presidential power, and so Taft appears as the defender of a bygone presidency tailored to a slower, older age—a "troubled president," in the words of presidential scholars Sidney M. Milkis and Michael Nelson; a "status quo president" when "the mood of the age was progressive," in the words of Michael A. Genovese.[3] Against the vigor of Roosevelt and the swirling controversies and globalism of the twentieth century, Taft is often presented as yesterday's news.

This traditional view of a doctrinaire dualism in the application of presidential prerogative, though, rests on two important fallacies. First is the idea that the presidency in the nineteenth century was a weak office, inextricably tied to the greater power of parties, the courts, or the Congress, and rarely flexing its muscles in the areas of policy development, public leadership, or administrative management and innovation. Notable presidents acted in all these fashions—George Washington, Thomas Jefferson, Andrew Jackson, James Polk, and Abraham Lincoln provide a few familiar examples. But other presidents also stood up to powerful interests, led on public issues, and directed the activities of the administrative state—John Quincy Adams and Ulysses S. Grant among them. The idea that Theodore Roosevelt's energetic presidency represents a revolutionary modernization of a "traditional" presidency is a misleading misrepresentation of U.S. political history.[4]

The second fallacy of counterpoising Roosevelt and Taft on presidential power is to anchor the analysis in that one quotation from that one passage from Taft. Taft was not a dogmatic believer in limited executive power, nor was he some kind of spongey doughball when events called on him to exert the office's authority. Taft's writings never stray into the kind of rigid formalism that many later writers ascribe to his view of presidential power. His criticism of the "undefined residuum of power which [the president] can exercise because it seems to him to be in the public interest" was a shot directed at Roosevelt's notion that, as president, *he* was the voice of the public interest—rather than Congress, the law, or the Constitution.

A few lines later in the same passage, Taft introduced a quotation from Roosevelt's secretary of interior, James R. Garfield, who told Congress that "full power under the Constitution was vested in the Executive Branch of the Government and the extent to which that power may be exercised is governed wholly by the discretion of the Executive unless any specific act has been prohibited either by the Constitution or by legislation." Taft disagreed, and followed with an extended and nuanced critique of Roosevelt's approach to the presidency. He called the Roosevelt-Garfield approach "an unsafe doctrine" that "might lead under emergencies to results of an arbitrary character, doing irremediable injustice to private right." Considering Roosevelt's actions to end the Pennsylvania coal strike in 1902, for example, Taft wrote, "The benevolence of his purpose no one can deny, but no one who looks at it from the standpoint of a government of law could regard it as anything but lawless."[5]

Taft concluded by writing that executive power does indeed enjoy legitimate grey areas, which serve as the basis for action. His closing lines make clear that an understanding of the presidency as inescapably bound by specific grants of authority in the Constitution was not Taft's position:

> The Constitution does give the President wide discretion and great power, and it ought to do so. It calls from him activity and energy to see that within his proper sphere he does what his great responsibilities and opportunities require. He is no figurehead, and it is entirely proper that an energetic and active clear-sighted people, who, when they have work to do, wish it done well, should be willing to rely upon their judgment in selecting their Chief Agent, and having selected him, should entrust to him all the power needed to carry out their governmental purpose, great as it may be.[6]

Taft, in fact, outlined a prominent executive role in the lawmaking process, writing elsewhere, "I think . . . we might advantageously give greater power to the President in the matter of legislation. One of the difficulties about a Congress—I say it with deference to that body—is that it does not know enough about the executive facts which ought to control legislation in the course of an efficient government."[7] Taft argued that Congress should give the floor to cabinet officers, allowing the president to inform and lead Congress and legislation directly.[8] Taft later supported Woodrow Wilson's return to oral delivery of messages to Congress, to help the president fix the public attention.[9] Taft explained the necessity of the executive's role in interpreting and administering statutes, arguing that Congress regularly conferred quasi-legislative and quasi-judicial authority on the president. He recommended giving the president a constitutional duty of framing a budget, developing the foundations of modern national budgeting examined in detail below. He favored limiting Congress's discretion over appropriations, and he opposed Congress's encroachments on the president's executive authority regarding dismissing executive officers (he had the last word on this as chief justice, cementing the president's dismissal powers with his opinion in *Myers v. United States*).[10] Taft believed that the president had constitutional powers which existed beyond the reach of Congress. "Taft's views on the Presidency are more or less conventional today," historian Rene N. Ballard concluded. "William Howard Taft helped to make them conventional."[11]

Taft promoted the active use of the president's veto as a tool in legislating, too, writing, "The Constitution makes the President's veto turn on the question whether he approves the bill or not. The term 'approve' is much too broad to be given the narrow construction by which it shall only authorize the President to withhold his signature when the reason for his disapproval of the bill is its invalidity." Taft argued, as did Andrew Jackson, that the president may at times better represent "the entire country" than does majority vote in both houses of Congress, and Taft stated that the president has (and should exercise) greater latitude than the Supreme Court in stopping legislation on its merits, short of a constitutional violation. He noted that only four presidents had not vetoed bills on their merits—one of them was John Quincy Adams—but he suggested that they might have benefited from friendly Congresses, open to other forms of persuasion to stop bills before they reached the president's desk. "There are other ways of killing a cat," Taft wrote, "than choking it with butter."[12] Among Taft's vetoes were that of Arizona's statehood because Taft believed its new state constitution inadequately protected judicial independence by allowing for the recall of judges, and a veto of an appropriations bill that included a provision which would have eliminated the Commerce Court that Taft's administration had worked to include in the Mann-Elkins Act.[13]

In foreign policy, Taft took an expansive view of the president's treatymaking authority, his commander-in-chief authority, and the president's role in making war, defending the landing of troops in Central America as completely justifiable under the Constitution.[14] He put forth a broad notion of the president's foreign policy authority, explained in the context of Roosevelt's involvement in Cuba and Panama.[15] While secretary of war, Taft "diverted" $2.5 million of army supplies to victims of the 1906 San Francisco earthquake, seeking and gaining legislative ratification of the move afterward—indicating his longstanding appreciation for executive action not strictly authorized by Congress.[16]

These statements and actions belie the commonly held perception of Taft as holding a passive, constrained view of executive power. Americans often forget Taft, and presidential scholars too often know him best from badly truncated quotations about the limits of presidential power.[17] Doomed to be forever contrasted with Theodore Roosevelt's radical vision of the presidency, Taft is perennially used as a foil for what we imagine about the development of presidential powers in the nineteenth and twentieth centuries. But this common view of Taft is incorrect when compared with what Taft actually said and wrote, and it is wrong when compared to what Taft actually did while president.

The synthesist, like the procedurist and the principled innovator, can deploy and defend a strong presidency. The claim by Roosevelt that he had authority to do whatever the Constitution did not explicitly forbid was, for Taft, too much. But that did not mean the president could only exercise those specific powers explicitly and specifically granted to the president by the text of the Constitution or by law. Taft's application of executive powers allowed a president to mobilize troops, negotiate arbitration agreement processes with the Senate, and push for new budgeting authority located in the presidency—but it did not, for example, allow him to seize private property without due process of law, as Roosevelt had threatened to do, and it did not allow executive officers to violate the law for what they perceived to be a higher public purpose, as he felt Roosevelt and Forest Service chief Gifford Pinchot had done in conservation. Taft's understanding did not allow him to circumvent the Senate's rejection of a treaty by signing an equivalent agreement by executive order, as Roosevelt had done with the Dominican Republic in 1905.[18]

Taft, like many presidents, made tactical choices depending on circumstances—laying back sometimes, acting more aggressively at others. He was not a passive president, though, reluctant to act, hamstrung by fealty to a doctrine of limited executive powers. Recognizing Taft as an active and engaged president, utilizing public communication, administrative leadership, and executive action tools to achieve results, is critical to understanding the relationship of the presidency and the state in the early twentieth century.

President Taft and the Administrative State

Taft used the president's authority over the administrative bureaucracy to initiate extensive reform and reorganization throughout the national government. He innovated broadly, retooling the federal machine for the twentieth century. Modernizing the government's budgeting and overseeing reform in its administrative operations set the foundations for a nation poised to become a dominant world power.

Presidential Budgeting

Taft's efforts to synthesize principled innovation with the lasting benefits of new laws, procedures, and rules is evident in the reforms he advocated related to the president's role in budgeting. Taft perceived the need for a national budget at a time when there was no overarching budget mechanism at the national level. He argued for locating central budgeting authority in the presidency, and he persuaded Congress to authorize a commission to study budgeting. Taft's efforts would eventually culminate in the landmark Budget and Accounting Act of 1921 and the institutionalization of the president's budget authority, a key foundation for twentieth-century presidential power. Taft's actions were creative, aggressive, and at the center of an ongoing argument about institutional powers related to the vast federal administrative state. Taft extended the presidency's scope and influence in the budget process, marrying principled innovation with measures destined for lasting procedural effectiveness.

Before Taft, each administrative agency sent its own budget requests to the Treasury Department, which just forwarded them to Congress. In 1909, Taft and the cabinet reviewed the departments' requests and cut $92 million from them before they were sent to Congress. This became what historian Donald F. Anderson calls "the first budget in modern American history."[19] In 1910, Taft asked for and received $100,000 from Congress to fund a Commission on Economy and Efficiency, which would examine budgeting issues across the federal government. The study was conducted by officials with deep experience analyzing public and private organizations and administration, such as Major Charles Hine, who had conducted similar studies for the Harriman railroad lines; Frederick Cleveland, famous for his work in New York's Bureau of Municipal Research; and Merritt Chance, a Washington insider who had experience at the Post Office and the War and Treasury Departments.[20] The commission also requested advice early on from "various firms specializing in accounting or business efficiency," including organizations that had produced studies of the Treasury Department, Interior Department, U.S. Navy, and Department of Justice over the years.[21] The focus on budgeting was new, but the idea of studying government and reorganizing for improved efficiency was not: government reorganization studies at the federal level go back to as early as 1789, both within the executive branch and stemming from Congress.[22]

Taft led his new effort directly, coordinating activity and ordering cooperation within the government. He ordered departments to form supporting committees and he set out a division of labor, in a manner reminiscent of his leadership of the Philippines commission. Taft reassured subordinates that the effort aimed at improving efficiency and government services, not at highlighting individual errors or harming people's careers.[23] As the initial inquiry evolved into the formal commission, Taft publicized the effort and worked to oversee its operations. Taft's initiatives on budgeting were laid out in careful and detailed public communications in his Second Annual Message, in a special message to Congress issued January 17, 1912, and in a special message to Congress on April 4, 1912.[24] Taft's public statements focused on detail and specifics, including General Technical Services, which was responsible for matters like repairs of government facilities, lighting, and transportation. He discussed a ridiculous amount of detail: the abolition of local offices and the classification of local officers, the cost of handling filing correspondence, the benefits of flat filing over folded paper, the office device exposition, the cost of copy work, insurance and travel costs, and waste in the distribution of public documents (sent from the Government Publishing Office all over the District of Columbia, only to return back to Union Station—a block away from the Government Publishing Office). He outlined proposals for improved purchasing, accounting, and reporting. The commission also recommended budget reform and expansion of presidential appointment powers within the executive branch.[25] The presentation was clear and accessible, rivaling John Quincy Adams's report on weights and measures in its precision and care. Both reflect the long tradition at the federal level of careful study and detailed reform analysis.

Wrapping all of this together, Taft offered a vision of a coordinated national budget emanating from the executive branch and from the agencies. Focusing as always on process and procedure, searching for systems that would run efficiently and effectively, and tying his innovations to the procedures and traditions of the past, Taft highlighted the fact that the vast operations of the government had never yet been studied systematically "as one piece of administrative mechanism."[26] He closed his argument with reference to the full-time expertise being employed at the city level and among private corporations to achieve similar ends—and he advocated for a full-time, funded commission to look into such matters for the federal government. Taft also noted the time it took to do such a study and arrive at significant conclusions based on careful evaluation. True to form, Taft emphasized the work of the commission to that point as an important work in progress, the benefits of which would be reaped in good time.

In 1912, Taft ordered the departments to follow a new process and submit their budgets through the commission before they went to Congress. Congress balked, belatedly perceiving the threat to its traditional turf in spending decisions. In August 1912, Congress attached to a civil bill a provision requiring that departments submit their budget estimates in the manner provided by Congress and in no other way, an effort to close off the route through the commission and the presidency. This sparked a constitutional dispute over core powers. Taft saw Congress's move as a threat to executive power: "Under the Constitution," he wrote during the fight, "the President is entrusted with the executive power, and is responsible for the acts of heads of department, and their subordinates as his agents, and he can use them to assist him in his constitutional duties, one of which is to recommend measures to Congress, and to advise it as to the existing conditions and their betterment."[27]

Taft engineered a workaround, instructing secretaries to obey Congress's provision but also to conform with his previous order to report through the commission. Taft accepted the reports and submitted the president's budget to Congress. He reasoned that departments must obey the law but, simultaneously, the president has a constitutional responsibility to submit to Congress "a regular statement and account of the receipts and expenditures." "The President," Taft later wrote, "who is the man that is responsible for the executive departments, ought to have the independent means of finding out through a body of experts whether or not a department is asking more than it ought to have."[28]

Taft defended his advocacy of systemic reform even as Congress ignored his submitted budget. A useful study had been produced by Taft's commission, but Congress withdrew the appropriation, much as it had starved Grant's efforts to implement civil service reform. "The Commission, however, did a great deal of most useful work," Taft wrote in the effort's epitaph, "and while the dust is accumulating on their reports at present, their investigations and conclusions were of permanent value, and some day they will be made the basis for further investigation and for definite measures of reform."[29] Taft's understanding of the long path to reform prevailed. His conclusions about the wisdom and improved efficiency of presidential budgeting were codified in the 1921 Budget and Accounting Act, for which Taft "deserves the credit," in the words of historian Rene N. Ballard.[30] The 1921 act modernized and solidified the president's central role in policy and spending decisions.[31]

Reform in the Bureaucracy

While Taft was no radical reformer in the spheres of Indian affairs, civil rights, immigration, religious minorities, or children's and women's issues, in all of these areas he worked through executive action and administrative leadership to encourage innovation.

Taft appointed the first woman to head a federal agency when, at the end of his presidency, he named Chicago-based reformer Julia Lathrop to head the brand-new Children's Bureau. Lathrop came from the settlement movement of Jane Addams and Florence Kelley, who were leading an effort to support and enhance the lives of people in inner cities, people in poverty, and people in other states of distress. Using statistics, data, and evidence to identify problems and craft appropriate, effective solutions, the settlement movement served as the foundation of many later efforts, public and private alike, to bring relief to inner cities with the same kind of Progressive-era approach to data that was driving Taft's presidential budgeting reforms. But as with the commission on efficiency, such use of "data" was hardly new in the Progressive era—the Indian service, for example, had long tracked various data points, now recognized as problematically ethnocentric, to track "improvement" among Native American populations, and John Quincy Adams had included cross-country comparisons in his report on weights and measures, leading him to conclude that adopting a metric system in the United States probably would not work.

In the case of the Children's Bureau, evidence suggested that children were in considerable danger in the United States, and Lathrop was among those advocating for creation of a new federal agency that would address the needs of children. The movement focused on the benefits to be had from a federal effort to tie together evidence and information about the nation's children, at the national level, where information could be aggregated and then disseminated for the benefit of Americans across the country. Activists pointed out that the federal government spent millions of dollars each year identifying and addressing problems of chickens—surely the same could be done for children.[32] The reformers got their agency, a permanent and forward-looking reform, and Taft was responsible for nominating its first chief. When the advocates settled on Lathrop as their choice—knowing that there existed no precedent for a woman heading a federal agency—Taft, ever-mindful of procedure, law, and tradition, asked Attorney General George Wickersham to determine whether there were any legal obstacles to the appointment of a woman. When Wickersham responded that he could find none, Taft went ahead with the appointment.[33] Even this mold-cracking appointment process had earlier precedent—Grant had asked *his* attorney general if there were any legal prohibitions on appointing an American Indian, Ely Parker, to head the Indian Office.[34]

Lathrop and the Children's Bureau left a lasting legacy. Among its successes were popular government pamphlets on mothering, for years the government's best-selling publications. The agency served as the first federal effort to focus attention on children, an effectively unrepresented group that had clear interests but few organized advocates. While Taft was not at the leading edge of the work being done on behalf of women, children, and the poor, he was able to use executive tools available to him through public commentary and a newly inclusive application of the appointment process to assist.[35]

Taft also used the appointment process to address racism. In the midst of the Jim Crow era, Taft in 1910 appointed William Henry Lewis, the first African American to serve as deputy U.S. assistant attorney general. Lewis overcame opposition to his nomination in the Senate and served from 1911 to 1913 in the highest post attained, to that time, by an African American. Taft is often criticized for not appointing more Blacks to federal posts, but the newspaper *The Freeman* editorialized in January 1910 that Taft was doing much more, and perhaps more important, work on behalf of Blacks in the United States. "Offices isn't everything to the race," the paper quoted one source as saying. "The men we now have at the helm are rendering gilt-edged service; why displace them for others who have neither their experience as officers nor their record as useful party leaders. . . . The President is doing some substantial things for the race that show his concern as to our well-being quite as effective as the handing out of a few jobs to individuals. He is doing a larger service for our people than the mere distribution of patronage." The writer cited Taft's efforts to battle the Strauss amendment in Maryland, which aimed to disenfranchise Black voters; his support of a bill promoting an exhibit at the semi-centennial exposition that would highlight the advances made by Blacks since emancipation; and his dedication to reimbursing the depositors of the defunct Freedmen's Bank, "in which the erstwhile ward of the nation was induced to place his savings . . . under a government guarantee of its soundness."[36]

As president, Taft also served on the board of the Jeanes Fund, the legacy of the late Philadelphia philanthropist Anna Jeanes, who left $1 million to improve education for Black children in southern rural areas. Taft invited the fund to hold its principal session at the White House, and in 1910 the board aimed to employ 152 teachers, covering 1,600 schools and 132 colleges.[37] Taft did not lead the fight for racial equality, but he added his efforts beneath the headlines. With appeals for racial justice and his work with Blacks, Taft "went further than would any president or presidential candidate down to Franklin

Roosevelt in seeking the political support of a once-enslaved people," writes Taft expert David H. Burton.[38]

Taft oversaw and encouraged reform at the Interior Department as well. He did not have a grand vision for Indian affairs in the Progressive era, a time characterized by a mélange of policies that its primary historian has called "the great confusion."[39] The era is too easily seen as merely the expression of an ideology of assimilation, though. Policies stemming from the period between Grant and Taft did indeed aim at breaking up tribal governments and distributing tribal lands to individual Natives and non-Natives. Assimilation programs sought to destroy Indigenous religions, languages, and lifeways. Reformers and "friends of the Indian" advocated boarding schools to teach Natives skills and trades but often did great damage to individuals and communities. While these are the dominant lines in the era's Indian affairs, and they get the most attention from historians, the Progressive era was also the birthplace of many of the reforms that would be celebrated when they came to fruition during the New Deal. Protection and encouragement of Native crafts and languages, support for Native governments and sovereignty, support for Native trade, and an attention to Indian health all took place in this era, especially during the Taft administration, as Taft's appointees slowly reoriented the Bureau of Indian Affairs away from the destruction of Natives and cultures and toward their protection and support.[40]

As an example, Taft's commissioner of Indian affairs, Robert Valentine, focused on assimilation but also on using Progressive approaches to efficiency, expertise, and economy to improve education and health outcomes. There were complex and arguably darker motives here—just as U.S. vaccination efforts protecting Natives against smallpox had sometimes been used to help facilitate U.S. removal efforts, Valentine was driven to improve health outcomes among Natives because he believed ill health hindered the efficient administration of assimilation policies on the reservations and placed nearby white settlers in danger.[41] Taft requested that the U.S. Public Health Service report on health status in Indian country, and Valentine pressed Congress to increase appropriations for treatment and prevention efforts fivefold between 1910 and 1912.[42] Valentine also worked for improved professionalism and accountability among the Indian Service's personnel, especially its schools and teachers. He tried to protect Native interests by auditing traders' claims for unpaid debts in an effort to identify and eliminate fraudulent claims, and he worked with the General Land Office to collect grazing fees due Native nations. He supported Indian rights to water on the Gila River Reservation and elsewhere, deep in the middle of one of the region's most contentious issues, and he restored to the Mescalero, Navajo, and other southwestern nations 2.5 million acres of forest land that had been seized by Theodore Roosevelt to create national forests two days before the end of Roosevelt's presidency. In tune with the Taft administration's penchant for legal processes, Valentine supported admitting Native claims to the U.S. Court of Claims and later advocated the creation of a specially constituted body to hear Native claims—an idea that reached fruition in 1946 with the creation of the Indian Claims Commission.[43]

Taft was personally involved in Indian affairs at key points. He sent Congress a special message on Indian health in 1912, explaining Valentine's efforts and requesting increases in funding.[44] In December 1910, Taft redrew treaty boundaries in Minnesota following public protests against Valentine's enforcement of treaty-based restrictions against liquor sales in three-fourths of the state. In February 1912, Taft revoked a circular issued by Valentine prohibiting religious garb or insignia from being worn by reservation school teachers; that circular had particularly offended Catholic nuns teaching at former mission schools.[45] Taft, like Grant, signed dozens of executive orders that reserved lands for Native nations.[46] When Taft issued a proclamation establishing the Navajo National Monument, he pulled no punches: "Warning is hereby expressly given to all unauthorized persons not to appropriate, excavate, injure, or destroy any of the ruins or relics hereby declared to be a national monument, or to locate or settle upon any of the lands reserved and made a part of this monument by this proclamation."[47]

Taft likewise advocated for the interests of immigrants and religious minorities. His postal savings bank initiative worked to immigrants' benefit and, in important ways, was built on their experiences, as detailed below. But Taft went beyond that, arguing vocally throughout his career that the federal government had an obligation to ensure the safety of aliens within the United States. After the 1912 election, Taft vetoed a restrictive immigration bill that included a literacy test and other means of excluding immigrants from the United States. He publicly argued that obligations in federal treaties made immigration a federal, not a state, matter.[48]

From 1909 to 1913, a time when discrimination followed immigrants and Natives, when Jim Crow laws dominated the landscape, and when women could not vote, Taft nudged the federal government toward race and gender equality. We need not press the matter too far: Taft was not an outspoken advocate of woman suffrage, he did not tackle Jim Crow head-on, and he did not seek fundamental reform of Indian affairs in the heart of the assimilation and allotment era. Many of his innovative acts here were situational, akin to Grant's efforts to respond to the locusts or to help James Webster Smith at West Point. But Taft acted strategically and effectively while staying true to a focus on traditions and established protocols. Lathrop and Lewis, for example, were experienced leaders, effective public servants, and collaborative managers, reflections of Taft himself. Lathrop's success at the Children's Bureau and the fight over the future direction of U.S. Indian policy established lasting, innovative foundations, just as the work of Attorney General George Wickersham, Interior Secretary Richard Ballinger, and others complemented Taft's collaborative, measured, and purposeful approach to active governance.[49] Social policy advocates, Black editors, and immigrant and Native American advocates alike respected Taft's use of appointments, executive tools, and public communication to forge new policies, programs, and departments.

As THE foregoing suggests, Taft's leadership fostered an organizational culture supportive of reform throughout his administration. At the State Department, Taft and his appointees updated the department's offices and procedures, reorganized State's offices and divisions, created an Asia section, and established Asia desks at existing bureaus. New divisions were created to focus on the Far East, the Near East, Latin America, and Western Europe, and a professional Foreign Service was created. A Division of Information was formed, legal advisors added, and the Bureau of Trade Relations expanded. The reorganization built a chief of staff system for organizational clarity, and an executive order instituted a merit system for foreign service officers. Taft and Secretary of State Philander Knox oversaw revisions of guidelines and hiring practices and reorganized the department's filing system so that it more reasonably and effectively matched the agency's business.[50] At the Department of the Navy, four permanent bureaus were established to handle naval operations, personnel, inspections, and materiel. Shipyards were reorganized and new budgeting procedures implemented. The Army Reserve was created at the War Department, and a comprehensive reform and reorganization begun. Taft broadened civil service protections for the federal workforce, particularly for postmasters, incorporating seventy thousand federal workers into the civil service, despite Congress's opposition at losing so many points of patronage, and he placed officials in the diplomatic corps up to embassy secretaries under a merit system and required examinations for appointment and promotion.[51]

Taft extended his focus on personnel into the judiciary: his appointments to the Supreme Court shared his views on the Constitution and governance and sought to expand Republican influence in the South. His appointments of Horace Lurton and Joseph Lamar helped pave the way for the Court's eventual acceptance of the constitutionality of Roosevelt-Taft reforms in the area of conservation.[52] Taft's appointees also paved the way for Court acceptance of Taft's interpretation of the Sherman Antitrust Act. Innovating again, Taft was the first president to appoint a new chief justice from among the sitting members of the Court. His circuit court appointments also reflected his views of the Constitution and governance, and emphasized judicial professionalism more than patronage for party or partisan allies.⁵³

Taft seeded his administration with people who were competent, experienced experts dedicated as much to Taft's understanding of the importance of procedural fairness and the rule of law as they were to Taft's progressive conservatism. He embraced the future, buying automobiles for the presidency, promoting the industry, and happily chugging about DC in experimental steam- and gasoline-powered cars after years in which Roosevelt had remained loyal to the horse.⁵⁴ Taft modernized the presidency, working to enshrine innovative approaches to national budgeting and administration in clearly defined rules and procedures.⁵⁵

President Taft and the Progressive State

Taft's major policy accomplishments and initiatives—among them conservation; international arbitration treaties; and reforms encompassing the tariff, taxation, and campaign finance—are addressed in detail in the next chapter. But that list is augmented by a variety of little-known or long-forgotten efforts by Taft to use his administration's experts, executive tools, and legislative actions to build new and enduring programs and processes, and to protect core institutions of republican governance. In a tense era, facing a fragmented Congress and a fractured Republican Party, President Taft laid out a host of initiatives including worker protections and postal savings banks, he influenced governance reform in Puerto Rico, and he worked to protect the independence of the judiciary.⁵⁶ Taft's approach to synthesizing law and principle never overlooked the human connections endemic to successful politics. He was driven by basic priorities: peace over war; restraint over aggression; cooperation over dominance. "The ultimate purpose of government and its limitations must be conceded to be the same," Taft wrote, "the promotion of the happiness of the average individual and his progress."⁵⁷ Taft's record as president is of many measures proposed, many measures enacted, and with the kind of detail that often frustrates entertaining narrative. Taft's focus throughout his career centered on demonstrable achievement.

The chances for success were not good, in large part because of the fragmentation of the Republican Party that resulted from Roosevelt's presidency.⁵⁸ Still, the legislative session that ended in June 1910 was characterized at the time, and by scholars since, as one of the most successful since the 1860s. Taft's leadership was critical to that success.⁵⁹ To see Taft as merely a manager, as many scholars have, ignores the leadership Taft exercised in articulating and pushing through a fractured Congress a diverse array of active, progressive legislation.

Taft did not shrink from recognizing, and publicizing, the federal government's responsibility to protect its citizens from harm. Throughout his presidential career, Taft trumpeted the legitimate role of the government in providing for the health and safety of workers. The Railroad Act, for example, restricted the working hours of train and telegraph operators, and improved inspections and health and safety requirements.[60] Taft argued that the bill was not only in the interests of workers but also in the interests of railroad companies by clarifying and making more uniform their operating environments and responsibilities. Taft promoted a worker's compensation bill, which addressed accidental injuries to employees or common carriers in the railroad industry, to provide predictability to railroads and standardize fair procedures. He laid out the details of his worker's compensation bill in a special message to Congress in February 1912.[61]

Taft oversaw a tightening of the Food and Drug Act, and he supported the complicated Payne-Aldrich tariff, a controversial measure discussed in more detail in the next chapter. He signed the historic Weeks Act in 1911, which appropriated $9 million for federal land purchases in the interests of conservation. One of numerous efforts to provide long-term legal stability to the conservation movement, the Weeks Act initially authorized purchase of 6 million acres of land in pursuit of conservation, wetlands protection, and fire control following the "year of the fires" in 1910. Over the next century, the act facilitated the creation of fifty-two national forests and the addition of close to 20 million acres of land. Discussion of the Weeks Bill in Congress was intentionally quiet, as Taft worked to secure legislation instead of working to inflame public awareness.[62]

Taft's Railroad Rate Bill became the landmark Mann-Elkins Act in 1910. Passage of the bill gave the Interstate Commerce Commission considerable authority to regulate railroads and codified "one of the most important Roosevelt policies to which he had been pledged."[63] The reforms empowered the commission to suspend or fix railroad rates and control facilities in radio, telephone, and telegraph, making it the precursor to the landmark 1934 Telecommunications Act. Taft secured passage of the bill despite fragmentation in Congress, and helped craft a bill satisfactory even to railroad interests, in part because the bill aimed to protect corporate interests and rights.[64] Mann-Elkins included penalties for disclosing information about railroad shipments when that information could be used to injure a shipper in favor of a competitor; it also made it unlawful to solicit such information.[65]

Consistent with Taft's focus on marrying innovation and procedure, Mann-Elkins also included a new Commerce Court to hear appeals. Taft wanted to ensure that there was a quasi-traditional judicial process to oversee the Interstate Commerce Commission's decisions, and the Commerce Court was designed to hear appeals of commission decisions—thus balancing the move toward strengthening a nominally independent commission with judicial review. Taft enjoyed industry support for the initiative, and (as expected) staffed the new Commerce Court with industry-friendly experts who were expected to temper any more radical actions by the newly strengthened commission. In some ways, the bill codified earlier, fundamental changes in the government's regulatory powers; in others it added new procedures and mechanisms, taking the government into new areas of operation. Taft led these reforms, having pushed them during the 1908 campaign and then, after his election, introducing legislation into Congress.[66]

TAFT'S SUPPORT for postal savings banks may be among his most intriguing initiatives, and it was one to which he returned again and again in speeches and messages. The Taft years preceded the widespread availability of savings banks, meaning that people had trouble saving and earning interest and that accumulating capital in developing regions of the country remained difficult. Officials at the Post Office had advocated for postal savings banks since the Grant administration, but little came of their efforts until Taft was in the White House. Over those forty years or so, the basic idea had changed little—what brought the plan to fruition in 1910 was the lobbying of a respected set of public servants at the Post Office and "the enthusiasm of Taft," in the words of political scientist Daniel P. Carpenter.[67] Taft pushed the idea during the 1908 campaign, proposing a $1,000 cap on individual deposits, with a required 2 percent quarterly interest payment from the postmaster general to depositors. The savings would be invested by the postmaster general, with the assistance of the attorney general and the treasury secretary, in a national bank in the same place where the deposit was received, or the one nearest the neighborhood of the deposit; if that proved impossible, then the money would be invested in local town, county, or state bonds. The government's investment could reap no more than 2.25 percent.[68] Initiating what Carpenter calls "arguably the most intrepid bureaucratic intrusion into private finance since the Second Bank of the United States," in 1910 Taft signed a postal savings bank bill that returned 2 percent on deposits.[69]

Taft supported the proposal based on an argument for the necessity of government involvement in areas where private capital would not, or had not yet, tread. He pointed out that while the East enjoyed the benefits of numerous banks and easily accessed locations, in only eleven of forty-five states did savings banking facilities even exist. In the Midwest the average distance from a post office to a bank of any kind was thirty-three miles; west of the Rockies the average distance was fifty-five miles. Taft invoked successes with postal savings banks in England and Europe, emphasizing that the plan would particularly aid immigrants, many of whom were familiar with such systems. He also pointed out that the United States had introduced such an idea successfully in the Philippines: "No private banking enterprise could possibly afford to establish savings banks throughout the thirty-five states where they have none, equal to the number of money-order offices.... These are all reasons for making it a Government matter." The banks would help ordinary people save; they would help business and banking grow and expand, providing money for investment; they would help immigrants adjust and assimilate; and they would help prevent runs on the banks by those small depositors who were skittish during banking panics.[70]

Taft noted in his Third Annual Message just how popular the system had become. After eleven months of operation, deposits had swollen to $11 million, distributed by more than 150,000 depositors across more than 2,700 banks, and Taft pointedly highlighted that the depositors represented 40 nationalities.[71] In his final annual message, in December 1912, Taft noted that the system had almost 13,000 depositories available, 300,000 depositors, and approximately $28 million in deposits.[72] By 1917, the system attracted more than $100 million in deposits at the U.S. Post Office.[73]

Taft's advances in postal service, in the interests of empowering ordinary American citizens, also included creation of a parcel post system—against opponents who feared that it would harm private carriers—and a rural delivery initiative, designed to bring U.S. postal service itself to isolated areas. Taft's explanation for these measures is clear evidence of his understanding of the needs of American citizens, of what might improve their lives, and of how it was government's responsibility to build capacity in areas underserved by private capital.

TAFT USED presidential tools clearly and aggressively in a variety of other issue areas. His response as president to an appropriations crisis in Puerto Rico reflected his willingness to act in divisive circumstances. Faced with a split in the island's leadership between independence advocates and interests aligned with its status as a U.S. territory, Taft provided complex administrative arrangements similar in many ways to those he had overseen in the Philippines. His earlier experience influenced his policy approaches to Puerto Rico, and the complexity of both situations suggests the deep expertise available to the president. Taft relied on his longtime aid George Colton, worked with Congress directly, and saw Congress pass his measure. Presidential control and influence over Puerto Rico set deeper, with Taft passing responsibilities on to the War Department and appointing Colton governor. Taft again used active measures, including public messaging, legislative action, and appointment powers.[74]

Taft utilized his veto most dramatically in defense of a core value of the American system, the independence of the judiciary. Taft vetoed the statehood petition of Arizona because Arizona's proposed constitution included provisions allowing for the recall of its judges. Taft repeatedly argued his case that such a measure threatened the people of Arizona, and should the idea grow in popularity, the people of the nation as a whole. Taft wrote, "I am discharging my constitutional function in respect to the enactment of laws, and my discretion is equal to that of the Houses of Congress.... [W]hen such a [proposed state] constitution contains something so destructive of free government as the judicial recall, it should be disapproved."[75] Taft discoursed here and elsewhere on the role of the independent judiciary and the important place of minority political interests, in passages reminiscent of James Madison's argument in *Federalist 10*. He wrote that good judges were *not* popular representatives,[76] nor were they supposed to act as a second legislature. He pointed out the danger of allowing popular passions and quick action to supersede judicial reflection, and suggested that such a recall system would invite pernicious control by unscrupulous political bosses and exacerbate the influence of muckraking journalism.[77] Later, he would defend the judiciary against Theodore Roosevelt's calls for judicial recall.[78]

In his final major domestic policy recommendation to Congress and the nation, Taft laid the groundwork for another enduring innovation: the Federal Reserve system. Long associated more with Woodrow Wilson than with Taft, it was Taft who first outlined reforms to create a path to national financial coherence and managed effectiveness. As always, Taft explained the constitutional issue, history, and argument for such reform, tying this to his perception of the needs of wage earners and their interest in a "safe and sane" banking and currency system.[79] Wilson embraced the measure, but its design owes far more to Taft.

All of these progressive measures aimed to protect the public—from overwork, fires, rural isolation, financial chaos—and to empower them—to earn, to save, to create and run small businesses. All combined innovative ideas with attention to lasting legislation and enduring procedural detail—the essence of the synthesist as president. Taft's legislative agenda remained remarkably consistent from the 1908 campaign through his presidency. By spring 1910, Taft's postal savings bill had been enacted; a conservation bill had been enacted, along with the 1910 General Dam Act; campaign finance regulation had been enacted; the Interstate Commerce Commission had been strengthened through Mann-Elkins; and a Commerce Court created.[80] A national deficit of roughly $57 million in 1908 had turned into an $11 million surplus by 1911.[81]

President Taft and International Affairs

In Asian, Latin American, and Canadian relations, Taft sought to advance American interests and did so with the creativity and purpose that he demonstrated in the contexts of administrative reform and domestic affairs. Taft's creative, pragmatic approaches to exercising presidential power appeared in narrower matters as well, such as protection for Jews in Russia, administration of the Panama Canal, and avoiding war with Mexico. Taft's efforts reflected a vision of an active, innovative presidency operating globally.

Critics see dollar diplomacy as an American-centered effort to use the nation's wealth and power to exploit weaker regions and peoples to the benefit of the United States and, often, its corporate interests. Taft argued that the goals were to focus on engagement, diplomacy, and trade, to benefit U.S. strategic and economic interests, stimulate commerce, and help provide stability and protection to the people of other nations.[82] Improving trade, expanding markets for American goods, and furthering the global reach of American finance and values were complementary priorities in the Taft years, as they had been for many previous presidents, including John Quincy Adams and Ulysses S. Grant. Taft worked to orient U.S. foreign policy behind a set of principles and procedures that would regularize and stabilize international relations with these goals in mind, but he paid particular attention to areas of the globe that he believed would be important to the United States in coming decades. Taft innovated in some areas, applying presidential effort in new ways. Without trying to untangle complex goals and controversies over motives and effects, and over assessing the relative weight of economic, political, strategic, and social purposes, we can take note of Taft's use of executive authority and executive action tools to pursue foreign policy.[83]

Taft foresaw big opportunities in Asia, especially China, and he expended considerable effort to enhance the position of the United States. "The great field of diplomatic care, attention and activity for the next thirty or forty years, so far as this country is concerned," Taft told an audience in January 1909, "is likely to be in the far Orient."[84] Taft's vision represented practical consideration for future generations, an effort to anticipate the future of world trade patterns.[85] The president's goal was to encourage American business and banking to enter China, to convince the Chinese government to let them in, and to force a wedge into the Four Powers' Open Door Policy that would propel the United States to the forefront of international economic growth, trade, banking, and finance.

Business leaders were not excited. China was in the last years of its dynastic period; it was perceived as a bad investment, and many feared that the central government would inevitably cede power to the provinces. Moreover, any activity favoring China entered a hornet's nest of international power politics involving not only France, England, and Germany but Russia, Japan, and Korea as well. It was risky; for example, E. H. Harriman had tried for years to gain enough support in China to extend a railroad across Manchuria, in the hope of creating a worldwide railway network, but he had seen little success.

Taft worked on three major endeavors in China: the Hukuang loan to finance railroad construction in the Yangtze Valley; the Chin-Ai Railway project, in which Taft worked to have American railroaders included in an effort to make of Manchuria a peaceful, neutral, international commercial zone; and a comprehensive currency loan to China.[86] Taft's process in these matters was strictly diplomatic; reading accounts of the very long and detailed negotiations reveals virtually no sense of pressure or foreboding—the negotiations were just negotiations. When they fell through, Taft refused to force his will or the nation's interest; he also refused to carp about wasted effort.[87]

In these negotiations, Taft innovated and proved surprisingly nimble. During the Hukuang loan negotiations, for example, Taft took the extraordinary action of contacting directly the Chinese government leader Prince Chun to express that he was disturbed at reports of Chinese opposition to U.S. involvement in the loan. The direct communication was highly unusual and illustrates both the significance Taft attached to the matter and his willingness to take action that cut new tracks in presidential diplomacy. Taft's action, taken at exactly the right time, secured U.S. involvement in the loan and established American finance as a player in China.[88] The Chin-Ai Railway project is generally seen as a failure, and the comprehensive currency loan failed to get an American named the loan's financial advisor, but Taft did manage to secure American financiers as the loan's backers.[89] Taft's China policy is thought of as largely unsuccessful in opening China to U.S. power, but it succeeded in improving the United States' standing with the major powers and in solidifying a role for the United States in international politics in Asia.

TAFT'S EFFORTS on behalf of American traders, companies, and citizens also drove his policy in Latin America, the centerpiece of dollar diplomacy's historiography. In nation after nation, Taft used diplomatic negotiation and commerce to build alliances, serve and promote American business interests, and empower citizens in America and abroad. Taft offered numerous lists reviewing his successful efforts and innovations in Latin America, including agreements on patents and trademarks, use of arbitration to resolve pecuniary claims, and even the purchase of American-made battleships by Argentina. This particular deal not only drew the two nations together and pushed European nations out; it helped American shipbuilders in a competitive market.

Taft promoted and secured millions of dollars in private American loans to Argentina, Guatemala, and Haiti, and contracts for submarines with Chile and Peru, for small warships with Brazil, and for railroad equipment with Argentina. He claimed a total of $50 million in new business—along with, perhaps more importantly, diplomatic benefits and advantages to the United States' geopolitical position in Latin America. Taft touted his good offices in helping resolve disputes between Peru and Ecuador, with the aid of Brazil, Argentina, and Chile.[90]

Taft's administration sent troops to influence affairs in Nicaragua and Honduras, flashpoints for dollar diplomacy's critics.[91] Secretary of State Philander Knox believed Nicaragua might be headed toward revolution. Emphasizing American input into choosing port collectors and insisting on privatization of railroads and other infrastructure, the Taft team used a military presence of 2,700 marines to influence outcomes after Juan Estrada seized power. Taft justified the action as acceptable because the United States was asked to help by Nicaragua's president, and Taft signed a 1911 agreement regularizing relations.[92]

Taft's focus on law and procedure was also a regular part of dollar diplomacy, however; Taft and his top team of Knox and others were "lawyers, not intellectual aristocrats like Roosevelt and Root," in the words of diplomatic historian Richard H. Collin.[93] Taft's team tried to build a claims commission in Nicaragua in 1911, for example, an innovative effort aimed at providing stability and impartial review of claims. Initially designed as a Nicaraguan court with two members from the United States and one from Nicaragua, the idea hit snags in Congress. Taft fell back on a deal worked out with American bankers and the government of Nicaragua to create a claims court immediately, with members appointed by the Nicaraguan government but only after being nominated by American bankers and approved by the U.S. secretary of state.[94] In Mexico, Taft removed ethically challenged operator David Thompson as ambassador to Mexico, replacing him with another active operator, the more reliable Henry Lane Wilson, as he tried to reestablish responsible oversight and supervision.[95]

In Honduras, fears of British involvement stemming from debt problems led the Taft team to intervene, guaranteeing loans and funds to stabilize the Honduran economy but leading to ongoing influence from American private financiers.[96] In Taft's view, the Honduras and Nicaragua efforts both aimed at ensuring those nations' financial stability so as to keep European powers out, promote investment, and secure U.S. control. The United States set itself up as guarantor of private loans to the countries. By securing the customs houses, Taft believed that revolution could be prevented, peace secured, American interests and investments protected, and commerce promoted.

It is in these types of efforts that critics have seen the heavy hand of U.S. imperialism and dominance. Taft argued that the long tradition of the Monroe Doctrine, often upheld by the *threat* of force, allowed the United States to perpetuate its commitment peacefully: "Our constant upholding and assertion of the Doctrine have enabled us, with the conflicting interests of European powers—the support of some and the acquiescence of others—to give effect to the Doctrine for now nearly a century, and that without the firing of a single shot." If the United States were to abandon the doctrine, Taft predicted, "it would be but a very short time before we would be forced into controversies that would be much more dangerous to the peace of this hemisphere than our continued assertion of the Doctrine properly understood and limited." "It is a national asset," he wrote, "and, indeed, an asset of the highest value for those who would promote the peace of the world."[97] The principles were traditional ones to Taft, sound and tested for almost a century. Crafting new and innovative agreements and arrangements would allow relations to stay current and address novel issues through negotiation and procedure.

WITH CANADA, Taft worked to bring about a reciprocity treaty that would have ensured free trade across the countries' borders. Anticipating the North American Free Trade Agreement by eighty years, Taft explained the benefits to be had by trading on a free-trade basis with Canada. The agreement that Taft submitted to Congress in January 1911 reduced duties on some products and eliminated them on others, in both directions across the border. Taft predicted that the effort might "blow me up politically," but he believed it to be good policy.[98]

Senate Republicans split on the treaty, leaving Taft in need of Democratic support in the Senate to secure passage. Even odder was Taft's association with the protectionist wing of the Republican Party. Taft's conclusion was that the future benefits to the arrangement far outweighed the costs to the nation as a whole. He was willing to lead the fight for it, even though it faced powerful opponents. The bill passed in the spring of 1911, in a significant victory for Taft.[99] In the end, the treaty was scuttled by two events out of Taft's control. Democratic House leader Champ Clark blundered into a statement that could be read as indicating his view that the treaty would redound to the disadvantage of Canada and diminish Canada into something of an American protectorate, fomenting Canadian opposition to the deal. Subsequent elections in Canada brought to power a government opposed to the treaty, and the initiative collapsed.[100]

In the short term, Taft's effort at Canadian reciprocity might be deemed a failure. But a main argument of the synthesist as president is focus on the long term. Taft's efforts on behalf of free trade with Canada, for better or worse, stand in a long line of American efforts to improve trade relations and secure trading partners. The "failure" here, like that of Taft's China policy, illustrates the work of the synthesist as much as the successes.

TAFT'S WILLINGNESS to apply presidential powers in foreign policy can perhaps best be seen in three more closely defined cases: protecting Jews in Russia, Panama Canal tolls, and avoiding war with Mexico.

Taft helped protect the rights of Jews in Russia by unilaterally abrogating an 1832 treaty between the United States and Russia over the then-highly publicized issue of Russian mistreatment of Jews. In the event, Taft outmaneuvered a Congress that was about to opt out of the treaty immediately. Recognizing the threat such congressional action posed to presidential supremacy in foreign affairs and diplomacy, and to the confidence other nations would have in American commitments, Taft gave public notice that he, as president, would take the United States out of the treaty in a year's time. Taft protected executive power and made his point on behalf of Russian Jews clearly and definitively.[101] This action, admirable though it may have been, damaged Taft's efforts to extend dollar diplomacy to the region, as the protection of Jews in Russia complicated efforts to build political and commercial relationships.

Taft had been working toward improving relations with Turkey as well, sending the experienced Oscar Straus to Turkey with the mandate to shift American efforts toward promoting commerce instead of protecting U.S. citizens. Straus's more traditional approach clashed with Taft's novel goals, though, complicating the initiative. Efforts to build relationships in Persia failed, too: Taft was likely behind the mission of William Morgan Shuster to go to Persia as a private financial advisor. Taft and Shuster had worked together in the Philippines, and when leaders in Persia asked the United States for help in stabilizing their economy, Taft reportedly recommended that Shuster go as a private citizen. Shuster's checkered career in Persia created no lasting gains. The effort to build relations and commercial exchanges with Russia, Turkey, and Persia, then, showed few lasting effects, but in each case Taft displayed his willingness to innovate and push boundaries in pursuit of long-term goals.[102]

Taft's efforts on behalf of American shipping in the case of tolls for the Panama Canal provide a good illustration of the synthesist at work on everyday foreign affairs issues. Leaders in Great Britain believed that all nations were under a treaty obligation to operate under similar restrictions, and pay equal tolls, once the Panama Canal opened. Taft, though, argued for elimination of the tolls for American shipping, or a reimbursement of those tolls to American companies. Taft put forward a legal brief on how eliminating the tolls for American shipping was not only fair and legal but just. The United States having built and paid for the canal, surely it had a responsibility to manage the canal in its own interests, Taft argued. It would never have placed itself on the exact same ground as other countries. Moreover, in terms of reimbursement, Taft pointed out that what countries did for their own ships was their business: if England, for example, wanted to reimburse its shippers for the cost of the tolls, it could do so—same as the Americans could. Finally, Taft asked that the ability to set tolls, allow exemptions, and otherwise manage the system be delegated clearly by Congress to the executive, not merely implied. In each dynamic of the case, Taft sought to protect and empower American interests, craft legal and constitutional rationales supporting such actions, and, importantly, expand the president's role and authority through clear and transparent interbranch process.[103]

Taft ultimately arranged for the president to get power from Congress to fix tolls through the Panama Canal. Debatable under international treaty, the case is a good example of Taft's justifying a questionable act by finding it in the national interest.[104] Taft was willing to submit the matter to arbitration when the British continued to protest. Taft's position empowered the United States and the merchant marine, and solidified U.S. hold over canal administration. Taft also secured discretionary authority to subsidize American shipping.

Taft then continued American maintenance of the Panama Canal Zone after congressional authorization had expired. He explained his actions: continued executive control took place "under the advice of the Attorney General that in the absence of action by Congress, there is necessarily an implied authority on the part of the Executive to maintain a government in a territory in which he has to see that the laws are executed." This action echoed John Quincy Adams's continuation of the Creek agency despite the absence of congressional reauthorization. In the Panama case, Taft carefully noted that the continuing, implied authority during ongoing construction of the canal could not be presumed to continue after construction was complete—Congress would need to take action: "Certainly, now that the canal is about to be completed and to be put under a permanent management, there ought to be specific statutory authority for its regulation and control and for the government of the zone, which we hold for the chief and main purpose of operating the canal."[105] Taft was hardly hemmed in by a narrow reading of the Constitution. He was working the levers of that document to his advantage, gaining strength in the matter of tolls by soliciting the support of Congress, and in the matter of canal maintenance by arguing that the president's authority continued even if not reauthorized.[106]

TAFT HAD encouraged private-sector banking and financial interests, tourists, and other investors into various initiatives around the globe as integral parts of dollar diplomacy. Mexico was no exception, where government activities included creating State Department pamphlets to tout investment opportunities and having U.S. and Mexican officials meet with tourists and prospective investors in Mexico.[107] As civil conflict within Mexico affected Texas and spilled into Arizona in 1911, though, violence in border areas spiked and calls for the president to take military action to protect Americans multiplied.

Taft avoided conflict and possibly war by utilizing rhetorical appeals to constrain his authority, even as he used the president's commander-in-chief authority and ambiguous powers under the Constitution to take concrete action and prepare for a broader conflict. Taft mobilized twenty thousand troops in Texas and ordered naval maneuvers in the Gulf of Mexico, keeping U.S. warships close to the action. Taft explained publicly that he was hoping to protect the border and encourage Mexico to act carefully to protect U.S. interests and citizens in Mexico. At the same time, Taft steadfastly refused appeals to move troops across the border. In his March 1911 instructions to his military commanders, Taft wrote that he did not think he possessed the procedural authority as president to invade Mexico:

> The assumption by the press that I contemplate intervention on Mexican soil to protect American lives or property is of course gratuitous, because I seriously doubt whether I have such authority under any circumstances, and if I had I would not exercise it without express congressional approval. . . . My determined purpose . . . is to be in a position so that when danger to American lives and property in Mexico threatens and the existing Government is rendered helpless by the insurrection, I can promptly execute congressional orders to protect them, with effect.[108]

Taft knew that a military exercise could be preparatory, and also an excellent opportunity to conduct exercises for experience and learning. In his instructions, he implored his commanders to act wisely and cautiously:

> Texas is a State ordinarily peaceful, but you can not put 20,000 troops into it without running some risk of a collision between the people of that State, and especially the Mexicans who live in Texas near the border and who sympathize with the *insurrectos,* and the Federal soldiers. For that reason I beg you to be as careful as you can to prevent friction of any kind. We were able in Cuba, with the army of pacification there of something more than 5,000 troops, to maintain them for a year without any trouble, and I hope you can do the same thing in Texas.[109]

In April 1911, fighting between Mexican government forces and rebels near Douglas, Arizona, left two Americans dead and eleven wounded—the third violent incident along the border. The disruptions worsened in May, as the revolutionaries overthrew Mexican president Porfirio Díaz. By July, continuing disruptions increased political pressure on Taft to take more aggressive and visible action. Republicans in particular wanted a muscular response, in hopes that a show of force would help their chances in the 1912 election. A strong, militant president would be a good sell, many thought, and Taft was urged to act so that he could build his support in the West. Theodore Roosevelt, of course, argued for vigorous intervention and for an end to chattering about the need to seek congressional approval.[110] Taft's expert advisors and the ambassador to Mexico, Henry Lane Wilson, though, worried that armed American intervention into Mexico might lead to massacres of Americans in border areas and the forfeiture of American property throughout the country.[111]

The crucial sequence came when the insurrection spilled into Douglas and resulted in the shooting of Americans on the U.S. side. Arizona's governor begged Taft for help: "In my judgment radical measures are needed to protect our innocent people, and if anything can be done to stop the fighting at Agua Prieta the situation calls for such action. It is impossible to safeguard the people of Douglas unless the town be vacated. Can anything be done to relieve situation, now acute?" But Taft held firm. In a dispatch made public, Taft noted that he could, of course, send troops "to cross the border and attempt to stop the fighting," or he could order them to fire at both groups of Mexican forces from the U.S. side of the border. "But if I take this step," he wrote, "I must face the possibility of resistance and greater bloodshed, and also the danger of having our motives misconstrued and misrepresented, and of thus inflaming Mexican popular indignation against many thousand Americans now in Mexico and jeopardizing their lives and property. The pressure for general intervention under such conditions it might not be practicable to resist." In short, Taft recognized the procedural authority he held under certain circumstances, but he anticipated the risk that any use of force along the border might paint him into a corner and propel the country into a general action within Mexico. Instead, Taft suggested an alternative: "I must ask you and the local authorities, in case the same danger recurs, to direct the people of Douglas to place themselves where bullets can not reach them and thus avoid casualty. I am loath to endanger Americans in Mexico, where they are necessarily exposed, by taking a radical step to prevent injury to Americans on our side of the border who can avoid it by a temporary inconvenience."[112]

Taft offered an extended public explanation of the events in his Third Annual Message, issued the winter following the crisis. Setting up the situation, Taft stated that the U.S. ambassador to Mexico had feared that the general uprising might eventually put at risk the forty thousand or more Americans living in Mexico, as well as "very large" American investments there. Taft assembled his troops in Texas while notifying Díaz not to be concerned. Taft quoted his earlier communications at length in the annual message, concluding, "I am glad to say that no further invasion of American rights of any substantial character occurred." He went on to bolster his argument for peace and attention to procedure in such situations: "The restraint exercised by our Government . . . was not due to a lack of force or power to deal with it promptly and aggressively, but was due to a real desire to use every means possible to avoid direct intervention in the affairs of our neighbor, whose friendship we valued and were most anxious to retain."[113]

Taft's position in this matter was neither absolute nor doctrinaire; instead, he shrewdly kept his options open. Taft's public avowals of the need for congressional action helped him fend off calls for intervention from aggressive Republicans, even as mobilizing troops gave Taft the ability to call them into action or send them to Mexico should circumstances deteriorate to where such an action was necessary—and, being necessary, such an action might become constitutional with or without Congress's input.[114] In other words, Taft deftly utilized a variety of executive action tools both to prepare for action *and* to defend his decision not to act more aggressively.

As he had done in other international matters related to China, Canada, Nicaragua, and elsewhere, Taft quickly and decisively chose a path that emphasized process, preparation, public education, and savvy application of his office's constitutional powers *and* its limitations. Taft consistently protected his options while respecting and even capitalizing on the constitutional separation of powers.

Conclusion

Taft's presidency was active and innovative, with lasting effect. The state, long-standing and fully functioning, was put to new purposes and adapted by the president and other actors to adjust to the new century and its issues. Taft used all of the tools traditionally at the disposal of the president to press his initiatives—legislative leadership, administrative action, public communication, and options like vetoes, executive orders, and appointments. As presidents had been doing for more than a century, Taft also relied on the accumulated expertise of specialists, experts, analysts, and institutions to provide specific and detailed advice and suggestions on a host of state activity both domestic and international. His work on budgeting, Panama Canal tolls, social legislation, dollar diplomacy, and a host of other areas reflects Taft's globe-trotting penchant for carefully managed progress.

Taft delivered demonstrable achievement, and his work was driven by a desire to build for the long term. At the end of his presidency, Taft summarized his tenure:

> I have strengthened the Supreme Bench, have given a good deal of new and valuable legislation, have not interfered with business, have kept the peace, and on the whole have led people to pursue their various occupations without interruption. It is a very humdrum, uninteresting administration, and does not attract the attention or enthusiasm of anybody, but after I am out, I think that you and I can look back with some pleasure in having done something for the benefit of the public weal.[115]

Taft's style was humble, good-humored, and collaborative. Eschewing bluster, he made it easy to overlook his achievements and his leadership as president.

7
Taft the Builder

PRESIDENT WILLIAM HOWARD TAFT combined the characteristics of the procedurist and those of the principled innovator. He pursued clear principles and simultaneously worked to craft innovations into lasting policy. He was a stickler in the Adams sense, believing deeply that rules and procedures mattered—they created stability, fairness, and inclusion. At the same time, Taft was an innovator as president—he not only supported innovations in numerous policy areas that broke new ground and set the federal government to new tasks, he helped design them.

The result is what I have referred to as a synthesist, but what might colloquially be called a builder: in areas like taxation, campaign finance regulation, conservation, and international arbitration treaties, Taft's ideas were big-picture innovations, and his efforts tried to work out small details. Taft built procedures and processes that ensured that his innovations lasted. He did this quite consciously, writing, for example, after his presidency:

> Real progress in government must be by slow stages. Radical and revolutionary changes, arbitrarily put into operation, are not likely to be permanent or to accomplish the good which is prophesied of them. My observation of new reform legislation of a meritorious character is that Congress and its members must be educated up to its value by those who have studied it and become convinced of its wisdom.
>
> It will be found that much of the good legislation that has gone on to the statute book has been pending before successive sessions of Congress and successive Congresses until Congress and the public have become familiar with the reasons for its adoption, until discussions lasting over from one Congress to another have subjected the proposals to useful scrutiny and amendment, and until it thus acquires a form that Congress is willing to adopt. Sessions therefore at which legislation is not finally adopted, in which there is much discussion of proposed legislation, may often be most useful to the public, both in defeating legislation which ought not to be enacted and in framing for future adoption legislation which will be useful.[1]

Taft understood the long game, as he had with presidential budgeting, administrative reforms, and his Asia policy: lasting reform takes time to develop and design, and it takes time to gain a critical mass of public and popular support. Taft's efforts to embed reforms in the governing system were of his time—efforts to cement approaches to progressive taxation and regulation, to ground conservation on a legal footing, and to develop a consensus behind the benefits of international arbitration treaties.

Progressive Taxation and Regulation

The Taft years saw the imbalances of corporate consolidations, trusts, and monopolies become a familiar part of conversation and of politics.[2] Theodore Roosevelt and the progressive reformers had helped awaken the public to the threats posed by corporate power and wealth. Reactions and reform proposals varied. The great issue of Taft's era was how to control the rapid changes and great consolidation of businesses, the great wealth of the American industrial titans, the great power of political machines, and the great poverty and need of millions of ordinary Americans.

Taft's goals for dealing with these issues were straightforward. As a conservative, he respected business achievement. He recognized benefits of efficiency and consolidation redounding to the improvement of an ordinary person's life, in lower prices, better goods, and faster service. Taft accepted "bigness," therefore—consolidation was not necessarily a bad thing. At the same time, Taft recognized that combinations could potentially be abusive. Efforts to dominate industry sectors could be beneficial if they truly served the public interest in efficiency and service, but efforts to corner markets and create monopolies for the purpose of profit, or to artificially control prices, or to destroy competition, raised serious dangers. And as companies translated their wealth into economic and especially political power, through market control, lobbying, and preferred access to government officials, the situation risked results that could work against the interests of the public.

For Taft as a progressive, an unregulated situation was untenable. It interfered with the public's ability to take advantage of modern business practices, bigness, and the scales of efficiency coming to dominate American business. It also interfered with the ability of ordinary people to get a fair deal from government: Taft worried that corporations, combinations, and their wealthy leaders could secure unfair advantages in campaigns and the selection of candidates, and exert unfair influence over the actions of elected representatives and unelected administrators tasked with regulating American society. The situation threatened to lock in a system where rules were obscure, enforcement played favorites, and ordinary people were vulnerable.

Taft believed that unchecked business growth, at its worst, threatened the viability of the American system. Unregulated corporate activity promised plutocracy, the control of government and business in the hands of the wealthy. Taft feared that plutocracy led to revolt: as more and more people got worse and worse off, inequality would become severe—and severe inequality invites revolution. Taft believed that responsible leaders needed to establish and update fair, open, and effective regulatory processes to manage the influence of the corporations, or else inequalities would result in takeover by radical elements. That takeover would likely lead to unpredictable and ever-increasing government intrusions on businesses, takeovers of industries like the railroads, and manipulation of political processes through measures like referenda and the recall of judges—radical responses all, threatening longstanding regime values and the viability of the American system.[3]

Taft the "progressive conservative" wanted to conserve what existed; he valued property rights and established traditions and protocols, believing that they had done well to develop the country and that allegiance to stable procedures and traditional ways of doing things remained the best path forward. At the same time, Taft understood the significant changes taking place around him, and he recognized that rules and procedures needed to be updated or invented to meet new challenges and address new issues. Taft was a builder throughout his career as a judge, as civilian governor in the Philippines, and as Roosevelt's secretary of war, as we saw in chapter 1. As president, Taft made decisions that sought to synthesize longstanding American economic rules and structures with innovative new ideas meant to provide lasting stability and fair processes for the future. Taft sought careful, thoughtful reform pushed through the established structures of governance—he wanted to use the system to manage and regulate, and to deter abuses, while allowing for growth and initiative to have real, tangible benefits for entrepreneurs, business owners, and the general public.

Taft offered a comprehensive reform approach to these issues, and he offered careful, reasoned, and public rationales for his proposals. He was successful in leading Congress and the nation to significant and lasting reform with judicial and administrative oversight. In addition to the issues addressed in the previous chapter, Taft's plan included comprehensive tax reform, antitrust enforcement, and campaign finance regulation. Taft's proposals, dealing with the most important and visible cluster of issues of the Progressive era, attracted public interest as well as focused attention within governing institutions.[4]

Tax Reform

The first pillar of Taft's efforts centered on reforming the tax structure through a tax on corporations and the legitimation of the personal income tax through ratification of the Sixteenth Amendment to the Constitution. President Taft led the charge on both topics, designing and engineering the compromise that secured both measures in a masterful and foundationally important bit of political leadership that belies Taft's reputation as a clumsy politician. Taft managed to defeat a dangerous effort to circumvent the Supreme Court's 1895 ruling against the income tax, thereby protecting the reputation of the Court and the independence of the judiciary—even as he maneuvered the income tax into becoming the Sixteenth Amendment by removing it from the House version of a controversial tariff reform bill and replacing it in that bill with the corporation tax.[5] In the end, he would get all three: the income tax, the corporation tax, and protection of the Court.

Once in office, it became clear to Taft that the tariff in general was failing to provide enough revenue to the government. Taft began to look for alternative processes, which included his longstanding interest in inheritance taxes and a corporation tax. With the income tax debate already very public and the subject of ongoing reform proposals, Taft dove into the nest of issues at the heart of the era.[6] He focused much of his administration's early attention on a revision of the tariff, and this became the vehicle for lasting changes. The tariff, for all its success in growing the domestic economy since the founding, had long bedeviled presidents and partisans. It was a matter so politically volatile in its direct help or harm to specific interests that Theodore Roosevelt had run away from the Republican Party's commitment to tariff reform while he was president—a politically smart, if not exactly courageous, decision. Taft embraced the necessity of reform and the party's commitment to it, and undertook the difficult and dangerous effort.[7]

Like all tariffs, the new Payne-Aldrich tariff encompassed a series of compromises on tariff rates that benefited some interests and were expected to hurt others. While the result has been commended as good policy by economists and historians, Taft was roundly criticized by many interests for the various tariff increases the bill contained.[8] Critics of the Taft administration see this as a signature failure on Taft's part—he would have been better off had he left the tariff alone or refused to sign the bill.[9] The Payne-Aldrich tariff, though, exemplifies Taft's willingness to enter treacherous waters in pursuit of protecting Americans and American interests, and his commitment to building mechanisms to aid decision making on thorny issues. In the following public explanation of his support for the controversial act, note how many times Taft touted the creation of regular processes that would benefit government and the public in a fair and consistent manner:

> The Payne-Aldrich Bill I approved, because, above all, it provided the *machinery* by which alone a just and intelligent revision of the tariff could be effected—a Tariff Board, which without political bias and free from political

pressure, would ascertain those facts essential to an intelligent adjustment of the rates of duty; because it clothed the Executive with power, *by means of maximum and minimum rates,* to compel just treatment from foreign nations of American products and exports; because it imposed a tax on profits of corporations that *at once gave to the government an insight into the operations* of these important instrumentalities of business, which it had in no other way been able to obtain, and because it provided the *machinery* whereby increased revenues could be collected in face of an emergency; because it granted to the Filipinos that measure of justice to which the nation stood pledged and which was essential to their prosperity; and, finally, because it effected a material reduction in the rates of duty—not so much of a reduction as I desired, but as much as I believe could be secured without the aid of that *machinery,* the Tariff Board, which it created.[10]

What is often overlooked is the place of Payne-Aldrich in Taft's work toward comprehensive tax reform. The Payne-Aldrich Act instituted a corporation tax, the first of its kind, launching a history of corporate taxation and oversight in the public interest that continues today. The act assessed a tax of 1 percent on net income of corporations with net annual earnings over $5,000.[11] Taft secured the innovative, landmark tax primarily to enable structured, fair government regulation of business activity. He utilized a variety of executive tools, including public communications as well as executive branch expertise and formal and informal interactions with Congress. Taft pushed reform steadily and emphasized his effort at key points by requesting and working out various permutations of reform proposals; by lobbying members of Congress at dinners, evening rides, golf outings, and other events; and through public communications like speeches, the Inaugural Address, and annual messages.[12]

Taft directed the course of debate through his dramatic June 1909 message to Congress, in which he expressed his wish for the corporation tax and support for an income tax amendment. According to leading studies of the law, Taft's message was "stunning" and "one of the shrewdest bits of strategy that could have been arranged." The message blindsided members of Congress with its full-throated endorsement of radical changes. Not only did Taft set the course for securing tax reform; he nimbly unified Republicans, whose support for various measures had been split. The move cemented the support of Republican Senate leader Nelson Aldrich, and it picked up support among Democrats.[13]

The corporation tax measure itself was drafted by Attorney General George Wickersham and Secretary of State Elihu Root, and then scrutinized by the Senate Finance Committee, with Taft's close supervision, so as to ensure passage of a law that would be acceptable to the Supreme Court. Taft's aide Archie Butt later related a conversation between Taft and Wickersham that took place on the day the measure was offered in the Senate. Taft said, "The strangest part is that the Congress was willing to have a member of the Cabinet draw up such an important amendment, for as a rule the Senate Committee on Finance is rather jealous of its prerogatives." Wickersham is said to have replied that "he was merely the instrument of the President himself, for while he had largely put the amendment into shape he only embodied the suggestions of the President."[14]

Taft continued his efforts to pass the corporation tax after introduction of the measure to the Senate, holding dinners with senators as the measures went to conference, and pushing the corporation tax in lieu of the House's preference for the income tax.[15] Taft was clear before, during, and after debates on this tax that, while it would serve to increase government revenue, the real benefit of a corporation tax was to regularize the government's ability to access information about corporate activity. The government would have regular information and a basis for decision making, and the public would have the ability to inspect corporate information and make informed judgments about corporate activities and investments.[16] The data-gathering from the corporation tax and for the Tariff Board would take place on a regular, systematic basis—not just during the politically tense times of tariff reform in Congress but at all times when the tariff was not garnering headlines and being riven by political brinksmanship. It was a first step toward business regulation to enable better governance.[17]

In his Second Annual Message, in 1910, Taft told Congress: "The corporation excise tax, proportioned to the net income of every business corporation in the country, has worked well. The tax has been easily collected. Its prompt payment indicates that the incidence of the tax has not been heavy. It offers, moreover, an opportunity for knowledge by the Government of the general condition and business of all corporations, and that means by far the most important part of the business of the country."[18]

THE CORPORATION tax itself would have been a significant achievement for President Taft. But there was much more: as part of the bargain that secured the corporation tax and public disclosure of corporate activity in the tariff bill, Taft simultaneously led the fight for the Sixteenth Amendment, which legitimated the personal income tax—fifteen years after it had been declared unconstitutional by the Supreme Court. Ever since, a movement had rumbled in Congress and the public aimed at passing new legislation repudiating the Court's ruling and reinstituting the tax. The proposed measures had considerable support and probably would have passed with President Taft's backing.[19]

Taft, however, recognized the constitutional and procedural dangers of Congress playing tit for tat with Supreme Court rulings. He was concerned that a legislative act that so directly invalidated a Supreme Court opinion on the meaning of the Constitution would upset the balance of power, bring the Court into disrepute, and set a dangerous (and easy) precedent for narrowing the scope of the judiciary's influence—all breaks with American tradition and threats to the principle of judicial independence.[20] Instead of supporting a law circumventing the Court, Taft took the harder route of a constitutional amendment to rectify what he saw as an error by the Court. Seeking to get the personal income tax but also to protect the authority and legitimacy of the Court and its rulings, Taft proposed a deal by which an income tax provision that had been included in early drafts of the tariff bill would be removed, replaced by Taft's corporation tax measure, and then made into a proposed constitutional amendment. The Sixteenth Amendment passed Congress and was ratified by the states, entering the Constitution in 1913.[21]

By cutting the income tax out of the tariff negotiations, sending an income tax amendment to the states, and inserting a corporation tax into Payne-Aldrich, Taft engineered a resounding victory for progressive reform.[22] These reforms were tremendously significant, and they showcase Taft's long-underrated political acumen. In one clever deal, Taft reinforced the separation of powers and the importance of the Constitution, and built the foundation of modern American tax policy.

Antitrust

Taft had been involved with antitrust issues since his days as a federal judge, and he was serving as solicitor general when the United States brought its first antitrust case in 1890.[23] He explained the target of his antitrust efforts during the 1908 presidential campaign:

> The economic and political history of the past four years is that of a great struggle between the national administration and certain powerful combinations in the financial world. . . . If the abuses of monopoly and discriminations cannot be restrained, if the concentration of power made possible by such abuses continues and increases, and it is manifest that under the system of individualism and private property the tyranny and oppression of an oligarchy of wealth cannot be avoided, then socialism will triumph, and the institution of private property will perish.[24]

Taft feared that an unrestrained free market would lead to socialism and what he saw as its threat to property rights. The only way to protect capitalism was *through* careful regulation, Taft believed, and the only way to do that was through the fair and transparent application of the rule of law.[25]

Theodore Roosevelt's approach to this issue had been problematic: his prosecution of Standard Oil, his acceptance of the abuses of J. P. Morgan, and his seemingly willful ignorance of U.S. Steel's efforts to monopolize the steel market, for example, have long stood as examples of presidential powers used for controversial, naive, and perhaps personally interested ends. Roosevelt's prosecutions focused on what he believed were "bad" trusts and encouraged informal gentlemen's agreements with "good" trusts to ensure compliance and good action. Roosevelt wanted government to help the good trusts through agreements, deals, and promises of immunity, and he had quickly pushed the new Bureau of Corporations into the political waters, turning what was designed as a neutral, data-gathering entity into a weapon for attacking some corporations and playing favorites with others. Two of Taft's antitrust targets would be U.S. Steel and International Harvester, corporations assured during the Roosevelt administration that, in exchange for their cooperation with the Bureau of Corporations, they would be immune from prosecution under the 1890 Sherman Antitrust Act.[26]

Taft was committed to trust busting, as were Roosevelt before and Woodrow Wilson after him. But where Taft stood out was in his commitment to judicial process and his discomfort with any attempt to evaluate, according to slippery and even arbitrary standards, "good" and "bad" trusts. Such efforts grated on Taft's understanding of equal application and enforcement of the laws. Taft favored prosecution of any company that had violated the clear intent of the law—regardless of whether they were good or bad trusts. For Taft, this was the only way to understand and fairly apply the law; as a result, he preferred judicial review of antitrust challenges to placing such a key responsibility among administrative commissions.[27] Taft's targeting of both U.S. Steel and International Harvester illustrates his commitment to enforcing the law fairly, without favoritism.[28] Taft also refused to go along with negotiated proposals and preapproved consolidations in the bituminous coal industry, and he bypassed the Bureau of Corporations in favor of prosecutory action.[29] Eschewing executive or personal judgments, Taft's administration tried to be guided by a neutral application of the law, particularly enforcement of the Sherman Antitrust Act, leading the Taft administration to bring more antitrust actions in Taft's four years than the Roosevelt administration had brought over the course of its nearly two full terms.[30] Taft implored Attorney General Wickersham to bring suits wherever they were appropriate. Over seven years, Roosevelt's administrations had brought fifty-four antitrust suits; in just four years, Taft's administration brought ninety.[31]

TAFT WAS A KEY influence in the development of the Sherman Antitrust Act from an instrument focused on price controls to one applicable to mergers and consolidations. His opinion as a federal circuit court judge in *Addyston Pipe & Steel Co. v. United States* (1899), initially resisted by the Supreme Court, eventually became the Court's position in *Standard Oil v. United States* (1911). Judge Taft had picked up on a dissent in the Supreme Court's 1897 ruling in *United States v. Trans-Missouri Freight* to help frame his opinion in *Addyston Pipe*, in which he found that the Sherman Act encompassed more than mere price restraints. Taft argued that the Sherman Act made naked restraints on commerce, like price restraints, unlawful, but ancillary restraints might be unlawful or lawful, depending on their reasonableness. The Supreme Court rejected that approach when it issued its 1904 decision in *Northern Securities Co. v. United States;* four justices in that case found the Sherman Act irrelevant to mergers. By the time of *Standard Oil* in 1911, though, Taft had appointed four justices to the Court and elevated Edward White to chief justice. The eight-to-one ruling in *Standard Oil* announcing the "rule of reason" essentially condemned actions that allowed the possibility of fixing prices or limiting production. In effect, the Court in *Standard Oil* adopted Taft's approach from *Addyston Pipe*.[32]

The Supreme Court issued its decisions in the landmark *Standard Oil* and *United States v. American Tobacco Company* cases midway through Taft's term. The decisions attracted sharp criticism, with many believing that the *Court* had taken it upon itself to decide which trusts would be considered good and bad. Now-president Taft immediately used the tools at his disposal to counter the popular and critical perception of the rulings. He argued in his Third Annual Message, in a post-presidential book, and in many speeches and lectures that the Court had articulated a clear standard, practical and consistent with prior rulings. He defended the Court as upholding a workable standard for companies going forward, and by so doing Taft helped to synthesize new applications of the law to new circumstances.[33]

Taft added that enforcement of the Sherman Act under these guidelines was also preventing new organizations of an objectionable kind from forming, and those big combinations that were being forged were being forged carefully. Existing companies operating close to the line of the law had adjusted their behaviors, he argued, and "many companies, rather than stand the test of litigation, are consenting to dissolution by agreement with government authorities."[34] Businesses were negotiating with the Justice Department, and Taft happily noted, "It seems possible to bring about these reorganizations without general business disturbance."[35]

When the Taft administration moved to consent decrees in the wake of *Standard Oil*, the key difference was the fact that consent decrees were legal documents enforceable through the judiciary—not gentlemen's agreements subject to the whims of personalities and circumstance. Taft argued in his Third Annual Message that the government's enforcement and the Court's rulings were having positive effects in other cases—specifically, decrees dissolving the combinations among electric lamp manufacturers, wholesale grocers, and orders involving the Powder Trust.[36] "Against evils" like contracts in restraint of trade, Taft wrote elsewhere, "wise laws protect individuals and the public by declaring all such contracts void."[37]

Taft's administration stands out in its commitment to bringing antitrust suits against major corporations. "If any president deserves the reputation as 'the Trust-Buster,'" writes economic historian Martin J. Sklar, "surely it is Taft."[38] Taft and his team accomplished this through an open, transparent, fair, and understandable execution of the law, utilizing the powers of the executive branch, cooperating with the laws passed by Congress, and defending the autonomy of the courts. The Taft effort combined innovative approaches to the new trusts with the procedurist's fealty to procedure and law. To drive the point home, Taft sketched an alternative world where his administration had not taken these actions. "But for these decisions," Taft wrote, "the work of concentrating all business of the country in a few hands would have gone on and we would have had our being and our comfort largely under control of a small number of iron monopolies."[39]

Economic historian Neil Fligstein notes the way that effective policy sometimes dooms political activity to obscurity; one thinks of early coastal defense policies or Grant's veto of the inflation bill. "Antitrust legislation and the debates they engendered," Fligstein writes, "seem like anachronisms today, precisely because they were effective. The practices they outlawed have generally been nonexistent in the business community since the 1920s. Firms had to develop alternative strategies for growth and profit, ones that did not constitute unfair trade practices nor restraints of trade."[40] Taft's prosecutions—and his judges—set the path of antitrust enforcement for the ensuing century.

Campaign Finance Reform

Taft's approach to the relationship of corporate power to campaign finance complemented his tax reforms and antitrust views: in all areas, Taft believed that concentrated power threatened the public interest. Taft worried that corporate power promised plutocracy in its ability to control government activity, and he worried that elections were vulnerable to well-heeled corporate interests through campaign contributions. Large and unregulated campaign contributions led to officeholders who were beholden to corporate financing—this included even judges, especially at the state level but also indirectly through the federal appointment process. Taft's efforts to manage the growing power of corporations in America included novel campaign finance law aimed at reducing the likelihood of nefarious connections between large corporate donors and elected officials.

Before he became president, Taft had asked one of his donors to reduce a $50,000 contribution to $10,000. Taft wanted to eliminate any appearance of a conflict of interest.[41] After his victory in 1908, Taft voluntarily publicized campaign contributions that had been made to the Republican National Committee during the 1908 campaign.[42] This was innovative, coming at a time when federal regulations mandated no such thing.[43] At the time, Taft wrote to Roosevelt,

> I am, as you are, in favor of the publicity of contributions and the receipts and expenditures. I think it is necessary to prevent the great use of money for corrupt or quasi-corrupt purposes, and I am willing to have it begin with this campaign, although it may work to our comparative disadvantage.... I am willing to undergo the disadvantage in order to make certain that in the future we shall reduce the power of money in politics for unworthy purposes.[44]

True to his penchant for both fair process and principled innovation in service of public goals, President Taft pushed for and signed the Publicity Act of 1910, the first campaign disclosure law at the national level. The Publicity Act—amended in 1911 and 1925 and renamed the Federal Corrupt Practices Act—continues to anchor a regulatory approach to federal elections and campaign finance more than a hundred years later. The original act set campaign spending limits on races for the U.S. House of Representatives and was the first federal act to require disclosure of political parties' spending—building on Taft's voluntary action following the 1908 election. In 1911, the act was amended to include U.S. Senate races and primaries. For the first time, candidates had to offer financial disclosures, and candidates for both House and Senate seats had to stay within expenditure caps.[45] Paired with his antitrust and tax efforts, Taft was helping to synthesize major, lasting reform at the intersection of business, wealth, influence, and governance.

TOGETHER WITH Taft's recommendations for an inheritance tax, for a federal incorporation tax, for organizing national budgeting under the president, and for rationalizing the banking and currency systems into what became the Federal Reserve, these measures coalesced into a landmark ordering of the national government's relationship to business, money, and wealth, affecting everyone from top to bottom in the American system.[46] The tax system these policies enshrined continues today in its basic form, the idea of government regulation of business through disclosure and publication of corporate activity continues, the bedrock philosophy of antitrust laws continues to center national and even international debates, and the principles of campaign finance rules involving disclosure and limits on contributions still survive, despite recent attacks.[47]

Taft secured these advances, and gave them lasting life, by avoiding the spotlights and pitfalls that come with a "strong leader" approach, and his role in such momentous developments remains obscured to this day as works on the presidency and the Progressive era skip quickly past Taft in favor of Roosevelt and Wilson. Taft did not monopolize the reform effort, and he did not center the reforms as presidentially owned. Instead, Taft worked for rational regulation, information, disclosure, transparency, and cooperation.

The measures affecting businesses were largely accepted by, even supported by, the businesses themselves. Taft convinced business leaders that a rational and transparent regulatory system was in their interests as much as it was in the public's. Taft touted the returns of the corporate income tax in its first year to demonstrate its effectiveness, and he explained repeatedly the effectiveness of his policies and the degree to which they integrated a workable, acceptable, and popular system. He touted the effectiveness of the decisions made by Congress, the courts, and the executive branch regarding antitrust enforcement. The process established for these measures, and their foundation in good law and constitutional amendment, meant that they would be lasting reforms—not easily subject to the changing whims of subsequent presidents or legislatures.

Taft explicitly recognized the need for cooperation among the branches, he did not shy away from testing the measures in the courts, and he emerged triumphant when the courts upheld them. He put to use the inherent strengths of a separation of powers system, achieving lasting results through leadership and collaboration in pursuit of clearly explained policies.[48] It was active government, and effective policymaking, with careful application of presidential leadership.

Conservation

Taft's approach to conservation further exemplifies the synthesist at work. Conservation is an issue where historians have often lionized Theodore Roosevelt and either ignored or even condemned Taft. Yet Taft was able to place more land under public protection in four years than Roosevelt had been able to do in almost eight. It was Taft's insistence on conserving land through a transparent and legal administrative process that so upset Roosevelt's supporters and has so affected historians seduced by Roosevelt's rhetoric ever since. This is not to suggest that Roosevelt was unimportant—as

Taft himself often noted, Roosevelt in a host of areas was able to make issues tangible to the public, generating awareness and activism on public health, peace, and conservation. Taft's enduring complaint against Roosevelt was the tendency of Roosevelt and his allies, like the Forest Service's Gifford Pinchot, to take matters into their own hands—to stir the public's ire and then to improvise unilateral executive action, make handshake deals, and cut corners on the route to what they saw as reform.

Taft's critique of Roosevelt echoes the critiques of Grant as principled innovator: those who agree with the goals often overlook or accept as the cost of reform the means employed to try to achieve those goals. For Taft, those means were often illegal, unconstitutional, or unethical—and any achievements gained through them risked fizzling out after a short time while eroding a system of laws and accountability. Taft worked to build an enduring legacy of conservation by worrying the difficult details and using legislation and process to enshrine innovation.[49]

Conservation stood at the intersection of the presidency and the state in the Progressive era. As in budgeting, tax, and campaign finance reform, Taft aimed to modernize policy and codify reforms for the twentieth century. His efforts to synthesize the old and new can be seen in his administration's approach to using executive action tools, in his leadership of the administrative bureaucracy during the Ballinger-Pinchot controversy, and in the oft-overlooked tenure of Walter L. Fisher, who succeeded Ballinger as interior secretary and who initiated reforms that lasted for decades.

Public Leadership beyond Awareness

Taft used all the executive tools at his disposal to pursue his goals in conservation policy. A good example of Taft's general approach and of his use of direct public communication can be seen in his address to the National Conservation Congress in St. Paul, Minnesota, on September 5, 1910.[50] President Taft laid out his vision for conservation in the speech, tapping the Constitution and addressing federalism, property rights, the public interest, the differences between public and private action, and the obligation to be concerned with future generations. It was a plea for reason and attention to detail over rhetoric and emotion in public policymaking.

Taft opened with a definition of the issue: "Conservation as an economic and political term has come to mean the preservation of our natural resources for economical use, so as to secure the greatest good to the greatest number." Taft then noted that, in the country's youth, this hardly seemed like an issue; in fact, anyone who hinted at conservation and thus suggested slowing down development and growth "was regarded as a traitor to his neighbors and an obstructor to public progress." But "now that the would-be pioneers have come to realize that all the richest lands in the country have been taken up, we have perceived the necessity for a change of policy in the disposition of our national resources so as to prevent the continuance of the waste which has characterized our phenomenal growth in the past. Today we desire to restrict and retain under public control the acquisition and use by the capitalist of our natural resources." Taft called attention to Roosevelt's role in popularizing the concern, and he argued that conservation was a national issue, not a sectional or partisan one: "It is a question that affects the vital welfare of all of us—of our children and our children's children."[51]

Taft's speech lacked the fire and energy of Roosevelt's oratory, instead offering a reasoned tone and an organized argument backed up by data—all of which may have been difficult to watch performed live, but which stands up a century later as a twenty-page guide to the conservation contexts and issues of the era. Taft divided his discussion into detailed sections on agricultural lands, mineral lands, forest lands, coal lands, oil and gas lands, and phosphate lands. Taft's presentation reflected the complexity of the issues in this era and the complex and fluid politics of conservation and development.[52]

The differences in tone and presentation highlight the difference between Roosevelt and Taft as orators but also the difference in their approaches as president to public policy reform. In his speech, Taft delineated approaches carefully tailored to specific issue areas, recommending slight adjustments to agricultural land policy, continuity in mineral lands policy, and experimentation in leasing coal lands. He divided regulation and administration of forest lands, advocating for state and private regulation of the timber lands that fell under their respective jurisdictions, combined with congressional deference to executive action regarding forest lands under federal control (particularly the process of distinguishing forest land that should be preserved from land more appropriate for homesteading). Taft emphasized the use of presidential authority, delegated by Congress, to make withdrawals of public lands by executive order.

When he approached the issue of oil and gas lands, Taft detailed his approach and his rationale:

> The principal underlying feature of such legislation [as regulating leasing of oil and gas lands] should be the exercise of beneficial control rather than the collection of revenue. As not only the largest owner of oil lands, but as a prospective large consumer of oil by reason of the increasing use of fuel oil by the navy, the federal Government is directly concerned both in encouraging rational development and at the same time insuring the longest possible life to the oil supply.[53]

Similar complex considerations governed Taft's discussion of phosphate lands and water-power sites.

After the presentation of the details and complexities—including a deferral to Congress in the controversy over the best method to handle water-power sites—Taft got down to the major difference between his approach and Roosevelt's, complementary though they might have been. In the passage, Taft emphasized the need to move beyond the rhetoric and passion of the principled innovator to the difficult work of synthesizing principles with the construction of rules and processes that would endure:

> I think it of the utmost importance that after the public attention has been roused to the necessity of a change in our general policy to prevent waste and a selfish appropriation to private and corporate purposes of what should be controlled for the public benefit, those who urge conservation shall feel the necessity of making clear how conservation can be practically carried out, and shall propose specific methods and legal provisions and regulations to remedy actual adverse conditions.
>
> I am bound to say that the time has come for a halt in general rhapsodies over conservation, making the word mean every known good in the world; for, after the public attention has been roused, such appeals are of doubtful utility and do not direct the public to the specific course that the people should take, or have their legislators take, in order to promote the cause of conservation. The rousing of emotions on a subject like this, which has only dim outlines in the minds of the people affected, after a while ceases to be useful, and the whole movement will, if promoted on these lines, die for want of practical direction and of demonstration to the people that practical reforms are intended.[54]

Taft understood that principled innovation does not necessarily last. It requires the creation of laws, rules, and processes to make it last. After noting the advances that had been made so far in withdrawing lands and establishing the legitimacy of such withdrawals, Taft returned to an appeal to the wisdom and ethics of conservation and its necessary attention to future generations: "Real conservation involves wise, nonwasteful use in the present generation, with every possible means of preservation for succeeding generations, and though the problem to secure this end may be difficult, the burden is on the present generation promptly to solve it and not to run away from it as cowards, lest in the attempt to meet it we may make some mistake."[55] Here one sees Taft's pep talk—motivational, responsible, and muscular, calling out laggards as cowards afraid to tackle the issue for fear of taking a misstep. Taft was aware of the presidency's potential to lead and shape public opinion. What he was doing here, though, was less calling attention to an issue and instead something much more difficult—rousing the public to *stay* engaged, to do the difficult work that follows awareness, and encouraging conservationists and experts to continue and secure the work that they were doing before they lost the opportunity. Simple awareness was not enough; awareness was not a high enough goal.

Taft made another appeal before concluding: "The problem is how to save and how to utilize, how to conserve and still develop; for no sane person can contend that it is for the common good that nature's blessings should be stored only for unborn generations."[56] Here is Taft's progressive conservatism, the era's compromise between conservation and development. We must conserve for future generations, Taft said, but the common good also allows use and development in the present.

In his conclusion, Taft underscored the need for specifics, for detail, as the next step after awareness and a better path than partisanship and inflamed rhetoric:

> I beg of you, therefore, in your deliberations and in your informal discussion, when men come forward to suggest evils that the promotion of conservation is to remedy, that you invite them to point out the specific evils and the specific remedies; that you invite them to come down to details in order that their discussions may flow into channels that shall be useful rather than into periods that shall be eloquent and entertaining, without shedding real light on the subject. The people should be shown exactly what is needed in order that they make their representatives in Congress and the state legislatures do their intelligent bidding.[57]

Taft's conservation efforts built on the attention that Roosevelt had brought to the issue, but Taft's vision for conservation differed from Roosevelt's. Roosevelt's efforts were often unilateral, ad hoc, built on executive action and informal agreements, infused with populism. Taft sought lasting success, codified in law and relying on clearly demarcated administrative responsibility.

Ballinger, Pinchot, and the Nature of Administrative Governance

Taft's use of executive tools and his leadership of the executive branch in pursuit of his reform goals can be seen in the Ballinger-Pinchot imbroglio. It is important to recognize that Taft not only had a different approach than Roosevelt to the details of policy, he had an entirely different approach to questions of governance and the use of presidential power. Taft's support for embattled Interior Secretary Richard Ballinger reflected Taft's core approach as a synthesist, in much the same way that John Quincy Adams's long-criticized tolerance of John McLean was consistent with Adams's procedurist approach to presidential decision making. What is seen by most scholars of this era as one of Taft's signature failures came when he alienated Roosevelt's forestry chief, the popular and charismatic Gifford Pinchot. Taft eventually forced Pinchot out of government, as he defended his own interior secretary against Pinchot, Roosevelt, and their followers. Taft's support for Ballinger and his break with the Roosevelt conservation wing is often seen as tone-deaf politics and a move away from Roosevelt's progressivism on the environment.[58] But what was really at issue was the approach to governing.[59]

Pinchot was, like Roosevelt, an aggressive, publicity-seeking leader of personal drive and mercurial action. Part of his approach to administering conservation had been to work out informal agreements with other departments and agencies that allowed Pinchot's Forest Service extensive de facto authority over lands and their use. Together with aggressive and shrewd use of public relations and the media, including writing for popular journals, Pinchot married popularity to personalized administration.[60] Roosevelt's interior secretary, James Garfield, while not as aggressive in the public arena as Pinchot, had a similar penchant for what political scientist Peri E. Arnold gently calls an "informal administrative style."[61] Less gently, Taft characterized Pinchot as "capable of any extreme act."[62] Abuses of executive power under Pinchot and Garfield, in the view of Taft and his allies, included informal agreements among executive departments that ignored congressionally demarcated divisions of authority, lack of planning on projects, closeness to preferred developers with unfair access to government bureaucrats, and ad-hoc and illegal administrative measures.[63] In short, the Pinchot team seemed to use handshake deals and friendly agreements inside and outside of government to run conservation efforts, skirting the law and endangering accountable administration.

Such behavior was not the Taft way.[64] Taft had appointed Ballinger head of the Department of Interior, which had legal authority over much of the land being managed by Pinchot and the Forest Service. Ballinger, like Taft, held an allegiance to law, procedure, and policy—he did not freelance, and he took seriously the administrative boundaries written into law by Congress. Ballinger balked at the informal deals made by Pinchot, deals that ignored these boundaries and, he believed, eroded institutional responsibility and accountability. Ballinger worked to reemphasize these lines, recover institutional authority lost to Pinchot, and regularize administration of conservation and forests.[65] In one of many examples, a program allowed forests on Native lands to be managed not by the Bureau of Indian Affairs, in Interior, but by the Forest Service. The program had been worked out by Pinchot and

Taft's commissioner of Indian affairs, Robert Valentine, but administrators at the bureau clashed with those from the Forest Service. Ballinger, responding to the disruptions, ruled the program illegal and ended it.[66] The approach taken by Taft and Ballinger saw law as a means to improved governmental outcomes—not as a brake on activity or a disincentive for action.

At the center of the controversy between Ballinger and Pinchot stood hundreds of thousands of acres of public lands to be used for water-power sites. Just before leaving office at the end of the Roosevelt administration in February 1909, Garfield had removed these thousands of acres from entry for sale to private entities, meaning they would remain under public control. Garfield appears not to have told his replacement, Ballinger, of the last-minute removals. When he learned of the removals, Ballinger—relying on law that stated that public land should be open to entry—found it beyond the authority of executive branch officials to remove the lands from entry. He reversed the withdrawal, making the lands once again able to be bid on and sold to private entities. Taft agreed.[67]

Pinchot and Louis Glavis, variously a functionary of the General Land Office and an activist on the West Coast, saw Ballinger's action as a rejection of their view, an insult to Pinchot's status as the nation's leading conservationist, and an abuse of executive authority in overturning *Garfield's* use of executive authority. Glavis charged Ballinger with having taken unlawful action years earlier in a case involving Alaskan coal lands. The battle became a front-page spectacle of charges, countercharges, and illegal and unethical behavior by the Pinchot-Glavis forces, all in a battle for the future direction of conservation policy and administration.[68]

The fight between the Roosevelt-Pinchot and Taft-Ballinger conceptions of conservation and environmentalism rumbled beneath a messy congressional investigation.[69] Taft eventually removed Glavis, who was fired in 1909.[70] Pinchot was forced to resign after directly and publicly confronting the president, and admitting insubordination, in a letter to Senator Jonathan Dolliver. Taft's dismissal of Pinchot was uncharacteristically sharp. For a man usually cheerful and calm, the tone of his letter to Pinchot is dramatic—and focuses on Pinchot's breach of procedure: "Your letter was in effect an improper appeal to Congress and the public to excuse in advance the guilt of your subordinates before I could act and against my decision in the Glavis case. . . . By your own conduct you have destroyed your usefulness as a helpful subordinate."[71]

Probably because of Roosevelt's reputation, the legal aspects of the controversy and the aspects that concern separation of powers and faithful execution of the laws tend to go missing from the historiography. Studies often paint the fight as Roosevelt's heroic conservationism and rugged use of executive power, on one hand, versus the reactionary conservatism of a complacent and corporation-friendly Taft administration, on the other. Pinchot's reputation as the zealous defender of the forests, and the czar of the Forest Service itself, seals the deal, usually, in favor of the Roosevelt forces. The quieter and literally more law-abiding Taft and Ballinger tend to be portrayed as reactionaries, standing in the way of a modern conception of eco-friendly policymaking.[72]

But Taft and Ballinger had a point, one that resurfaces every time a president uses executive powers to protect wilderness areas or direct environmental policy by executive orders and agreements. For Taft, much of this was best, and most lastingly, done through explicit lawmaking. Ballinger saw himself as standing against government by decrees issued by unelected bureaucrats pursuing a "public interest" that was closer to favoritism for the rich and connected.[73] He focused much of his effort on the limits of executive discretionary authority, the battle between Interior and the Forest Service, and on control of the Reclamation Service within Interior.[74] Ballinger saw Pinchot's relationships as favoring established industries and discriminating against newer ones, and historian James Penick Jr. wrote of Ballinger that "when he took refuge in the law it was as a haven against the arbitrary whim of individual administrators."[75]

Progressivism and following the law could certainly work together in promoting the conservation of wilderness spaces. The legal implications of the controversial Hetch Hetchy Dam's development outside of San Francisco, for example, led the Taft–Ballinger–Walter L. Fisher team to become the biggest obstacle to its construction. The Roosevelt and Wilson administrations worked assiduously in favor of constructing the dam, anticipating benefits that would accrue to San Francisco developers. Taft, Ballinger, and Fisher all deferred in the matter to Congress, believing that it was Congress's responsibility to make a final decision. Congress and the Supreme Court eventually clarified the executive's authority, effectively sanctioning the Taft administration's call for legislative clarity about the executive's authority to temporarily withdraw lands. Taft followed Roosevelt's lead in withdrawing public lands from private entry, but he asked (and received) congressional authorization.[76]

As leader of his administrative team, Taft stuck by Ballinger against forces that were angry at the opposition to the dynamic duo of Roosevelt and Pinchot. But Taft believed Ballinger was innocent of any wrongdoing in the cases at the heart of the congressional investigation. Later scholars have agreed, and Interior Secretary Harold Ickes in 1940 released the findings of an Interior Department investigation of Ballinger titled *Not Guilty*.[77] At great political cost then and afterward, Taft remained loyal to legal and administrative processes that he believed were the basis of forward-looking innovation, and he remained loyal to an expert administrator caught in the maelstrom of political infighting over policy. "If I were to turn Ballinger out, in view of his innocence and in view of the conspiracy against him," Taft wrote, "I should be a white-livered skunk."[78] Taft echoed Adams's loyalty to law-abiding subordinates, in service of principled innovations in conservation policy.

Taft and his appointees, in short, believed that the old ways of dealing with the environment had to be modernized—to pursue new goals, many of which had been articulated by Roosevelt, but also to ensure a balance between the people's welfare and private rights. Measures were carefully designed to promote government action through policies that simultaneously *contained* government action. When Ballinger resigned in 1911 and Taft replaced him with Fisher, Taft again emphasized law and administrative experience. Generally overlooked amid the glare of the Ballinger-Pinchot controversy, Fisher's tenure was professional and effective, achieving reforms as well as one of Taft's key goals: getting the spotlight off the Interior Department and its conservation efforts. Fisher was a friend of Pinchot's, a well-known and respected progressive conservationist, yet more moderate in tone than Pinchot. Fisher's reforms dominated activity at the Interior Department for the next twenty years and grounded lasting policy efforts in the Taft-Fisher approach to law and accountability.[79]

Surrendering to Pinchot would have meant surrendering deeply held commitments to administrative process, delegation of lawful authority, and the end result of lasting and effective conservation policy. Historians who view Taft as politically clumsy for his choices here miss the point entirely. This was a battle for policy, an important enough goal. But it was also a battle over the means by which policy is made and by which administrators carry out their charges. Notably, Taft won—Roosevelt is the poster child for conservation and the modern environmental movement, but his style of unilateral action in favor of the environment has never been universally accepted and has often been divisive and unstable—exemplified by the back and forth over unilateral executive actions to protect or develop public lands that has taken place across virtually every recent presidential administration. By contrast, Taft's approach—careful, deliberate, and with the strength and solidity of cooperative action, in tune with the rule of law and constitutional procedure—achieved lasting success on environmental issues. As mentioned above, Taft's administration conserved far more land than Roosevelt's had.[80]

International Arbitration Agreements

We have already seen that the Grant administration in the 1871 Treaty of Washington established a firm stance in favor of international arbitration treaties. Designed to help peacefully resolve conflicts and disagreements that might lead to war, according to a set and stable process, such arbitration treaties are the basis for international agreements like the North American Free Trade Agreement and the agreements governing the World Trade Organization, and international organizations like the United Nations. Taft bridged the gap between Grant's early efforts and the successful founding of lasting institutions based on arbitration and process as means of addressing international disputes. Taft was perhaps the most visible advocate in the early twentieth century for international arbitration agreements and international organizations. Taft's efforts to promote arbitration treaties were as visionary as his reforms in budgeting, taxation, regulation, and conservation, as he put the weight of his presidency and significant effort after he left office into laying the groundwork for an expanded set of international arbitration agreements.

Taft was no dreamer—he understood that war was unlikely to be eliminated. At the same time, Taft recognized that such treaties and organizations could go a long way toward establishing peaceful processes that would make war less likely and less frequent. Taft argued that world peace was possible, and he held up the effect of John Quincy Adams's Monroe Doctrine in Latin America as evidence. Taft emphasized the role that could be played by arbitration treaties in identifying justiciable issues in advance and creating a fair process for reaching resolution of disputes.[81] In campaign speeches, his Inaugural Address, and throughout his presidency, Taft promoted the Hague Tribunal and other measures.[82] Taft pressed the issue in a nationwide speaking tour in October 1911.[83] He made his case for peace: "We had the War of 1812," he said, "in which our neighbor, England, asserted rights that she would not now think of pressing. I think that war might have been settled without a fight and ought to have been. So with the Mexican War. So I think with the Spanish War." Taft received fulsome praise from the *New York Times* and other media outlets, and his initiatives won strong support among activists, peace organizations (whose memberships were dominated by lawyers and business leaders), and the general public.[84] In 1913 and 1914, Taft gave a series of four lectures published as *The United States and Peace*.

While the Roosevelt administration had been moving in the same direction, Taft balked at the approach Roosevelt had taken toward the process of securing the agreements. The track record on arbitration agreements from the Roosevelt presidency, in fact, served as a reminder of the weakness of principled innovation on its own. Roosevelt's secretary of state John Hay negotiated nine arbitration treaties, but executive agreements were the mechanism for implementing them. These efforts failed when the Senate scuttled the agreements.[85] The Senate understandably wanted a role, perhaps by sanctioning "special treaties" to get it done. Taft, in contrast, favored arbitration agreements crafted and codified as full treaties, sanctioned under the rules of the Constitution by a two-thirds vote of the Senate. Taft believed that this would create better policy, broader support, and more lasting effects than executive agreements.[86]

Another aspect of the Roosevelt administration's efforts bothered Taft's commitment to fairness and fair process. Elihu Root negotiated twenty-four other arbitration agreements for Roosevelt, which would have become activated if two-thirds of the Senate approved a special treaty in the particular case. These were flawed, in Taft's view, because they included a loophole demanded by U.S. senators—an off-ramp that would allow the United States to opt out of its arbitration agreements and commitments if the issue involved the "honor, independence, and vital interests" of the United States.[87] Of course, this then bound nothing and created no clear process and no commitment to having the arbitration agreement in the first place. If a major issue came up, in other words, and the United States could back out of arbitration by arguing that the new issue was in its vital interest, no serious matter would ever reach arbitration as a way of addressing and resolving it. Taft would argue for years that the "vital interest" loophole undermined the whole idea.[88]

Critically, Taft pointed out that the United States had to be ready to lose in arbitration—it had to be ready to be wrong, and to be willing to accept an adverse ruling if the arbitration process so concluded. "We cannot win every case," he wrote. "Nations are like individuals; they are not always right, even though they think they are, and if arbitration is to accomplish anything, we must be willing to lose and abide by the loss."[89] Taft was the first head of any government to endorse arbitration agreements without the loophole of "national honor and vital interests."[90]

President Taft signed arbitration treaties with France and Britain on August 3, 1911.[91] Article 2 of these treaties created a Joint High Commission of Inquiry, consisting of three Americans appointed by the president and three members from the other country, which would decide if an issue were justiciable. If so found, by vote of at least five of the six commissioners, the agreements called for arbitration by the Permanent Court of Arbitration at The Hague or by a special tribunal created by executive agreement. Article 2 covered all issues—without the vital interest loophole.

Taft's effort to synthesize the principled innovations of arbitration treaties with a new and lasting process failed. In the view of critics, Taft's agreements undercut the constitutional role of the Senate in examining individual treaties. But Taft argued that if the Senate could bind the United States to arbitrate a single question, it could also bind the country for *all* questions. In other words, Taft's view of the sharing of foreign policy powers included grey areas that allowed for flexibility among the branches, and he linked his innovations to procedural tradition. Taft argued that this was an area that would benefit from a balance of process and politics in the very real, very pragmatic sense: "If the

Senate can not now bind us to abide by the judgment of an arbitral court as to whether a question is justiciable, it can never bind us, and if the Senate can not bind us, the nation can not bind us, and this peace-loving people is forever incapable of taking a step along the great path which all the world wishes to tread, and along which all the world thinks America best fitted to lead."[92]

In seeking passage, Taft compromised with the Senate and tried to work out a more inclusive process. The Senate would, for example, approve all presidential nominees to the Joint High Commission.[93] The Senate would also have an effective "veto" over matters declared justiciable, by requiring the negotiation of a special agreement defining the powers of the arbitrators and the questions to be arbitrated.[94] Critically, Senate amendment also excluded from the process any questions involving the Monroe Doctrine, immigration rules, state debts, and territorial disputes. In the end, as loopholes and exceptions multiplied, Taft became dissatisfied. He refused to submit the reworked agreements to France and Britain.[95]

Taft's reaction to the demise of the treaties, however, was forward-looking: "It was not that those treaties would have abolished war; nobody said they would; but it was that they were a step in the right direction toward the practical ideal under which war would have been impossible. Other nations might have followed our lead with one another, and we would have an interlacing of treaties."[96] For Taft, the effort was a practical one, to make arbitration the initial go-to place to address disputes. Deliberation and compromise, as in the United States system, would bend toward thoughtful and peaceful resolution. The entire system would be governed by a stated process, a new rule of law, far beyond what had been contained in peace treaties, and expanding the sway of fair process and the rule of law in international affairs.

Taft would continue his efforts on behalf of arbitration treaties after leaving the presidency. He was a prominent advocate of the "League to Enforce Peace," speaking on its behalf at the Century Club in New York in the fall of 1914. Taft became the league's president when it was officially formed in 1915, and he traveled the country on behalf of its principles.

Conclusion

Taft summed up his presidential experience at the Lotus Club in New York, ten days after losing the 1912 presidential election:

> The Presidency is a great office to hold. It is a great honour and it is surrounded with much that makes it full of pleasure and enjoyment for the occupant, in spite of its heavy responsibilities and the shining mark that it presents for misrepresentation and false attack.... Of course the great and really the

only lasting satisfaction that one can have in the administration of the great office of President is the thought that one has done something permanently useful to his fellow countrymen. The mere enjoyment of the tinsel of office is ephemeral, and unless one can fix one's memory on real progress made through the exercise of presidential power there is little real pleasure in the contemplation of the holding of that or any other office, however great its power or dignity or high its position in the minds of men.[97]

Taft always began with a belief in the wisdom of concerted, collaborative action. He believed that the entire governing system functioned best when presidential leadership and innovation were tied intimately to the functionings and powers of other departments, other people, and other points of view. Lasting policy was best enacted through legislation—not through presidential fiat—to adapt to modern circumstances, to achieve lasting effects, and to build predictable processes. The interactions of institutions like Congress and the courts helped ensure a republican system of government, helped protect individual rights and competing groups, and helped individuals and collective interests achieve effective representation.

Taft operated in a world encased in Jim Crow racism, anti-Native paternalism, and anti-woman subjugation. He faced a world of deep labor unrest, with a growing laborers' movement that had been organizing strikes and operating in conflict with owners and the wealthy for decades. Taft also faced a divided political scene, one exacerbated by the unpredictable actions taken for almost eight years by Theodore Roosevelt.

In our appreciation of Roosevelt's achievements, though, it is often easy to forget just how divisive a figure he was—a provocateur with a radical conception of the presidency and its powers under the Constitution. Taft faced the expectations of Roosevelt's supporters as well as the fears of those who thought he went too far, and Taft justified his loss to Woodrow Wilson in the 1912 presidential campaign on the basis of having prevented a return of Roosevelt to the presidency. Taft pointedly stated after winning the Republican nomination that "no matter what happens, Roosevelt cannot be elected. I draw my consolation and satisfaction from that." After the election, Taft would drive the point home: "If he [Roosevelt] had been elected, I don't think anybody could measure the damage he would have done."[98]

Taft pushed his innovative ideas not into open space but into established procedures and the constitutional system. He did this because he trusted that patience and hard work in that system would produce the best creative results. "One of the propositions that I adhere to," Taft wrote, "is that it is a very dangerous method of upholding reform to violate the law in so doing, even on the ground of high moral principle, or saving the public."[99] Taft encouraged constitutional discussion and debate in promoting his major initiatives, and he shrewdly managed the institutional mechanisms involved. He helped conserve impressive quantities of public resources for future generations through new laws and procedures, he led the reordering of the legal and economic relationships between business and government, and he helped increase the relevance of modern structures of international peace, which today include the United Nations and the International Criminal Court. Taken together, Taft's syntheses of principled innovations and enduring processes helped set the foundation for the American century.

CONCLUSION
THE NON-DEVELOPMENT OF THE AMERICAN PRESIDENCY AND THE NEW SCHOLARSHIP OF THE AMERICAN STATE

IT IS CLEAR from the foregoing that centering a traditional-modern dichotomy in the development of the American presidency may not be the best way to conceive of the presidency over time. The administrations of John Quincy Adams, Ulysses S. Grant, and William Howard Taft featured presidents pushing specific legislative agendas, engaging in public communication, leading the administrative bureaucracy, and utilizing executive action tools to influence policymaking and other issues. But what of the state? The scholars who have discerned a change in the twentieth-century presidency have attributed that development to changes in the scope and significance of state activity. But these aspects of the state did not change much either: the state and its administrative capacity have been robust in America since the Washington administration. The idea that changes in the state's capacities and relevance have driven changes in the presidency is flawed on both sides of the equation.

So what *has* changed?

My answer lies in exploring changes in the nature of the state's goals more than in its scope, as the modern liberal state became increasingly enmeshed in mediating conflicts at the intersection of state power and individual rights. While exploring this dynamic fully is beyond the scope of this book, the analysis in the preceding chapters suggests the significance of post–Civil War juridical and constitutional changes. What explains the difference of the twentieth century is the revised Constitution's effects on the polity, and the effects that judges have had on the state. Those dynamics are far more important, and far more significantly altered, from the early republic to the twentieth and twenty-first centuries than are either the scope of state activity or the policy and leadership tools of presidents. This chapter examines consistencies in state capacity and presidential leadership over time, addresses the changes to state goals after the Civil War, and highlights the importance of individual character, integrity, and decision-making approaches when seeking to understand presidential behavior in any era.

Misreading the Twentieth Century by Misunderstanding the Nineteenth

The perceived—yet largely undemonstrated—twentieth-century increase in the use of presidential direct action, popular communication, and legislative and administrative leadership has often been tied to one of four dynamics generally presented as "modern," and therefore explanatory of the perceived increase in opportunities to exercise presidential powers: (1) the rise of the administrative state, (2) the arrival of the United States on the global stage, (3) the increase in the significance of modern crises, and (4) increasing partisanship and gridlock. All of these, in various combinations, have been presented as drivers of increased presidential use of direct-action tools and increased presidential action in relation to legislation, administrative leadership, and public communication. These explanations for the increased use of presidential action, however, are ripe for reassessment. Recent scholarship suggests the presence of an intrusive and expansive administrative state in the nineteenth-century United States. Foreign policy issues drove significant executive action in the nineteenth century, particularly when we recognize the hybrid foreign-domestic policy nature of many key issue areas in these years. Crises in the nineteenth century were perceived by presidents and other observers as existential threats to the nation. Partisanship and divided government were frequent features of nineteenth-century politics.

ONE LINE of explanation for the perceived increase in the use of presidential direct-action tools sees the presidency as responding to the federal government's expanding functions in the late nineteenth and early twentieth centuries. As the federal government took on more responsibilities and the administrative state became more influential in policymaking and in people's lives, the argument goes, presidents capitalized on the vague grant of "executive power" in the Constitution to take the reins of policy and administrative leadership. This argument is often presented as a clean, linear development: administration supposedly moved from congressional control exercised through detailed laws and careful oversight in the nineteenth century, to expert control and then interest group control in the late nineteenth and early twentieth centuries, and finally to presidential control.[1] A classic misstatement of American development came from Woodrow Wilson in his *Congressional Government*.[2] More recently, scholars like Elena Kagan have seen Congress's role as originally one of providing detailed regulatory statutes and the president's role as late-developing, but such work generally relies on the era of the Interstate Commerce Commission as its starting point—which is about ninety years too late.[3] Presidents are seen as adapting to an increasing state, as when Sidney M. Milkis introduces his essay in *The Oxford Handbook of American Political Development* with a series of rhetorical questions, including, "How has presidential power been affected by the emergence of 'big government' during the first six decades of the twentieth century and the rancorous political contest over its authority that has endured ever since?"[4] Important works like Stephen Skowronek's *Building a New American State: The Expansion of National Administrative Capacities, 1877–1920*; Daniel P. Carpenter's *The Forging of Bureaucratic Autonomy: Reputations, Networks, and Policy Innovation in Executive Agencies, 1862–1928*; and Richard Franklin Bensel's *Yankee Leviathan: The Origins of Central State Authority in America, 1859–1877* all locate significant state development in various ways late in the nineteenth century.[5]

These works, though, misunderstand the early development of administrative functions at the federal level. Their approach has been challenged by voluminous recent scholarship, with William Novak leading the charge against the "myth" of the weak American state. In critical policy areas like land acquisition, land policy, Indian affairs, customs enforcement, and diplomacy, early Congresses passed broad laws delegating vast authority over administrative detail to presidents and executive branch subordinates. As we have seen in the Adams, Grant, and Taft administrations, such details were overseen by presidents and also relied on the work of expert administrators, skilled and experienced technicians, and others to whom were delegated policymaking authority over complicated public issues.[6] Numerous independent boards and commissions, composed of a variety of experts and interest group representatives, supplemented these efforts; see, for example, multiple bodies established to adjudicate land and title disputes, the Bernard Board on national defense, the Freedman's Commission, and the Board of Indian Commissioners.

To rest conclusions about the development of presidential authority on a misunderstanding of the development of the administrative state invites serious error. As with the capacity of the president to act unilaterally, the office's relationship to administration developed fast, early, and in a way that looks remarkably as it does today. If leadership of the American administrative state is an explanation for presidential action, then leading the administrative state would have tempted earlier presidents.

THE UNITED STATES' entry on the world stage in the twentieth century is often seen as opening up opportunities in foreign policy that effectively expanded presidential powers and responsibilities.[7] This approach, though, misconstrues the presence of the United States in international politics throughout the nineteenth century. Adams's entire career; Grant's efforts in Europe, Korea, and the Caribbean; and Taft's global presence all suggest wide opportunity for executive action in foreign affairs long before the heart of the twentieth century. These presidents' choices to deploy or not to deploy executive authority should be examined, not dismissed.

An argument about the state and the presidency that focuses on the state's international position in the twentieth century also misleads because it is difficult to draw bright lines between foreign and domestic affairs involving the federal government in the late eighteenth and nineteenth centuries. While many of the earliest uses of unilateral action tools and administrative leadership in critical issues seem to have involved essentially foreign policy matters, like the Neutrality Proclamation and the Louisiana Purchase, the complexity of the nation's policy environment makes drawing distinctions between executive action in foreign affairs versus domestic affairs difficult. In other words, because rare, high-profile examples dealt with matters generally considered to be foreign affairs, like the Neutrality Proclamation, and because we have only recently begun to recognize the depth of the nineteenth-century federal government's involvement in domestic administration, there has been a tendency to draw a bright line between unilateral executive capacity in foreign and domestic affairs. This is misleading.

There were many unilateral actions touching on clearly domestic affairs, and there were many unilateral actions in areas that were a complex blend of foreign and domestic concerns. U.S. Indian policy involved both foreign and domestic affairs simultaneously, for example, in a manner that blurs easy distinctions. Land acquisition, treaty negotiations, territorial governance, removal of white squatters, and fur-trade regulation can all be seen as both domestic and foreign, in some senses dealing with internal matters and in others dealing with relations among nations and foreign entities. Similar arguments might be made about commissions examining Spanish land-grant controversies; extensions of criminal justice authority into territorial regions like the Dakotas, Puerto Rico, and the Philippines; and the work generally of administrative units like the War Department, Treasury Department, and Customs Service throughout the nineteenth century. If foreign affairs and international politics are explanations for presidential action, then leading in international and hybrid domestic-foreign affairs contexts would have tempted earlier presidents.

ANOTHER EXPLANATION for a perceived rise in executive action and presidential leadership sees presidential opportunities expanding as the severity of crises facing the United States increased in the twentieth century. Authors like Terry M. Moe and William G. Howell, while acknowledging the difficulty of tracking presidential action, conclude that "consequential" presidential actions have increased over time. They base their conclusion in part on the large crises of the twentieth century.[8] It is not clear, though, why the Cold War or the 1990s

Gulf Crisis as it appeared to twentieth-century presidents necessarily loomed as more significant "crises" than did Spanish control of the Mississippi River in the 1790s, the War of 1812, or Custer's defeat in the minds of presidents confronted with choices about how, and whether, to use executive powers unilaterally. John Quincy Adams believed that the crisis with Georgia over the Creek treaties threatened to produce civil war in the 1820s, as we have seen. Grant understood Reconstruction and western expansion to be existential issues confronting the United States, and Taft perceived unrestrained capitalism and inequality—among other issues—as threats to the viability of the American experiment. Were President Barack Obama's executive orders on immigration, or President Donald Trump's on tariffs, more consequential than Grant opening the Black Hills to white encroachment? Are those modern actions more consequential than Adams's unilateral actions to spur the Pacific Expedition? Are they more consequential than Taft's innovations regarding the president's role in national budgeting, or his veto of Arizona's statehood application in order to protect the independence of the judiciary? It is not clear why events related to Indian affairs, westward expansion, nineteenth-century diplomacy, or other crises would not have opened the same executive action opportunities for earlier presidents. If crisis and threat are explanations for presidential action, leading the responses to crises and threats would have tempted earlier presidents.

FINALLY, INCREASING partisanship and attendant gridlock in Congress is often cited as an explanation for the increased use by presidents of direct-action tools.[9] Yet the three presidencies examined closely in this book existed in times of great partisan strife, notably Adams's divisive battles with the growing influence of Jacksonian Democrats; Grant's battles with often violent Democrats and splinter factions within his own Republican Party; and Taft's battles with Democrats, Socialists, and fragments of his own Republican Party at the height of the Progressive era, which led to the historic four-way presidential election of 1912. There is nothing inherently more partisan, or inherently more likely to lead to gridlock, in the Democrats' mid-twentieth-century dominance or the party battles being fought since the Reagan era. If partisanship and gridlock are explanations for presidential action, the partisanship and gridlock of earlier eras also would have tempted earlier presidents.

IT IS THUS LIKELY *not* the twentieth-century presence of significant administrative capacity, the role of foreign policy, the perceived significance of crises, or partisanship that explains any apparent increase in recent presidents' willingness to use tools of direct action, to lead on administrative and legislative policymaking, or to engage in public communication. All of these dynamics of the state and the presidency are characteristic of the eighteenth and nineteenth centuries. What we confront is a presidency that has always enjoyed a state with significant administrative capacity, a presidency that has always possessed the tools for taking direct action, a presidency that has always been involved in foreign policymaking and has regularly faced what were seen as significant crises, and a presidency that has often faced partisan and institutional obstacles to leadership.

U.S. presidents have always had the capacity to act unilaterally and to lead. Institutional tools and opportunities for executive action have long existed, a fact evident in both our familiar tales of unilateral executive action and in new information coming to the fore as scholars examine issue areas in which presidential and administrative action have long gone unnoticed. Leadership tools available to presidents developed, and were deployed, early. Executive privilege, executive orders, presidential proclamations, public rhetoric and communication, and a defense of presidential prerogative and presidential control of the executive branch all date back to the earliest presidential administrations. Terry Moe and William Howell's listing of executive capacities, for example, is as true of the early presidency as it is of the presidency since the turn of the twentieth century. Presidents from George Washington forward have had an independent base of authority that enhanced the executive nature of the job. They have had the operations of government in their hands (including what Moe and Howell refer to as the reconciliation of conflicting values). They have had "at their disposal a tremendous reservoir of expertise, experience, and information, both in the institutional presidency and in the bureaucracy at large." They have been "ideally suited to be *first movers* and to reap agenda powers that go along with it."[10]

Each of the main subjects in this book came to the presidency having directly witnessed these dynamics, including significant uses of unilateral executive authority: Adams was in Congress for the Louisiana Purchase, he was in the cabinet as Jackson invaded Florida, and he wrote James Monroe's Monroe Doctrine. Grant witnessed Abraham Lincoln's unprecedented actions during the Civil War as well as the fights between Andrew Johnson and Congress over executive authority. Taft had been an integral part of nation-building under William McKinley and Theodore Roosevelt, and then an important cabinet member during Roosevelt's precedent-shattering presidency.

Certainly the three knew that they *could* take unilateral action, and certainly they understood that such action would likely be supported and approved by their own parties and perhaps by the broader public, as had been the case in all of these examples. There were calls for Adams to fight slavery more directly, calls for Grant to act more decisively to build Republican Party strength in the South, calls for Taft to invade Mexico. Fully aware of prior examples, John Quincy Adams, Ulysses S. Grant, and William Howard Taft each enjoyed opportunities to take unilateral action, and in certain situations they availed themselves of the office's potential and took action. Sometimes, they chose not to: Adams, Grant, and Taft consciously and willingly interacted with Congress and the courts in some of the most critical issue areas they faced, eschewing opportunities to exercise unilateral power on such issues and instead placing their own favored priorities at risk by working through a system of separated powers that imperiled, and sometimes defeated, their preferences, as we have seen.

In short, if the foundations of traditional studies of the presidency are limited by having overlooked state and administrative action in the nineteenth century, and have misread the opportunities available for presidential leadership in these years, then the basic narrative of presidential development may be as fundamentally misleading as the myth of a weak state that has long dominated scholarship in American history and political development.

The President and the People's Welfare

So, to ask again, what has changed?

William Howard Taft served at the center of the shift in American governmental priorities from what William Novak, in his landmark book, called *The People's Welfare*.[11] Novak described state and local governance from the republic's earliest days that valued and pursued the people's welfare, *salus populi*, in a manner somewhat foreign to Americans today. Government was expected to work for the benefit of the populace, and it did, with little interference from or traction gained by those who saw individual rights, particularly property rights, being negatively affected. Novak tracked examples of communities tearing down private structures that blocked public rights of way, of communities enacting quarantines on ships and sailors (many of which interfered directly with profits), of cities preventing private construction on public land and seaways, and of the intentional destruction of private warehouses to allow for firebreaks. Lawsuits claiming that the regulation or destruction of private property was unlawful were consistently rejected by the courts, which saw the maintenance and protection of the people's welfare as clearly prioritized over individual rights.

While Novak's book focuses on the state and local levels, in other places he has addressed these issues at the national level, and together his work suggests a possible explanation for the puzzle of American state development when neither the presidency nor the capacity of the state seem to have changed much since the late eighteenth and early nineteenth centuries.[12] The new literature on American state development in the nineteenth century supports the interpretation that much was done in service of the people's welfare at the national level: land policy, health policy, Indian affairs, infrastructure development, and economic regulation, for example. Many of these policy areas had negative effects on private property, and the courts generally favored the federal government's pursuit of the public welfare above the claimed rights of individuals.[13] Much more research is needed to make this case decisively, but it is clear in cases like *Johnson v. McIntosh* (1823) and in the absence of legal challenges to laws like the 1790 "Act for the Government and Regulation of Seamen in the Merchants Service," the 1798 "Act for the Relief of Sick and Disabled Seamen," or the Indian Trade and Intercourse Acts (1790–1834) that national policy did not succumb easily to challenges from individuals claiming damage to their rights and property.[14] John Quincy Adams's approach to the presidency and to governing clearly fell within this tradition. Most notably, Adams's vibrant promotion of internal improvements furthered the idea that government existed to improve the lives of the people.

Novak argued that this began to change at the state and local level in the latter part of the nineteenth century. Fear of advancing government action after the Civil War raised concerns that sparked growth in efforts to defend the rights of individuals against the power of government and its effects on people's lives. Previously, when such clashes were decided by the courts, they were decided easily in favor of governmental efforts to improve conditions for everyone. Increasingly, though, courts began to see violations of individual rights by government, and a period of tensions arose.

Grant's presidency is near the beginning of these developments, and one can see the tensions arising from the Civil War amendments to which Grant and his presidency were so committed. The amendments sought to ensure equality, justice, and other improvements for all people, and yet they also began to be utilized to defend against government intrusions into private and corporate life. The Department of Justice sought to protect individuals, even as temporary congressional authorizations of presidential action aimed to place limits on Grant and his administration's ability to intrude into people's lives. Congress's fading Reconstruction efforts, and the Supreme Court's increasing opposition to governmental interference, whittled away at Grant's ability to use the national government to protect and further the people's welfare. The battle between traditional *salus populi* and the strengthening individual rights tradition, especially exemplified by controversies surrounding the application of the Fourteenth Amendment, characterized that era.

I agree with Novak when he writes, "The central question of the late nineteenth-century polity was what would hold it all together." The era from 1877 to 1937 was one of great transformation in the state and the society:

"Liberal constitutionalism thrived on (and reinforced) the separation of public from private, state power from individual right. Indeed, its identity and strength hinged on its role as the principal guardian of the sacrosanct boundaries between power and liberty. The invention of this constitutional law entailed fundamentally new rationalities of regulation, social governance, and public order." Moreover, "Between 1877 and 1937, then, American conceptions of state power, individual rights, and the rule of law were fundamentally transformed"—so fundamentally that Novak noted how difficult it is for us to even see it.[15]

At the center of this sixty-year period stand many important figures. Among them is William Howard Taft: federal judge in its developing years, president at its center, and chief justice of the Supreme Court in its later period. Taft played a unique and indispensable role in defining and codifying the new balances that defined the twentieth-century American polity. Taft's presidency landed square in the middle of this transition, as the republic moved from its century-long tradition of majoritarian policymaking to its second-century deference to the rights of individuals and minority groups. Taft served at the peaked intersection of these two grand approaches to the state, and Taft the synthesist built new principles into enduring policies and programs. In this, President Taft becomes a central figure in the creation of twentieth-century America.

Novak wrote that the new regime's "central attribute was the simultaneous pursuit of two seemingly antagonistic tendencies—the *centralization of power* and the *individualization of subjects*. The two would be ultimately mediated (and, again simultaneously, promoted) by the *constitutionalization of law*." He continued, "Power and liberty, formerly interwoven in the notion of self-regulating, common law communities, were now necessary antipodes kept in balance only through the magnetic genius of an ascendant American constitutionalism." For Novak, it was the Civil War and the constitutional amendments following that conflict that began to reorganize and transform public life and its relationship to private right. The changes emanating from the Thirteenth, Fourteenth, and Fifteenth Amendments were argued in courts and realized in practice:

> The constitutional clauses "involuntary servitude," "privileges and immunities," "due process," "equal protection," and "right of citizens of the United States" embodied a whole new political philosophy. The heart of that philosophy was a radical reconstruction of individual rights. Abolitionism, emancipation, and radical Republicanism renewed interest in the inherent, natural, and absolute rights of individuals, dethroning a public-spirited common law as the source of American fundamental law. In contrast to the law of *salus populi*, this new

"higher" constitutionalism emphasized individual freedoms and personal autonomy rather than the duties incumbent upon members of organized and regulated communities. These were the roots of distinctly modern notions of individual civil rights and civil liberties.[16]

The three presidents examined in this book reflect this evolution. Adams's focus on the common welfare sought to better society through internal improvements, adherence to federal supremacy and law, and well-understood common traditions and procedures anchored in Novak's nineteenth-century state, even at the federal level, with a vast diversity of application in western areas.[17] Grant's innovations and adaptations after the Civil War reflect the landscape-altering impact of the Civil War amendments, as the national state tried simultaneously to reunite the Union, construct a new union, and extend across the continent in the following decades, even as courts (including the Supreme Court) and judges (eventually including Taft) worked to calibrate the balances between state activity and individual rights.[18] By the time of Taft's presidency, the novel legal approaches to those amendments and to the new liberal constitutionalism had become ripe for comprehensive approaches in national policy—the effort to reconcile and balance the ever-increasing state, an increasingly diverse population studded with new rights for previously unrepresented and enslaved groups, and growing private rights and accumulations of private wealth and property. At the national level, President Taft helped lead a significant part of the effort to codify new, written rules governing the intersection of private right and the public welfare.

Taft built the foundation for reconciling these competing goals in a kind of symbiotic tension that would characterize American governance in the twentieth century. Having dealt with some of these issues as a judge, President Taft worked to cement government's ability to provide for the people's welfare through the personal income tax, a corporation tax, and campaign finance regulation. And yet, those laws also recognized and established limits on government's intrusive capabilities in an effort to strike a balance between the power of the state to act for all and the power of the state to intrude on the one or the few.

In Taft's "Special Message on the Employers' Liability and Workmen's Compensation Commission," for example, Taft addressed the constitutional question related to the due process clause of the Fifth Amendment. He noted for Congress that the report recommending the measure examined the issue and satisfied the president that the measure was constitutional.[19] With the corporation tax, Taft touted the transparency of government access to corporate records but allowed that the law made it difficult for ordinary citizens to access sensitive data. Taft was well aware of the balance he was trying to create between government and public goals, on one hand, and private property rights and privacy on the other. A 1910 amendment to the law restricted access to corporate filings, making them "open to inspection only upon the order of the President under rules and regulations to be prescribed by the Secretary of the Treasury and approved by the President."[20] In his Second Annual Message, Taft discussed the president's role in issuing regulations and the process that had been designed to ensure public transparency and access to those records, while including provisions that protected business interests and privacy.[21] When the Supreme Court upheld the act in 1911, it specifically ruled on the balancing act properly enacted between the needs of the larger society and the interests of corporations under the Fourth and Fifth Amendments.[22] Such balancing is characteristic of Taft administration efforts in antitrust and conservation as well.[23]

Notably, in my understanding, it is Theodore Roosevelt who represents the dying breaths of the old order, not Taft. Roosevelt's efforts to solve problems on behalf of the people, sometimes through executive power alone and a radically reoriented view of the presidency, rested on an older tradition that easily prioritized *salus populi* over individual rights. Roosevelt's best-known policy efforts and his philosophy of governance are much closer to those of John Quincy Adams than they are to the twentieth-century world of individual rights and property interests understood to be in direct conflict with governmental efforts to regulate on behalf of the people. It was Taft who believed in the need to balance the tensions, and their benefits, in a world that was already well on its way toward the concentration of individual wealth, on one hand, and the awesome power of the state to divide or threaten that wealth, on the other. It was Taft who helped define and codify the scope and limits of governmental authority in a manner that effectively carved out space for pursuit of the people's welfare while simultaneously crafting procedural protections for individual rights and property.

The days of the president and the state working together to pursue the people's welfare had seen government actions to restrict and control land acquisition, build infrastructure, regulate alcohol sales, provide healthcare, and much more upheld by federal courts against minimal private challenges. Those days had transitioned to the novel battles between government action and legal and constitutional restraint characteristic of the post–Civil War years. By the time Taft left office, Roosevelt's effort to use the presidency to hold on to the glory days of the people's welfare had been modernized by Taft: the state was now clearly ensconced in continued activity, as it always had been, and the presidency was still an office of energy, legislative initiatives, public communication, and unilateral action, as it always had been. But the effort to balance that activity against private right and interest had been codified in the tax system, antitrust enforcement, campaign finance regulation, and conservation efforts, forcing the president into a new role as balancer-in-chief.[24]

From the late eighteenth century to the early twentieth, it was not the presidency that changed, and it was not state capacity that changed. It was not even the populace that had changed that much, as there had always been challenges to government action. What changed was an ethos of governance, including the increasing willingness of federal judges to hear—and accept—the constitutional challenges to national government action that they had previously dismissed as less worthy than government efforts to provide for the people's welfare.

Presidential Choice and Decision Making

If what has changed over time is not the use of presidential tools and resources, and it is not the existence of a robust and intrusive American state, but rather the purposes to which the state and presidency are put, then we are back to recognizing the importance of traditional study of individual presidents, their character, and their decision making. It is important that Taft the jurist-administrator was at the center of so much activity between the end of the Civil War and the New Deal. Taft matters for what his background was and what he did in office, and how he made decisions, in the same way that Theodore Roosevelt and Woodrow Wilson matter as individuals. Three very different people occupying the same office, with different approaches to the fundamental questions of the era, they innovated differently and addressed established rules and procedures with different degrees of respect. There continues to be value in studying the people who hold the office, including their formative years, early careers, and even what lessons can be gleaned from their post-presidencies.

Adams, Grant, and Taft deployed consistent—if very different—decision-making approaches to the matters they faced as presidents. Each shared an understanding that unilateral executive action was appropriate and necessary. All three presidents were what we often think of as strong presidents, when "strong" is characterized by the exercise of unilateral executive authority paired with aggressive defenses of presidential independence. All three presidents exercised presidential authority aggressively, and all three collaborated with Congress on critical issues. Yet the three left legacies of different natures corresponding to their decision-making ethics.

The procedurist often leaves a legacy free of controversy and challenges. John Quincy Adams, for example, is rarely the subject of debate about his motives or the rationale for his decisions. What debate surrounds Adams is usually about what is perceived as his clumsiness as president—for a man so

CONCLUSION 221

steeped in politics and leadership, historians especially have often been bewildered at his apparent failures in the presidency. But many of those "failures," as we have seen, were the result of a consistently procedurist approach: the failure to remove John McLean, the failure to appoint delegates to the Panama Congress unilaterally, the apparent (but untrue) failure to persuade the country to continue to support national involvement in a host of domestic policies and programs. But the criticisms are about the choices, from a policy or political standpoint. Adams is rarely if ever the subject of serious questions about his consistency, his integrity, or the basis for his decisions. Thus does the procedurist gain safe harbor by relying on rules and traditions. The procedurist leaves a quiet, safe, and secure legacy, vulnerable only to charges that more might have been done if only the procedurist had been willing to take more risks.

By contrast, the principled innovator leaves a trail of controversy and debate. They are the most argued about and debated presidents because of their approach. Fighting for what was "right," making ad-hoc and unpredictable tactical decisions, and innovating in pursuit of broad goals, Grant as president sought to reform and redirect the state apparatus in a series of innovations toward new ends and to advance broad principles. This presidential approach to decision making is often controversial, and the roller-coaster ride of historical assessments of President Grant bear this out. The merits and limitations of his initiatives and his decision making are endlessly debated. Those who agree with Grant's priorities portray him as a near-great president striving desperately to secure goals like freedom, justice, and equality, and doing whatever he could to get the job done. Grant's detractors, though, have seen in Grant an instinctive, ad-hoc decision maker who lacked consistency or long-term effectiveness. It is difficult to find consensus about such a president. The pursuit of higher ideals makes a principled innovator vulnerable to criticism of those ideals, preference for other ideals, or simply criticism of tactics and policy choices about means. This occurs in a manner rarely visited upon the procedurist. And there is no fallback—where the procedurist seeks solace in procedures and fairness, even aloofness, the principled innovator remains in the thick of it, unprotected by neutral procedures approved by broad consensus among individuals who disagree.[25]

Among the three decision-making approaches described here, the synthesist secures the most lasting and most lauded legacy. One of the few great and consistent synthesists, President Taft led the creation of enduring innovations that in many ways set the foundations for the American state over the course of the American century. Taft helped integrate new understandings of individual rights, thrown up against state activity after the Civil War. Where the principled innovator leaves a controversial personal legacy, the synthesist leaves a lasting national legacy. This analysis, in fact, suggests strongly that a broader reevaluation of Taft's presidency may be in order.

John Quincy Adams, Ulysses S. Grant, and William Howard Taft governed with integrity. Their presidential leadership was consistent with their pre-presidential careers, and each applied a consistent decision-making ethic to the issues they faced as president. Their individual legacies follow in good order: the safe reputation of the procedurist, the controversial debates about the principled innovator, and the lasting contributions of the synthesist.

REEXAMINATIONS OF the state have led to an understanding of a vibrant, influential, extensive, and intrusive American state in the late eighteenth and nineteenth centuries. Reexamination of the presidency's place in that state reveals rich examples of presidential leadership and the steady use of modern executive tools throughout American history. Bringing to studies of the presidency a more careful assessment of the president's actions in the nineteenth- and early twentieth-century administrative state—meaning examining presidential actions related to territorial and cultural expansion, land acquisition, the development of infrastructure and social programs, Indian affairs, race relations, diplomacy, and leadership in public administration, among other matters—reveals an active and independent presidency in three very different eras.

BIBLIOGRAPHICAL ESSAY
THE AMERICAN STATE AND THE UNDERSTUDIED PRESIDENCY

The field of presidency studies has long underestimated the presidency before Theodore Roosevelt. This is an understandable outgrowth of our long misunderstanding about the scope and complexity of the American state before the Progressive era, but earlier works in this field are thus often incomplete. These works have been indispensable touchstones that have helped us organize the field of presidency studies and identify themes and dynamics that stretch across presidencies and are worthy of study. At the same time, scholarship about the presidency must keep pace with new revelations about American state development.[1]

The dominant literature about the presidency and the American state engages at least five main lines of analysis: administrative leadership, executive direct action, diplomacy and war-making, legislative leadership, and popular communication. Studies focusing on the president's administrative leadership rely on an assumption of a small and immature state administrative apparatus in the nineteenth century, and find a presidency that exercised little administrative leadership before the Progressive era and which then struggled to keep up with the increasing scope of twentieth-century governance. Studies of executive direct action similarly present earlier presidents as rarely utilizing tools of direct executive action, such as executive orders, signing statements, and proclamations; when they did use such tools, their use is generally thought to have been for mostly ceremonial or minor issues. Scholars of the president's commander-in-chief authority have generally overlooked the vast amount of war-making and violence in North America in the nineteenth century, and have taken little serious notice of the president's role in regular but significant international diplomacy. Another set of studies focuses on the president's legislative agenda, generally seeing the eighteenth- and nineteenth-century president as one that neither proposed nor pushed for specific legislative initiatives and who rarely tried to lead Congress on policy—in part because the president lacked the administrative and information resources to do so, and in part because the president was beholden to party dynamics and therefore was much less of an independent force than we are used to today. Finally, the eighteenth- and nineteenth-century presidents are seen as eschewing popular leadership, failing to rally the public, talk politics, or use moral suasion. Part of this is related to the assumedly limited resources at the president's disposal, but part is tied to an argument about etiquette and tradition that deterred presidents from going "over the head" of Congress and speaking directly to the people.

Each of these five standard building blocks of our understanding of the eighteenth- and nineteenth-century presidency is built more on a foundation of assertion and assumption than on one of evidence and analysis, to the detriment of our understanding of the office's actual activities and its relationship to the state. Recent efforts to fill the nineteenth-century gap in these subfields are important, but they have not yet offered a thorough analysis of the presidency in eighteenth-, nineteenth-, and early twentieth-century contexts.

Administrative Leadership

Assumptions about the nineteenth-century American state have driven conclusions about the president's minimal role as administrative leader. The central assumption of much of this scholarship needs to be discarded.

The dominant tale is sometimes presented in a generalized view of a small state, limited national governance, and a weak presidency compared with its modern counterpart. Presidency scholar Michael A. Genovese summarizes a familiar progression: "Over time, the presidency would evolve from chief clerk to chief executive to national leader to Imperial President."[2] Constitutional scholar Cass R. Sunstein offered a similar narrative: "It cannot be disputed that the original understanding of the presidency called for much less presidential authority than is taken for granted today." "It is a simple truth that the national government has far more authority than the framers of the Constitution originally envisaged." "There is no question that the current President is quite different from the founders' President."[3] These are bold, absolutist statements that discourage inquiry.

Many studies of the presidency go into further detail, seeing that office functioning within a small, immature state, requiring more of a clerk than a leader of policy or administration. Kenneth R. Mayer's book on executive orders captures the prevailing wisdom about the presidency's relationship to the administrative state:

> While there were earlier examples of expanding presidential power, most notably during the Jackson and Lincoln administrations, they were temporary episodes in an otherwise unexceptional story. Most nineteenth-century presidents lacked the inclination to assert their executive power, and they lacked the resources necessary for strong leadership. The federal government was small, and its powers were hemmed in by narrow interpretations of the

commerce clause. Government positions were doled out as congressionally controlled patronage. The president's ability to exert leadership was limited, because there were no administrative mechanisms or organizational processes that enabled him to supervise or control the executive branch.[4]

Government scholar Peri E. Arnold offers a similar perspective in his influential book *Making the Managerial Presidency*. Arnold writes, "Administration was simple in the Founding era," and he adds an explanation: "Around 1900 the development of the American administrative state increased the importance of administrative activity in national governance." He summarizes the changes over time, writing, "The past [twentieth] century has seen the growth of a vast administrative apparatus within an 18th-century, pre-bureaucratic American regime."[5]

Revealingly, in *Making the Managerial Presidency*, Arnold offers a long list of citations supporting his conclusions about the modern presidents while offering little evidentiary support for his assertions about the nineteenth century. Mayer's conclusion about the early state and the presidency is offered without much specific support. Elsewhere, Arnold did expand on the development and specialization of administration in the late nineteenth century. Following Leonard D. White's studies and also Daniel P. Carpenter's influential book on the development of bureaucratic autonomy, Arnold writes, "Once clerical and routine in its work, the federal public service [in the Progressive era] saw increasing demand for specialists. The early twentieth-century public service required technicians and professionals, that is, knowledge specialists. . . . The old conception was that administration was the implementation of specifically drawn legislation." Arnold continues, describing "those who advised in the traditional presidency" as "cabinet members, members of Congress, leaders of the president's party, and business leaders."[6]

Arnold's baseline, like that of many scholars, is to see the Progressive-era presidency as navigating novel challenges, particularly the marriage of new expectations of, and need for, presidential leadership, combined with the absence of institutional support in a weak state and absence of informational support from a largely undeveloped executive branch. "How were presidents able," Arnold writes, "to initiate and pursue policy at a time when the presidency lacked the informal political resources, such as means for information acquisition, analysis, and liaison?"[7]

But there is a bad assumption here: that presidents lacked such information resources. This notion is belied by longstanding resources available to presidents in Indian affairs, land policy, internal improvements, the Post Office, civil rights enforcement, foreign policy, and the many issues addressed by the federal government in the nineteenth century. Progressive-era presidents benefited from the vast array of institutional resources developed over more than a century of American governance. They may have lacked resources in some areas, but a blanket generalization informing our understanding of the presidency as an institution is unjustified without further evidence.

Missing from such traditional presentations about the development of the president as administrative leader are all of the eighteenth and nineteenth centuries' expert administrators, people like Henry Knox, Alexander Hamilton, Indian affairs superintendent Thomas McKenney, William Thornton (head of the Patent Office from 1802 to 1828), and Joseph Totten (the U.S. Army's chief engineer from 1818 to 1864). Leaders at the Corps of Topographical Engineers, experienced diplomats, and people serving across a variety offices—like O. O. Howard, military field officer and head of the Freedmen's Bureau, or Francis Walker, leader of the 1870 census and then commissioner of Indian affairs—offered subject-matter expertise as well as experience in leading government units. Many others advised the president on varied matters of state throughout the nineteenth century. Many of these administrative advisors were "tied to the president's agenda by their own preferences, and their relationships to the president furthered their own bureaucratic interests," as Arnold describes Gifford Pinchot and Frederick Newell in the Progressive era—other examples include John Quincy Adams and Postmaster John McLean, Ulysses Grant and Commissioner of Indian Affairs Ely Parker, and William Howard Taft and Interior Secretary Richard Ballinger.[8]

In conservation and land policy, for example, Arnold suggests that Theodore Roosevelt's initiatives had little prior context and that little in the way of institutional resources or expertise were available to him. Yet as early as the Washington administration, the elimination of game as well as changing approaches to land use had been major elements of decision making about land and Indian policy. John Quincy Adams faced issues of conservation in Alaskan seal territory, northeastern fisheries, and Florida live oak trees. Advising him was Samuel Humphreys, appointed by Adams in 1826 as chief naval constructor of the United States, an office he served until 1846. Humphreys's father, Joshua—often referred to as the "Father of the American Navy"—had communicated to members of Congress and the executive branch about naval construction in the 1790s and served as chief constructor in that era, and Samuel Humphreys's son Andrew served as an engineer and carried communications between Ulysses Grant and Robert E. Lee at the end of the Civil War before eventually becoming part of President Grant's Isthmian Canal Commission and offering other extensive service to the country.[9] President Grant dealt with issues of conservation and environment in the contexts of the Desert Land and Timber Culture Acts, as well as the question of destroying buffalo populations and the creation of the first national park at Yellowstone. Federal land and timber policy, often driven by executive branch field administrators, went well back into the nineteenth century. Arnold places heavy emphasis on Roosevelt's willingness to lean on the U.S. Geological Survey for information—but the survey dates back to 1879, with administrative and institutional roots in federal mapping and related efforts that go back long before that.[10]

Expertise went even deeper. Albert Lepawsky wrote of the conservation subfield of water resources in these years, and Todd Shallat adds, "Doubtless the influence of bureaucracy has swelled in our lives, but the history of water policy is evidence of gradual, seldom radical, transition. It shows credentialed experts in government a century before the first degrees in public administration. Scientific management, statistical reporting, and other tools of implementation were antebellum tactics, the Whig-Hamiltonian response to cut throat localism and chaos in public works."[11] Taft and Roosevelt would hardly have had to hunt for sources of information, or justify presidential innovation, in a policy area that had existed at the federal level since the 1790s and which by 1831 had already been the subject of executive and administrative action, lawsuits and public controversy, and at least five major laws. To see in the Progressive era some new creation of federal administrative expertise, and to see presidents as only then coming to exploit opportunities in administrative leadership, is to miss more than a century of state activity being overseen by presidents.

THE ASSUMED absence of robust administrative capacity and expertise in the nineteenth century grounds a puzzle that scholars have tried to solve about the president's relationship to the administrative state supposedly being created in the late nineteenth century. In large part, such efforts present the early twentieth-century presidencies of Roosevelt, Taft, and Wilson as struggling to deal with the new scope of the state and its new interactions in policy matters, even as presidents enjoyed newfound opportunities to manage and direct administration.[12] Kenneth Mayer refers, for example, to "an increasing level of congressional delegation to the executive branch" in the late nineteenth century.[13] Richard W. Waterman opens his introduction to a *Presidential Studies Quarterly* symposium by stating, "The essays in this symposium examine the administrative presidency strategy. That leadership strategy originally was initiated by the Richard M. Nixon administration as an attempt to accomplish administratively what it could not do legislatively."[14] Lewis L. Gould sees the "essence" of the modern presidency as what presidents did in the twentieth century, including winning two world wars and achieving a regular celebrity: "They championed legislation, oversaw the economy, traveled around the world, and articulated American values."[15]

Yet, to Gould's approach, one might point out that earlier presidents won a series of violent wars against Native Americans and the Confederacy, many could be considered celebrities, most championed legislation, some oversaw the economy in key ways, and all articulated American values—certainly Adams, Grant, and Taft fit these categories in important ways. Intriguingly too, all three traveled extensively outside North America before and after their presidencies. As for Waterman's claim about the novelty of an administrative presidency strategy, variations of that strategy were employed by John Quincy Adams in his fight to undermine slavery and put into motion what would become the Pacific Expedition of 1838, by Grant to reform Indian policy and lead disaster relief in directions that Congress rejected, and by Taft to modernize presidential budgeting.

Comparisons like these have too often been made too easily, based on assumptions about the nineteenth-century presidency and without serious effort to support statements offered about presidents in earlier eras. After examining the presidency and the state in the nineteenth century more carefully, it is not clear at all why Progressive-era presidents would have suddenly had to justify their authority for innovation *or* acquire new political resources to achieve their aims. Such had been the way of presidents for more than a century.

AT TIMES, the failure to see the administrative state and grapple with how that affects our understanding of the presidency before the Progressive era is merely a matter of miscounting. Scholars often cite how few federal employees there were in Washington, DC, without recognizing the significance of public servants outside of the capital working on land surveys and in land offices, working as Indian agents and reservation superintendents, or working as soldiers and officers in the military.[16] These studies also generally fail to apply to the early government calculations like Paul C. Light's studies of the "true size" of government.[17] Light's work draws attention to the private contract employees and state and local officials who carry out federal mandates in contemporary government. His point is as true about the nineteenth century as it is about the twenty-first, and we should consider the implications for our understanding of state activity and presidential influence when we look at contractors supplying the military with tents, weapons, and uniforms; contractors delivering the mails on private stagecoach lines; private entities overseeing Indian removal, and so on. When one considers the workers digging the National Road in 1810, people designing and building canals supported by federal subscription, missionaries operating with federal support, storekeepers moonlighting as Post Office employees, and the like, the count of employees at the seat of government becomes a terrifically misleading indicator by which to gauge government scope and capacity.

Old habits die hard. Many scholars rely on Leonard D. White's important but now more than sixty-year-old works to inform discussions of how few people worked in the executive branch. Yet White's exclusion of Indian affairs from *The Jeffersonians* is a red flag, especially as he asserted that "the process of dispossession of the Indian is not pursued here, since it was a political rather than an administrative problem."[18] This approach is a misleading trivialization of how difficult it was to dispossess and relocate tens of thousands of people. Yet the sentiment recurred more than fifty years later in Morton Keller's well-received 2007 book, *America's Three Regimes*. In that work, Keller perpetuates the vision of a small and insubstantial federal government, the tasks of which were somehow simple and uncontroversial, writing, "The result was a stunted national state, which remained that way well into the twentieth century. A small military, a spoils-ridden bureaucracy, and distributive rather than dirigiste land, tariff, and chartering policies kept the government's profile low and (save for slavery and territorial expansion) unmenacing. The American state was not one of bureaucrats and armies but of parties and courts."[19] The parenthetical identifies what remains unconsidered in many works, sliding gently past further analysis of two of the era's most significant, salient, and complicated issue areas.

These studies tend to miss the complex dynamics of managing so many people in such diverse and complicated fields of operation, and they miss the constant efforts at managerial reform and reorganization led by presidents. Arnold writes, "Prior to 1905, administrative reform was a congressional province from which presidents were excluded through most of the 19th century." Contrastingly, he writes, "Since Theodore Roosevelt, American presidents have assumed responsibility for administrative efficiency in the executive branch. In the 20th century, the president became managerial.... Eleven of the [twentieth] century's fifteen presidents have been involved in peace-time comprehensive reorganization. In sharp contrast, the managerial dimension of the presidency has little foundation or precedent in either 19th-century practice (after the first third of the century) or in the Constitution." Yet presidents were involved in reforms in the federal bureaucracy throughout the nineteenth century that encompassed Indian affairs, the State Department, land policy, criminal justice policy, civil rights enforcement in the Justice Department, the War Department, the Office of Indian Trade, and many other units. Washington initiated reform of the military after Arthur St. Clair's defeat, John Quincy Adams and Andrew Jackson oversaw reform at the Indian Office behind the landmark 1826 Cass-Clark report, and Ulysses Grant appointed Ely Parker head of the Bureau of Indian Affairs primarily to carry out administrative reform. Reform was ongoing, as presidents reorganized federal bureaus and departments to serve their policy interests. So when Arnold asks, "Why did the initiative for reform shift from Congress to the presidency, and why did presidents initiate administrative reform?" he centers an interesting question on an untested foundation: it is not at all clear that the initiative for reform shifted. The question of why presidents initiated reform is an intriguing one, but one that is as relevant for studying the nineteenth century as it is for studying the twentieth and twenty-first.[20]

In sum, our understanding of the president's relationship to the administrative state changes dramatically when we recognize the scope and influence of the American state in the eighteenth and nineteenth centuries, revealed in recent scholarship on a host of policy issues. The federal government was involved in so much more than we used to think. It is time to look deeper at the administrative presidency in these years, to explore just how presidents and federal administrators were involved in overseeing, managing, and reforming the design and implementation of national policies. Some efforts have already been made by Jerry L. Mashaw, Max M. Edling, and Peter Kastor, among others, and have revealed exciting new findings.[21] We should be open to using this new work to reassess the extent of real development in the president's role as administrative leader in the Progressive and modern eras.

Direct Executive Action

Scholars who study the use of direct executive action tools have often failed to examine closely the use of such tools in the eighteenth and nineteenth centuries. Like scholars of the administrative state, experts in the study of direct-action tools like executive orders, signing statements, and proclamations too often begin with an embedded presumption that the presidency did not do much in its first century or so, and that direct actions from the president would have been largely ceremonial or would have affected minor policy areas and few people.

The dominant narrative of the presidency sees early use of administrative leadership and executive action tools as rare and exceptional. This basic narrative, most lastingly outlined by Terry Moe and William Howell in their late 1990s studies of executive power, suggests that the twentieth century witnessed the increasing regularization of the use of such tools and actions. Moe and Howell argued that "central to an understanding of presidential power" was a matter so important

> that it virtually defines what is distinctively modern about the modern American presidency. This is the president's formal capacity for taking unilateral action and thus for making law on his own. Often, presidents do this through executive orders. Sometimes they do it through proclamations or executive

agreements or national security directives. But whatever vehicles they may choose, the end result is that presidents can and do make new law—and thus shift the existing status quo—without the explicit consent of Congress.[22]

Moe and Howell acknowledged that historic actions such as Washington's Neutrality Proclamation, Jefferson's Louisiana Purchase, and Lincoln's Emancipation Proclamation accomplished similar results, often through formal mechanisms, from the earliest days of the presidency. But they revert quickly to an assertion of modernity: "Presidents have always acted unilaterally to make law. It is just that their power to do so has grown over time and become more consequential."[23] Fang-Yi Chiou and Lawrence S. Rothenberg recently echoed this idea, writing, "Not surprisingly, with the great expansion of government in its size, reach and complexity in the years after the New Deal, the relevance of presidential unilateral action has risen greatly." Yet when they write that "no understanding of the modern presidency in terms of its operation or its power can take place without sensitivity to the role that unilateral action plays," they offer no analysis of why the same cannot be said of the presidency in the eighteenth and nineteenth centuries.[24] This subfield of presidency studies is also ripe for reassessment as we internalize the scope and activities of the presidency and the state in the eighteenth and nineteenth centuries.

Executive Orders

Kenneth Mayer defines executive orders as, "loosely speaking, presidential directives that require or authorize some action within the executive branch (though they often extend far beyond the government). They are presidential edicts, legal instruments that create or modify laws, procedures, and policy by fiat."[25] Phillip J. Cooper offers this more specific but still broad definition: "Executive orders are directives issued by the president to officers of the executive branch, requiring them to take an action, stop a certain type of activity, alter policy, change management practices, or accept a delegation of authority under which they will henceforth be responsible for the implementation of law."[26] Other scholars have offered different definitions, and often with a declaration that a clear and accepted definition does not exist, suggesting the difficulty of trying to nail down a precise definition of presidential leadership orders.[27]

Studies of executive action tend to rely on unsupported assertions about the eighteenth- and nineteenth-century presidency. Echoing scholars specializing in presidential administrative leadership, Mayer writes, for example, "Most executive orders in the eighteenth and nineteenth centuries in fact involved routine administrative procedures," followed by a reference to an order issued by Washington to make sure that department heads kept good accounts of their operations. He then references orders from 1880 to 1900 that primarily addressed civil service matters and public lands—without recognition of the significance of the public lands issue at the time, and leaving the impression that such orders were only relevant after 1880. Public lands come back later in his analysis but again without any suggestion that these would have been critically important matters with direct effects on people, Native nations, and investments.[28] The approach is thus a localized application of the notion that presidents were clerks and that state action was routine and noncontroversial.

Mayer closes with a numerical comparison of Theodore Roosevelt's executive orders, which in number dwarfed those issued by prior presidents. Mayer writes, without evidence or support, "It is no accident that the first president to make extensive use of executive orders, Theodore Roosevelt, was also responsible for elucidating the modern 'stewardship' notion of presidential power; nor that Franklin Roosevelt, whose administration marked the development of the modern institutional presidency, issued far more orders than any other president."[29] But given Mayer's relatively loose definition of executive orders, how are we really to compare either Roosevelt's actions with earlier presidencies? And how carefully have we counted executive orders to this point?

The absence of good data on the use of specific executive action tools makes drawing conclusions about such developments shaky. While Grant standardized the format of executive orders, for example, consistent data on their issue begins only in 1935.[30] Mayer's analysis of executive orders is predominantly a study of the period from 1936 to 1999, and the only action he describes that predates the twentieth century is the Louisiana Purchase: "Technically, although the term was not in use at the time, the Louisiana Purchase was carried out by an executive order."[31] The American Presidency Project fails to include numerous executive orders issued by President Grant related to Indian lands, and the list of Indian land–related orders from President Taft is also incomplete. The list also omits John Quincy Adams's order establishing an agricultural station in Florida and Grant's orders reserving lands for the Kumeyaay in southern California and patenting lands for individual Potawatomi and Kickapoo.[32] Phillip Cooper, in his excellent study of executive action tools, rightly states that numerical counts of such actions tell us little.[33]

Numerical counts also fail to reveal context. For example, as of this writing the American Presidency Project's dataset of executive orders omits Zachary Taylor's 1850 order to remove Chippewa peoples from Wisconsin and revoke treaty-based hunting and fishing rights. This order was, of course, centrally important at the time to Native Americans as well to new settlers, traders, business and transportation interests, land speculators, and so on. And it was important not just in the moment—that presidential order sparked more than a century and half of activity, as the Ojibwe and others opposed the action, other interests defended it, and the U.S. Supreme Court—in 1999—upheld a district court ruling invalidating the order. Suggesting an interesting study in the reversal of an executive order, the controversy's trajectory was not confined to litigation. As interests continued to operate as though the order were still in effect, battles by Ojibwe and others to stay on their land and defend their interests in hunting and fishing rights guaranteed by treaty—and controversies over whether treaties of 1837 and 1842 had been abrogated by Taylor's executive order—continued. As federal courts upheld treaty rights and violent protests ensued, those events affected efforts to alter Wisconsin school curricula to include education about Native American rights and the history and importance of the treaties. All of this has as a central event an executive order signed in 1850, which is not included in a prominent dataset by which presidency scholars study executive orders.[34]

Categorization can also obscure context. Mayer's criteria for a "significant" executive order—"press attention, congressional notice, presidential emphasis, litigation, or creation of institutions with substantive policy responsibility"—would clearly apply to Taylor's Ojibwe order as well as to much of what went on in the nineteenth century. Included in this would be most executive actions involving Indian affairs generally, given the amount of attention to this central area of federal policymaking; Adams's initial efforts to create the Pacific Expedition; actions regarding public lands; and a host of other actions that, while not categorized as formal executive orders, would easily meet the criteria delineated by Mayer.[35]

In a related effort, Raymond Williams's analysis of "significant" executive orders follows Mayer and David Mayhew in defining "significant." This method lays heavy emphasis on "contemporary and/or retrospective coverage."[36] Williams's historical dataset, though, relies on New York Times mentions of executive orders. Such coverage is a shaky foundation for analysis, given the fact that until recently many historians, presidency scholars, and even journalists had a very different approach to government actions affecting Native Americans or nineteenth-century government policies and programs. In other words, an executive order affecting particular Native lands in California or directing education policy on western reservations may not have received much contemporary and/or retrospective coverage in the New York Times. Executive orders were the dominant form of creating and affecting Indian reservations after the formal end of treatymaking in 1871, a utilization of executive orders between 1855 and 1919 that is of tremendous significance to Natives and non-Natives alike but which easily may have escaped coverage in the Times.[37]

Moreover, in his controls for war, Williams includes the Civil War and the Spanish-American War but not wars on the Plains, in the Southwest, or anywhere else with Native nations and confederacies. In short, Williams is exactly right to examine the nineteenth-century presidency in detail according to the excellent theoretical work provided by Mayer and others. But his study remains incomplete in what it can reliably tell us about the presidency at a time when executive action focused on westward expansion and wars with Native peoples, and when contemporary accounts may have overlooked such actions because of attitudes associated with Manifest Destiny. After all, even retrospective accounts are just starting to incorporate such topics as significant policy areas of federal governance and executive action.

Without careful study of earlier presidencies and more subtle understanding of policy contexts, we are blind to earlier presidents' use of executive orders—how many, how significant, under what circumstances they were issued, and what we can learn about opposition or challenges to such exercises of executive power. Importantly, if the administrative state existed in the nineteenth century, then the assumed natural connection between Theodore Roosevelt's or Franklin Roosevelt's use of executive orders and the capacity of the administrative state actually suggests that nineteenth-century presidents were likely to have issued far more executive orders than has been generally assumed.

Signing Statements and Proclamations

Other executive actions receive similar treatment in scholarly studies. Phillip J. Cooper writes that "the signing statement has been used as a tool of presidential direct action since the Reagan administration." He notes the occasionally significant presidential proclamation, defining the proclamation in general as "an instrument that states a condition, declares the law and requires obedience, recognizes an event, or triggers the implementation of a law (by recognizing that the circumstances in law have been realized)." He adds that the usual understanding of the difference between an executive order and a proclamation is that the former is directed at officers of the government while the latter is directed at "those outside government."[38]

Like others, though, Cooper underestimates the early government. He writes in his section on proclamations, "In the early days, the president had little in the way of an executive branch to implement policies, and those agencies that did exist did not have any systematic methods in place to issue the kinds of rules needed to implement policies across a large and rapidly growing nation."[39] This defaults to the traditional understanding of the limited nineteenth-century state. But Grant used signing statements, for example, and he made broad use of proclamations. Taft signed fifty-five proclamations just putting into effect the Payne-Aldrich tariff.[40] And while Cooper evinces a greater willingness to see nineteenth-century actions as significant, his case studies and analyses are overwhelmingly dominated by twentieth-century examples.[41] Likewise, Mayer examines the use of presidential boards and commissions in American history, many of which interrelate with executive orders, signing statements, and proclamations, but the examples he examines most closely are almost all from the twentieth century.[42] Presidents also made specific arguments and justifications within proclamations aimed at particularly significant policy areas, in contrast to assertions made by Jeffrey Tulis in his classic *The Rhetorical Presidency*.[43]

There have been efforts to fill in a more detailed picture of the nineteenth century. Jeremy D. Bailey and Brandon Rottinghaus have found that proclamations became ceremonial largely in the twentieth century. Prior to that, many addressed policy matters, with nearly four hundred policy proclamations issued, by their count, prior to the Theodore Roosevelt administration. Roughly a quarter were "settle down" proclamations responding to domestic unrest, to anticipated action by Americans against foreign entities, or "giving notice to citizens that they will be subject to law enforcement or military action if they continue to break the laws and/or disturb the peace."[44] From the standpoint of presidency studies, these authors have uncovered a terrific new avenue by which we can better understand the eighteenth and nineteenth centuries, and they underscore the fact that many of these proclamations dealt with matters regarding Native Americans, land, and slavery.

Graham G. Dodds offers a marvelous introduction to all of this in his book *Take Up Your Pen*. Dodds acknowledges the difficulties involved in categorizing and counting what he calls "unilateral presidential directives," including executive orders and proclamations. And while he reverts to assertions about increased usage from Theodore Roosevelt forward, Dodds offers an analysis uncommonly receptive to eighteenth- and nineteenth-century usage of such tools. Dodds documents that earlier presidents used such tools regularly, on matters significant and mundane (and everywhere in between), and he suggests the benefits of further research that is open to accepting nineteenth-century presidents as more assertive and unilaterally inclined than we often think. In fact, Dodds singles out Grant, who by his count issued 217 executive orders: "No president [before Grant] had issued even 80 executive orders, and most had issued far fewer."[45]

We should be open to using this new work to reassess the extent of real development in the president's use of direct executive action tools in the Progressive and modern eras. Congress delegated significant authority to the president in Indian affairs, land management, infrastructure development, pension administration, and other affairs. Congressional delegation to the executive on the host of issues that characterize national governance in the nineteenth century created vast opportunities for executive direct action before the Progressive era.

Diplomacy and War

One of the most important aspects of presidential power, and a basis for contemporary concern for what is seen as the rapidly growing influence of the presidency in relation to Congress, is the war-making power. Cass Sunstein and others have repeated the familiar charge that the "modern" presidency is far freer to deploy military force without a declaration of war from Congress: "The president has been permitted to initiate military activity in circumstances in which the original understanding would have required congressional authorization. On the founding view, a congressional declaration of war was a precondition for war. The only exception was that a President could act on his own in order to repel a sudden attack on the United States."[46] Saikrishna Bangalore Prakash writes more recently, "No one doubts that presidential powers have accreted over time. Where once the office was weak, it is now strong.... The president's military authority has swollen with the times."[47]

Many studies for many years have asserted a similar conclusion without examining eighteenth- and nineteenth-century contexts, while omitting or minimizing conflicts with Native Americans. For example, studies by Abbot Smith in 1942 and by David Gray Adler in 1988 use, as their earliest examples, the U.S. response to the 1793 war between France and Great Britain; they ignore war-making and military action in the Old Northwest, which just two years prior had led to General Arthur St. Clair's defeat and the loss of a significant portion of the military's personnel and equipment.[48] Adler omits discussion of any conflicts with Native nations, including the Seminole Wars, despite discussing in detail other matters arising during the Jackson administration.[49] Studies that begin their analyses of the president's authority in diplomacy and war with Washington's 1793 Neutrality Proclamation or debates surrounding quasi-wars with France and England miss critically important, and significant, examples of how presidential war-making powers were understood and realized at the time.[50]

Traditional studies of the president and war overlook constant military deployments and violent battles between U.S. forces and Native nations in the eighteenth and nineteenth centuries, none of which were accompanied by a declaration of war. The loss of most of the American army under St. Clair in 1791, the long war with the Seminoles in the 1830s and 1840s, and conflict with the Sioux in the 1850s, 1860s, 1870s, 1880s, and 1890 are just a few instances of the kind of national, ongoing war-making that were never accompanied by declarations of war. It is an unexplained oversight to leave these out and see the twentieth century as the birthplace of executive-driven war-making. Scholars have overlooked other deployments, and diplomatic efforts entangled with military maneuvers and deterrent threats, as well, including John Quincy Adams's use of the military to interdict slave ships and to control conflict between the Creek Nation and the state of Georgia, and Grant's military foray into Korea.

Other authors include U.S.-Native conflicts but trivialize them. William D. Adler calls these early conflicts "small wars," and Robert J. Delahunty and John Yoo call them "smaller conflicts."[51] In an earlier time but with similar disregard, Arthur M. Schlesinger Jr. wrote that "military action against Indians—stateless and lawless by American definition—pirates, slave traders, smugglers, cattle rustlers, frontier ruffians or foreign brigands was plainly something different from warfare against organized government."[52] This is clearly incorrect on both the technical aspects—American Indian nations were considered states, were recognized by treaties, and were protected by laws—and on context—being conflicts against "organized government" that *could* "lead to full-scale war," as American leaders always worried.

More recently, in his analysis of the president as commander in chief, Norman A. Graebner expanded on the effort to outline the exceptions to the war-making understanding of the founders by including but then downplaying the significance of conflict with Native Americans in the eighteenth and nineteenth centuries. When Graebner mentioned conflict with Natives, like other authors he saw them as exceptions—conflicts "where the threat was too trivial to require congressional approval."[53] This is an assessment that would have surprised Washington, St. Clair, Congress, and Native communities in the Old Northwest in the founding era, and numerous presidents, Congresses, and Native nations throughout the nineteenth century.

Yet Graebner did acknowledge more than 170 instances of presidents' utilizing the armed forces, with only five declarations of war, and concluded that the division of authority outlined in the Constitution has been ineffective.[54] The confusion is more dire than Graebner found, because events like Washington's military efforts in the Old Northwest and Grant's efforts on the Plains, largely excluded from Graebner's attention, were neither trivial nor so immediate that Congress could not be consulted, and those events certainly were neither prevented nor terminated by Congress. One study, in fact, finds more than 1,800 battles between U.S. and Native forces between 1790 and 1897, the vast majority of which took place between 1830 and 1880.[55] Other studies track the high proportion of federal spending dedicated to Indian affairs and the military in these years.[56] This should provide a vast trove of information begging for inclusion in studies of the president as war-maker and commander in chief. Such a study would be likely to strengthen Graebner's conclusion that "the Constitution always permitted the executive to do whatever the public would approve," which would add to what we know of the nineteenth century and dramatically alter our perception of what has—or more likely, has not—changed in the twentieth and twenty-first centuries.[57]

Related aspects of nineteenth-century diplomacy and deployments of force also get short shrift in much scholarship about the presidency. Terry Moe and William Howell, for example, failed to count dozens of U.S.-Indian treaties in their analysis of treaties and executive actions in foreign affairs. Moe and Howell tallied just three treaties for the period 1790–99, seven for the period 1800–1809, and seven for the period 1810–19, for a total of seventeen. By contrast, Francis Paul Prucha, tallying only ratified treaties with American Indian nations, counted ten from 1790 to 1799, thirty from 1800 to 1809, and fifty from 1810 to 1819—a total of ninety.[58] Executive leadership of military action, proclamations targeting Indian treaties or boundary enforcement, executive order reservations, and pardons of Native American leaders have been largely overlooked, even though such executive actions were directly related to some of the most important and prominent aspects of public policy in the nation's first century and a quarter.

Scholars have begun to consider U.S.-Native conflicts more fully when examining war-making powers, including in particular the early efforts of the Washington administration.[59] These studies have added robust debate about the Washington administration's war-making against Native nations, but there is still much to be done. The state was doing more than we previously thought, and the administrative components of that state and the executive actions taken by its presidents were more developed and more influential. Presidents were engaged in far more consequential executive action related to war-making and diplomacy than has generally been recognized.

The President's Legislative Agenda

Studies of the president's role in setting a legislative agenda and leading the fight to pass particular legislation have also tended to overlook the president's role in important eighteenth- and nineteenth-century legislation, especially legislation related to Indian affairs, westward expansion, and other matters too long missing from our understanding of American governance before the twentieth century.

These studies often assert that the president was not a legislative leader in the nineteenth century and did not generally propose legislation or come to office with goals of pushing for passage of specific measures. Mayer, for example, easily passes off the standard assertion in his study of executive orders: "Some aspects of this relationship [between the president and Congress] are modern developments (particularly the expectation that presidents would prepare a comprehensive legislative agenda, which became common only in the twentieth century)."[60] In a popular textbook on the presidency, George C. Edwards III and Stephen J. Wayne write, "The president's domestic policy role did not evolve gradually; it developed in response to policy problems during the twentieth century and has continued into the twenty-first." While acknowledging that presidents recommended measures in the nation's first century, the authors write that "they did not formulate domestic policy on a regular basis."[61] No evidence supports these statements, and there is no effort to examine, for example, George Washington's leadership of Indian policies passed into law, John Quincy Adams's leadership on internal improvements and scientific exploration, or Ulysses Grant's leadership on civil rights and Indian affairs.

As in the case of administrative leadership, executive direct action, and war-making, studies which merely assert that the eighteenth- and nineteenth-century president did not act as a legislative leader often fail to recognize the centrality of Indian policy, internal improvements, diplomacy, and even matters such as healthcare policy and education to the federal government's efforts in these years. As such, they are prone to overlooking the president's role in proposing and pushing for legislation in those areas. Washington, for example, made policy and legislative recommendations to Congress in efforts to influence the questions before it, and he did so regularly, as did John Quincy Adams and Ulysses S. Grant.[62] A major study that has examined this area carefully, by political scientist Jeffrey E. Cohen, finds that Washington and other eighteenth- and nineteenth-century presidents throughout American history have had defined legislative agendas and have utilized the annual/State of the Union message and other tools to identify and recommend specific measures. In fact, Cohen identifies Indian affairs as being at the heart of presidential legislative agendas in the nineteenth century. Yet even Cohen's study excludes a wide variety of presidential actions in relation to Congress, most notably requests that Congress *not* act, and requests that were made privately, orally, or through intermediaries—including administration officials.[63]

As we recognize the vast scope of state activity in foreign and domestic affairs, what we find is a presidency that since its inception has been willing to press specific legislative proposals and agendas to Congress on a broad array of issues. And when we include activities like informal lobbying of Congress, recommendations made to Congress by administrative agencies with the president's imprimatur, and specific requests that Congress *refrain* from acting, as occurred throughout the John Quincy Adams, Ulysses S. Grant, and William Howard Taft administrations, we see even more evidence to support the conclusion that presidents have pursued and promoted significant, specific legislative agendas since the first presidency.

Popular Leadership and Presidential Communication

A last category that has attracted the attention of presidency scholars relates to popular leadership and communication. Here, the field is dominated by the argument that nineteenth-century presidents rarely used popular communications to influence the public. Jeffrey Tulis argued that the "rhetorical presidency," wherein the president speaks directly to the public about policy matters, developed only in the twentieth century. He wrote that efforts by nineteenth-century presidents to speak directly to the public or to directly influence the course of legislation animated a strong backlash. Voters and legislators, he argued, worked to punish the breach of etiquette created by rare instances of active, communicative presidents.[64]

In his introduction to *The Rhetorical Presidency*, Tulis wrote, "Today it is taken for granted that presidents have a *duty* constantly to defend themselves publicly, to promote policy initiatives nationwide, and to inspirit the population. And for many, this presidential 'function' is not one duty among many, but rather the heart of the presidency—its essential task." He added, "Our pre-twentieth-century polity proscribed the rhetorical presidency as ardently as we prescribe it."[65] Tulis's basic argument persists in academic works and textbooks, despite steady debate over the years.[66] Ryan L. Teten, for example, following Tulis and moving through prominent methods of presidential communication, wrote in 2003 that "in the past, speech making [by presidents], as well as public appeal in the content of speeches, was not only infrequent but discouraged due to precedent and technology."[67] Michael Nelson nails down the dominant historical argument compactly: "To say that presidents in the eighteenth and nineteenth century were to be seen but not heard is an overstatement—but not by much."[68]

But there is not much analysis of content in these works, with authors looking only briefly at pre–Progressive-era presidencies. When Nelson writes, "What the first president did not do was equally precedent setting, namely, use the inaugural address as an occasion to exercise his constitutional power to make 'recommendations of particular measures' to Congress," he overlooks Washington's favorable attention in his First Inaugural Address to ratifying the proposed Bill of Rights amendments. The misunderstanding is compounded if we ignore examples like Jefferson's discussion of the Louisiana Purchase in his Second Inaugural Address, and John Quincy Adams's discussion of internal improvements in his Inaugural Address, examined in chapter 3.[69] And as for the president's annual message, in Teten's article only a few brief passages covered presidential delivery of the annual message prior to the Woodrow Wilson administration.[70] Teten turned quickly from brief attention to content to a focus on mechanical aspects of the speeches like word count and connection to the public through use of "we" and "our"—there was no further attempt to examine or compare policy content.[71]

Teten's subsequent research, though, delved more deeply into the historical record and became more skeptical of Tulis's thesis.[72] Challenges have been raised by Mel Laracey and other scholars, who have looked more broadly at presidential communications beyond spoken rhetoric.[73] Indeed, even Tulis's original argument, which so influenced scholarship in this area, was built on some shaky foundations. For example, a memorable anecdote from early in *The Rhetorical Presidency*, used to frame the larger discussion, features a problematically truncated quotation. Tulis discussed an appearance by president-elect Abraham Lincoln in Pittsburgh in February 1861, on his way to Washington, DC. Tulis presented "the attitude toward popular rhetoric captured a century ago by a newspaperman who provided a verbatim account" of the speech and the audience's reaction. Lincoln stated—to great applause—that "to touch upon it at all [meaning the "present distracted condition of the country"] would involve an elaborate discussion of a great many questions and circumstances, which would require more time than I can at present command, and would perhaps, unnecessarily commit me upon matters which have not yet fully developed themselves." Tulis seized on the reporter's commentary: "Immense cheering, and cries of 'good!' 'that's right!'" "Lincoln refused to speak about an impending civil war and was applauded," Tulis concluded. "It is hard to imagine a crowd cheering any instance of 'stonewalling' today."[74]

Yet immediately after the cheering died down—and unreported by Tulis—Lincoln launched into exactly that discussion. The president-elect offered a thoughtful discourse on "the condition of the country," calling it an "extraordinary" one and arguing that, "notwithstanding the troubles across the river [in Ohio], there is really no crisis, springing from anything in the government itself. In plain words, there is really no crisis except an *artificial one!*" After discoursing on this for a while and offering advice to citizens "to keep cool," Lincoln then moved to a detailed discussion of the tariff, of all things, even going so far as to read to the audience a section of the Republican Party's 1860 platform, highlighting that "there are shades of difference in construing even this plank of the platform." He went on to discuss labor, production, the condition of the national treasury, "the tariff bill now before Congress," the theory behind representative government, and the "varied interest of our common country," identifying "the coal and iron of Pennsylvania, the corn of Illinois, and the 'reapers of Chicago.'"[75]

Lincoln, in short, did not refuse to speak about the impending civil war—his entire speech used that "extraordinary" condition as a takeoff point from which he recommended general approaches and particular actions related to that general context, and to other specific matters then before Congress. And in case that is not enough to demonstrate that presidents spoke politics, let us look at the public reaction. Tulis left off with Lincoln being cheered for not getting into the details, but the full report of Lincoln's speech ends with Lincoln saying, with the public's reactions added in brackets by the reporter, "But I am trespassing upon your patience—[cries of 'no!' 'no!' 'Go on—we'll listen!'] and must bring my remarks to a close. Thanking you most cordially for the kind reception which you have extended me, I bid you all adieu. [Enthusiastic applause.]"[76] Tulis used his presentation of the Lincoln event as a springboard to argue that Lincoln's reticence stands in for general attitudes of presidents and the public in the nineteenth century. But Lincoln's speech actually demonstrates the exact opposite of Tulis's conclusion: rather than being cheered for not talking politics, Lincoln talked politics—and the public loved it.

Another weakness in the argument for seen-but-not-heard presidents in the nineteenth century is frequent misjudgment of what constituted the issues of the day. By not recognizing matters like Indian affairs and westward expansion as salient policy areas to presidents and their audiences—or by assuming that a minimal state made discussion of internal improvements in the 1820s idealistic—Tulis, Nelson, and others have failed to see that presidents *were* "talking politics" when their addresses and speeches discussed such matters. Tulis, for example, wrote, "The relatively few popular speeches that were made differed in character from today's addresses. Most were patriotic orations for ceremonial occasions, some raised constitutional issues, and several spoke to the conduct of war. Very few were domestic 'policy speeches' of the sort so common now, and attempts to move the nation by moral suasion in the absence of war were almost unknown."[77] Tulis's book then turns to the form of delivery of the annual message and the formalities and procedures in the early presidency, while Teten's early article turned to identifying the intended audience. Neither analysis goes much farther on content.

Yet as early as the first presidency, George Washington regularly addressed political issues in his annual messages, including matters related to the makeup of the military, war and diplomacy in the Old Northwest, and the policy and regulatory requirements of westward expansion and Indian relations—all of which were hotly contested issues at the time and critical to the nation's future. Congress acted swiftly and directly to put the president's suggested initiatives into effect.[78] When John Quincy Adams discussed internal improvements, or Ulysses Grant discussed westward expansion, they were not discussing naturally occurring events, Manifest Destiny, and population movement by osmosis—they were outlining public policy direction, arguing for preferred options, and leading public opinion. Adams, Grant, and Taft talked politics in public and popular communication, they used moral suasion, and they addressed details and engaged in partisan fights on the issues of the day.

To whom were these messages directed? Tulis's approach in *The Rhetorical Presidency* is narrow, centering on presidential speeches delivered orally; later scholars have expanded the universe of public communications to be considered when assessing overall presidential behavior.[79] Presidents in the eighteenth and nineteenth centuries, of course, did not enjoy the kind of direct access to millions of citizens afforded by radio, television, the internet, and now social media. But that should not obscure the fact that presidents discussed with the public what they could, how they could. In particular, even though annual messages and inaugural addresses were formally directed to members of Congress, presidents were well aware that, as Tulis acknowledged, these communications would be disseminated and discussed by a wide public. According to Tulis, in the early republic the annual messages and veto messages "received the most scrutiny and were the most carefully crafted presidential remarks."[80]

From the very beginning, presidential messages were crafted with the public audience in mind, and assessing audience for presidential communications gets easier when taking context fully into account. Washington, for example, clearly assessed the public audience when determining the content of his First Inaugural Address and his Third Annual Message, and his communications to individuals and organizations regularly engaged public and controversial matters.[81] John Quincy Adams had the public in his sights when he offered his Inaugural Address and his First Annual Message. Grant had the public audience in mind with his message accompanying his 1874 veto of the inflation bill, in the runup to his 1873 annual message, and in his 1874 special message, actively anticipated by the public and by officials in Cuba and Europe for what Grant would say regarding the Cuban rebellion and the execution of American citizens following the seizure of the ship *Virginius*. Presidents who made speeches directly to the public discussed specific proposals and policy options, including Washington and James Monroe on their southern tours, Lincoln at the train station, and Grant outside the Executive Mansion, speaking to firefighters about the relocation of Washington, DC.[82] Presidential speeches and formal communications were "fashioned for all" and regularly included discussion of particular policy issues and specific policy proposals.

IN A FULL-THROATED 2009 defense of *The Rhetorical Presidency* against its challengers, particularly Mel Laracey, David A. Crockett reinforced the idea that it was the identification of a change in constitutional interpretation and philosophy in the Progressive era that remained the book's signal contribution. Among the factors Crockett highlighted were, "First, we have with the rhetorical presidency a transformation of the constitutional order into a presidency-centered system." Crockett seized on the question of whether, and to what extent, presidents "addressed policy matters on a continuous basis, as is done now," to argue that this is "precisely the distinction" between the traditional president and the president from the Progressive era forward.[83]

But it seems clear that John Quincy Adams addressed policy matters continuously in public communication, given his continuous leadership as a main protagonist in matters like internal improvements, treaty policy and federal supremacy, and Pacific exploration, and given the way he nimbly avoided the spotlight he attracted in some areas in order to lead a hidden-hand effort to erode the foundations of slavery. Grant was a main, continuous, and visible protagonist in national politics related to Reconstruction, westward expansion, opening the Black Hills, relieving populations decimated by locusts, and so on. It becomes ever less clear that there is a significant difference between the Progressive era and earlier eras when it comes to presidents' willingness to go public, use tools of public communication, and interact with media in order to achieve policy ends and reinforce efforts to push legislative initiatives and deploy unilateral executive action tools.

These cases and others challenge the idea that presidents did not communicate with the public through formal messages and a variety of forms of public communication. And if we expand the frame of reference to a broader understanding of the rhetorical presidency, we are likely to find many more examples of presidential efforts to get "individuals, organizations, and governments to either make different decisions than they would otherwise make, support causes they might otherwise neglect, or embrace goals they might otherwise not elevate," in the words of political scientist Roger B. Porter.[84] Ryan Teten's later articles pressed this case forward from his earlier works.[85] Mel Laracey's approach to presidential communications adds to all of this the utilization of presidentially influenced party newspapers, as well as "the use of other nineteenth-century presidential communications tools, such as the interview, the press release, and letters written by presidents to be read in public or published in newspapers." Ultimately, Laracey finds that "half of the nineteenth century presidents managed to engage in a form of going public—communicating their policy positions rather clearly to the American public—even though only a few made policy speeches. . . . Among other things, it means that there could not have been a universally felt, constitutionally based norm against going public, as has been asserted."[86]

As we recalibrate our understanding of the salient issues of the eighteenth- and nineteenth-century United States, and as we begin to recognize extensive and ongoing efforts by presidents in these years to lead national policymaking, we will recognize more and more examples of presidents speaking directly to the public, leading public opinion in a variety of direct and indirect ways, and promoting and defending specific positions in presidential rhetoric and communications.

Conclusion

A thin rendering of the nineteenth century is often the foil for analysis of what is assumed to be the new leadership of the Progressive era and the twentieth century. If we have been wrong about the nineteenth century, though, then the changes seen in the Progressive era may not actually be changes. Renewed study of John Quincy Adams gives us better insight into the presidency and the state in the 1820s, and study of Ulysses Grant helps contextualize executive behavior and the state after the Civil War. A reassessment of Progressive-era presidents like William Howard Taft helps us understand how the Progressive-era presidency built on an *existing,* broad state apparatus and more than a century of use of executive action tools, presidential leadership of administration and policy, and public communication. Taft, Theodore Roosevelt, and Woodrow Wilson were not presidents building executive capacity largely from scratch. They were presidents utilizing long-existing executive action tools and leadership strategies to influence administration, legislation, and the public.

The Progressive era and the New Deal seem far less revolutionary when we understand the scope and intrusiveness of the American state in the republic's first century. The presidency seems far less evolutionary when we better understand the actions of presidents in the full context of their times.

NOTES

INTRODUCTION

1. For example, see Jeffrey K. Tulis, "The Two Constitutional Presidencies," in *The Presidency and the Political System*, 11th ed., ed. Michael Nelson (Thousand Oaks, CA: CQ Press, 2018), 1–33; Peri E. Arnold, *Making the Managerial Presidency: Comprehensive Reorganization Planning, 1905–1996*, 2nd ed. (Lawrence: University Press of Kansas, 1998); Stephen Skowronek, *Building a New American State: The Expansion of National Administrative Capacities, 1877–1920* (Cambridge: Cambridge University Press, 1982); Daniel P. Carpenter, *The Forging of Bureaucratic Autonomy: Reputations, Networks, and Policy Innovation in Executive Agencies, 1862–1928* (Princeton, NJ: Princeton University Press, 2001); Kenneth R. Mayer, *With the Stroke of a Pen: Executive Orders and Presidential Power* (Princeton, NJ: Princeton University Press, 2001); Phillip J. Cooper, *By Order of the President: The Use and Abuse of Executive Direct Action* (Lawrence: University Press of Kansas, 2002); Terry M. Moe and William G. Howell, "The Presidential Power of Unilateral Action," *Journal of Law, Economics, and Organization* 15 (1999): 132–79; Terry M. Moe and William G. Howell, "Unilateral Action and Presidential Power: A Theory," *Presidential Studies Quarterly* 29 (December 1999): 850–72; Jeffrey K. Tulis, *The Rhetorical Presidency* (Princeton, NJ: Princeton University Press, 1987); and Samuel Kernell, *Going Public: New Strategies of Presidential Leadership*, 2nd ed. (Washington, DC: CQ Press, 1993).

2. See, for example, Brian Balogh, *A Government Out of Sight: The Mystery of National Authority in Nineteenth-Century America* (Cambridge: Cambridge University Press, 2009); Paul Frymer, *Building an American Empire: The Era of Territorial and Political Expansion* (Princeton, NJ: Princeton University Press, 2019); Max M. Edling, *A Hercules in the Cradle: War, Money, and the American State, 1783–1867* (Chicago: University of Chicago Press, 2014); William D. Adler, *Engineering Expansion: The U.S. Army and Economic Development, 1787–1860* (Philadelphia: University of Pennsylvania Press, 2021); William J. Novak, "The Myth of the 'Weak' American State," *American Historical Review* 113 (2008): 752–72; Stephen Sawyer and William J. Novak, "Emancipation and the Creation of Modern Liberal States in America and France," *Journal of the Civil War Era* 3 (2013): 467–500; and William J. Novak, "A State of Legislatures," *Polity* 40 (2008): 340–47. On the persistence of the idea of the "weak" state, see William J. Novak, "Long Live the Myth of the Weak State? A Response to Adams, Gerstle, and Witt," *American Historical Review* 115 (2010): 792–800. On the administrative state, see the definition John A. Rohr adapts from Dwight Waldo in *To Run a Constitution: The Legitimacy of the Administrative*

State (Lawrence: University Press of Kansas, 1986), xi, 217n11; Dwight Waldo, *The Administrative State* (New York: Ronald Press, 1948); and Stephen J. Rockwell, *Indian Affairs and the Administrative State in the Nineteenth Century* (Cambridge: Cambridge University Press, 2010).

3. Jon C. Rogowski, "Presidential Influence in an Era of Congressional Dominance," *American Political Science Review* 110 (2016): 325. See also Jon C. Rogowski, "Presidential Incentives, Bureaucratic Control, and Party Building in the Republican Era," *Presidential Studies Quarterly* 45 (2015): 796–811.

4. Rogowski, "Presidential Influence," 340. See also Rogowski, "Presidential Incentives."

5. Graham G. Dodds, *Take Up Your Pen: Unilateral Presidential Directives in American Politics* (Philadelphia: University of Pennsylvania Press, 2013); Jeffrey E. Cohen, *The President's Legislative Policy Agenda, 1789–2002* (Cambridge: Cambridge University Press, 2012); Mel Laracey, *Presidents and the People: The Partisan Story of Going Public* (College Station: Texas A&M University Press, 2002).

6. John R. Van Atta, *Securing the West: Politics, Public Lands, and the Fate of the Old Republic, 1785–1850* (Baltimore: Johns Hopkins University Press, 2014); Gregory Ablavsky, *Federal Ground: Governing Property and Violence in the First U.S. Territories* (New York: Oxford University Press, 2021); Frymer, *Building an American Empire*; Jerry L. Mashaw, *Creating the Administrative Constitution: The Lost One Hundred Years of American Administrative Law* (New Haven, CT: Yale University Press, 2012); David F. Ericson, *Slavery in the American Republic: Developing the Federal Government, 1791–1861* (Lawrence: University Press of Kansas, 2011); Matthew Karp, *This Vast Southern Empire: Slaveholders at the Helm of American Foreign Policy* (Cambridge, MA: Harvard University Press, 2016); Michele Landis Dauber, *The Sympathetic State: Disaster Relief and the Origins of the American Welfare State* (Chicago: University of Chicago Press, 2013); Larry C. Skogen, *Indian Depredation Claims, 1796–1920* (Norman: University of Oklahoma Press, 1996); Laura Jensen, *Patriots, Settlers, and the Origins of American Social Policy* (Cambridge: Cambridge University Press, 2003); Theda Skocpol, *Protecting Soldiers and Mothers: The Political Origins of Social Policy in the United States* (Cambridge, MA: Harvard University Press, 1995).

7. Max M. Edling, *A Revolution in Favor of Government: Origins of the U.S. Constitution and the Making of the American State* (New York: Oxford University Press, 2003); Max M. Edling and Peter Kastor, eds., *Washington's Government: Charting the Origins of the Federal Administration* (Charlottesville: University of Virginia Press, 2021). For other references, see the notes throughout this book and the review essay by Gautham Rao, "The New Historiography of the Early Federal Government: Institutions, Contexts, and the Imperial State," *William and Mary Quarterly*, 3rd series, 77 (2020): 97–128.

8. Maggie McKinley, "Lobbying and the Petition Clause," *Stanford Law Review* 68 (2016): 1131–1205; Daniel P. Carpenter, *Democracy by Petition: Popular Politics in Transformation, 1790–1870* (Cambridge, MA: Harvard University Press, 2021).

9. Skowronek, *Building a New American State*, 3. On "big government," see Rockwell, *Indian Affairs*, 26–37, 303–28.
10. David K. Nichols, *The Myth of the Modern Presidency* (University Park: Pennsylvania State University Press, 1994), 173.
11. William J. Novak, *The People's Welfare: Law and Regulation in Nineteenth-Century America* (Chapel Hill: University of North Carolina Press, 1996).

1. Choices within the State, 1776–1930

1. Harlow Giles Unger, *John Quincy Adams* (Boston: Da Capo Press, 2012), 126–35.
2. Robert Lee, "Accounting for Conquest: The Price of the Louisiana Purchase of Indian Country," *Journal of American History* 103 (March 2017): 924. Lee calculates the total cost adjusted for inflation at over $8.5 billion in 2012 dollars.
3. Unger, *Adams*, 129, 132; Lynn Hudson Parsons, *The Birth of Modern Politics: Andrew Jackson, John Quincy Adams, and the Election of 1828* (New York: Oxford University Press, 2009), 21. In 1834, U.S. Representative Adams would question plans for an Indian territory for similar reasons. Francis Paul Prucha, *The Great Father: The United States Government and the American Indians* (Lincoln: University of Nebraska Press, 1984), 305–6.
4. Jerry L. Mashaw, *Creating the Administrative Constitution: The Lost One Hundred Years of American Administrative Law* (New Haven, CT: Yale University Press, 2012), 91.
5. Unger, *Adams*, 141; Robert V. Remini, *John Quincy Adams* (New York: Times Books, 2002), 38. John F. Kennedy's *Profiles in Courage* (1956; reprint New York: Harper, 2006), 23–50, offers the classic account of Adams's independent streak in the early 1800s.
6. On Adams's independence and voting record, see also Mary W. M. Hargreaves, *The Presidency of John Quincy Adams* (Lawrence: University Press of Kansas, 1985), 24; Unger, *Adams*, 123–34; Remini, *Adams*, 33–49; and John T. Morse Jr., *John Quincy Adams* (Boston: Houghton Mifflin, 1882), 57–61.
7. Mashaw, *Creating the Administrative Constitution*, chap. 6.
8. Unger, *Adams*, 138–40.
9. Remini, *Adams*, 31; Samuel Flagg Bemis, *John Quincy Adams and the Foundations of American Foreign Policy* (New York: Knopf, 1949), 93–95.
10. Unger, *Adams*, 154; Samuel Flagg Bemis, "John Quincy Adams and Russia," *Virginia Quarterly Review* 21 (1945): 553–68; David W. McFadden, "John Quincy Adams, American Commercial Diplomacy, and Russia, 1809–1825," *New England Quarterly* 66 (1993): 613–29.
11. Unger, *Adams*, 167, 169–76; Remini, *Adams*, 44–49.
12. Unger, *Adams*, 173–74; Remini, *Adams*, 46.
13. Quoted in Unger, *Adams*, 176; see also quotation at 264–65.
14. Unger, *Adams*, 184–85, 200.

15. Unger, *Adams*, 187; see also 186–88; William Earl Weeks, *John Quincy Adams and American Global Empire* (Lexington: University Press of Kentucky, 1992), 8, 46.
16. Lester Harris, "The Cession of Florida and John Quincy Adams, Secretary of State, U.S.A.," *Florida Historical Quarterly* 36 (1958): 225, examines how Secretary Adams's Florida policy intertwined with his efforts in Latin America and on the West Coast.
17. Weeks, *Adams*, 178. See also Unger, *Adams*, 209–11, and Hargreaves, *Presidency*, 24–25.
18. Harris, "The Cession of Florida," 238.
19. Quoted in Unger, *Adams*, 209.
20. For details on the complexity and duration of issues arising from Spanish land grants in Florida after the Adams-Onís Treaty, see Edward F. Keuchel and Joe Knetsch, "Settlers, Bureaucrats, and Private Land Claims: The 'Little Arredondo Grant,'" *Florida Historical Quarterly* 68 (1989): 201–17. Harlow Giles Unger points out that the agreement led to later issues involving Missouri and the extension of slavery. Unger, *Adams*, 211ff.
21. Unger, *Adams*, 217–18.
22. Weeks, *Adams*, 31–32; Bemis, *Adams and the Foundations*, 278–80.
23. Unger, *Adams*, 200–203; Bradford Perkins, *Castlereagh and Adams: England and the United States, 1812–1823* (Berkeley: University of California Press, 1964), 262.
24. For detailed descriptions of Adams's day-to-day activities as secretary of state, see Walker Lewis, "John Quincy Adams and the Baltimore 'Pirates,'" *American Bar Association Journal* 67 (1981): 1010–14, and Charles Wilson Hackett, "The Development of John Quincy Adams's Policy with Respect to an American Confederation and the Panama Congress, 1822–1825," *Hispanic American Historical Review* 8 (1928): 496–526. For an analysis of young Adams and republicanism, public virtue, and his core values as a statesman, see Cory M. Pfarr, "John Quincy Adams's Republicanism: 'A Thousand Obstacles Apparently Stand before Us,'" *Massachusetts Historical Review* 16 (2014): 73–121. For studies of the interrelationships of ethics, philosophy, and Adams's approach to foreign policy, see Greg Russell, "John Quincy Adams: Virtue and the Tragedy of the Statesman," *New England Quarterly* 69 (1996): 56–74; Greg Russell, "John Quincy Adams and the Ethics of America's National Interest," *Review of International Studies* 19 (1993): 23–38; and Daniel G. Lang and Greg Russell, "The Ethics of Power in American Diplomacy: The Statecraft of John Quincy Adams," *Review of Politics* 52 (1990): 3–31.
25. Unger, *Adams*, 200–201; Weeks, *Adams*, 49–58.
26. Unger, *Adams*, 216–20; Hackett, "Development of John Quincy Adams's Policy."
27. See Weeks, *Adams*, 180–81, and Morse, *Adams*, 137.
28. See Weeks, *Adams*, 67, 98, 125, 131.
29. Remini, *Adams*, 55; Weeks, *Adams*, 156–75. On Adams and Florida, see also William Earl Weeks, "John Quincy Adams's 'Great Gun' and the Rhetoric of

American Empire," *Diplomatic History* 14 (1990): 25–42; Harris, "The Cession of Florida"; and Frederick Cubberly, "John Quincy Adams and Florida," *Florida Historical Society Quarterly* 5 (1926): 88–93.
30. On Adams and Jackson, see Unger, *Adams*, 204; Parsons, *Birth of Modern Politics*, 50–54; Weeks, *Adams*, 105–26; Harris, "The Cession of Florida," 227–28; and Lynn Hudson Parsons, "'A Perpetual Harrow upon My Feelings': John Quincy Adams and the American Indian," *New England Quarterly* 46 (1973): 346–49. On Amelia Island and Galveston, see Weeks, *Adams*, 57.
31. Weeks, *Adams*, 162–63; Harris, "The Cession of Florida"; Weeks, "John Quincy Adams's 'Great Gun.'"
32. Weeks, *Adams*, 165; see also 145, 157–60, 170–71, 64–65, 94–104.
33. Weeks, *Adams*, 59; Unger, *Adams*, 200; Hargreaves, *Presidency*, 212.
34. See Irwin F. Greenberg, "Justice William Johnson: South Carolina Unionist, 1823–1830," *Pennsylvania History* 36 (1969): 307–34; Alan F. January, "The South Carolina Association: An Agency for Race Control in Antebellum Charleston," *South Carolina Historical Magazine* 78 (1977): 194–97; William M. Wiecek, *The Sources of Anti-Slavery Constitutionalism in America, 1760–1848* (Ithaca, NY: Cornell University Press, 2018), 136–40; and Philip M. Hamer, "Great Britain, the United States, and the Negro Seamen Acts, 1822–1848," *Journal of Southern History* 1 (1935): 3–12. Gerald L. Neuman highlights the relevance of the Seamen's Acts to the nation's history of immigration contexts. Neuman, "The Lost Century of American Immigration Law (1776–1875)," *Columbia Law Review* 93 (1993): 1873–78. Michael Schoeppner addresses these issues explicitly in the context of Novak's work on the people's welfare. Schoeppner, "Peculiar Quarantines: The Seamen Acts and Regulatory Authority in the Antebellum South," *Law and History Review* 31 (2013): 559–86. The cases were also notable because Judge William Johnson's defense of national supremacy in interstate commerce questions, trumping state action, predated *Gibbons v. Ogden* and was later sanctioned by Attorney General William Wirt in May 1824, after he was asked by Secretary Adams to offer an opinion. Wiecek, *Sources*, 137. See also Greenberg, "Justice William Johnson"; January, "South Carolina Association," 195–96; and Hamer, "Great Britain," 10–12. Adams revisited the issue when he was in Congress in 1843. Wiecek, *Sources*, 139–40; Hamer, "Great Britain," 21–22. See also David Waldstreicher and Matthew Mason, *John Quincy Adams and the Politics of Slavery: Selections from the Diary* (New York: Oxford University Press, 2017), and Francis D. Adams and Barry Sanders, *Alienable Rights: The Exclusion of African Americans in a White Man's Land, 1619–2000* (New York: Perennial, 2003), 143. South Carolina ignored federal court rulings, and eventually the government's position was reversed by Jackson's attorney general, John Berrien. Adams and Sanders, *Alienable Rights*, 143.
35. John Quincy Adams, *Report upon Weights and Measures* (Washington, DC: Gales and Seaton, 1821), 14. On civil society generally, see, for example, 10, 11, 12.
36. See Unger, *Adams*, 272–73; Marlana Portolano, *The Passionate Empiricist: The Eloquence of John Quincy Adams in the Service of Science* (Albany: State

University of New York Press, 2009); A. Hunter Dupree, *Science in the Federal Government: A History of Policy and Activities to 1940* (Cambridge, MA: Belknap Press of Harvard University Press, 1957), chap. 4; and William H. Goetzmann, *Beyond the Revolution: A History of American Thought from Paine to Pragmatism* (New York: Basic, 2009), 180–83.

37. "The House 'Gag Rule,'" History, Art and Archives, U. S. House of Representatives, https://history.house.gov/Historical-Highlights/1800-1850/The-House-of-Representatives-instituted-the-%E2%80%9Cgag-rule%E2%80%9D/; Daniel P. Carpenter, *Democracy by Petition: Popular Politics in Transformation, 1790–1870* (Cambridge, MA: Harvard University Press, 2021), 311, chap. 10; Maggie McKinley, "Lobbying and the Petition Clause," *Stanford Law Review* 68 (2016): 1131–1205.
38. *John Quincy Adams: Diaries,* ed. David Waldstreicher (New York: Library of America, 2017), 2:422; see also 2:521–22, 578–80, 584–85, 603; Carpenter, *Democracy by Petition,* 73–74, 310–12.
39. See William Lee Miller, *Arguing about Slavery: John Quincy Adams and the Great Battle in the United States Congress* (New York: Vintage, 1995); Joseph Wheelan, *Mr. Adams's Last Crusade: John Quincy Adams's Extraordinary Post-Presidential Life in Congress* (New York: Public Affairs, 2008); Unger, *Adams,* 266–303; Remini, *Adams,* 137–45; and Robert P. Ludlum, "The Antislavery 'Gag-Rule': History and Argument," *Journal of Negro History* 26 (1941): 203–43.
40. See Miller, *Arguing,* 233, 349–50, and Nancy Isenberg and Andrew Burstein, *The Problem of Democracy: The Presidents Adams Confront the Cult of Personality* (New York: Viking, 2019), 413–15.
41. See Waldstreicher, ed., *Adams: Diaries,* 2:587, 609–10.
42. Howard Jones, *Mutiny on the Amistad: The Saga of a Slave Revolt and Its Impact on American Abolition, Law, and Diplomacy* (New York: Oxford University Press, 1987), 142, 176–82. For a concise summary of the events, see Patricia Roberts-Miller, "John Quincy Adams's *Amistad* Argument: The Problem of Outrage; or, The Constraints of Decorum," *Rhetoric Society Quarterly* 32 (2002): 6–11.
43. Jones, *Mutiny,* 81, 153.
44. J. David Hacker, "Decennial Life Tables for the White Population of the United States, 1790–1900," *Historical Methods* 43 (April–June 2010): esp. 23, 35 (fig. 6).
45. Jones, *Mutiny,* 145–48; see also 205–6, 212–20.
46. Jones, *Mutiny,* 179; see 164–80 generally.
47. *United States v. The Libellants and Claimants of the Schooner* Amistad, *Her Tackle, Apparel, and Furniture, Together with Her Cargo, and the Africans Mentioned and Described in the Several Libels and Claims* (40 U.S. 518) (1841); emphasis added. This clarifying passage appears just prior to the section often labeled "Conclusion," in which Adams offered an emotional farewell to the Court and a motivating speech appealing to the justices. See also Michele Valerie Ronnick, "Virgil's *Aeneid* and John Quincy Adams's Speech on Behalf of the *Amistad* Africans," *New England Quarterly* 71 (1998): 473–77.

48. Christopher McGrory Klyza, "The United States Army, Natural Resources, and Political Development in the Nineteenth Century," *Polity* 35 (2002): 5–6. On Grant in Detroit, Sacketts Harbor, and on the West Coast, see Geoffrey Perret, *Ulysses S. Grant: Soldier and President* (New York: Modern Library, 1999), 78–102; Ronald C. White, *American Ulysses: A Life of Ulysses S. Grant* (New York: Random House, 2017), 102–21; and Ulysses S. Grant, *Personal Memoirs* (New York: Library of America, 1990), 135–40. On Grant and American Indians in Washington Territory, see White, *American Ulysses*, 115.
49. See, for example, Grant, *Memoirs*, 68–69, 260, 261, 410; Ulysses S. Grant, *The Papers of Ulysses S. Grant*, ed. John Y. Simon et al. (Carbondale: Southern Illinois University Press, 1967–2012), 19:40, 109–10, 110; 25:168; 27:294 (hereafter *USG*); Albert D. Richardson, *A Personal History of Ulysses S. Grant* (Washington, DC: National Tribune, 1898), 536; and Louis A. Coolidge, *The Life of Ulysses S. Grant* (Boston: Houghton Mifflin, 1922), 290, 490n1, 381, 423–24 (quotation); see also 561.
50. "The Racial Views of Ulysses S. Grant," *Journal of Blacks in Higher Education* 66 (2009–10): 26; Joan Waugh, *U.S. Grant: American Hero, American Myth* (Chapel Hill: University of North Carolina Press, 2009), 42. See also Grant, *Memoirs*, 143–51, 419, 773.
51. Waugh, *Grant*, 28, 37–38; see also 30.
52. Grant, *Memoirs*, 55, 60, 63, 160–61, 173; *USG*, 19:197; 25:9–19, 24, 98–99, 106–7, 108, 109; 27:294–96, 305–8.
53. Grant, *Memoirs*, 74, 82, 165–66, 387–88, 246, 313, 646, 284–86. Cf. O. O. Howard, *Autobiography of Oliver Otis Howard, Major-General, United States Army* (New York: Baker and Taylor, 1908; reprint London: Forgotten Books, 2012), 2:179–80.
54. Grant, *Memoirs*, 146–47, 765–66.
55. James M. McPherson, *Battle Cry of Freedom: The Civil War Era* (New York: Oxford University Press, 1988), 848–50.
56. Grant, *Memoirs*, 739; see 739–41 generally.
57. White, *American Ulysses*, 407.
58. For example, see Grant, *Memoirs*, 712–13; *USG*, 19:43; and William Gillette, *Retreat from Reconstruction, 1869–1879* (Baton Rouge: Louisiana State University Press, 1979), 174, 401n9.
59. In general, see Brooks D. Simpson, *Let Us Have Peace: Ulysses S. Grant and the Politics of War and Reconstruction, 1861–1868* (Chapel Hill: University of North Carolina Press, 1991), 172–74, 190–92, 203, 225–36. See also Hans L. Trefousse, *Andrew Johnson: A Biography* (1989; reprint New York: Norton, 1997), 277, 290–331.
60. Quoted in Simpson, *Let Us Have Peace*, 190.
61. For more on Grant's post-presidential career, see Waugh, *Grant*, 156–65; Coolidge, *Life*, 534–60; and White, *American Ulysses*, 613–31.
62. On Grant and the *Memoirs*, see, for example, Waugh, *Grant*, 168–213; Coolidge, *Life*, 560–65; and White, *American Ulysses*, 638–52.

63. Jonathan Lurie, *William Howard Taft: The Travails of a Progressive Conservative* (Cambridge: Cambridge University Press, 2012), 33.
64. Herbert S. Duffy, *William Howard Taft* (New York: Minton, Balch, 1930), 48; see also 33–52; Lurie, *Taft*, 20–25, 28–38; David H. Burton, *William Howard Taft: Confident Peacemaker* (Philadelphia: St. Joseph's University Press, 2004), 20–23.
65. Lurie, *Taft*, 34–36; Rene N. Ballard, "The Administrative Theory of William Howard Taft," *Western Political Quarterly* 7 (1954): 65–74.
66. Lurie, *Taft*, 26; Alpheus Thomas Mason, *William Howard Taft: Chief Justice* (New York: Simon and Schuster, 1964), 18. Herbert S. Duffy counts twenty-seven cases. Duffy, *Taft*, 33.
67. Duffy, *Taft*, 28; Lurie, *Taft*, 27, 26.
68. On Taft in the Philippines generally, see Lurie, *Taft*, 49–53. For background on the war, see, for example, Burton, *Taft*, 29–37; Paul A. Kramer, *The Blood of Government: Race, Empire, the United States, and the Philippines* (Chapel Hill: University of North Carolina Press, 2006); Stuart Creighton Miller, *"Benevolent Assimilation": The American Conquest of the Philippines, 1899–1903* (New Haven, CT: Yale University Press, 1982), chaps. 5, 9–13; Richard Drinnon, *Facing West: The Metaphysics of Indian Hating and Empire Building* (New York: Schocken, 1990), 307–32; and Scott Nearing and Joseph Freeman, *Dollar Diplomacy: A Study in American Imperialism* (New York: B. W. Huebsch, 1925), 201–3. These studies offer sharp contrast with the assessment of Peri E. Arnold, who dismisses Taft's leadership in the Philippines as subordinate actions that "entailed specific goals [given to him by Elihu Root] and clear supervision [by Roosevelt]." Arnold concludes that Taft was "a superlative subaltern" with a "passive" career and "no clear ideological stance." Arnold, *Remaking the Presidency: Roosevelt, Taft, and Wilson, 1901–1916* (Lawrence: University Press of Kansas, 2009), 85, 99, 94; see also 72, 95, 98. In contrast, see Julian Go, *American Empire and the Politics of Meaning: Elite Political Cultures in the Philippines and Puerto Rico during US Colonialism* (Durham, NC: Duke University Press, 2008), chap. 3, and Kramer, *Blood of Government*, chaps. 2–3.
69. See Duffy, *Taft*, 80–82, 151–52; Go, *American Empire*, 47, 194–96; Kramer, *Blood of Government*, chap. 2, 194, 198–208, 237–38; Miller, *"Benevolent Assimilation,"* 134; and Carl Sferrazza Anthony, *Nellie Taft: The Unconventional First Lady of the Ragtime Era* (New York: William Morrow, 2005), 173. O. O. Howard drew a line explicitly from the Freedmen's Bureau, through Grant's Peace Policy, to "the work of education in the Philippine Islands." Howard, *Autobiography*, 2:203. Critical reviews of Taft and the Taft Commission appear in Kenneth E. Bauzon, *Capitalism, the American Empire, and Neoliberal Globalization: Themes and Annotations from Selected Works of E. San Juan, Jr.* (Singapore: Palgrave Macmillan, 2019), 55–59, 87, 107, 123, and Drinnon, *Facing West*, 316–17.
70. See, for example, Lurie, *Taft*, 42, 43n21; Miller, *"Benevolent Assimilation,"* 135, 166–67, 210; cf. 213–15, 263; and Anthony, *Nellie Taft*, 136–45.

71. *Reports of the Taft Philippine Commission* (Washington, DC: U.S. Government Printing Office, 1901), 15.
72. Duffy, *Taft*, 103–4.
73. Duffy, *Taft*, 122.
74. See Lurie, *Taft*, 44. Taft also resolved the thorny subject of "Friars' lands" held by Catholic denominations dating to the years of Spanish control of the islands, engineering the purchase of those lands by the United States and their sale back to Filipinos. See Duffy, *Taft*, 105–13, 138–50.
75. Duffy, *Taft*, 137; see also 164.
76. Duffy, *Taft*, 140. See also the nuanced discussions of Taft's legacy in Go, *American Empire*, 114–17, 140–41, 193–200, and Michael S. Kugelman, "Winning Hearts and Minds through 'Actual Deeds': U.S. Public Diplomacy during the Occupation of the Philippines in Comparison with the American Involvement in Iraq Today" (MA thesis, Tufts University, 2005).
77. Lurie, *Taft*, 50. See also Duffy, *Taft*, 124–30, and Kugelman, "Winning Hearts and Minds," 38.
78. Cathleen D. Cahill, *Federal Fathers and Mothers: A Social History of the United States Indian Service, 1869–1933* (Chapel Hill: University of North Carolina Press, 2011), 88, 209.
79. Quoted in Lurie, *Taft*, 50. See also Burton, *Taft*, 29–37, and Anthony, *Nellie Taft*, esp. chap. 8.
80. See Donald F. Anderson, *William Howard Taft: A Conservative's Conception of the Presidency* (Ithaca, NY: Cornell University Press, 1973), 18, and Burton, *Taft*, 37–40. On Taft's understanding of the constitutional basis for executive action in Panama in the absence of congressional authorization, see L. Peter Schultz, "William Howard Taft: A Constitutionalist's View of the Presidency," *Presidential Studies Quarterly* 9 (1979): 407–8.
81. Stanley D. Solvick, "William Howard Taft and Cannonism," *Wisconsin Magazine of History* 48 (1964): 50 (quotation), 55, 56.
82. Duffy, *Taft*, 167–77.
83. Ralph Eldin Minger, "William Howard Taft's Forgotten Visit to Russia," *Russian Review* 22 (1963): 149–56.
84. Ralph Eldin Minger described Taft's rationale for why U.S. action was constitutional and legal. Minger, "William H. Taft and the United States Intervention in Cuba in 1906," *Hispanic American Historical Review* 41 (1961): esp. 78, 80–81, 82, 87, 89. See also Schultz, "William Howard Taft," 406–7, and Nearing and Freeman, *Dollar Diplomacy*, 178–83. Cf. Anderson, *Taft*, 18–20, and Burton, *Taft*, 40–44.
85. Duffy, *Taft*, 303–4; Mark Alden Branch, "Big Man on Campus," *Yale Alumni Magazine*, March–April 2013, https://yalealumnimagazine.org/articles/3632-big-man-on-campus.
86. Lurie, *Taft*, 178n22, 184, 197, 185–90. Lurie notes how surprisingly pro-labor Taft managed to be on the Labor Board.

87. Congressional Research Service (CRS), "Supreme Court Nominations, 1789–2020: Actions by the Senate, the Judiciary Committee, and the President," March 8, 2022, 35, https://crsreports.congress.gov/product/pdf/RL/RL33225. Taft's confirmation is often reported as unanimous, but the CRS and the U.S. Senate each report it as sixty to four. See CRS, "Supreme Court Nominations," 35; U.S. Senate, "Supreme Court Nominations (1789–Present)," https://www.senate.gov/legislative/nominations/SupremeCourtNominations1789present.htm#9. Note e on page 46 of the CRS report offers an explanation based on Senate procedure during Taft's confirmation.
88. Mason, *Taft*. See also Justin Crowe, "The Forging of Judicial Autonomy: Political Entrepreneurship and the Reforms of William Howard Taft," *Journal of Politics* 69 (2007): 73–87.
89. See, for example, Bernard Schwartz, *A History of the Supreme Court* (New York: Oxford University Press, 1993), 207–8, and Mason, *Taft*, 133–37, 148–49.
90. See Mason, *Taft*, esp. chaps. 5–6, 283, 283n.
91. On Taft as chief justice generally, see Mason, *Taft*; Schwartz, *History of the Supreme Court*, 213–19; Lucas A. Powe Jr., *The Supreme Court and the American Elite, 1789–2008* (Cambridge, MA: Harvard University Press, 2009), 192–200; and Peter Charles Hoffer, Williamjames Hull Hoffer, and N. E. H. Hull, *The Supreme Court: An Essential History* (Lawrence: University Press of Kansas, 2007), 217–38.
92. Mason, *Taft*, chaps. 7, 9; see also 97, 199, 204, 219, 223, 263. On the Taft Court's activism, see 292–93; on its efficiency, see 195ff, 231.
93. Mason, *Taft*, chap. 4, esp. 112, 114, 120; see also 97, 104, 234; Hoffer, Hoffer, and Hull, *Supreme Court*, 220; Schwartz, *History of the Supreme Court*, 217.

2. President John Quincy Adams and the American State in the 1820s

1. On the Revolutionary War bill, see John Quincy Adams, *Memoirs of John Quincy Adams, Comprising Portions of his Diary*, ed. Charles Francis Adams (Philadelphia: J. B. Lippincott, 1874–77; reprint London: Forgotten Books, 2011), 7:541; 8:15 (hereafter *JQA*). On other problems of implementation, see *JQA*, 8:20, 34–35, 39, 68. Adams suggested that Attorney General William Wirt not work for a Baltimore railroad in their dispute with the Chesapeake & Ohio Canal so as to avoid a conflict of interest, given that the United States had subscribed $1 million to the canal company. *JQA*, 8:33. For a similar case involving government lawyers and land claims in Florida, see *JQA*, 8:72–73.
2. John T. Morse Jr., *John Quincy Adams* (Boston: Houghton Mifflin, 1882), 195. In contrast, Paul Nagel casually dismissed Adams's "hugely unsuccessful administration" in *John Quincy Adams: A Public Life, a Private Life* (Cambridge, MA: Harvard University Press, 1997), 303. Stephen Skowronek refers to Adams's "hapless struggle for credibility" in *The Politics Presidents Make: Leadership from John Adams to Bill Clinton* (Cambridge, MA: Belknap Press of

Harvard University Press, 1993), 112. Mary W. M. Hargreaves is a rare modern instance of an author who gives the Adams presidency a generally positive assessment, in *The Presidency of John Quincy Adams* (Lawrence: University Press of Kansas, 1985).
3. Fred Kaplan, *John Quincy Adams: American Visionary* (New York: HarperCollins, 2014), 425. See also Nancy Isenberg and Andrew Burstein, *The Problem of Democracy: The Presidents Adams Confront the Cult of Personality* (New York: Viking, 2019), 380–81, and John Lauritz Larson, *Internal Improvement: National Public Works and the Promise of Popular Government in the Early United States* (Chapel Hill: University of North Carolina Press, 2001), 173–77.
4. *JQA*, 7:111, 129, 265, 286, 493; 8:78, 95 (quotations); see also 7:455–56; 8:100–101.
5. Lynn Hudson Parsons, *The Birth of Modern Politics: Andrew Jackson, John Quincy Adams, and the Election of 1828* (New York: Oxford University Press, 2009), 115; see also 129, 154.
6. Robert V. Remini, *John Quincy Adams* (New York: Times Books, 2002), 85–86, 111–13. See also Hargreaves, *Presidency*, 179.
7. Francis Paul Prucha, *Broadax and Bayonet: The Role of the United States Army in the Development of the Northwest, 1815–1860* (1953; reprint Lincoln: University of Nebraska Press, 1995), 25ff, 134–48.
8. See Larson, *Internal Improvement*, 191, table 4; Daniel M. Mulcare, "Restricted Authority: Slavery Politics, Internal Improvements, and the Limitation of National Administrative Capacity," *Political Research Quarterly* 61 (2008): 683nn1, 5; Victor L. Albjerg, "Jackson's Influence on Internal Improvements," *Tennessee Historical Magazine* 2 (1932): 259–69, esp. 261–63; Victor L. Albjerg, "Internal Improvements without a Policy," *Indiana Magazine of History* 28 (1932): 168n1; and William H. Goetzmann, *Army Exploration in the American West, 1803–1863* (Lincoln: University of Nebraska Press, 1959), 9; see, generally, 3–61. See also Goetzmann's *Beyond the Revolution: A History of American Thought from Paine to Pragmatism* (New York: Basic, 2009), 174–77, 178–80, 273, and his review of contemporaneous critiques of Jacksonian democracy at 258–63; and Emilie Connolly, "Fiduciary Colonialism: Annuities and Native Dispossession in the Early United States," *American Historical Review* 127 (March 2022): 223–53. For other data, see W. J. Donald, "Land Grants for Internal Improvements in the United States," *Journal of Political Economy* 19 (1911): 404–10, and David F. Ericson, *Slavery in the American Republic: Developing the Federal Government, 1791–1861* (Lawrence: University Press of Kansas, 2011), 13 and the citations at 197n66. Approximately one-third of the funds spent on internal improvements from 1789 to 1861 was spent during Jackson's eight years as president. Albjerg, "Internal Improvements without a Policy," 174. On Jackson's support for internal improvements, see Carlton Jackson, "The Internal Improvement Vetoes of Andrew Jackson," *Tennessee Historical Quarterly* 25 (1966): 261. In his time in Congress, Jackson supported seven internal improvement bills and opposed none. Albjerg, "Jackson's Influence on Internal Improvements," 260. See also Albjerg, "Internal Improvements

without a Policy," 173–74. As president, he signed off on more infrastructure projects than he rejected. Jackson, "Internal Improvements without a Policy," 261–62.

9. Cf. A. Hunter Dupree, who writes that Adams's commitment to science came to nothing. Dupree, *Science in the Federal Government: A History of Policy and Activities to 1940* (Cambridge, MA: Belknap Press of Harvard University Press, 1957), 39–43.

10. Dupree, *Science in the Federal Government*, 56–61, 62–63.

11. Marlana Portolano, *The Passionate Empiricist: The Eloquence of John Quincy Adams in the Service of Science* (Albany: State University of New York Press, 2009), 55. See also Dupree, *Science in the Federal Government*, 64; Jean Heffer, *The United States and the Pacific: History of a Frontier* (Notre Dame, IN: University of Notre Dame Press, 2002), 84; and John R. Van Atta, *Securing the West: Politics, Public Lands, and the Fate of the Old Republic, 1785–1850* (Baltimore: Johns Hopkins University Press, 2014), 242.

12. *JQA*, 8:233–34.

13. Quoted in Harlow Giles Unger, *John Quincy Adams* (Boston: Da Capo Press, 2012), 119.

14. Hargreaves, *Presidency*, 42.

15. William Earl Weeks, *John Quincy Adams and American Global Empire* (Lexington: University Press of Kentucky, 1992), 18.

16. On Adams and internal improvements generally, see Larson, *Internal Improvement*, 157–80; Hargreaves, *Presidency*, 5–9, 42, 165–87; and Unger, *Adams*, 220–21. See also Van Atta, *Securing the West*; Weeks, *Adams*, 92–93; John Lauritz Larson, "'Bind the Republic Together': The National Union and the Struggle for a System of Internal Improvements," *Journal of American History* 74 (1987): 363–87; and Carter Goodrich, "American Development Policy: The Case of Internal Improvements," *Journal of Economic History* 16 (1956): 449–60. On internal improvements and state constitutions, see Carter Goodrich, "The Revulsion against Internal Improvements," *Journal of Economic History* 10 (1950): 145–69. On rhetoric and ideas, 1808–17, see Michael J. Hostetler, "The Early American Quest for Internal Improvements: Distance and Debate," *Rhetorica* 29 (2011): 53–75. On land grants for canals and wagon roads, including discussion of the federal government and Ohio and Indiana in the 1820s, see Donald, "Land Grants." For a brief literature review of the scholarship in this area and the development of overarching interpretations, see Mulcare, "Restricted Authority," 674–75.

17. On the Gallatin report, see Larson, "'Bind the Republic Together,'" 372–76; Larson, *Internal Improvement*, 59–63; Lawrence G. Hines, "The Early 19th Century Internal Improvements Reports and the Philosophy of Public Investment," *Journal of Economic Issues* 2 (1968): 384–92; Carter Goodrich, "National Planning of Internal Improvements," *Political Science Quarterly* 63 (1948): 16–28; Rozann Rothman, "Political Method in the Federal System: Albert Gallatin's Contribution," *Publius* 1 (1972): 123–41; and Van Atta, *Securing the West*, 75–78.

18. Hargreaves, *Presidency*, 29; Parsons, *Birth of Modern Politics*, 113; Van Atta, *Securing the West*, 130 and chap. 4 generally.
19. Hargreaves, *Presidency*, 173–78.
20. Hargreaves, *Presidency*, 175; Leland R. Johnson, "Army Engineers on the Cumberland and Tennessee, 1824–1854," *Tennessee Historical Quarterly* 31 (1972): 149–69; S. Charles Bolton, "'Like a Bridge Finished to the Middle of a Stream,'" *Arkansas Historical Quarterly* 78 (2019): 339–64; Todd Shallat, "Building Waterways, 1802–1861: Science and the United States Army in Early Public Works," *Technology and Culture* 31 (1990): 18–50 (focusing on water projects); Todd Shallat, "Engineering Policy: The U.S. Army Corps of Engineers and the Historical Foundation of Power," *Public Historian* 11 (1989): 6–27; Richard D. Durbin and Elizabeth Durbin, "Wisconsin's Old Military Road: Its Genesis and Construction," *Wisconsin Magazine of History* 68 (1984): 2–42 (which offers extensive Adams-era background regarding a project mostly associated with the Jackson years); Mulcare, "Restricted Authority"; Carter Goodrich, "Internal Improvements Reconsidered," *Journal of Economic History* 30 (1970): 289–311; Goodrich, "American Development Policy." John Lauritz Larson emphasizes the public-private and local-national mixtures of policymaking. Larson, "'Bind the Republic Together'"; Larson, *Internal Improvement*. J. Ledlie Klosky and Wynn E. Klosky emphasize international links in "Men of Action: French Influence and the Founding of American Civil and Military Engineering," *Construction History* 28 (2013): 83–84.
21. Robert G. Angevine, *The Railroad and the State: War, Politics, and Technology in Nineteenth-Century America* (Stanford, CA: Stanford University Press, 2004), 16–17. On the General Survey Act generally, see Johnson, "Army Engineers," 150–51; and Durbin and Durbin, "Wisconsin's Old Military Road," 7–8. See also Forest G. Hill, "Formative Relations of American Enterprise, Government and Science," *Political Science Quarterly* 75 (1960): 408–10.
22. Todd Shallat, "Water and Bureaucracy: Origins of the Federal Responsibility for Water Resources, 1787–1838," *Natural Resources Journal* 32 (1992): 16–17, 19; Albjerg, "Internal Improvements without a Policy," 171–73; Robert G. Angevine, "Individuals, Organizations, and Engineering: U.S. Army Officers and the American Railroads, 1827–1838," *Technology and Culture* 42 (2001): 297–98, 307–8.
23. Harold L. Nelson, "Military Roads for War and Peace—1791–1836," *Military Affairs* 19 (1955): 1–14.
24. Hargreaves, *Presidency*, 175–76; Albjerg, "Internal Improvements without a Policy," 173, 173n26.
25. Geneal Prather, "The Struggle for the Michigan Road," *Indiana Magazine of History* 39 (1943): 1–24.
26. See, for example, Shallat, "Building Waterways," esp. 31–38; Shallat, "Engineering Policy"; Prather, "Struggle for the Michigan Road," 8; Albjerg, "Internal Improvements without a Policy," 172–73; Julian P. Bretz, "Early Land Communication with the Lower Mississippi Valley," *Mississippi Valley*

Historical Review 13 (1926): 3–29; Christopher McGrory Klyza, "The United States Army, Natural Resources, and Political Development in the Nineteenth Century," *Polity* 35 (2002): 5–6; and Alan D. Watson, "North Carolina and Internal Improvements, 1783–1861: The Case of Inland Navigation," *North Carolina Historical Review* 74 (1997): 48.

27. Shallat, "Water and Bureaucracy," 18–24; Larson, "'Bind the Republic Together,'" 385. For interesting analysis of the connections between historical efforts and more contemporary infrastructure debates, see Bruce Seely, "A Republic Bound Together," *Wilson Quarterly* 17 (1993): 18–39, and Adam J. White, "Infrastructure Policy: Lessons from American History," *New Atlantis* 35 (2012): 3–31.
28. Prather, "Struggle for the Michigan Road," 7–11.
29. Angevine, "Individuals, Organizations, and Engineering," 309–11.
30. Angevine, "Individuals, Organizations, and Engineering," 308; Angevine, *Railroad and the State*, 73–78.
31. Hargreaves, *Presidency*, 173. Projects were "of paramount interest." Albjerg, "Internal Improvements without a Policy," 168; see also 174–76. For a list of well-executed projects, see Goodrich, "American Development Policy," 456–57. On the popularity of a North-South road to Indianapolis, and of improvement projects in the region generally, see Prather, "Struggle for the Michigan Road."
32. *JQA*, 8:6, 27, 7 (quotation).
33. Watson, "North Carolina and Internal Improvements," 60–62, 73. See also Alan D. Watson, "Battling 'Old Rip': Internal Improvements and the Role of State Government in Antebellum North Carolina," *North Carolina Historical Review* 77 (2000): 179–204; Harry L. Watson, "Squire Oldway and His Friends: Opposition to Internal Improvements in Antebellum North Carolina," *North Carolina Historical Review* 54 (1977): 105–19; and Hill, "Formative Relations." For the Bernard-Totten report on New Jersey's Morris Canal in 1823, see Hines, "Early 19th Century Internal Improvements Reports," 388–89. Generally, see Todd A. Shallat, "American Gibraltars: American Engineers and the Quest for a Scientific Defense of the Nation, 1815–1860," *Army History* 66 (2008): 4–19; Shallat, "Water and Bureaucracy," 16–17; Shallat, "Building Waterways"; Klosky and Klosky, "Men of Action"; and Angevine, *Railroad and the State*. On the Gallatin report and the sophistication of analysis and cost-benefit analysis at the time, see Hines, "Early 19th Century Internal Improvements Reports," and Lawrence G. Hines, "Precursors to Benefit-Cost Analysis in the Early United States Public Investment Projects," *Land Economics* 49 (1973): 310–17. See also Hostetler, "Early American Quest." On the general trend from sophisticated analysis to public benefit arguments, from Albert Gallatin to Secretary of War Peter Porter (1810) to John C. Calhoun (1817), see Hostetler, "Early American Quest," and Larson, "'Bind the Republic Together,'" 372–85. On differential expertise, see Shallat, "Water and Bureaucracy," 19–21, and Todd Shallat, "Science and the Grand Design: Origins of the U.S. Army Corps of Engineers," *Construction History* 10 (1994): 17–27.
34. *JQA*, 6:526, 532; 7:217, 246, 251, 393, 395; 8:16, 33–34.

35. Prucha, *Broadax and Bayonet*, 134. See also Remini, *Adams*, 85–86, and Weeks, *Adams*, 92.
36. Hargreaves, *Presidency*, 176; Van Atta, *Securing the West*.
37. Secretary of War, Annual Report from the Department of War, with the President's Message, in *American State Papers: Military Affairs*, vol. 4, 20th Congress, 2nd session, December 2, 1828, 14, 39–40, 625–30, http://memory.loc.gov/cgi-bin/ampage?collId=llsp&fileName=019/llsp019.db&Page=1. See also Nelson, "Military Roads," 10.
38. Hargreaves, *Presidency*, 187, 166.
39. *JQA*, 8:15.
40. *JQA*, 8:15.
41. Hargreaves, *Presidency*, 168–73; Heffer, *United States and the Pacific*, 84–88. Adams was also an important figure in the coastal survey of the eastern seaboard. *JQA*, 7:119, 453.
42. William D. Adler, *Engineering Expansion: The U.S. Army and Economic Development, 1787–1860* (Philadelphia: University of Pennsylvania Press, 2021), 123, 128, and chap. 4 generally; Goetzmann, *Army Exploration*, 8–10.
43. Dupree, *Science in the Federal Government*, 5.
44. Hargreaves, *Presidency*, 12–15, 314–17.
45. Hargreaves, *Presidency*, 181.
46. *JQA*, 7:145–46. Adams continued this theme in December 1826, with a sarcastic contrast of a military academy's presentation with the commencement at Columbia College, which Adams attended the next day. *JQA*, 7:214.
47. Hargreaves, *Presidency*, 182–87; *JQA*, 8:47. On the Bank and globalization, see Parsons, *Birth of Modern Politics*, 61, 85–86.
48. Hargreaves, *Presidency*, 197–99; Van Atta, *Securing the West*, 129–38.
49. *JQA*, 7:59–63, 349–50, 178, 189–92, 363, 52.
50. *JQA*, 7:293, 298.
51. *JQA*, 7:297–98, 299–300. Adams habitually swam naked in the Potomac, which may explain his "comparative coolness" at hearing of the new requirement for naked examinations.
52. *JQA*, 7:291.
53. *JQA*, 7:159. Also, in 1827 Adams refused to add his name to a contribution list for a minister collecting funds to support educating people for the ministry. Joseph G. Smoot, "A Presbyterian Minister Calls on President John Quincy Adams, November 7–9, 1827," *New England Quarterly* 34 (1961): 379–82.
54. For other examples of Adams's approach, see *JQA*, 7:13, 14–15, 250–55. On process, principle, and decisions on pardons, see *JQA*, 7:204. On process managing the battle between Edward Gaines and Winfield Scott for command of the army, which started before Adams was president and ended after he was out of office, see *JQA*, 7:252–54. On courts-martial and courts of enquiry at West Point, regarding process, standard operating procedures, and deference to the chain of command, see *JQA*, 7:19, 23–24, 29, 35, 45, 46, 265–66, 271, 297–98, 457, 476, 505–7; 8:13–15, 42–43. On anticipating issues

regarding Peter Porter in the Caribbean, see *JQA*, 7:289–90. For other general examples, see *JQA*, 6:544–45; 7:363, 372, 384. On examining the papers on slave claims and cases before rendering decisions, see *JQA*, 7:171–72, 236. On silence, see *JQA*, 7:409. On using text of the Constitution in decision making, see *JQA*, 7:52. On using text of laws, treaties, and regulations, see *JQA*, 6:434 (to solve a dispute in Monroe's cabinet over Porter's authorization to land in Puerto Rico in pursuit of pirates); 6:453–54, 445 (on piracy and Cuba); 6:479 (information and documents given to Joel R. Poinsett, who would be appointed U.S. minister to Mexico by Adams and who had asked for guidance on authorizations for landing on foreign territory in pursuit of pirates); 7:17 (on stationing a ship along the Northeast Coast to protect fishermen, relying on the 1818 Convention with Great Britain and other materials); 7:7, 254, 296–97, 307, 231–32 (on Indian affairs and Georgia); 7:254, 256 (on Britain and the colonial trade question); 7:308 (on dismissing army cadets for misconduct); 7:503–4, 509 (on slavery and shipwrecks); 7:66 (on increasing the pay of surgeons in military service).

55. Treaty quoted in Francis Paul Prucha, *American Indian Treaties: The History of a Political Anomaly* (Berkeley: University of California Press, 1997), 142–43. See also C. Joseph Genetin-Pilawa, *Crooked Paths to Allotment: The Fight over Federal Indian Policy after the Civil War* (Chapel Hill: University of North Carolina Press, 2012), 17.
56. Prucha, *American Indian Treaties*, 143–44.
57. Prucha, *American Indian Treaties*, 144, appendix B. Terry M. Moe and William G. Howell count only twenty-three treaties in the entire period from 1820 to 1829; see Terry M. Moe and William G. Howell, "The Presidential Power of Unilateral Action," *Journal of Law, Economics, and Organization* 15 (1999): 164 (table 1).
58. Francis Paul Prucha, *The Great Father: The United States Government and the American Indians* (Lincoln: University of Nebraska Press, 1984), 259; Hargreaves, *Presidency*, 201; Herman J. Viola, *Diplomats in Buckskins: A History of Indian Delegations in Washington City* (Bluffton, SC: Rivilo Books, 1995), 97–99.
59. John K. Mahon, *History of the Second Seminole War, 1835–1842* (Gainesville: University of Florida Press, 1992), 57–72; *JQA*, 7:65.
60. Laurence M. Hauptman, *Conspiracy of Interests: Iroquois Dispossession and the Rise of New York State* (Syracuse, NY: Syracuse University Press, 1999), 144–61; *JQA*, 7:371, 388, 453, 464, 465, 484–85, 8:22–23, 55, 58, 98; Daniel P. Carpenter, *Democracy by Petition: Popular Politics in Transformation, 1790–1870* (Cambridge, MA: Harvard University Press, 2021), 135–41. Hauptman writes that despite the formal failure of the treaty, it was "allowed to stand," with white settlement overrunning Seneca territory and the Senecas receiving monetary compensation only in the 1960s and 1970s. See Hauptman, *Conspiracy of Interests*, 160–61.
61. *JQA*, 7:411, 422; see also 7:442, 444–45.
62. *JQA*, 7:502–3.

63. Quoted in Prucha, *American Indian Treaties*, 147.
64. *JQA*, 7:502–3, 516, 518, 523, 526, 539. For more on the Cherokees and the land at issue, see Brad Agnew, "The Cherokee Struggle for Lovely's Purchase," *American Indian Quarterly* 2 (1975–76): esp. 356.
65. See Agnew, "Cherokee Struggle"; on the president's role, see esp. 353–56. See also Derek R. Everett, "On the Extreme Frontier: Crafting the Western Arkansas Boundary," *Arkansas Historical Quarterly* 67 (2008): 1–26.
66. While treaties can be seen as classic elements of foreign policy, they were in many ways also elements of domestic land and expansion policy, and were seen as such by many state and congressional leaders. As examples, see Richard J. Hryniewicki, "The Creek Treaty of Washington, 1826," *Georgia Historical Quarterly* 48 (1964): 425–41; Richard J. Hryniewicki, "The Creek Treaty of November 15, 1827," *Georgia Historical Quarterly* 52 (1968): 1–15; and William G. McLaughlin, "Georgia's Role in Instigating Compulsory Indian Removal," *Georgia Historical Quarterly* 70 (1986): 619–20. See also Jay Gitlin, "Private Diplomacy to Private Property: States, Tribes, and Nations in the Early National Period," *Diplomatic History* 22 (1998): 92–99. For an example of the executive, especially the president and attorney general, at loggerheads with Congress over implementing claims under treaties with the Creeks, see Larry C. Skogen, *Indian Depredation Claims, 1796–1920* (Norman: University of Oklahoma Press, 1996), 73–79, 230n59.
67. Hargreaves, *Presidency*, 67–163; Weeks, *Adams*, 20.
68. Hargreaves, *Presidency*, 89; Remini, *Adams*, 104.
69. Remini, *Adams*, 104. On the Hanseatic treaties, see *JQA*, 8:26.
70. The settlement also put to rest a mediation commission led by the Russian czar, which Adams had negotiated in 1822. Hargreaves, *Presidency*, 68–69.
71. Hargreaves, *Presidency*, 82 (quotation), 76–85.
72. Prucha, *American Indian Treaties*, 140–41.
73. See Prucha, *Great Father*, 259–61; Hargreaves, *Presidency*, 201; Viola, *Diplomats in Buckskins*, 97–99; and Prucha, *Broadax and Bayonet*, 23–24.
74. Prucha, *Broadax and Bayonet*, 69, 24.
75. Here, the conflict lay with white Arkansas residents upset at the amount of valuable land secured in the treaty to Choctaws removing from the East to the region. Prucha, *American Indian Treaties*, 148.
76. David LaVere, *Contrary Neighbors: Southern Plains and Removed Indians in Indian Territory* (Norman: University of Oklahoma Press, 2000), 54–55.
77. Prucha, *American Indian Treaties*, 138–40. The treaty with the Choctaws having allowed funds for education, for example, Adams supported the establishment of the Choctaw Academy in 1825. Herman J. Viola, *Thomas L. McKenney, Architect of America's Early Indian Policy: 1816–1830* (Chicago: Sage, 1974), 189; Ronald N. Satz, *American Indian Policy in the Jacksonian Era* (Lincoln: University of Nebraska Press, 1975), 250–51.
78. Hargreaves, *Presidency*, 81–82, 157. Provisions insisted on by Jacksonian forces that would have guaranteed protection against attacks by Native Americans

and the return of fugitive enslaved people led to the rejection of the treaty with Mexico by the Mexican senate.

79. Charles Wilson Hackett, "The Development of John Quincy Adams's Policy with Respect to an American Confederation and the Panama Congress, 1822–1825," *Hispanic American Historical Review* 8 (1928): 521–26.

80. William Earl Weeks, "John Quincy Adams's 'Great Gun' and the Rhetoric of American Empire," *Diplomatic History* 14 (1990): 41–42; John Quincy Adams, First Annual Message, December 6, 1825, American Presidency Project, https://www.presidency.ucsb.edu/documents/first-annual-message-2; John Quincy Adams, "Message Regarding the Congress of American Nations," December 6, 1825, Miller Center, https://millercenter.org/the-presidency/presidential-speeches/december-6-1825-message-regarding-congress-american-nations. See also Hackett, "Development of John Quincy Adams's Policy," 525, and Light T. Cummins, "John Quincy Adams and Latin American Nationalism," *Revista de Historia de America* 86 (1978): 228.

81. L. Paul Gresham, "The Public Career of Hugh Lawson White," *Tennessee Historical Quarterly* 3 (1944): 301.

82. Hargreaves, *Presidency*, 152–53; Cummins, "Adams and Latin American Nationalism," 225–31.

83. See Hargreaves, *Presidency*, 129–31, 147–58. See also Remini, *Adams*, 102; Kaplan, *Adams*, 405–10; Parsons, *Birth of Modern Politics*, 119; Cummins, "Adams and Latin American Nationalism"; and Morse, *Adams*, 192. Cf. Samuel Flagg Bemis, *John Quincy Adams and the Union* (New York: Knopf, 1956), 77, and Samuel Flagg Bemis, *John Quincy Adams and the Foundations of American Foreign Policy* (New York: Knopf, 1949), 544–61.

84. Opposing slavery had been mentioned prominently in the invitation sent by Colombian minister Jose Maria de Salazar to Henry Clay in November 1825; Hackett, "Development of John Quincy Adams's Policy," 518. On regional politics, see Weeks, *Adams*, 85–104.

85. Hargreaves, *Presidency*, 69–84.

86. Skogen, *Indian Depredation Claims*, 36, 41–51, 71–79, 231n74.

87. See, for example, on Georgia: *JQA*, 7:545, 8:47–48; on Florida: *JQA*, 7:74, 8:31–32, 72–73; on Arkansas: *JQA*, 8:35.

88. Emanuel Raymond Lewis, *Seacoast Fortifications of the United States: An Introductory History* (Annapolis, MD: Naval Institute Press, 1979), including maps at 10, 13; J. E. Kaufmann and H. W. Kaufmann, *Fortress America: The Forts That Defended America, 1600 to the Present* (Cambridge, MA: Da Capo Press, 2004), 175–234.

89. Kaufmann and Kaufmann, *Fortress America*, 219.

90. Hargreaves, *Presidency*, 215.

91. On the Treasury, see *JQA*, 7:109; 8:32, 39. On the U.S. Navy, see *JQA*, 8:66, and Hargreaves, *Presidency*, 228–35. On the War Department, see *JQA*, 8:58, 67, 15, 18, 27, 39, 84. See also Hargreaves, *Presidency*, 214.

92. *JQA*, 6: 520–21, 521 (quotations). On Crawford's effort, see *JQA*, 6:514, 521. On Adams and continuity in office generally, see *JQA*, 6:474–75; 7:154–55, 162, 163–64, 180, 316–17, 390, 424–25, 441, 544. On Clay and the replacement of official publishers and presses, see Hargreaves, *Presidency*, 262–70.
93. On Adams's efforts regarding administration appointments, see Hargreaves, *Presidency*, 53–66, 258, 261, 282; Parsons, *Birth of Modern Politics*, 116; and *JQA*, 6:546.
94. Hargreaves, *Presidency*, 65–66, 204, 230ff; Morse, *Adams*, 197–201; *JQA*, 7:272–73, 319, 478–79, 482, 496; 8:61.
95. Hargreaves, *Presidency*, 62.
96. Weeks, *Adams*, 72, 131, 136–37, 149.
97. See, for example, *JQA*, 6:435–37, 442, 462–63, 532; 7:179, 190–91, 200, 227–28, 274, 280, 283, 310, 393, 466, 482, 487, 495, 498–99, 502, 504, 516, 519–20, 529, 539; 8:29, 66, 85–87.
98. See, for example, *JQA*, 7:231, 235–37.
99. *JQA*, 7:377, 455, 197, 408, 497.
100. Hargreaves, *Presidency*, 223–24.
101. Scott's appeal to Congress failed, as Congress sanctioned Adams's action. Adams considered publishing his views on the matter, but Attorney General William Wirt convinced him not to. Hargreaves, *Presidency*, 226–27.
102. Prucha, *Great Father*, 259; Hargreaves, *Presidency*, 201; Viola, *Diplomats in Buckskins*, 97–99; Prucha, *Broadax and Bayonet*, 23–24.
103. *JQA*, 6:427; 7:402, 421, 536, 117. See also Fred Kaplan, *Lincoln and the Abolitionists: John Quincy Adams, Slavery, and the Civil War* (New York: HarperCollins, 2017), 135.
104. See Weeks, *Adams*, 57–58, 67; *JQA*, 8:20–21; and Bemis, *Adams and the Foundations*, 307–8, 313, 344, 345, 349.
105. Unger, *Adams*, 271, 302; Weeks, *Adams*, 115–19.
106. Weeks, *Adams*, 67–69, 94–104, 205n41. See also the quotation from William Duane about Adams's interference in Weeks, *Adams*, 104. For a discussion of Adams's pre-presidency use of the media, see Isenberg and Burstein, *Problem of Democracy*, 336–38.
107. Quoted in Prucha, *Great Father*, 190; see also 187–91; Judith A. Boughter, *Betraying the Omaha Nation, 1790–1916* (Norman: University of Oklahoma Press, 1998), 29–30; *JQA*, 7:117.
108. McLaughlin, "Georgia's Role," 626–27.
109. Hargreaves, *Presidency*, 169, 171.
110. *JQA*, 8:54.
111. Prucha, *Great Father*, 230–31; Mahon, *History of the Second Seminole War*, 58–72.
112. See, for example, *JQA*, 6:461, 536, 541, 543; 7:11–12, 264, 280, 301–2, 307–8, 359, 541; 8:4–5, 62–63, 68–69, 146–47.
113. Kaplan, *Adams*, 429. See also Wheelan, *Mr. Adams's Last Crusade*, 117–19, and Marta McDowell, *All the Presidents' Gardens: Madison's Cabbages to Kennedy's*

Roses—How the White House Grounds Have Grown with America (Portland, OR: Timber Press, 2016), 77–79.

114. Kaplan, *Adams*, 429. See also *JQA*, 7:121, 269–70, 352, 486, and Bemis, *Adams and the Union*, 123.
115. William R. Adams, "Florida Live Oak Farm of John Quincy Adams," *Florida Historical Quarterly* 51 (1972): 129–31.
116. Adams, "Florida Live Oak Farm," 129, 132, 135. See also Ernest A. Engelbert, "Political Parties and Natural Resources Policies: An Historical Evaluation, 1790–1950," *Natural Resources Journal* 1 (1961): 233–34.
117. Adams, "Florida Live Oak Farm," 138–42.
118. Adams, "Florida Live Oak Farm," 136, 134, 129.
119. Adams, "Florida Live Oak Farm," 133, 134.
120. *JQA*, 7:100.

3. Presidential Decision Making and the Administrative State

1. Terry L. Cooper, *The Responsible Administrator: An Approach to Ethics for the Administrative Role*, 5th ed. (San Francisco: Jossey-Bass, 2006). See also Craig E. Johnson, *Meeting the Ethical Challenges of Leadership: Casting Light or Shadow* (Thousand Oaks, CA: Sage, 2001), 172–83.
2. Lynn Hudson Parsons, *The Birth of Modern Politics: Andrew Jackson, John Quincy Adams, and the Election of 1828* (New York: Oxford University Press, 2009), 47; Mary W. M. Hargreaves, *The Presidency of John Quincy Adams* (Lawrence: University Press of Kansas, 1985), 200; Harlow Giles Unger, *John Quincy Adams* (Boston: Da Capo Press, 2012), 173.
3. See Lynn Hudson Parsons, "'A Perpetual Harrow upon My Feelings': John Quincy Adams and the American Indian," *New England Quarterly* 46 (1973): 346–59; William Earl Weeks, *John Quincy Adams and American Global Empire* (Lexington: University Press of Kentucky, 1992), 193–94; Parsons, *Birth of Modern Politics*, 47.
4. Tim Alan Garrison, "Beyond *Worcester*: The Alabama Supreme Court and the Sovereignty of the Creek Nation," *Journal of the Early Republic* 19 (1999): 423–50; Lynda Worley Skelton, "The States Rights Movement in Georgia, 1825–1850," *Georgia Historical Quarterly* 50 (1966): 391–412. See also Tim Alan Garrison, *The Legal Ideology of Removal: The Southern Judiciary and the Sovereignty of Native American Nations* (Athens: University of Georgia Press, 2002).
5. On Jackson's novel approaches, see, for example, Ronald N. Satz, *American Indian Policy in the Jacksonian Era* (Lincoln: University of Nebraska Press, 1975), esp. 41–42. On ethnic cleansing and genocide, see Alan Wolfe, *Political Evil: What It Is and How to Combat It* (New York: Knopf, 2011), chaps. 6–7, and Benjamin Madley, *An American Genocide: The United States and the California Indian Catastrophe* (New Haven, CT: Yale University Press, 2016).

6. See, for example, John K. Mahon, *History of the Second Seminole War, 1835–1842* (Gainesville: University of Florida Press, 1992), 57.
7. John Quincy Adams, *Memoirs of John Quincy Adams, Comprising Portions of his Diary*, ed. Charles Francis Adams (Philadelphia: J. B. Lippincott, 1874–77; reprint London: Forgotten Books, 2011), 6:511 (hereafter *JQA*). For background, see Satz, *American Indian Policy*, 3–6, 11–12.
8. Francis Paul Prucha, *The Great Father: The United States Government and the American Indians* (Lincoln: University of Nebraska Press, 1984), 220–21.
9. See *JQA*, 6:528, regarding Adams's consent to the ratification of the treaty. For background on the situation, see Parsons, "'A Perpetual Harrow upon My Feelings,'" 351–59; Christopher D. Haveman, *Rivers of Sand: Creek Indian Emigration, Relocation, and Ethnic Cleansing in the American South* (Lincoln: University of Nebraska Press, 2016), 6–7, 12, chap. 1; Michael D. Green, *The Politics of Indian Removal: Creek Government and Society in Crisis* (Lincoln: University of Nebraska Press, 1985); James W. Silver, "General Gaines Meets Governor Troup: A State-Federal Clash in 1825," *Georgia Historical Quarterly* 27 (1943): 248–70; Richard J. Hryniewicki, "The Creek Treaty of Washington, 1826," *Georgia Historical Quarterly* 48 (1964): 425–41; and Skelton, "States Rights Movement."
10. *JQA*, 7:3–4, 5–6, 11.
11. Silver, "General Gaines," 257. Silver's article offers an excellent discussion of federal-state issues focused on a dissection of communications and negotiations between Gaines and Troup. See also Haveman, *Rivers of Sand*, 14, 19, 20–21.
12. Haveman, *Rivers of Sand*, 11–24, 39–41; Green, *Politics of Indian Removal*, 69–125; Hargreaves, *Presidency*, 202–8; Francis Paul Prucha, *American Indian Treaties: The History of a Political Anomaly* (Berkeley: University of California Press, 1997), 148–51; Nancy Isenberg and Andrew Burstein, *The Problem of Democracy: The Presidents Adams Confront the Cult of Personality* (New York: Viking, 2019), 344. Haveman's book highlights the effective resistance strategies of the Creeks.
13. *JQA*, 7:12, 29.
14. *JQA*, 7:33–34.
15. Robert Remini, *John Quincy Adams* (New York: Times Books, 2002), 93; see generally 88–100.
16. *JQA*, 7:34.
17. Quoted in Remini, *Adams*, 94.
18. *JQA*, 7:49.
19. Quoted in Silver, "General Gaines," 253n20, 254–55, 263–67.
20. E. Taylor Parks and Alfred Tischendorf, "Cartagena to Bogota, 1825–1826: The Diary of Richard Clough Anderson, Jr.," *Hispanic American Historical Review* 42 (1962): 222.
21. Prucha, *American Indian Treaties*, 150.
22. Remini, *Adams*, 98. See also *JQA*, 7:66, 68, 69, 71, 72–73, 78–79, 87, 89–92, 106, 108, 109, 110.

23. Remini, *Adams*, 98.
24. Hargreaves, *Presidency*, 204. When Habersham suggested that he would not put the warrants into effect because of his personal loyalty to the state, Clay replaced him. Hargreaves, *Presidency*, 204.
25. JQA, 7:232–33. See also Hargreaves, *Presidency*, 203–5. Troup's tirade to the United States is quoted in Silver, "General Gaines," 255–56.
26. JQA, 7:73–74; 8:53–54.
27. JQA, 7:90, 89.
28. JQA, 7:90; emphasis added.
29. JQA, 7:92.
30. JQA, 7:92.
31. JQA, 7:219. Troup prepared his forces in anticipation. James C. Bonner, "Journal of a Mission to Georgia in 1827," *Georgia Historical Quarterly* 44 (1960): 74–75. See also Carl J. Vipperman, "The 'Particular Mission' of Wilson Lumpkin," *Georgia Historical Quarterly* 66 (1982): 295–96.
32. Cooper, *Responsible Administrator*, 24–30.
33. JQA, 7:219.
34. JQA, 7:219.
35. JQA, 7:219.
36. JQA, 7:219–20, 233.
37. John Quincy Adams, "Message Regarding the Creek Indians," February 5, 1827, Miller Center, https://millercenter.org/the-presidency/presidential-speeches/february-5-1827-message-regarding-creek-indians.
38. JQA, 7:221.
39. See, for example, JQA, 8:19, in which Adams reported that a representative from Virginia "urges the necessity of removing [squatters in Indian lands] by military force." Lieutenant John Vinton, Adams's envoy, wrote in his diary that "this looks like Civil War!" when he read in the newspapers Troup's responses to Adams and his call for resisting federal action ordered by the president. Bonner, "Journal of a Mission," 80.
40. JQA, 7:231–32.
41. See Richard J. Hryniewicki, "The Creek Treaty of November 15, 1827," *Georgia Historical Quarterly* 52 (1968): 1–15; Remini, *Adams*, 99; and JQA, 7:409–10.
42. See, for example, Hargreaves's ambivalent conclusion in *Presidency*, 207–8; Remini, *Adams*, 100; and Fred Kaplan, *John Quincy Adams: American Visionary* (New York: HarperCollins, 2014), 399–400, 424. Paul Nagel omits the Creek story entirely. Nagel, *John Quincy Adams: A Public Life, A Private Life* (Cambridge, MA: Harvard University Press, 1997).
43. Haveman, *Rivers of Sand*, chap. 2.
44. Hargreaves, *Presidency*, 206–7. Troup explicitly denounced Adams for exceeding his authority as president in trying to resolve the issues involved. Skelton, "States Rights Movement," 393; *Macon [GA] Telegraph*, November 20, 1827; Hryniewicki, "The Creek Treaty of Washington," 438–39.

45. See, for example, Hargreaves, *Presidency*, 156, and Kenneth O'Reilly, *Nixon's Piano: Presidents and Racial Politics from Washington to Clinton* (New York: Free Press, 1995), 31.
46. Quoted in Joseph Wheelan, *Mr. Adams's Last Crusade: John Quincy Adams's Extraordinary Post-Presidential Life in Congress* (New York: Public Affairs, 2008), 98. On Adams's youth, family, and development, see David F. Musto, "The Youth of John Quincy Adams," *Proceedings of the American Philosophical Society* 113 (1969): 269–82, and William Jerry MacLean, "Othello Scorned: The Racial Thought of John Quincy Adams," *Journal of the Early Republic* 4 (1984): 147.
47. Quoted in Unger, *Adams*, 212.
48. See Wheelan, *Mr. Adams's Last Crusade*, 212.
49. Unger, *Adams*, 303–4.
50. Weeks, *Adams*, 191–96; Unger, *Adams*, 212.
51. George A. Lipsky, *John Quincy Adams: His Theory and Ideas* (New York: Thomas Y. Crowell, 1950), 210–15, 228–29; Burrus M. Carnahan, *Act of Justice: Lincoln's Emancipation Proclamation and the Law of War* (Louisville: University Press of Kentucky, 2007), esp. 7–10; David Brion Davis, *Inhuman Bondage: The Rise and Fall of Slavery in the New World* (New York: Oxford University Press, 2006), 313; Garry Wills, *Lincoln at Gettysburg: The Words That Remade America* (New York: Simon and Schuster, 2006).
52. See Matthew Karp, *This Vast Southern Empire: Slaveholders at the Helm of American Foreign Policy* (Cambridge, MA: Harvard University Press, 2016).
53. Fritz Hirschfeld, *George Washington and Slavery: A Documentary Portrayal* (Columbia: University of Missouri Press, 1997).
54. Henry Wiencek, *An Imperfect God: George Washington, His Slaves, and the Creation of America* (New York: Farrar, Straus and Giroux, 2003), 271–75.
55. David F. Ericson, *Slavery in the American Republic: Developing the Federal Government, 1791–1861* (Lawrence: University Press of Kansas, 2011), esp. chap. 6.
56. See, for example, Hirschfeld, *George Washington and Slavery*, 71, 112–17, and Wiencek, *Imperfect God*.
57. Mashaw, *Creating the Administrative Constitution*, 13, 16.
58. Fred I. Greenstein, *The Hidden-Hand Presidency: Eisenhower as Leader* (New York: Basic Books, 1982), 5, 59.
59. Greenstein, *Hidden-Hand Presidency*, 4–5.
60. John Quincy Adams, First Annual Message, December 6, 1825, American Presidency Project, https://www.presidency.ucsb.edu/documents/first-annual-message-2.
61. Donald L. Canney, *Africa Squadron: The U.S. Navy and the Slave Trade, 1842–1861* (Washington, DC: Potomac Books, 2006), 15–27; Ericson, *Slavery in the American Republic*, 36–41.
62. *JQA*, 7:509. See also *JQA*, 7:418–19, 420–21, 423, 503–4.

63. Jenny S. Martinez, *The Slave Trade and the Origins of International Human Rights Law* (New York: Oxford University Press, 2012), 46–48, 51–66, 124–26; Ericson, *Slavery in the American Republic*, 40–41, 48; John T. Noonan Jr., *The Antelope: The Ordeal of the Recaptured Africans in the Administrations of James Monroe and John Quincy Adams* (Berkeley: University of California Press, 1977), 82–92; Canney, *Africa Squadron*, 18–20.
64. *JQA*, 6:427–28; 6:427 (quotation). See also Hargreaves, *Presidency*, 33.
65. John T. Morse Jr., *John Quincy Adams* (Boston: Houghton Mifflin, 1882), 191–92; *JQA*, 7:103–4.
66. John R. Van Atta, *Securing the West: Politics, Public Lands, and the Fate of the Old Republic, 1785–1850* (Baltimore: Johns Hopkins University Press, 2014), 36; Ericson, *Slavery in the American Republic*, 123, 172; Patrick Rael, "The Long Death of Slavery," in *Slavery in New York*, ed. Ira Berlin and Leslie M. Harris (New York: New Press, 2005), 137; *JQA*, 6:466–67; Fred Kaplan, *Lincoln and the Abolitionists: John Quincy Adams, Slavery, and the Civil War* (New York: HarperCollins, 2017), 121–22, 140ff.
67. *JQA*, 6:523. See also Adams's effort to nominate the outspoken and virulently antislavery Charles Hammond to the U.S. Supreme Court. William Henry Smith, *Charles Hammond and His Relations to Henry Clay and John Quincy Adams* (Chicago: Chicago Historical Society, 1885), esp. 11, 30, 31, 56, 58, 61–72.
68. See Richard R. John, "John Quincy Adams," in *The Reader's Companion to the American Presidency*, ed. Alan Brinkley and Davis Dyer (New York: Houghton Mifflin, 2000), 88. See also Daniel M. Mulcare, "Restricted Authority: Slavery Politics, Internal Improvements, and the Limitation of National Administrative Capacity," *Political Research Quarterly* 61 (2008): 671–85; Harry L. Watson, "Squire Oldway and His Friends: Opposition to Internal Improvements in Antebellum North Carolina," *North Carolina Historical Review* 54 (1977): 107–9, 119, and generally; John Majewski, "Who Financed the Transportation Revolution? Regional Divergence and Internal Improvements in Antebellum Pennsylvania and Virginia," *Journal of Economic History* 56 (1996): 763–88; John Majewski, "Commerce and Community: Internal Improvements in Virginia and Pennsylvania, 1790–1860," *Journal of Economic History* 56 (1996): 467–69; Daniel Feller, *The Public Lands in Jacksonian Politics* (Madison: University of Wisconsin Press, 1984); Pamela L. Baker, "The Washington National Road Bill and the Struggle to Adopt a Federal System of Internal Improvement," *Journal of the Early Republic* 22 (2002): 447, 463; Bruce Seely, "A Republic Bound Together," *Wilson Quarterly* 17 (1993): 22–23; Jeffrey Normand Bourdon, "'All Must Have a Say': Internal Improvements and Andrew Jackson's Political Rise in North Carolina in 1824," *North Carolina Historical Review* 91 (2014): 67, 89–92; and Carter Goodrich, "National Planning of Internal Improvements," *Political Science Quarterly* 63 (1948): 36–37. David F. Ericson notes that the U.S. government, the military, and its contractors utilized slave labor for internal improvement projects, complicating the analysis here and suggesting the need

for further study. Ericson, *Slavery in the American Republic*, 135–51, and chap. 6 generally.

69. *JQA*, 8:233. See also John Lauritz Larson, "'Bind the Republic Together': The National Union and the Struggle for a System of Internal Improvements," *Journal of American History* 74 (1987): 386; Baker, "Washington National Road Bill"; Mulcare, "Restricted Authority," 676–77; and William H. Goetzmann, *Beyond the Revolution: A History of American Thought from Paine to Pragmatism* (New York: Basic, 2009), 294.
70. Richard R. John, *Spreading the News: The American Postal System from Franklin to Morse* (Cambridge, MA: Harvard University Press, 1995), 256; Paul Starr, *The Creation of the Media: Political Origins of Modern Communications* (New York: Basic Books, 2004), 88–89.
71. As just one example, John Lauritz Larson calls Adams's refusal to remove McLean "singularly stupid." Larson, *Internal Improvement: National Public Works and the Promise of Popular Government in the Early United States* (Chapel Hill: University of North Carolina Press, 2001), 178.
72. *JQA*, 7:275, 363–64. See also other plaudits described in John, *Spreading the News*, 69; data at 51, table 2.1, and chap. 3 generally.
73. John, *Spreading the News*, 66, 81, 90–100, 107, and chap. 3 generally. McLean's top two assistants included a pro-Jackson operator but also a pro-Adams senior clerk. John, *Spreading the News*, 69–71.
74. Hargreaves, *Presidency*, 239–40.
75. See, for example, *JQA*, 7:282, 344–45, and Hargreaves, *Presidency*, 239.
76. *JQA*, 7:343.
77. *JQA*, 7:536, 544; 8:25, 51. See also Hargreaves, *Presidency*, 50–53.
78. *JQA*, 8:109–10; see also 8:112.
79. John, *Spreading the News*, 72–73.
80. Jon C. Rogowski, "Presidential Influence in an Era of Congressional Dominance," *American Political Science Review* 110 (2016): 325–41.
81. Greenstein, *Hidden-Hand Presidency*, 237.
82. On Adams's legislative agenda, see Jeffrey E. Cohen, *The President's Legislative Policy Agenda, 1789–2002* (Cambridge: Cambridge University Press, 2012), 16n5, 26n14, 29n16, 105, 151, 262.
83. The idea of government's functions being to protect and empower comes from George Lakoff, *The Political Mind: A Cognitive Scientist's Guide to Your Brain and Its Politics* (New York: Penguin, 2009).
84. William J. Novak, *The People's Welfare: Law and Regulation in Nineteenth-Century America* (Chapel Hill: The University of North Carolina Press, 1996).
85. Weeks, *Adams*, 18.
86. See, for example, Remini, *Adams*, 77–81; Nagel, *Adams*, 298–305; Kaplan, *Adams*, 394–98; A. Hunter Dupree, *Science in the Federal Government: A History of Policy and Activities to 1940* (Cambridge, MA: Belknap Press of Harvard University Press, 1957), 39–43; and Isenberg and Burstein, *Problem of Democracy*, 354–55, 372.

87. John Quincy Adams, Inaugural Address, March 4, 1825, in *Fellow Citizens: The Penguin Book of U.S. Presidential Inaugural Addresses*, ed. Robert V. Remini and Terry Golway (New York: Penguin, 2008), 73–80. Quotations in this section are from this address unless noted otherwise.
88. *JQA*, 7:63. Rush was in favor; Clay opposed making the statement, even though he felt Congress had the power and that "if they did not exercise them there would be a dissolution of the Union by the mountains." *JQA*, 7:63. Ultimately, Adams wrote that Barbour withdrew his objection, Clay approved the theme but not the delineation of details, Rush approved, and Southard "said scarcely anything."
89. Adams, First Annual Message. Quotations in this section are from this message unless otherwise noted.

4. President Grant and the American State after the Civil War

1. See, for example, Morton Keller, *America's Three Regimes: A New Political History* (New York: Oxford University Press, 2007); Michael A. Genovese, *A Presidential Nation: Causes, Consequences, and Cures* (Boulder, CO: Westview Press, 2013); Sidney M. Milkis, "Presidents, Refoundings, and the 'Living Constitution,'" in *The Presidency: Facing Constitutional Crossroads*, ed. Michael Nelson and Barbara A. Perry (Charlottesville: University of Virginia Press, 2021), 200–226; Saikrishna Bangalore Prakash, "The Living Presidency: Always at a Crossroads," in Nelson and Perry, eds., *The Presidency*, 7–27; Peri E. Arnold, *Remaking the Presidency: Roosevelt, Taft, and Wilson, 1901–1916* (Lawrence: University Press of Kansas, 2009); Daniel P. Carpenter, *The Forging of Bureaucratic Autonomy: Reputations, Networks, and Policy Innovation in Executive Agencies, 1862–1928* (Princeton, NJ: Princeton University Press, 2001); and Jeffrey K. Tulis, *The Rhetorical Presidency* (Princeton, NJ: Princeton University Press, 1987).
2. Ulysses S. Grant, First Annual Message, December 6, 1869, American Presidency Project, https://www.presidency.ucsb.edu/documents/first-annual-message-11; Seventh Annual Message, December 7, 1875, American Presidency Project, https://www.presidency.ucsb.edu/documents/seventh-annual-message-3.
3. Grant, First Annual Message.
4. References to Grant's annual messages are from the American Presidency Project, https://www.presidency.ucsb.edu/people/president/ulysses-s-grant.
5. Grant, First Annual Message.
6. Grant, First Annual Message.
7. Grant, First Annual Message.
8. See, for example, Ulysses S. Grant, *The Papers of Ulysses S. Grant*, ed. John Y. Simon et al. (Carbondale: Southern Illinois University Press, 1967–2012), 20:46, 21:44–45; 24:274–84; 25:288–90; 28:69–70 (hereafter *USG*).
9. *USG*, 28:69–70; see also, for example, 20:44, 45; 22:264; 25:287–88.

NOTES TO PAGES 97-99   273

10. Ulysses S. Grant, Fifth Annual Message, December 1, 1873, American Presidency Project, https://www.presidency.ucsb.edu/documents/fifth-annual-message-3.
11. Kenneth R. Bowling, "'Federal Town' to 'National Capital': Ulysses S. Grant and the Reconstruction of Washington, D.C.," *Washington History* 14 (2002): 14; see also 19–20, 24n2; Whit Cobb, "Democracy in Search of Utopia: The History, Law, and Politics of Relocating the National Capital," *Dickinson Law Review* 99 (1995): 527–611.
12. Ulysses S. Grant, Sixth Annual Message, December 7, 1874, American Presidency Project, https://www.presidency.ucsb.edu/documents/sixth-annual-message-3.
13. Namely the availability of education, prohibition on sectarian teaching supported by the government or by tax dollars, the separation of church and state, the driving out of "immorality, such as polygamy and the importation of women for illegitimate purposes," and a sound currency. Grant, Seventh Annual Message.
14. Grant, Seventh Annual Message. See also, for example, *USG*, 21:47, 65; 22:265, 266, 278n14, 278–79n17; 25:252–53, 288–92; 26:418–27; 28:70–73, 72n6.
15. For Grant's speech, see *USG*, 21:95; see also 95–97nn. For background, see Bowling, "'Federal Town,'" 14–15.
16. Bowling, "'Federal Town,'" 16. See also Frederick Gutheim and Antoinette J. Lee, *Worthy of the Nation: Washington, DC, from L'Enfant to the National Capitol Planning Commission*, 2nd ed. (Baltimore: Johns Hopkins University Press, 2009), 88–92.
17. Bowling, "'Federal Town,'" 18. See also Cobb, "Democracy in Search of Utopia," esp. 561–83.
18. Tulis, *Rhetorical Presidency*, 64, 66.
19. See Tulis, *Rhetorical Presidency*, 64, 66, and compare, for example, *USG*, 20:50 (on race); 21:95–97 (on moving the capital to the West); 22:157 (speech hoping for harmony among the sections); 23:144–46 (to Oglala Sioux); 23:201n3 (August 1872 correspondent interview in which Grant discussed his purposes in running for reelection); 23:289–90 (speaking about race, justice, and equality to a group of Black Philadelphians); 24:291 and editorial note, 291–92 (the Washington *Evening Star* reported that Grant addressed a delegate of the National Colored Convention and spoke in favor of enfranchisement and equal rights, including arguing that legislation seemed necessary to secure those rights following emancipation); 24:292n2 (Grant made similar comments to another group and projected that Congress should and would pass "a civil rights bill"; see also 20:50); 25:51–52 (Grant lectured a South Carolina taxpayers' group about the war, federalism, and discriminatory tax structures); 25:252–57 (three speeches to Cherokee, Choctaw, and Creek delegations); 26:343–44, 369, 532 (strongly in favor of free schools and opposed to any public funding for sectarian schools; for public reactions, see 26:344–51); 26:366 (on the upcoming election and Republican control of government); 26:343 (decrying politics or partisanship in discussing issues); 26:119–20 (to a

Sioux delegation addressing treaties, population dynamics, gold, and the Black Hills); and 19:17–22, 25–28 (on religious tolerance).
20. Ulysses S. Grant, *Personal Memoirs* (New York: Library of America, 1990), 166–67.
21. *USG*, 19:213; see also 19:243; cf. 19:216 and, generally, 215ff; Louis A. Coolidge, *The Life of Ulysses S. Grant* (Boston: Houghton Mifflin, 1922), 341; Josiah Bunting III, *Ulysses S. Grant* (New York: Times Books, 2004), 94–95. See also Irwin Unger, *The Greenback Era: A Social and Political History of American Finance, 1865–1879* (Princeton, NJ: Princeton University Press, 1964), 93–94; Joan Waugh, *U.S. Grant: American Hero, American Myth* (Chapel Hill: University of North Carolina Press, 2009), 130–31; and Frank J. Scaturro, *President Grant Reconsidered* (Lanham, MD: Madison Books, 1999), 49–50.
22. Unger, *Greenback Era*, 169ff; Waugh, *Grant*, 131; Coolidge, *Life*, 339–49; *USG*, 19:244–45, 255–59.
23. Unger, *Greenback Era*, 171–72, 172n48, 194.
24. Unger, *Greenback Era*, chap. 7, 220–28; *USG*, 25:68.
25. Unger, *Greenback Era*, 235, 236; see also, generally, 233–45.
26. Irwin Unger, "The Business Community and the Origins of the 1875 Resumption Act," *Business History Review* 35 (1961): 251.
27. *USG*, 25:65 (quotation).
28. *USG*, 25:74, 75–76. See also Allan Nevins's discussion in *Hamilton Fish: The Inner History of the Grant Administration* (1936; reprint New York: Frederick Ungar, 1957), 2:712, and chap. 29 generally, illustrating Grant's interactions with his cabinet experts in such an important matter.
29. See *USG*, 25:65–81.
30. *USG*, 27:90–91, 103–7, 184–85, 268–72.
31. See Act of April 5, 1869, chap. 10, §§1–2, 16 Stat. 6, 6–7, cited in "ArtII.S2.C2.3.15.3 Removals in Jacksonian America through the Nineteenth Century," Constitution Annotated: Analysis and Interpretation of the U.S. Constitution, https://constitution.congress.gov/browse/essay/artII-S2-C2-3-15-3/ALDE_00013109/#ALDF_00018955, and William Howard Taft, *The President and His Powers*, in *The Collected Works of William Howard Taft*, vol. 6, ed. W. Carey McWilliams and Frank X. Gerrity (1916; reprint Athens: University of Ohio Press, 2003), 49.
32. *USG*, 27:273–75; 25:43–44.
33. See Grant's Annual Messages, and *USG*, 27:88–89, 107–10.
34. Wilbur R. Miller, "The Revenue: Federal Law Enforcement in the Mountain South, 1870–1900," *Journal of Southern History* 55 (1989): 211.
35. *USG*, 19:17–22, 25–28, 37–39. See also Jonathan D. Sarna, *When Grant Expelled the Jews* (New York: Nextbook/Schocken, 2012).
36. "Executive Orders," American Presidency Project, https://www.presidency.ucsb.edu/statistics/data/executive-orders; Nevins, *Fish*, 2:833–34. Grant's census order is at *USG*, 21:208–9.

37. "Proclamations," American Presidency Project, https://www.presidency.ucsb.edu/documents/app-categories/written-presidential-orders/presidential/proclamations.
38. *USG*, 20:151; 21:336–37; 27:329–30, 334, 335.
39. *USG*, 19:189–91; see especially the letter at 191 applauding Grant for using his practical mind against the "learned decision of a self-puffed lawyer," Grant's attorney general, who disagreed with this interpretation of the law.
40. *USG*, 23:103–4.
41. Grant, *Memoirs*, 147; see also 325–26, 749–50; *USG*, 19:147–49. See also Albert D. Richardson, *A Personal History of Ulysses S. Grant* (Washington, DC: National Tribune, 1898), 542, and Bunting, *Grant*, 91. Cf. Phillip J. Cooper, *By Order of the President: The Use and Abuse of Executive Direct Action* (Lawrence: University Press of Kansas, 2002), 70–80.
42. Sidney Ratner, "Was the Supreme Court Packed by President Grant?" *Political Science Quarterly* 50 (1935): 343–58.
43. Thomas G. Alexander, "Federal Authority versus Polygamic Theocracy: James B. McKean and the Mormons, 1870–1875," *Dialogue: A Journal of Mormon Thought* 1 (1966): 86, 87.
44. Andrew Gyory, *Closing the Gate: Race, Politics, and the Chinese Exclusion Act* (Chapel Hill: University of North Carolina Press, 1998), 71, 186–87. See also *USG*, 27:3–9.
45. Bruce E. Stewart, "Attacking 'Red-Legged Grasshoppers': Moonshiners, Violence, and the Politics of Federal Liquor Taxation in Western North Carolina, 1865–1876," *Appalachian Journal* 32 (2004): 26–48, esp. 42.
46. David M. Emmons, "Theories of Increased Rainfall and the Timber Culture Act of 1873," *Forest History Newsletter* 15 (1971): 13. On implementation of the bill, see C. Barry McIntosh, "Use and Abuse of the Timber Culture Act," *Annals of the Association of American Geographers* 65 (1975): 347–62.
47. See Mark Wahlgren Summers, *The Era of Good Stealings* (New York: Oxford University Press, 1993), 99–103.
48. Leonard D. White, *The Republican Era, 1869–1901: A Study in Administrative History* (New York: Macmillan, 1958), 281–87, 224.
49. White, *Republican Era*, 281–87; Coolidge, *Life*, 398–404; *USG*, 25:59–60, 283 85 (Sixth Annual Message); Ari Hoogenboom, *The Presidency of Rutherford B. Hayes* (Lawrence: University Press of Kansas, 1988), 144–46.
50. On the effects of the Desert Land Act, see John T. Ganoe, "The Desert Land Act in Operation, 1877–1891," *Agricultural History* 11 (1937): 142–57, and John T. Ganoe, "The Desert Land Act since 1891," *Agricultural History* 11 (1937): 266–77. On the Arnell Act, see Sylvia G. L. Dannett, "Belva Ann Lockwood, Feminist Lawyer," *Courier* 8 (1971): 43–44, and Julia Hull Winner, "Belva A. Lockwood—That Extraordinary Woman," *New York History* 39 (1958): 333. Campaign finance scholar Kurt Hohenstein sees the 1876 Anti-Assessment Act as the foundation of efforts to regulate campaign finance at the national

level. Hohenstein, *Coining Corruption: The Making of the American Campaign Finance System* (DeKalb: Northern Illinois University Press, 2007), 21–25, 144–45.

51. *USG*, 21:31; William P. Vaughn, "West Point and the First Negro Cadet," *Military Affairs* 35 (1971): 101; Brain G. Shellum, "The 'Silencing' of Early Black Cadets at West Point," *Journal of Blacks in Higher Education* 51 (2006): 72. Cf. Eric Foner, *Reconstruction: America's Unfinished Revolution, 1863–1877* (New York: Perennial, 1988), 531, 545.
52. Smith's wealthy patron, David Clark of Hartford, Connecticut, accused Grant and Howard of trying to run Smith out of the academy. Yet Clark wrote in the same letter that Grant had told him directly that he would see Smith's rights protected. See *USG*, 21:31–32. See also Vaughn, "West Point." Cf. Ron Chernow, *Grant* (New York: Penguin, 2017), 768–70. Grant's son was implicated in events that aimed at harassing and intimidating Black cadets. *USG*, 21:28–34.
53. Shellum, "The 'Silencing,'" 72; Vaughn, "West Point," 102.
54. Shellum, "The 'Silencing,'" 72–73. See also Henry Ossian Flipper, *The Colored Cadet at West Point: Autobiography of Henry Ossian Flipper, U.S.A., First Graduate of Color from the U.S. Military Academy* (New York: Homer Lee, 1878; reprint via Amazon for Kindle, Etext prepared by Tony Adam), esp. 182–90.
55. See the discussion in Gillette, *Retreat from Reconstruction*, 73–75.
56. Paul Kahan, *The Presidency of Ulysses S. Grant: Preserving the Civil War's Legacy* (Yardley, PA: Westholme, 2018), 60–61; Chernow, *Grant*, 641.
57. "African American Postal Workers in the 19th Century," United States Postal Service, October 2017, https://about.usps.com/who/profile/history/pdf/african-american-workers-19thc.pdf.
58. "Ebenezer D. Bassett: America's First African American Chief of Mission," National Museum of American Diplomacy, https://diplomacy.state.gov/u-s-diplomacy-stories/ebenezer-d-bassett-champion-of-human-rights/; Walter L. Williams, "Nineteenth Century Pan-Africanist: John Henry Smyth, United States Minister to Liberia, 1878–1885," *Journal of Negro History* 63 (1978): 18–19; James A. Padgett, "Ministers to Liberia and Their Diplomacy," *Journal of Negro History* 22 (1937): 58–59.
59. Jill Norgren, *Belva Lockwood: The Woman Who Would Be President* (New York: New York University Press, 2007), 50–51. Lockwood ran for president in 1884 and 1888.
60. Michael L. Tate, *The Frontier Army in the Settlement of the West* (Norman: University of Oklahoma Press, 1999), 217–22. See also Walter N. Trenerry, "The Minnesota Legislator and the Grasshopper, 1873–77," *Minnesota History* 36 (1958): 54–61; Stanley D. Casto, "The Rocky Mountain Locust in Texas," *Southwestern Historical Quarterly* 111 (2007): 182–204; and Clyde A. Milner II, *With Good Intentions: Quaker Work among the Pawnees, Otos, and Omahas in the 1870s* (Lincoln: University of Nebraska Press, 1982), 166–68. Congressional efforts to provide disaster relief were common, with "more than ninety separate relief measures" being authorized between 1860 and 1930. Michele

Landis Dauber, *The Sympathetic State: Disaster Relief and the Origins of the American Welfare State* (Chicago: University of Chicago Press, 2013), 25; see also 56–57 and generally.
61. A. S. Packard Jr., "The Migrations of the Destructive Locust of the West," *American Naturalist* 11 (1877): 28.
62. Packard, "Migrations," 28. See also Casto, "Rocky Mountain Locust," 195, and H. T. Fernald, "Insects: The People and the State," *Scientific Monthly* 27 (1928): 196.
63. Casto, "Rocky Mountain Locust," 195. For more background, including efforts to begin to collect data in the 1830s and the Department of Agriculture's numerous entomology reports in the 1860s and 1870s, see Fernald, "Insects."
64. Fernald, "Insects," 204. See also William H. Dusenberry, "The Mexican Agricultural Society, 1879–1914," *The Americas* 12 (1956): 391–92.
65. Tate, *Frontier Army*, 217–22. On the Mississippi River, Texas, and Red Cloud Agency, see *USG*, 25:113–14; 27:52–53, 86–88.
66. See Coolidge, *Life*, 496–520; Scaturro, *President Grant*, 43; Nevins, *Fish*, 2:chap. 35; and Gillette, *Retreat from Reconstruction*, 325–34. Generally, see Roy Morris Jr., *Fraud of the Century: Rutherford B. Hayes, Samuel Tilden, and the Stolen Election of 1876* (New York: Simon and Schuster, 2003).
67. On expertise, see, for example, Joseph G. Dawson III, *Army Generals and Reconstruction: Louisiana, 1862–1877* (Baton Rouge: Louisiana State University Press, 1982); Gregory P. Downs, *After Appomattox: Military Occupation and the Ends of War* (Cambridge, MA: Harvard University Press, 2015), 214–15; and Lou Falkner Williams, *The Great South Carolina Ku Klux Klan Trials, 1871–1872* (Athens: University of Georgia Press, 2004). On Grant and his understanding of administration and management, see, for example, Grant, *Memoirs*, 36, 51, 59, 121–23, 131–33, 153, 154, 268, 285–86, 325–26, 423–24, 476–78, 597ff, 739, 642–45, and chap. 22 generally, and *USG*, 19:43, 117–18; 25:88–91, 361. On Grant's delegation and respect for discretionary authority, and his opposition to micromanagement, see, for example, Grant, *Memoirs*, chap. 22, pp. 69–70, 215, 304–5, 473–74, 535–36, 541–42, 583, and *USG*, 19:3, 58; 27:219–20. Of course, Grant also weighed in, often strongly, when he felt that was necessary and appropriate; see, for example, Downs, *After Appomattox*, 219–21.
68. See Bunting, *Grant*, 87.
69. Foner, *Reconstruction*, 444–45; Nevins, *Fish*, 1:chap. 6; Kenneth M. Stampp, *The Era of Reconstruction, 1865–1877* (New York: Vintage, 1965), 187.
70. Coolidge, *Life*, 379. For an analysis of Grant's appointees as reformers, see Summers, *Era of Good Stealings*, 185–89, 190–99, and chap. 13 generally.
71. Coolidge, *Life*, 277; Unger, *Greenback Era*, 164; Foner, *Reconstruction*, 445; Nevins, *Fish*, 1:139.
72. Foner, *Reconstruction*, 534.
73. Unger, *Greenback Era*, 171–72, 191–92.
74. Nevins, *Fish*, 1:139–40, 176. Grant encouraged U.S. acceptance of steamships built for the mails. *USG*, 25:162–63.
75. Nevins, *Fish*, 2:719–22, 824–25; White, *Republican Era*, 262.

76. C. Joseph Genetin-Pilawa, *Crooked Paths to Allotment: The Fight over Federal Indian Policy after the Civil War* (Chapel Hill: University of North Carolina Press, 2012), 67; Jules Witcover, *The American Vice Presidency: From Irrelevance to Power* (Washington, DC: Smithsonian Books, 2014), 174–81.
77. On Washburne, see David McCullough, *The Greater Journey: Americans in Paris* (New York: Simon and Schuster, 2011), esp. chap. 10, and Nevins, *Fish*, 1:404–6. On Alphonso Taft see, for example, *USG*, 27:75–76.
78. Robert G. Athearn, *William Tecumseh Sherman and the Settlement of the West* (1956; reprint Norman: University of Oklahoma Press, 1995); Tate, *Frontier Army*.
79. Foner, *Reconstruction*, 454, 457–59; Robert J. Kaczorowski, *The Politics of Judicial Interpretation: The Federal Courts, Department of Justice, and Civil Rights, 1866–1876* (New York: Fordham University Press, 2005), 64, chap. 4.
80. Nevins, *Fish*; Andrew Priest, "Thinking about Empire: The Administration of Ulysses S. Grant, Spanish Colonialism and the Ten Years' War in Cuba," *Journal of American Studies* 48 (2014): 547; Jay Sexton, "The United States, the Cuban Rebellion, and the Multilateral Initiative of 1875," *Diplomatic History* 30 (2006): 336–38, 345–46. On Fish's appointment, see, for example, Nevins, *Fish*, 1:40–41, 90, and chap. 5, and *USG*, 19:149.
81. See, for example, Nevins, *Fish*, 2:716, 823–24, 832, and Kaczorowski, *Politics of Judicial Interpretation*, 41, 57, 111ff, and chap. 4 on the Department of Justice.
82. Genetin-Pilawa, *Crooked Paths*, 30–72; William H. Armstrong, *Warrior in Two Camps: Ely S. Parker, Union General and Seneca Chief* (Syracuse, NY: Syracuse University Press, 1978).
83. Genetin-Pilawa, *Crooked Paths*, 59, 20, 62–90; David H. DeJong, *Paternalism to Partnership: The Administration of Indian Affairs, 1786–2021* (Lincoln: University of Nebraska Press, 2022), 139–45.
84. Donald R. McCoy, "The Special Indian Agency in Alaska, 1873–1874: Its Origins and Operation," *Pacific Historical Review* 25 (1956): 355–67, esp. 367n40.
85. A. Hunter Dupree, *Science in the Federal Government: A History of Policy and Activities to 1940* (Cambridge, MA: Belknap Press of Harvard University Press, 1957), 186; *USG*, 27:83–86, 338–42. See also Grant's signing of the Rivers and Harbors Act in 1876. *USG*, 27:268–71.
86. See *USG*, 25:361, 324, 332, and Robert J. Chandler, "An Uncertain Influence: The Role of the Federal Government in California, 1846–1880," *California History* 81 (2003): 255–56.
87. James Rodger Fleming, "Storms, Strikes, and Surveillance: The U.S. Army Signal Office, 1861–1891," *Historical Studies in the Physical and Biological Sciences* 30 (2000): 319–20; *USG*, 25:150–51.
88. Erik D. Craft, "Private Weather Organizations and the Founding of the United States Weather Bureau," *Journal of Economic History* 59 (1999): 1063, 1069; Dupree, *Science in the Federal Government*, 184–90. The Weather Bureau would be transferred from the Signal Service to the new Department of Agriculture in 1891. Fred A. Shannon, *The Farmer's Last Frontier: Agriculture, 1860–1897* (1945; reprint New York: Holt, Rinehart and Winston, 1963), 288.

89. See *USG*, 28:168, 204, and Fleming, "Storms, Strikes, and Surveillance," 324–27.
90. Dupree, *Science in the Federal Government*, 195–204. See also William H. Goetzmann, *Exploration and Empire: The Explorer and the Scientist in the Winning of the American West* (Austin: Texas State Historical Association, 2000), 481, 488, 533–36.
91. Genetin-Pilawa, *Crooked Paths*, 82–90, 94–111; Armstrong, *Warrior in Two Camps*, 152–65; *USG*, 25:346–47. The congressional investigation ultimately found problems but no evidence of fraud in Parker's case. On scandal frames in the era, see Summers, *Era of Good Stealings*, and Margaret Susan Thompson, *The "Spider-Web": Congress and Lobbying in the Era of Grant* (Ithaca, NY: Cornell University Press, 1985).
92. Kaczorowski, *Politics of Judicial Interpretation*, 69, 75–76, xv, 80, 81; Foner, *Reconstruction*, 458; William S. McFeely, *Grant: A Biography* (New York: Norton, 1981), esp. 372–74.
93. Genetin-Pilawa, *Crooked Paths*, 99; Coolidge, *Life*, 387–89, 490–91; Nevins, *Fish*, 2:465–69.
94. Coolidge, *Life*, 279–80, 293–311; John Bassett Moore, "Introduction," in Nevins, *Fish*, xv; Tom Bingham, "The *Alabama* Claims Arbitration," *International and Comparative Law Journal* 54 (2005): 1; Jay Sexton, "The Funded Loan and the 'Alabama' Claims," *Diplomatic History* 27 (2003): 476–77. See also Bunting, *Grant*, 105–6; Nevins, *Fish*, 2:511–51; and Richardson, *Personal History*, 543.
95. For general background and analysis, see Bingham, "*Alabama* Claims," and Sexton, "Funded Loan."
96. Sexton, "Funded Loan," 461; Harold T. Pinkett, "Efforts to Annex Santo Domingo to the United States, 1866–1871," *Journal of Negro History* 26 (1941): 37. See also Unger, "Business Community," 250, on the effects of both events.
97. Sexton, "Funded Loan," 474–75.
98. Coolidge, *Life*, 311. See also Bingham, "*Alabama* Claims," 24–25, and Sexton, "Funded Loan," 465–66, 476. Sexton emphasizes the significance of the *Alabama* claims as part of the United States' postwar financial goals, and he describes key roles played by financial players in the negotiations. At 461–62 he describes how Fish worked with Congress to pass a debt funding bill, setting a more promising stage for the complicated negotiations. For analysis of the great number of multipartite administrative treaties involving the United States, see Henry Reiff, "The Enforcement of Multipartite Administrative Treaties in the United States," *American Journal of International Law* 34 (1940): 661–79.
99. For example, the case of the *Virginius* is not mentioned in Ron Chernow's 1,074-page biography of Grant.
100. Ulysses S. Grant, Fifth Annual Message; Coolidge, *Life*, 523–25; *USG*, 25:3–7.
101. Sexton, "The United States, the Cuban Rebellion," 349; Priest, "Thinking about Empire," 551–52.
102. See Myres S. McDougal, William T. Burke, and Ivan A. Vlasic, "The Maintenance of Public Order at Sea and the Nationality of Ships," *American Journal of International Law* 54 (1960): 56–62, 114–16; Priest, "Thinking about

Empire," 551; and Sexton, "The United States, the Cuban Rebellion," 347. For a discussion that includes the position taken by Britain, which also had citizens aboard the *Virginius*, see Anna Van Zwanenberg, "Interference with Ships on the High Seas," *International and Comparative Law Quarterly* 10 (1961): 793–96.

103. See Henry A. Kmen, "Remember the *Virginius:* New Orleans and Cuba in 1873," *Louisiana History* 11 (1970): 313–31; Priest, "Thinking about Empire"; Sexton, "The United States, the Cuban Rebellion"; George H. Gibson, "Attitudes in North Carolina Regarding the Independence of Cuba, 1868–1898," *North Carolina Historical Review* 43 (1966): 43–65; Luis Martinez-Fernandez, "Political Change in the Spanish Caribbean during the United States Civil War and Its Aftermath, 1861–1878," *Caribbean Studies* 27 (1994): 37–64; and Gerald E. Poyo, "Cuban Revolutionaries and Monroe County Reconstruction Politics, 1868–1876," *Florida Historical Quarterly* 55 (1977): 407–22.

104. Gibson, "Attitudes in North Carolina," 46; Priest, "Thinking about Empire," 555–56.

105. Quoted in Priest, "Thinking about Empire," 551; see also 552–53.

106. Gibson, "Attitudes in North Carolina," 47.

107. Sexton, "The United States, the Cuban Rebellion," 347, 351ff.

108. Sexton, "The United States, the Cuban Rebellion," 335, 358–63; Scaturro, *President Grant*, 54–55; Priest, "Thinking about Empire," 554.

109. Sexton, "The United States, the Cuban Rebellion," 335, 364; see also 349, 354–55; *USG*, 20:45. See also Bunting, *Grant*, 102.

110. See Coolidge, *Life*, 312–34, and Bunting, *Grant*, 102–6.

111. *USG*, 20:156–57.

112. Coolidge, *Life*, 315–22; Nevins, *Fish*, 1:chaps. 12, 14, esp. 317–20.

113. Pinkett, "Efforts to Annex Santo Domingo," 36.

114. Coolidge, *Life*, 315–34; Pinkett, "Efforts to Annex Santo Domingo," 32.

115. Pinkett, "Efforts to Annex Santo Domingo," 32–34, 40–43.

116. Ulysses S. Grant, Eighth Annual Message, December 5, 1876, American Presidency Project, https://www.presidency.ucsb.edu/documents/eighth-annual-message-3.

117. Foner, *Reconstruction*, 494–97; Nevins, *Fish*, 2:chap. 19, esp. 464–65; Coolidge, *Life*, 328–29.

118. Ronald J. Jensen, "The Politics of Discrimination: America, Russia and the Jewish Question, 1869–1872," *American Jewish History* 75 (1986): 280–95; 282 (quotation).

119. On Puerto Rico, see Nevins, *Fish*, 2:619–31. On Cuba, see Nevins, *Fish*, 2:chap. 26. See also Grant's Annual Messages.

120. On the Cuban filibuster, see *USG*, 19:210–12. On Boss Tweed, see Coolidge, *Life*, 527–28. On Charles Lawrence, see Andrew Wender Cohen, "Smuggling, Globalization, and America's Outward State, 1870–1909," *Journal of American History* 97 (2010): 392.

121. *USG*, 27:147–55.
122. For example, treaties of commerce and/or extradition with El Salvador, Honduras, Peru, Guatemala, Nicaragua, and Belgium, noted by Grant at *USG*, 25:321, 360.
123. See Nevins, *Fish*, 1:414–48; 2:476–81, 483ff.
124. Gordon H. Chang, "Whose 'Barbarism'? Whose 'Treachery'? Race and Civilization in the Unknown United States-Korea War of 1871," *Journal of American History* 89 (2003): 1331–65.
125. Richard B. Morris, ed., *Encyclopedia of American History*, 6th ed. (New York: Harper and Row, 1982), 335, and Scaturro, *President Grant*, 55. On Grant and Pacific Islands, see *USG*, 27:96–103.

5. Presidential Decision Making and the Evolving State

1. Henry G. Waltmann, "Circumstantial Reformer: President Grant and the Indian Problem," *Arizona and the West* 13 (1971): 330–31; Jennifer Graber, "'If a War It May Be Called': The Peace Policy with American Indians," *Religion and American Culture* 24 (2014): 40. Waltmann tallies more than two hundred military actions in these years. Waltmann, "Circumstantial Reformer," 338 n37. See also Robert A. Trennert, "John H. Stout and the Grant Peace Policy among the Pimas," *Arizona and the West* 28 (1986): 45–68.
2. Eric Foner, *Reconstruction: America's Unfinished Revolution, 1863–1877* (New York: Perennial, 1988), 532–33. The Jurisdiction and Removal Act also passed with Grant's signature in 1875. Foner, *Reconstruction*, 555–57.
3. Robert J. Kaczorowski, *The Politics of Judicial Interpretation: The Federal Courts, Department of Justice, and Civil Rights, 1866–1876* (New York: Fordham University Press, 2005), chap. 1, 57.
4. William Gillette, *The Right to Vote: Politics and the Passage of the Fifteenth Amendment* (Baltimore: Johns Hopkins University Press, 1969), 43, 49, 55, 146, 157–58; Max J. Skidmore, *Maligned Presidents: The Late 19th Century* (New York: Palgrave Macmillan, 2014), 30–32.
5. Ulysses S. Grant, *The Papers of Ulysses S. Grant*, ed. John Y. Simon (Carbondale, IL: University of Southern Illinois Press, 2005), 20:130–31 (hereafter *USG*); Louis A. Coolidge, *The Life of Ulysses S. Grant* (Boston: Houghton Mifflin, 1922), 369. On the partisan reaction to Grant's proclamation, see Gillette, *Right to Vote*, 144, 161, 161n1.
6. Coolidge, *Life*, 459. See also Gillette, *Right to Vote*, 162–65, and the careful analysis in Skidmore, *Maligned Presidents*, 25–49.
7. Ulysses S. Grant, *Personal Memoirs* (New York: Library of America, 1990), 752–53.
8. *USG*, 27:205–6.
9. William L. Barney, *Battleground for the Union: The Era of the Civil War and Reconstruction, 1848–1877* (Englewood Cliffs, NJ: Prentice-Hall, 1990), 274. See also Kaczorowski, *Politics of Judicial Interpretation*, 66; *USG*, 27:206; and Lou

Falkner Williams, *The Great South Carolina Ku Klux Klan Trials, 1871–1872* (Athens: University of Georgia Press, 2004), 45–46, 124–30.

10. See, for example, on Georgia, *USG*, 19:83–84, 87, 114–17; 27:210–11, 213, 214–15. On Alabama, *USG*, 27:208. On Arkansas, *USG*, 19:111–14; 25:61–65, 83–87, 93–103, 106–11. On Louisiana, *USG*, 19:113–14, 249–50; 25:213–28, 234–43; 27:237–39, 296–301. On Virginia, *USG*, 19:158–59, 163–64, 164–72, 247–49; 27:209, 216. On Mississippi, *USG*, 19:164, 171–72, 204–8, 221–23; 25:156–59; 27:236–37, 239–40, 320–24. On Texas, *USG*, 19:214–19; 25:9–19, 326–27; 27:208–9. On Tennessee, *USG*, 25:228–32; 27:211. On Florida, *USG*, 27:212. On Kansas, *USG*, 27:212. On Kentucky, *USG*, 19:263–66; 27:215. On South Carolina, *USG*, 25:51–54; 27:200–208, 230–36, 329–36. On Missouri, *USG*, 27:216. See, generally, *USG*, 25:187–201, 339–41; 27:199–216, 296–301, 320–24.

11. See Allan Nevins, *Hamilton Fish: The Inner History of the Grant Administration* (1936; reprint New York: Frederick Ungar, 1957), 2:591; see also 2:601–2; *USG*, 19:67; 25:51–54, 63, 87, 98, 99, 106–11, 187–201, 228–32; 27:199–200, 231, 237.

12. *USG*, 27:329–36. See also Gregory P. Downs, *After Appomattox: Military Occupation and the Ends of War* (Cambridge, MA: Harvard University Press, 2015), chap. 9, and Graham G. Dodds, *Take Up Your Pen: Unilateral Presidential Directives in American Politics* (Philadelphia: University of Pennsylvania Press, 2013), 111–13, 118–19.

13. See, for example, *USG*, 25:9–19.

14. Downs, *After Appomattox*. On declining troop levels and other constraints on their actions, see, for example, Allen W. Trelease, *White Terror: The Ku Klux Klan Conspiracy and Southern Reconstruction* (New York: Harper, 1971), xxxiv–xxxv, and William Gillette, *Retreat from Reconstruction, 1869–1879* (Baton Rouge: Louisiana State University Press, 1979), 35.

15. In general, see Foner, *Reconstruction*, 454–59, and Kaczorowski, *Politics of Judicial Interpretation*, 13–20.

16. See Coolidge, *Life*, 372–73.

17. Williams, *Great South Carolina Ku Klux Klan Trials*, 42–43; Coolidge, *Life*, 374–75; Foner, *Reconstruction*, 457–59; Joan Waugh, *U.S. Grant: American Hero, American Myth* (Chapel Hill: University of North Carolina Press, 2009), 141–42.

18. Ron Chernow, *Grant* (New York: Penguin, 2017), 704–5 (quotation); for a concise review of Grant's efforts to lead Congress and his own cabinet to act decisively against the Klan, see 700–11. On Grant's commitment to the Civil War amendments, see Chernow, *Grant*, 744–45.

19. Brooks D. Simpson, "Ulysses S. Grant and the Failure of Reconciliation," *Illinois Historical Journal* 81 (1988): 279–80.

20. James M. McPherson, "Abolitionists and the Civil Rights Act of 1875," *Journal of American History* 52 (1965): 504.

21. Jed Handelsman Shugerman, "The Creation of the Department of Justice: Professionalization without Civil Rights or Civil Service," *Stanford Law Review* 66 (2014): 121–72.

22. On details of the Department of Justice's activities, see, for example, Stephen Cresswell, "Enforcing the Enforcement Acts: The Department of Justice in Northern Mississippi, 1870–1890," *Journal of Southern History* 53 (1987): 421–40. On the formation of the Department of Justice, see Shugerman, "Creation of the Department of Justice," esp. 125–26, and Norman W. Spaulding, "Professional Independence in the Office of the Attorney General," *Stanford Law Review* 60 (2008): 1931–79, esp. 1957–68. On Hoar's removal as attorney general, see Shugerman, "Creation of the Department of Justice," 157–59, 162–63, and Sidney Ratner, "Was the Supreme Court Packed by President Grant?" *Political Science Quarterly* 50 (1935): 349.
23. Foner, *Reconstruction*, 459.
24. Skidmore, *Maligned Presidents*, 42.
25. Kaczorowski, *Politics of Judicial Interpretation*, xv, xxiv–xxv, 70ff, 83ff, 91–92; Cresswell, "Enforcing the Enforcement Act."
26. Kaczorowski, *Politics of Judicial Interpretation*, chaps. 4–5, 81–83; Williams, *Great South Carolina Ku Klux Klan Trials*, 124.
27. Kaczorowski, *Politics of Judicial Interpretation*, 22–23, 46ff, 51–61, 69–70, 75.
28. Foner, *Reconstruction*, 258; Kaczorowski, *Politics of Judicial Interpretation*, 7–12, chap. 1.
29. Kaczorowski, *Politics of Judicial Interpretation*, 55–56.
30. Kaczorowski, *Politics of Judicial Interpretation*, 57–58; Skidmore, *Maligned Presidents*, 35–38.
31. On the critical nature of the Supreme Court's decisions in this era, see, for example, Foner, *Reconstruction*, 529–34; Kaczorowski, *Politics of Judicial Interpretation*, esp. xxv, xvi–xvii, chaps. 6–9; and Lawrence Goldstone, *Inherently Unequal: The Betrayal of Equal Rights by the Supreme Court, 1865–1903* (New York: Walker, 2011).
32. Kaczorowski, *Politics of Judicial Interpretation*, 155–60. By November 1875, only 921 officers and men remained in Louisiana, 575 in South Carolina, 480 in Virginia, 311 in Georgia, 293 in Florida, 247 in North Carolina, 210 in Tennessee, 178 in Mississippi, and 89 in Arkansas. Joseph G. Dawson III, *Army Generals and Reconstruction: Louisiana, 1862–1877* (Baton Rouge: Louisiana State University Press, 1982), 222. See also Downs, *After Appomattox*, 9, 89–111, 141–42, 188–90, 232–33, and the useful appendices at 257–65.
33. Robert M. Goldman, *Reconstruction and Black Suffrage: Losing the Vote in Reese and Cruikshank* (Lawrence: University Press of Kansas, 2001), 68–70.
34. Kaczorowski, *Politics of Judicial Interpretation*, 150, chap. 8 generally; Goldman, *Reconstruction and Black Suffrage*, 42–59.
35. For background and analysis of *Reese* and *Cruikshank*, see Goldman, *Reconstruction and Black Suffrage*, and Ronald B. Jager, "Charles Sumner, the Constitution, and the Civil Rights Act of 1875," *New England Quarterly* 42 (1969): 350–72.
36. *USG*, 27:204.

37. *USG*, 27:299; see also 27:298–99, 320, 324.
38. Kaczorowski, *Politics of Judicial Interpretation*, 178. See also Williams, *Great South Carolina Ku Klux Klan Trials*, chap. 7, esp. 141.
39. See Alan Wolfe, *Political Evil: What It Is and How to Combat It* (New York: Knopf, 2011), 171–73.
40. Coolidge, *Life*, 280. See also Kenneth M. Stampp, *The Era of Reconstruction, 1865–1877* (New York: Vintage, 1965), especially his evaluation at 207–15.
41. Douglas R. Egerton, *The Wars of Reconstruction: The Brief, Violent History of America's Most Progressive Era* (New York: Bloomsbury Press, 2014). See also Foner, *Reconstruction*, xxiii, 8–9, 291, 410–11.
42. See Foner, *Reconstruction*, chaps. 3, 7, 8.
43. Foner, *Reconstruction*, 351–64, 291, 317–33, 485–88, 537–53, 602–3 (quotation).
44. See, for example, Francis Paul Prucha, *The Great Father: The United States Government and the American Indians* (Lincoln: University of Nebraska Press, 1984), 586–93.
45. See, for example, H. Craig Miner, *The Corporation and the Indian: Tribal Sovereignty and Industrial Civilization in Indian Territory, 1865–1907* (1976; reprint Norman: University of Oklahoma Press, 1989).
46. See, for example, Gary Clayton Anderson, *Massacre in Minnesota: The Dakota War of 1862, the Most Violent Ethnic Conflict in American History* (Norman: University of Oklahoma Press, 2019); Corinne L. Monjeau-Marz, *The Dakota Indian Internment at Fort Snelling, 1862–1864* (St. Paul: Prairie Smoke Press, 2006); Stan Hoig, *Sand Creek Massacre* (Norman: University of Oklahoma Press, 1974); Ari Kelman, *A Misplaced Massacre: Struggling over the Memory of Sand Creek* (Cambridge, MA: Harvard University Press, 2015); and Prucha, *Great Father*, 447–61. See also Benjamin Madley, *An American Genocide: The United States and the California Indian Catastrophe* (New Haven: Yale University Press, 2016), and Karl Jacoby, *Shadows at Dawn: A Borderlands Massacre and the Violence of History* (New York: Penguin, 2008).
47. Douglas Firth Anderson, "'More Conscience Than Force': U.S. Indian Inspector William Vandever, Grant's Peace Policy, and Protestant Whiteness," *Journal of the Gilded Age and Progressive Era* 9 (2010): 173. See also Waltmann, "Circumstantial Reformer," 327–28, 331, and Christine Bolt, *American Indian Policy and American Reform: Case Studies of the Campaign to Assimilate the American Indians* (London: Allen and Unwin, 1987), 75–81.
48. C. Joseph Genetin-Pilawa, "Ely Parker and the Contentious Peace Policy," *Western Historical Quarterly* 41 (2010): 202. See also William H. Armstrong, *Warrior in Two Camps: Ely S. Parker, Union General and Seneca Chief* (Syracuse: Syracuse University Press, 1978), 140–41.
49. *USG*, 19:43; Prucha, *Great Father*, 513–14.
50. Quoted in *USG*, 19:193. See also *USG*, 19:191–98. On Parker's controversy in particular, see *USG*, 19:194–96; 25:346.
51. Robert H. Keller Jr., *American Protestantism and United States Indian Policy, 1869–82* (Lincoln: University of Nebraska Press, 1983), 21.

52. Waltmann, "Circumstantial Reformer," 334–35; R. Pierce Beaver, "The Churches and President Grant's Peace Policy," *Journal of Church and State* 4 (1962): 177; Keller, *American Protestantism*, 20–21; Genetin-Pilawa, "Ely Parker," 206; Anderson, "'More Conscience Than Force,'" 176–78.
53. Waltmann, "Circumstantial Reformer," 335.
54. Grant chose two of nine himself and relied on Interior Secretary Jacob Cox and friend and influential activist George Stuart to select the others. Waltmann, "Circumstantial Reformer," 335–36; Genetin-Pilawa, "Ely Parker," 207. Almost all came from the dry goods, mineral extraction, and transportation industries. Genetin-Pilawa, "Ely Parker," 208. See also *USG*, 19:196–97.
55. Beaver, "Churches," 176–77.
56. *USG*, 19:191–93.
57. *USG*, 19:193–98.
58. Armstrong, *Warrior in Two Camps*, 144.
59. Law quoted by Genetin-Pilawa, "Ely Parker," 207.
60. See *USG*, 19:194; Genetin-Pilawa, "Ely Parker"; and Armstrong, *Warrior in Two Camps*, 143–50 and chap. 13 generally.
61. Genetin-Pilawa, "Ely Parker," 207, 210–11.
62. Genetin-Pilawa, "Ely Parker"; Armstrong, *Warrior in Two Camps*, 139.
63. C. Joseph Genetin-Pilawa, *Crooked Paths to Allotment: The Fight over Federal Indian Policy after the Civil War* (Chapel Hill: University of North Carolina Press, 2012), esp. chaps. 3–5; Armstrong, *Warrior in Two Camps*, 152–65.
64. Anderson, "'More Conscience Than Force,'" 179ff.
65. Genetin-Pilawa, *Crooked Paths*.
66. For review of the Peace Policy, see Cathleen D. Cahill, *Federal Fathers and Mothers: A Social History of the United States Indian Service, 1869–1933* (Chapel Hill: University of North Carolina Press, 2011), 18–20; Jacoby, *Shadows at Dawn*, 124–28; Robert M. Utley, *Frontier Regulars: The United States Army and the Indian, 1866–1891* (Lincoln: University of Nebraska Press, 1973), 188–218; Prucha, *Great Father*, 501–33; and Keller, *American Protestantism*.
67. Waltmann, "Circumstantial Reformer," 326; Armstrong, *Warrior in Two Camps*, 150. On the paradoxes of the Peace Policy and Quaker religious views, see Graber, "'If a War.'" On the Peace Policy and Indian religious freedom, see Beaver, "Churches," 183–85. On the Peace Policy and religious bigotry and discrimination among Christians, see Robert L. Whitner, "Grant's Indian Peace Policy on the Yakima Reservation, 1870–82," *Pacific Northwest Quarterly* 50 (1959): 135–42.
68. Waltmann, "Circumstantial Reformer," 334. For breakdown by denominations, see Beaver, "Churches," 179–80.
69. Genetin-Pilawa, *Crooked Paths*, 78–80; *USG*, 25:346.
70. Prucha, *Great Father*, 534–35; Graber, "'If a War,'" 40; Robert E. Ficken, "After the Treaties: Administering Pacific Northwest Indian Reservations," *Oregon Historical Quarterly* 106 (2005): 446–7; John W. Ragsdale Jr., "The Chiricahua Apaches and the Assimilation Movement, 1865–1886: A Historical

Examination," *American Indian Law Review* 30 (2005–6): 309, 320–63; Frank Pommersheim, "The Black Hills Case: On the Cusp of History," *Wicazo Sa Review* 4 (1988): 19; *USG*, 25:345–47; Ulysses S. Grant, Fifth Annual Message, December 1, 1873, American Presidency Project, https://www.presidency.ucsb.edu/documents/fifth-annual-message-3. See also Armstrong, *Warrior in Two Camps*, 142, on Parker's willingness to use force.

71. Ulysses S. Grant, First Inaugural Address, March 4, 1869, in *Fellow Citizens: The Penguin Book of U.S. Presidential Inaugural Addresses*, ed. Robert V. Remini and Terry Golway (New York: Penguin, 2008), 186.
72. Ulysses S. Grant, Second Inaugural Address, March 4, 1873, in Remini and Golway, eds., *Fellow Citizens*, 191–92.
73. Robert Wooster, *The Military and United States Indian Policy, 1865–1903* (Lincoln: University of Nebraska Press, 1988), 132.
74. On transfer generally, see Prucha, *Great Father*, 473–78, 552ff.
75. *USG*, 19:80–81, 99. Grant also initially opposed reductions to the military while the Indian wars continued. *USG*, 19:81.
76. Genetin-Pilawa, "Ely Parker," 205; Waltmann, "Circumstantial Reformer."
77. See, for example, Robert M. Utley, *The Indian Frontier of the American West, 1846–1890* (Albuquerque: University of New Mexico Press, 1984), 124–201, and Robert G. Athearn, *William Tecumseh Sherman and the Settlement of the West* (1956; reprint Norman: University of Oklahoma Press, 1995), 248.
78. Prucha, *Great Father*, 513ff, 552ff. On transfer, see, for example, *USG*, 25:336, 343, 345, 346–47, 356; 27:176, 177, 179, 180–83.
79. David D. Smits, "The Frontier Army and the Destruction of the Buffalo: 1865–1883," *Western Historical Quarterly* 25 (1994): 312–38, esp. 324–26, 330–31.
80. *USG*, 26:84–85. See also G. B. Morey, "Newton Horace Winchell, the George Armstrong Custer Expedition of 1874, and the 'Discovery' of Gold in the Black Hills, Dakota Territory, U.S.A.," *Earth Sciences History* 18 (1999): 86.
81. *USG*, 26:163.
82. Catharine R. Franklin, "Black Hills and Bloodshed: The U.S. Army and the Invasion of Lakota Land, 1868–1876," *Montana* 63 (2013): 26–41, 90–93; Grant K. Anderson, "The Black Hills Exclusion Policy: Judicial Challenges," *Nebraska History* 58 (1977): 1–24; *USG*, 26:162–63.
83. See, for example, Jeffrey L. Patrick, "To the Black Hills Gold Fields: The Letters of Samuel M. Zent, Hoosier Prospector, 1875–1876," *Indiana Magazine of History* 91 (1995): 262–87, and Anderson, "Black Hills Exclusion Policy." See also, for example, *USG*, 25:342, 26:159–65.
84. Franklin, "Black Hills and Bloodshed," 39; Anderson, "Black Hills Exclusion Policy"; *USG*, 26:84–89, 145–47, 159–65, 208–15.
85. Anderson, "Black Hills Exclusion Policy," 21. It is interesting to note the parallel effect that court rulings had on Reconstruction policy in the South.
86. *USG*, 26:163.
87. Franklin, "Black Hills and Bloodshed," 39; *USG*, 26:163. See also J. S. Radabaugh, "Custer Explores the Black Hills 1874," *Military Affairs* 26 (1962–63): 162–70;

Morey, "Newton Horace Winchell"; Eugene McAndrews, "Custer's Engineer—William Ludlow," *Military Engineer* 61 (1969): 200–202; and Hyman Palais, "Some Aspects of the Black Hills Gold Rush Compared with the California Gold Rush," *Pacific Historical Review* 15 (1946): 59–67. For the significance of this era's federal actions over the next century and a half, see Pommersheim, "Black Hills Case"; Edward Lazarus, *Black Hills White Justice: The Sioux Nation versus the United States, 1775 to the Present* (New York: HarperCollins, 1991); Alan L. Neville and Alyssa Kaye Anderson, "The Diminishment of the Great Sioux Reservation: Treaties, Tricks, and Time," *Great Plains Quarterly* 33 (2013): 237–51; and Patrick, "To the Black Hills."

88. Ulysses S. Grant, Eighth Annual Message, December 5, 1876, American Presidency Project, https://www.presidency.ucsb.edu/documents/eighth-annual-message-3; *USG*, 27:127–28, 169–83. For review and analysis, see Utley, *Frontier Regulars*, 243–48 and chap. 14 generally, and James C. Olson, *Red Cloud and the Sioux Problem* (Lincoln: University of Nebraska Press, 1965).

89. See Franklin, "Black Hills and Bloodshed," 27–28. Cf. Patrick, "To the Black Hills," 277.

90. Keith A. Murray, *The Modocs and Their War* (Norman: University of Oklahoma Press, 1959), chaps. 12, 13.

91. Larry C. Skogen, *Indian Depredation Claims, 1796–1920* (Norman: University of Oklahoma Press, 1996), 89; see also 87–89. For more on indemnity claims, the role of the Indian Office, and interactions among the executive, Congress, and the states during the Grant administration, see 89–102 and chap. 6.

92. "Message from the President of the United States, Communicating, in Compliance with a Resolution of the Senate of April 23, 1872," S. Exec. Doc. No. 70, 42nd Cong., 2nd sess. (1872), 1. See also Kelly K. Agnew, "The Goingsnake Tragedy: Conflict and Compromise, Cherokee Style," *OAH Magazine of History* 2 (1987): 33–38, and Jeffrey Burton, *Indian Territory and the United States, 1866–1906: Courts, Government, and the Movement for Oklahoma Statehood* (Norman: University of Oklahoma Press, 1995), 33–45.

93. John B. Jones to H. R. Clum, acting commissioner of Indian affairs, October 29, 1873, Foreman Transcripts, Letters and Documents: Cherokee, 1826–1884, 153–54, Indian Archives Division, Oklahoma Historical Society, Oklahoma City, quoted in Daniel F. Littlefield Jr. and Lonnie E. Underhill, "The Trial of Ezekiel Proctor and the Problem of Judicial Jurisdiction," *Chronicles of Oklahoma* 48 (1970), https://www.houseofproctor.org/genealogy/showmedia.php?mediaID=15527.

94. Some sources report that everyone involved was granted amnesty by Grant in 1873. See Agnew, "Goingsnake Tragedy," and Will Chavez, "'Tragedy at Goingsnake' Occurred 149 Years Ago," *Cherokee Phoenix*, April 15, 2021, https://www.cherokeephoenix.org/culture/tragedy-at-goingsnake-occurred-149-years-ago/article_066217de-9dee-11eb-9f44-ebca978e17e7.html.

95. See, for example, an excerpt of the congressional debate at Vine Deloria Jr. and Raymond J. DeMallie, *Documents of American Indian Diplomacy: Treaties,*

Agreements, and Conventions, 1775-1979 (Norman: University of Oklahoma Press, 1999), 1:246.
96. Waltmann, "Circumstantial Reformer," 336, 330; Prucha, *Great Father,* 527-33; Jill St. Germain, *Indian Treaty-Making Policy in the United States and Canada, 1867-1877* (Toronto: University of Toronto Press, 2001).
97. Francis Paul Prucha, *American Indian Treaties: The History of a Political Anomaly* (Berkeley: University of California Press, 1997), 339-43.
98. Generally, see Prucha, *American Indian Treaties,* 311-45.
99. Prucha, *American Indian Treaties,* 313-26.
100. See Deloria and DeMallie, *Documents,* 1:233-52; Prucha, *American Indian Treaties,* 313-26; and Arthur Spirling, "U.S. Treaty Making with American Indians: Institutional Change and Relative Power, 1784-1911," *American Journal of Political Science* 56 (2012): 84-97.
101. Prucha, *American Indian Treaties,* 326-29.
102. Waltmann, "Circumstantial Reformer," 337, 337nn35, 36; Beaver, "Churches," 178ff.
103. Prucha, *American Indian Treaties,* 326.
104. Prucha, *American Indian Treaties,* 331 (quotation), 329-33.
105. See, for example, *USG,* 21:201-2. Treaties regularly specified presidential authority to allot lands. Ficken, "After the Treaties," 454-56.
106. Ragsdale, "Chiricahua Apaches," 312. Grant also abolished the reservation in 1876. Ragsdale, "Chiricahua Apaches," 315.
107. Michael P. Malone and Richard B. Roeder, "1876 on the Reservations: The Indian 'Question,'" *Montana: The Magazine of Western History* 25 (1975): 55. See also Prucha, *American Indian Treaties,* 314-15.
108. *USG,* 26:123. On Indian-related orders and executive order reservations, see also Malone and Roeder, "1876 on the Reservations," 55; Ficken, "After the Treaties," 442, 451, 457n1; Ragsdale, "Chiricahua Apaches," 308-9, 312; Jeffrey P. Shepherd, "At the Crossroads of Hualapai History, Memory, and American Colonization: Contesting Space and Place," *American Indian Quarterly* 32 (2008): 23-24; David M. Brugge, *The Navajo and Hopi Land Dispute: An American Tragedy* (Albuquerque: University of New Mexico Press, 1999); Tanis C. Thorne, "On the Fault Line: Political Violence at Campo Fiesta and National Reform in Indian Policy," *Journal of California and Great Basin Anthropology* 21 (1999): 183-86; Christina Gish Hill, "'General Miles Put Us Here': Northern Cheyenne Military Alliance and Sovereign Territorial Rights," *American Indian Quarterly* 37 (2013): 356-63; Martha C. Knack, "A Short Resource History of Pyramid Lake, Nevada," *Ethnohistory* 24 (1977): 54; and Prucha, *American Indian Treaties,* 329-33.
109. See *Executive Orders Relating to Indian Reservations from May 14, 1855 to July 1, 1912* (Washington, DC: U.S. Government Printing Office, 1932), 43-44; Robert H. Keller and Michael F. Trek, *American Indians and National Parks* (Tucson: University of Arizona Press, 1998), 109, 121; and Cahill, *Federal Fathers and Mothers,* 174, chap. 7.

NOTES TO PAGES 152–153   289

110. On reserving or protecting lands, see *USG*, 25:353, 357, 362, 363; 27:52–53, 86–88, 89. For context on executive orders relating to Indian lands and withdrawals of public lands, see Phillip J. Cooper, *By Order of the President: The Use and Abuse of Executive Direct Action* (Lawrence: University Press of Kansas, 2002), 37. On removing squatters, see *USG*, 25:25, 26; Clyde A. Milner II, *With Good Intentions: Quaker Work among the Pawnees, Otos, and Omahas in the 1870s* (Lincoln: University of Nebraska Press, 1982), 141; and Knack, "Short Resource History," 52–53. On Pawnee timber, see Milner, *With Good Intentions*, 72.
111. See, for example, Milner, *With Good Intentions*, 120.
112. Prucha, *American Indian Treaties*, 331–32.
113. Utley, *Frontier Regulars*, 297; Alvin M. Josephy Jr., *The Nez Perce Indians and the Opening of the Northwest* (Boston: Houghton Mifflin, 1965), 456–68; Ari Hoogenboom, *The Presidency of Rutherford B. Hayes* (Lawrence: University Press of Kansas, 1988), 154–55.
114. On Mission Indians, see *Executive Orders Relating to Indian Reservations from May 14, 1855 to July 1, 1912*, 43–44. For similar examples, see 6, 7, 23, 24, 39, 45, 46, 58, 59, 60, 62, 72, 76–77, 86, 88, 89, 90, 91, 92, 95, 96, 97, 98, 114, 115, 117, 118, 121–22, 133, 135, 148, 149, 157, 159, 160, 162, 163, 195, 196, 197, 199, 205, 206, 206–7, 208.
115. Prucha, *American Indian Treaties*, 332; Ragsdale, "Chiricahua Apaches," 316–20; Knack, "Short Resource History."
116. David E. Wilkins, *American Indian Politics and the American Political System* (Lanham, MD: Rowman and Littlefield, 2007), 87. See also "Tribal Property Interests in Executive-Order Reservations: A Compensable Indian Right," *Yale Law Journal* 69 (1960): 627–42, and Prucha, *American Indian Treaties*, 333. For context in the field, see Knack, "Short Resource History," and Ragsdale, "Chiricahua Apaches," 317n218.
117. "Tribal Property Interests," 628. Congress ended the practice in Arizona and New Mexico in 1918, and generally in 1919. Prucha, *American Indian Treaties*, 332–33.
118. On the Peace Policy and its era generally, see Leonard D. White, *The Republican Era, 1869–1901: A Study in Administrative History* (New York: Macmillan, 1958). Cf., for example, Alysa Landry, "Ulysses S. Grant: Mass Genocide through 'Permanent Peace' Policy," *Indian Country Today*, May 3, 2016, https://ictnews.org/archive/ulysses-s-grant-mass-genocide-through-permanent-peace-policy. For a clear explanation of some of the historiographical debates surrounding Grant and Indian affairs, see Waltmann, "Circumstantial Reformer."
119. For details of unique local and regional circumstances, politics, and issues, and how state action under the Peace Policy affected local and regional interests, Natives, traders, educators, men, women, white settlers, tradesmen, dry goods industries, transportation, and so on, see David S. Trask, "Episcopal Missionaries on the Santee and Yankton Reservations: Cross-Cultural Collaboration and President Grant's Peace Policy," *Great Plains Quarterly* 33 (2013): 87–101; Trennert, "John H. Stout"; Whitner, "Grant's Indian Peace Policy"; Henry E.

Stamm IV, "The Peace Policy at Wind River: The James Irwin Years, 1871–1877," *Montana* 41 (1991): esp. 65–66, 68–69; Anderson, "'More Conscience Than Force,'" esp. 180–84; Graber, "'If a War,'" esp. 45–54; J. C. Imoda and Francis J. Weber, "Grant's Peace Policy: A Catholic Dissenter," *Montana* 19 (1969): 55–63; Ficken, "After the Treaties"; and Knack, "Short Resource History." On complexities in Indian affairs policy, see, for example, *USG*, 25:23–29, 81–83, 113–14, 344–47, 357–58; 27:125–30, 249–59.

120. See, for example, Trennert, "John H. Stout," 49–51, 53–54, and Graber, "'If a War,'" 44. On popular awareness of the policy and opposition to it, with Grant's response in sending O. O. Howard to Arizona Territory to work it out, see Trennert, "John H. Stout," 55–58. Grant received many letters and communiqués expressing support for the Peace Policy and offering stories and evidence that it was working; see, for example, *USG*, 25:375–79.

121. Grant, Fifth Annual Message.

6. President Taft and the 125-Year-Old American State

1. See, for example, Rene N. Ballard, "The Administrative Theory of William Howard Taft," *Western Political Quarterly* 7 (1954): esp. 66–69; Harlan Hahn, "President Taft and the Discipline of Patronage," *Journal of Politics* 28 (1966): 368–90; Truman R. Clark, "President Taft and the Puerto Rican Appropriation Crisis of 1909," *The Americas* 26 (1969): 152–70; L. Peter Schultz, "William Howard Taft: A Constitutionalist's View of the Presidency," *Presidential Studies Quarterly* 9 (1979): 402–14; Donald F. Anderson, "The Legacy of William Howard Taft," *Presidential Studies Quarterly* 12 (1982): 30–33; David H. Burton, "The Learned Presidency: Roosevelt, Taft, Wilson," *Presidential Studies Quarterly* 15 (1985): 492; and Michael J. Korzi, "Our Chief Magistrate and His Powers: A Reconsideration of William Howard Taft's 'Whig' Theory of Presidential Leadership," *Presidential Studies Quarterly* 33 (2003): 305–24.

2. William Howard Taft, *The President and His Powers*, in *The Collected Works of William Howard Taft*, vol. 6, ed. W. Carey McWilliams and Frank X. Gerrity (1916; reprint Athens: University of Ohio Press, 2003), 104. For use of this quotation, see, for example, Andrew Rudalevige, *The New Imperial Presidency: Renewing Presidential Power after Watergate* (Ann Arbor: University of Michigan Press, 2006), 28; Sidney M. Milkis and Michael Nelson, *The American Presidency: Origins and Development, 1776–2018*, 8th ed. (Washington, DC: CQ Press, 2019), 282; Michael A. Genovese, *The Power of the American Presidency, 1789–2000* (New York: Oxford University Press, 2000), 116–17; Mark J. Rozell, *Executive Privilege: Presidential Power, Secrecy, and Accountability*, 2nd rev. ed. (Lawrence: University Press of Kansas, 2002), 7–8; and Michael Nelson, ed., *The Evolving Presidency: Landmark Documents*, 6th ed. (Thousand Oaks, CA: Sage, 2019), 127–32.

3. Milkis and Nelson, *American Presidency*, 244; Genovese, *Power of the American Presidency*, 115.

4. David K. Nichols, *The Myth of the Modern Presidency* (University Park: Pennsylvania State University Press, 1994); Louis Fisher, "Teaching the Presidency: Idealizing a Constitutional Office," *PS: Political Science and Politics* 45 (2012): 17–31. Cf. Samuel J. Kornhauser, "President Taft and the Extra-Constitutional Function of the Presidency," *North American Review* 192 (1910): 577–94.
5. Taft, *President and His Powers*, 105–6, 108, 109. For further discussion, see Louis Fisher, "Teaching the Presidency," 21–22, and Edmund Morris, *Theodore Rex* (New York: Random House, 2001), 131–37, 150–69.
6. Taft, *President and His Powers*, 116–17.
7. William Howard Taft, *Ethics in Service* (1914; reprint Cabin John, MD: Wildside Press, 2006), 36. See also Taft, *President and His Powers*, 63–79.
8. Ballard, "The Administrative Theory of William Howard Taft," 67–68.
9. Taft, *President and His Powers*, 38; Taft, *Ethics in Service*, 36.
10. Taft, *President and His Powers*, 63–79, 16, 49; *Myers v. United States* (1926) (272 U.S. 52).
11. Ballard, "The Administrative Theory of William Howard Taft," 69; see also 67.
12. Taft, *President and His Powers*, 21; see also 11–29, 47.
13. Nathaniel L. Nathanson, "The Administrative Court Proposal," *Virginia Law Review* 57 (1971): 1912. See also James A. Huston, *The Sinews of War: Army Logistics 1775–1953* (Washington, DC: Center of Military History, 1997), 294–95.
14. Taft, *President and His Powers*, 80–93, 74–76. On Taft and commander-in-chief authority, see Schultz, "William Howard Taft," 410–11.
15. Taft, *President and His Powers*, 69–70, 73. See also Schultz, "William Howard Taft," 406–7 (Cuba), 407–8 (Panama).
16. Ballard, "The Administrative Theory of William Howard Taft," 68.
17. On overlooking Taft, see, for example, John Tirman, *The Deaths of Others: The Fate of Civilians in America's Wars* (New York: Oxford University Press, 2011), 47, and Stephen G. Walker and Mark Schafer, "Theodore Roosevelt and Woodrow Wilson as Cultural Icons of U.S. Foreign Policy," *Political Psychology* 28 (2007): 749n4.
18. Donald F. Anderson, *William Howard Taft: A Conservative's Conception of the Presidency* (Ithaca, NY: Cornell University Press, 1973), 20–21.
19. Anderson, *Taft*, 86. See also Ballard, "The Administrative Theory of William Howard Taft," 69–74.
20. Ballard, "The Administrative Theory of William Howard Taft," 69; Bess Glenn, "The Taft Commission and the Government's Record Practices," *American Archivist* 21 (1958): 278–83; Lewis L. Gould, *The William Howard Taft Presidency* (Lawrence: University Press of Kansas, 2009), 122–24.
21. Glenn, "Taft Commission," 278.
22. See, for example, David H. DeJong, *Paternalism to Partnership: The Administration of Indian Affairs, 1786–2021* (Lincoln: University of Nebraska Press, 2022), 10, 12, 13, and summaries of specific administrators' efforts throughout, and Gustavus A. Weber, *Organized Efforts for the Improvement*

of Methods of Administration in the United States (New York: D. Appleton, 1919).

23. Glenn, "Taft Commission," 280–86. For one example of a department's response to the effort, see Cathleen D. Cahill, *Federal Fathers and Mothers: A Social History of the United States Indian Service, 1869–1933* (Chapel Hill: The University of North Carolina Press, 2011), 217–23, esp. 220.
24. William Howard Taft, Second Annual Message, December 6, 1910, in *The Collected Works of William Howard Taft*, vol. 4, *Presidential Messages to Congress*, ed. David H. Burton (Athens: University of Ohio Press, 2002), 71–73 (hereafter *Presidential Messages*); Taft, Special Message, January 17, 1912, in *Presidential Messages*, 225–49; Taft, Special Message, April 4, 1912, in *Presidential Messages*, 260–71. See also Fourth Annual Message, December 6, 1912, in *Presidential Messages*, 318.
25. Ballard, "The Administrative Theory of William Howard Taft," 71–74, 70.
26. Taft, Special Message, January 17, 1912, in *Presidential Messages*, 244ff, 226.
27. Quoted in Anderson, *Taft*, 89.
28. Ballard, "The Administrative Theory of William Howard Taft," 72, 73.
29. Taft, *President and His Powers*, 54. See also Peri E. Arnold, *Making the Managerial Presidency: Comprehensive Reorganization Planning, 1905–1996*, 2nd ed. (Lawrence: University Press of Kansas, 1998), 39.
30. Ballard, "The Administrative Theory of William Howard Taft," 73.
31. Anderson, *Taft*, 90. See also Camilla Stivers, *Bureau Men, Settlement Women: Constructing Public Administration in the Progressive Era* (Lawrence: University Press of Kansas, 2000), 72–73, 154n39, and chap. 4 generally, and Arnold, *Making the Managerial Presidency*, 15–21, chap. 2.
32. Kriste Lindenmeyer, *"A Right to Childhood": The US Children's Bureau and Child Welfare, 1912–46* (Urbana: University of Illinois Press, 1997); Stivers, *Bureau Men, Settlement Women*.
33. Lindenmeyer, *"A Right to Childhood,"* 27–29.
34. Ulysses S. Grant, *The Papers of Ulysses S. Grant*, ed. John Y. Simon et al. (Carbondale: Southern Illinois University Press, 1967–2012), 19:197 (hereafter *USG*); William H. Armstrong, *Warrior in Two Camps: Ely S. Parker, Union General and Seneca Chief* (Syracuse: Syracuse University Press, 1978), 135–36.
35. See also Jonathan Lurie, *William Howard Taft: The Travails of a Progressive Conservative* (Cambridge: Cambridge University Press, 2012), 7, and Carl Sferrazza Anthony, *Nellie Taft: The Unconventional First Lady of the Ragtime Era* (New York: William Morrow, 2005), 60, 240–42, 284–87, 368–71.
36. R.W. Thompson, "At the National Capital," *Freeman* (Indianapolis), January 1, 1910, https://news.google.com/newspapers?nid=FIkAGs9z2eEC&dat=19100101&printsec=frontpage&hl=en, 1. See also Taft, Inaugural Address, March 4, 1909, in *Fellow Citizens: The Penguin Book of U.S. Presidential Inaugural Addresses*, ed. Robert V. Remini and Terry Golway (New York: Penguin, 2008), 278; Taft, "The Future of the Negro," speech delivered at Allen Temple, Cincinnati, September 15, 1908, in *The Collected Works of William Howard Taft*, vol. 2, *Political Issues*

and Outlooks, ed. David H. Burton (Athens: Ohio University Press, 2001), 52–57 (hereafter *Political Issues and Outlooks*); Taft, "Hopeful Views of Negro Difficulties," delivered in Big Bethel Church, Atlanta, January 16, 1909, *Political Issues and Outlooks,* 179–82; Taft, "The Young Men's Christian Association," delivered at Tabernacle Baptist Church, Augusta, GA, January 17, 1909, *Political Issues and Outlooks,* 192; and Taft, Second Annual Message, December 6, 1910, in *Presidential Messages,* 70 (on the Freedmen's Bank and the Negro Exposition). For criticism of Taft, see Paolo E. Coletta's note about Taft's Inaugural Address, in Remini and Golway, eds., *Fellow Citizens,* 268; Gould, *Taft Presidency,* 131–32; and Alpheus Thomas Mason, *William Howard Taft: Chief Justice* (New York: Simon and Schuster, 1964), 141, 275. On Taft and racial tolerance, see also Sidney M. Milkis, *Theodore Roosevelt, the Progressive Party, and the Transformation of American Democracy* (Lawrence: University Press of Kansas, 2009), 169, 193–94, 201, 274–76, and Anthony, *Nellie Taft,* 15, 65, 150–51, 390.

37. Thompson, "At the National Capital," 1; Taft, "Young Men's Christian Association," 192; Taft, "The Outlook of Negro Education," delivered at the Haines Normal and Industrial School, Augusta, GA, January 19, 1909, in *Political Issues and Outlooks,* 197.
38. David H. Burton, "Preface," in *Political Issues and Outlooks,* 6. See also Taft, Inaugural Address, in Remini and Golway, eds., *Fellow Citizens,* 277–79.
39. Tom Holm, *The Great Confusion in Indian Affairs: Native Americans and Whites in the Progressive Era* (Austin: University of Texas Press, 2005). See also Cahill, *Federal Fathers and Mothers,* 209–35, and Schultz, "William Howard Taft," 405.
40. Holm, *Great Confusion;* Francis Paul Prucha, *The Great Father: The United States Government and the American Indians* (Lincoln: University of Nebraska Press, 1984), 841–53.
41. On vaccinations and Indian removal, see J. Diane Pearson, "Lewis Cass and the Politics of Disease: The Indian Vaccination Act of 1832," *Wicazo Sa Review* 18 (2003): 9–35; and Ruth Bloch Rubin, "State Preventive Medicine: Public Health, Indian Removal, and the Growth of State Capacity, 1800–1840," *Studies in American Political Development* 34 (2020): 24–43. On Valentine, health, and assimilation, see Diane T. Putney, "Robert Grosvenor Valentine (1909–12)," in *The Commissioners of Indian Affairs, 1824–1977,* ed. Robert M. Kvasnicka and Herman J. Viola (Lincoln: University of Nebraska Press, 1979), 234–35.
42. DeJong, *Paternalism to Partnership,* 241, 244–45; Putney, "Robert Grosvenor Valentine," 234–35.
43. DeJong, *Paternalism to Partnership,* 240–45; Putney, "Robert Grosvenor Valentine," esp. 238. On Gila River, see John Shurts, *Indian Reserved Water Rights: The Winters Doctrine in Its Social and Legal Context, 1880s-1930s* (Norman: University of Oklahoma Press, 2000), 184, 186, 187–222, chaps. 9–10 generally. On reforms in education, see Cahill, *Federal Fathers and Mothers,* 223–29.
44. Putney, "Robert Grosvenor Valentine," 234–35; Prucha, *Great Father,* 850.

45. Putney, "Robert Grosvenor Valentine," 238, 240.
46. See *Executive Orders Relating to Indian Reservations from May 14, 1855 to July 1, 1912*, 11, 12, 13, 13–14, 15–16, 22, 23, 24, 27, 28, 29, 30, 37, 45, 52, 53, 54–55, 61, 63, 69, 73, 94, 110, 125–26, 130, 168, 169, 174–75, and *Executive Orders Relating to Indian Reservations from July 1, 1912 to July 1, 1922* (Washington, DC: U.S. Government Printing Office, 1932), 32, 42, 46, 47, 50, 72.
47. Reprinted in *Executive Orders Relating to Indian Reservations from July 1, 1912 to July 1, 1922*, 11.
48. Gould, *Taft Presidency*, 206–7.
49. See, for example, commentary on Lathrop in Lindenmeyer, "A Right to Childhood"; Stivers, *Bureau Men, Settlement Women*, 60–61, 98–100; Cecelia Tichi, *Civic Passions: Seven Who Launched Progressive America (and What They Teach Us)* (Chapel Hill: University of North Carolina Press, 2009), 93–5, 114, 117; background on Ballinger in Paolo E. Coletta, *The Presidency of William Howard Taft* (Lawrence: University Press of Kansas, 1973), 82–84, and James Penick Jr., *Progressive Politics and Conservation: The Ballinger-Pinchot Affair* (Chicago: University of Chicago Press, 1968), chap. 2, 186–96; and George Wickersham, *The Changing Order: Essays on Government, Monopoly, and Education, Written During a Period of Readjustment* (New York: Putnam, 1914). On Roosevelt holdovers in the administration, see Anderson, *Taft*, 64, and Herbert S. Duffy, *William Howard Taft* (New York: Minton, Balch & Company, 1930), 284–85.
50. Anderson, *Taft*, 68–72, 90–93, 238–39; David H. Burton, *William Howard Taft: Confident Peacemaker* (Philadelphia: St. Joseph's University Press, 2004), chap. 3.
51. Anderson, *Taft*, 91–92.
52. Daniel S. McHargue, "President Taft's Appointments to the Supreme Court," *Journal of Politics* 12 (1950): esp. 509–10; Lawrence Rakestraw, "Conservation Historiography: An Assessment," *Pacific Historical Review* 41 (1972): 285–86.
53. Rayman L. Solomon, "The Politics of Appointment and the Federal Courts' Role in Regulating America: U.S. Courts of Appeals Judgeships from T.R. to F.D.R.," *American Bar Foundation Research Journal* 9 (1984): 285–343.
54. Michael L. Bromley, *William Howard Taft and the First Motoring Presidency* (Jefferson, NC: McFarland, 2003); Theodore Roosevelt to Charles Hughes, October 8, 1905, manuscript image, https://www.shapell.org/manuscript/theodore-roosevelt-did-not-like-cars/#transcripts.
55. Lurie, *Taft*, xiii.
56. Duffy, *Taft*, 252; Anderson, *Taft*, 125–26; Gould, *Taft Presidency*, 95; Lurie, *Taft*, 103–8, 160, 169–70; Anderson, "The Legacy of William Howard Taft," 28–29. For a good treatment of Taft in the midst of the Republican split, see Stanley D. Solvick, "William Howard Taft and Cannonism," *Wisconsin Magazine of History* 48 (1964): 48–58.
57. William Howard Taft, *Popular Government*, reprinted in *The Collected Works of William Howard Taft*, vol. 5, *Popular Government and The Anti-Trust Act*

and the Supreme Court, ed. David Potash and Donald F. Anderson (Athens: Ohio University Press, 2003), 22; see also 21 (hereafter *Popular Government*).
58. For example, see Duffy, *Taft*, 230–31. On how Taft approached the split within the Republican Party and made decisions to support Joe Cannon and the old guard, in pursuit of demonstrable policy achievements, see Solvick, "William Howard Taft and Cannonism."
59. Anderson, *Taft*, 134–35; E. Merton Coulter, "The Attempt of William Howard Taft to Break the Solid South," *Georgia Historical Quarterly* 19 (1935): 134–44; McHargue, "Taft's Appointments," esp. 509–10.
60. Lurie, *Taft*, 169; Tichi, *Civic Passions*, 54–55.
61. Taft, Special Message, February 20, 1912, in *Presidential Messages*, 250–53.
62. "The Battle for the Weeks Bill," *American Forestry* 16 (1910): 133. See also Stephen J. Pyne, *Year of the Fires: The Story of the Great Fires of 1910* (New York: Viking, 2001); George W. Williams, "The Beginnings of the National Forests in the South: Protection of Watersheds," paper presented to the 14th Annual Environment Virginia Conference (2003), revised, https://foresthistory.org/wp-content/uploads/2017/02/ProtectionofWatersheds_Williams.pdf; and Lincoln Bramwell, "1911 Weeks Act: The Legislation that Nationalised the US Forest Service," *Journal of Energy and Natural Resources Law* 30 (2012): 325–36.
63. Anderson, *Taft*, 132. See also Gould, *Taft Presidency*, 101.
64. Anderson, *Taft*, 131–32; Lurie, *Taft*, 169.
65. Frank Haigh Dixon, "The Mann-Elkins Act, Amending the Act to Regulate Commerce," *Quarterly Journal of Economics* 24 (1910): 624–25.
66. See Dixon, "Mann-Elkins Act," 615–24; J. Newton Baker, "The Commerce Court: Its Origin, Its Powers and Its Judges," *Yale Law Journal* 20 (1911): 555–62; William R. Doezema, "Railroad Management and the Interplay of Federal and State Regulation, 1885–1916," *Business History Review* 50 (1976): esp. 170–72; George E. Dix, "The Death of the Commerce Court: A Study in Institutional Weakness," *American Journal of Legal History* 8 (1964): 249–50, 254–56; Nathanson, "Administrative Court," 1004–8; Marc Winerman, "The Origins of the FTC: Concentration, Cooperation, Control, and Competition," *Antitrust Law Journal* 71 (2003): 30; Gould, *Taft Presidency*, 97–98; and Patrick J. McGinnis, "A Case of Judicial Misconduct: The Impeachment and Trial of Robert W. Archbald," *Pennsylvania Magazine of History and Biography* 101 (1977): 506–20. The Commerce Court was disbanded in 1913.
67. Daniel P. Carpenter, *The Forging of Bureaucratic Autonomy: Reputations, Networks, and Policy Innovation in Executive Agencies, 1862–1928* (Princeton: Princeton University Press, 2001), 162.
68. William Howard Taft, "Postal Savings Banks and the Guaranty of Bank Deposits," delivered at St. Paul, MN, September 28, 1908, in *Political Issues and Outlooks*, 107–8.
69. Carpenter, *Forging of Bureaucratic Autonomy*, 162; see also his discussion and analysis, 149–63.
70. Taft, "Postal Savings Banks," 108–11; 109 (quotation).

71. Taft, Third Annual Message, December 21, 1911, in *Presidential Messages*, 218–19. Daniel P. Carpenter's data also indicate that the postal savings banks were a hit with, and supported by, immigrants. Carpenter, *Forging of Bureaucratic Autonomy*, 157–61.
72. Taft, Fourth Annual Message, December 19, 1912, in *Presidential Messages*, 339–40. See also Taft, Inaugural Address, in Remini and Golway, eds., *Fellow Citizens*, 275; Taft, Second Annual Message, December 6, 1910, in *Presidential Messages*, 43, 46–47; Taft, Third Annual Message, December 21, 1911, in *Presidential Messages*, 218–20; Taft, "Postal Savings Banks," 107–21; and Gould, *Taft Presidency*, 95.
73. Carpenter, *Forging of Bureaucratic Autonomy*, 157.
74. Clark, "President Taft and the Puerto Rican Appropriation Crisis of 1909."
75. Taft, Veto Message, August 22, 1911, in *Presidential Messages*, 150–51; H. A. Hubbard, "The Arizona Enabling Act and President Taft's Veto," *Pacific Historical Review* 3 (1934): 307–22.
76. See Taft, Veto Message, August 22, 1911, in *Presidential Messages*, 152. See also Taft, *Popular Government*, 112–13, 120, 137.
77. Taft, Veto Message, August 22, 1911, in *Presidential Messages*, 154. See also Taft, *Popular Government*, 107–32.
78. See Milkis, *Theodore Roosevelt*, 55–62, 156–57, 217; Lewis L. Gould, *Four Hats in the Ring: The 1912 Election and the Birth of Modern American Politics* (Lawrence: University Press of Kansas, 2008), 25–26, 58–59; Anderson, *Taft*, 231–33; Duffy, *Taft*, 280–81; and Mason, *Taft*, 56–58.
79. See Taft, Fourth Annual Message, December 6, 1912, in *Presidential Messages*, 317. See also Taft, Fourth Annual Message, December 6, 1912, in *Presidential Messages*, 314–17; Korzi, "Our Chief Magistrate and His Powers," 311; and Taft, *Popular Government*, 31.
80. Charles K. McFarland, "The Federal Government and Water Power, 1901–1913: A Legislative Study in the Nascence of Regulation," *Land Economics* 42 (1966): 449. McFarland writes that the 1920 Federal Water Power Act is based on Progressive-era fights.
81. U.S. Office of Management and Budget, "Federal Surplus or Deficit," Federal Reserve Bank of St. Louis, March 13, 2023, https://fred.stlouisfed.org/series/FYFSD.
82. See, for example, Burton, *Taft: Confident Peacemaker*, chap. 3; Scott Nearing and Joseph Freeman, *Dollar Diplomacy: A Study in American Imperialism* (New York: B. W. Huebsch, 1925), 264–67; Robert D. Schulzinger, *US Diplomacy since 1900*, 4th ed. (New York: Oxford University Press, 1998), 39; Robert Freeman Smith, "Cuba: Laboratory for Dollar Diplomacy, 1898–1917," *Historian* 28 (1966): 586–609; D. H. Dinwoodie, "Dollar Diplomacy in the Light of the Guatemalan Loan Project, 1909–1913," *The Americas* 26 (1970): 237–53; Cyrus Veeser, "Inventing Dollar Diplomacy: The Gilded-Age Origins of the Roosevelt Corollary to the Monroe Doctrine," *Diplomatic History* 27 (2003): 301–26; David M. Pletcher, "Reciprocity and Latin America in the Early 1890s: A Foretaste of Dollar Diplomacy," *Pacific Historical Review* 47 (1978): 53–89;

and Richard M. Abrams, "Review: United States Intervention Abroad: The First Quarter Century," *American Historical Review* 79 (1974): 83–86. For the strategy of supervised loans, see Emily S. Rosenberg, "Revisiting Dollar Diplomacy: Narratives of Money and Manliness," *Diplomatic History* 22 (1998): 161; for commerce, see Naomi W. Cohen, "Ambassador Straus in Turkey, 1909–1910: A Note on Dollar Diplomacy," *Mississippi Valley Historical Review* 45 (1959): 632–42; for customs collectorships, see Dana G. Munro, "Dollar Diplomacy in Nicaragua, 1909–1913," *Hispanic American Historical Review* 38 (1958): 211.

83. Richard H. Collin, "Symbiosis versus Hegemony: New Directions in the Foreign Relations Historiography of Theodore Roosevelt and William Howard Taft," *Diplomatic History* 19 (1995): 473–97; Abrams, "Review: United States Intervention Abroad"; Smith, "Cuba," 586–87; Dinwoodie, "Dollar Diplomacy"; Joseph O. Baylen, "American Intervention in Nicaragua, 1909–33: An Appraisal of Objectives and Results," *Southwestern Social Science Quarterly* 35 (1954): 129; Benjamin T. Harrison, "Woodrow Wilson and Nicaragua," *Caribbean Quarterly* 51 (2005): 25–36; Pletcher, "Reciprocity and Latin America," 54–55; David Sheinin, "The New Dollar Diplomacy in Latin America," *American Studies International* 37 (1999): 81–99. As imperialism, see, for example, Walter E. Leuchtenburg, "Progressivism and Imperialism: The Progressive Movement and American Foreign Policy, 1898–1916," *Mississippi Valley Historical Review* 39 (1952): 483–504. As symbiosis more than hegemony, see William Schell Jr., "American Investment in Tropical Mexico: Rubber Plantations, Fraud, and Dollar Diplomacy, 1897–1913," *Business History Review* 64 (1990): 217–54; Collin, "Symbiosis versus Hegemony"; Munro, "Dollar Diplomacy," 231–33; and Baylen, "American Intervention" (on complexity).

Most analysts conclude that the policies generally failed. See Collin, "Symbiosis versus Hegemony"; Dinwoodie, "Dollar Diplomacy" (Guatemala); Gail L. Owen, "Dollar Diplomacy in Default: The Economics of Russian-American Relations, 1910–1917," *Historical Journal* 13 (1970): 272 (Russia, Persia, Far East); Cohen, "Ambassador Straus," 642 (Turkey); Kamyar Ghaneabassiri, "U.S. Foreign Policy and Persia, 1856–1921," *Iranian Studies* 35 (2002): 145–75 (Persia); Abrams, "Review: United States Intervention Abroad," 79–81 (Japan and elsewhere); Anderson, "The Legacy of William Howard Taft," (Taft's legacies and effects were neither significant nor lasting); Baylen, "American Intervention" (Taft is presented as effective at three stated goals; failure is result of later backlash: 154); and Munro, "Dollar Diplomacy," 233 (results "unfortunate" and effective but also based on effects on other countries).

84. Taft, "The Winning of the South," delivered at Atlanta, January 15, 1909, in *Political Issues and Outlooks*, 178.
85. Anderson, *Taft*, 238.
86. Walter V. Scholes and Marie V. Scholes, *The Foreign Policies of the Taft Administration* (Columbia: University of Missouri Press, 1970), 124–46, 174–94, 196–220; Anderson, *Taft*, 245–58; Schulzinger, *US Diplomacy since 1900*, 40–44.

87. Scholes and Scholes, *Foreign Policies*. See also Owen, "Dollar Diplomacy," 251–52.
88. Anderson, *Taft*, 245–50; Gould, *Taft Presidency*, 84.
89. Anderson, *Taft*, 250–53, 255; Gould, *Taft Presidency*, 86–87; Nearing and Freeman, *Dollar Diplomacy*, 40–51, 60ff.
90. Anderson, *Taft*, 263–65.
91. On Nicaragua and Honduras, see, for example, Baylen, "American Intervention," 130–33, 143; Harrison, "Woodrow Wilson and Nicaragua," 25–26; and Munro, "Dollar Diplomacy."
92. Taft, *President and His Powers*, 75; Taft, Second Annual Message, December 6, 1910, in *Presidential Messages*, 12–15; see also Third Annual Message, December 7, 1911, in *Presidential Messages*, 182.
93. Collin, "Symbiosis versus Hegemony," 491.
94. Munro, "Dollar Diplomacy," 220–32.
95. Schell, "American Investment," 249–54.
96. Anderson, *Taft*, 258ff. On Taft policy in Central America and the Caribbean, see Schulzinger, *US Diplomacy since 1900*, 44–51.
97. William Howard Taft, *The United States and Peace*, reprinted in *The Collected Works of William Howard Taft*, vol. 6, ed. W. Carey McWilliams and Frank X. Gerrity (1914; reprint Athens: University of Ohio Press, 2003), 138, 139.
98. Taft quoted in Anderson, *Taft*, 137.
99. Anderson, *Taft*, 143.
100. Clark had said, "I hope to see the day when the American flag will float over every square foot of the British North American possession clear to the North Pole." Quoted in Anderson, *Taft*, 222. See 222ff. for politics and reciprocity—the postal rate hike, a compromise pro-media tariff adjustment, and the role of the Hearst papers. See also Duffy, *Taft*, 263–67.
101. Taft, *President and His Powers*, 88–89; Gould, *Taft Presidency*, 172. See also Taft, *The United States and Peace*, 148–66. Taft's father had been instrumental in protecting Jews in Russia during his service in the Grant administration: Anthony, *Nellie Taft*, 150.
102. Owen, "Dollar Diplomacy," 252–55; Cohen, "Ambassador Straus," 632–35; Ghaneabassiri, "U.S. Foreign Policy and Persia"; "The Situation in Persia: America and Mr. Shuster's Position," *Glasgow Herald*, December 11, 1911.
103. Anderson, *Taft*, 240–41.
104. Taft, Memorandum [to accompany the Panama Canal Act], August 24, 1912, in *Presidential Messages*, 276–82.
105. Taft, Third Annual Message, December 21, 1911, in *Presidential Messages*, 211.
106. Anderson, *Taft*, 240–41; Gould, *Taft Presidency*, 187–89. Wilson led a retreat from the position, and Congress repealed the tolls exemption in 1914.
107. Schell, "American Investment," 225–40. For examples of the government leading reluctant private interests elsewhere, see also Rosenberg, "Revisiting Dollar Diplomacy," 160; Pletcher, "Reciprocity and Latin America," 55; Abrams,

"Review: United States Intervention Abroad"; and Munro, "Dollar Diplomacy," 212–13.
108. Taft, Third Annual Message, December 7, 1911, in *Presidential Messages*, 177.
109. Taft, Third Annual Message, December 7, 1911, in *Presidential Messages*, 178.
110. Anderson, *Taft*, 271–73; Leuchtenburg, "Progressivism and Imperialism," 492.
111. Anderson, *Taft*, 274.
112. Taft, Third Annual Message, December 7, 1911, in *Presidential Messages*, 180.
113. Taft, Third Annual Message, December 7, 1911, in *Presidential Messages*, 176–77, 180–81.
114. Anderson, *Taft*, 265–75; Coletta, *Presidency of William Howard Taft*, 175–81.
115. William Howard Taft to Nellie Taft, July 22, 1912, in *My Dearest Nellie: The Letters of William Howard Taft to Helen Heron Taft, 1909-1912*, ed. Lewis L. Gould (Lawrence: University Press of Kansas, 2011), 235.

7. Taft the Builder

1. William Howard Taft, *The President and His Powers*, in *The Collected Works of William Howard Taft*, vol. 6, ed. W. Carey McWilliams and Frank X. Gerrity (1916; reprint Athens: University of Ohio Press, 2003), 19 (paragraph breaks added).
2. Tony Freyer, *Regulating Big Business: Antitrust in Great Britain and America, 1880-1990* (Cambridge: Cambridge University Press, 1992), 111; Marc Winerman, "The Origins of the FTC: Concentration, Cooperation, Control, and Competition," *Antitrust Law Journal* 71 (2003): 1, 6.
3. In general, see Alpheus Thomas Mason, *William Howard Taft: Chief Justice* (New York: Simon and Schuster, 1964), chap. 2.
4. Freyer, *Regulating Big Business*, 113; Neil Fligstein, *The Transformation of Corporate Control* (Cambridge, MA: Harvard University Press, 1990), 91, table 3.3. See also Roy G. Blakey and Gladys C. Blakey, *The Federal Income Tax* (London: Longman, Green, 1940), 45n102.
5. *Pollock v. Farmers' Loan & Trust Co.*, 157 U.S. 429 (1895). See Sheldon D. Pollack, "Origins of the Modern Income Tax, 1894–1913," *Tax Lawyer* 66 (2013): 295–330, and Blakey and Blakey, *Federal Income Tax*, 43–45.
6. Blakey and Blakey, *Federal Income Tax*, 23, 40. For discussions of economic factors driving tax reform, see also Ajay K. Mehrotra, "American Economic Development, Managerial Corporate Capitalism, and the Institutional Foundations of the Modern Income Tax," *Law and Contemporary Problems* 73 (2010): 25–61, and Bennett D. Baack and Edward John Ray, "Special Interests and the Adoption of the Income Tax in the United States," *Journal of Economic History* 45 (1985): 607–25. For more on the progression in Taft's thinking, see Pollack, "Origins of the Modern Income Tax," 312–15.
7. Donald F. Anderson, *William Howard Taft: A Conservative's Conception of the Presidency* (Ithaca, NY: Cornell University Press, 1973), 96; Lewis L. Gould,

The William Howard Taft Presidency (Lawrence: University Press of Kansas, 2009), 49; Sidney M. Milkis, *Theodore Roosevelt, the Progressive Party, and the Transformation of American Democracy* (Lawrence: University Press of Kansas, 2009), 29; Paolo E. Coletta, *The Presidency of William Howard Taft* (Lawrence: University Press of Kansas, 1973), 57; Peri E. Arnold, *Remaking the Presidency: Roosevelt, Taft, and Wilson, 1901–1916* (Lawrence: University Press of Kansas, 2009), 109–16; David A. Lake, "International Economic Structures and American Foreign Economic Policy, 1887–1934," *World Politics* 35 (1983): 532; Stanley D. Solvick, "William Howard Taft and the Payne-Aldrich Tariff," *Mississippi Valley Historical Review* 50 (1963): 424, 426.

8. For favorable views of the tariff, see Anderson, *Taft*, 111–25; Herbert S. Duffy, *William Howard Taft* (New York: Minton, Balch, 1930), 238; Solvick, "William Howard Taft and the Payne-Aldrich Tariff."

9. On the tariff's key role in the 1912 election, see Lewis L. Gould, *Four Hats in the Ring: The 1912 Election and the Birth of Modern American Politics* (Lawrence: University Press of Kansas, 2008), x, 8–11.

10. Quoted in Duffy, *Taft*, 241; emphasis added. See also Coletta, *Presidency of William Howard Taft*, 63–64. Congress refused to appropriate funds for the Tariff Board, though, rendering it a nonentity. Anderson, *Taft*, 146. For summary and discussion of the act's provisions, see Anderson, *Taft*, 118, and Jonathan Lurie, *William Howard Taft: The Travails of a Progressive Conservative* (Cambridge: Cambridge University Press, 2012), 140–41.

11. On specific provisions of the law, see Blakey and Blakey, *Federal Income Tax*, 53–54; for revenue data 58–59; Pollack, "Origins of the Modern Income Tax"; and Duffy, *Taft*, 240–41.

12. Blakey and Blakey, *Federal Income Tax*, 43–44; Pollack, "Origins of the Modern Income Tax," 316–18, 318n140.

13. Pollack, "Origins of the Modern Income Tax," 316; Blakey and Blakey, *Federal Income Tax*, 44; Coletta, *Presidency of William Howard Taft*, 67.

14. Butt quoted in Blakey and Blakey, *Federal Income Tax*, 46n104; see also 52. Wickersham also drafted a bill extending the authority of the Interstate Commerce Commission (which eventually became Mann-Elkins) and a federal incorporation law (which was popular but did not pass). Wilfred E. Binkley, "The President as Chief Legislator," *Annals of the American Academy of Political and Social Science* 307 (1956): 94–95; Melvin I. Urofsky, "Proposed Federal Incorporation in the Progressive Era," *American Journal of Legal History* 26 (1982): 160–83. See also Dana G. Munro, "Dollar Diplomacy in Nicaragua, 1909–1913," *Hispanic American Historical Review* 38 (1958): 219.

15. Blakey and Blakey, *Federal Income Tax*, 47.

16. Solvick, "William Howard Taft and the Payne-Aldrich Tariff," 435–36; Francis W. Bird, "Constitutional Aspects of the Federal Tax on the Income of Corporations," *Harvard Law Review* 24 (1910): 31–46.

17. Solvick, "William Howard Taft and the Payne-Aldrich Tariff," 440–42; Blakey and Blakey, *Federal Income Tax*, 43; see also 57–58. Similarly, Taft's proposed

tariff commission was not permitted to set rates itself, but it was empowered to gather data on which rates could be set.
18. Taft, Second Annual Message, December 6, 1910, in *The Collected Works of William Howard Taft*, vol. 4, *Presidential Messages to Congress*, ed. David H. Burton (Athens: University of Ohio Press, 2002), 25–26 (hereafter *Presidential Messages*). Cf. Blakey and Blakey, *Federal Income Tax*, 57–59.
19. On urban and immigrant support for the income tax, see John D. Buenker, "Urban Liberalism and the Federal Income Tax Amendment," *Pennsylvania History* 36 (1969): 192–215. On agriculture's support, see Douglas K. Barney and Tonya K. Flesher, "A Study of the Impact of Special Interest Groups on Major Tax Reform: Agriculture and the 1913 Income Tax Law," *Accounting Historians Journal* 35 (2008): 71–100. Generally, see Pollack, "Origins of the Modern Income Tax," 303–4, 314–15. For useful background on *Pollock*, see Pollack, "Origins of the Modern Income Tax," and Samuel B. Pettengill, "The History of a Prophecy: Class War and the Income Tax," *American Bar Association Journal* 39 (1953): 473–76, 521–22.
20. On *Pollock* and public opinion of the Court, see Roy G. Blakey, "The New Income Tax," *American Economic Review* 4 (1914): 25; Blakey and Blakey, *Federal Income Tax*, 45n101; and Pollack, "Origins of the Modern Income Tax," 316–17.
21. See Henry F. Pringle, *The Life and Times of William Howard Taft: A Biography* (1939; reprint Norwalk, CT: Easton Press, 1967), 1:431–36, and Anderson, *Taft*, 229–30.
22. Rene N. Ballard, "The Administrative Theory of William Howard Taft," *Western Political Quarterly* 7 (1954): 65; Blakey and Blakey, *Federal Income Tax*, 42, 42n92, 60–61; Pettengill, "History of a Prophecy"; Lurie, *Taft*, 106–7; Michael L. Bromley, *William Howard Taft and the First Motoring Presidency* (Jefferson, NC: McFarland, 2003), 250; Solvick, "William Howard Taft and the Payne-Aldrich Tariff," 434–35; Pollack, "Origins of the Modern Income Tax," 296, 299, 306, 327–29; Anderson, *Taft*, 108–10.
23. Winerman, "Origins of the FTC," 27n153.
24. Quoted in Duffy, *Taft*, 204.
25. See William Howard Taft, *The Anti-Trust Act and the Supreme Court*, reprinted in *The Collected Works of William Howard Taft*, vol. 5, *Popular Government and The Anti-Trust Act and the Supreme Court*, ed. David Potash and Donald F. Anderson (Athens: Ohio University Press, 2003), esp. 174 (hereafter Taft, *Anti-Trust Act*).
26. See James C. German Jr., "Taft, Roosevelt, and United States Steel," *Historian* 34 (1972): 598–613; Freyer, *Regulating Big Business*, 31, 72–75, 110–23, 132–50; Jonathan Chausovsky, "From Bureau to Trade Commission: Agency Reputation in the Statebuilding Enterprise," *Journal of the Gilded Age and Progressive Era* 12 (2013): 343–78; Martin J. Sklar, *The Corporate Reconstruction of American Capitalism, 1890–1916* (Cambridge: Cambridge University Press, 1988); Arthur M. Johnson, "Theodore Roosevelt and the Bureau of Corporations,"

Mississippi Valley Historical Review 45 (1959): 571–90, reprinted in Robert F. Himmelberg, ed., *Business and Government in America since 1870*, vol. 2, *The Monopoly Issue and Antitrust, 1900–1917* (New York: Garland, 1994), 85–104; and Edmund Morris, *Theodore Rex* (New York: Random House, 2001), 65, 478, 495.

27. Winerman, "Origins of the FTC," 29–32.
28. Sklar, *Corporate Reconstruction*, 375. See also James C. German Jr., "The Taft Administration and the Sherman Antitrust Act," *Mid-America* 54 (1972): 172–86, reprinted in Himmelberg, ed., *Business and Government*, 22–36, and German, "Taft, Roosevelt."
29. William Graebner, "Great Expectations: The Search for Order in Bituminous Coal, 1890–1917," *Business History Review* 48 (1974): 63; Chausovsky, "From Bureau to Trade Commission," 353–55; Winerman, "Origins of the FTC," 30.
30. Anderson, *Taft*, 81; Gould, *Taft Presidency*, 98, 165; German, "Taft, Roosevelt"; Winerman, "Origins of the FTC."
31. Anderson, *Taft*, 79; German, "Taft Administration," 22.
32. Winerman, "Origins of the FTC," 7–15. See also Robert H. Wiebe, "Business Disunity and the Progressive Movement, 1901–1914," *Mississippi Valley Historical Review* 44 (1958): 664–85, and William R. Doezema, "Railroad Management and the Interplay of Federal and State Regulation, 1885–1916," *Business History Review* 50 (1976): 153–78.
33. Taft, Third Annual Message, December 5, 1911, in *Presidential Messages*, 171–72, 161; Taft, *Anti-Trust Act*, esp. 175, 222–23, 232–38, 241; John R. Carter, "From Peckham to White: Economic Welfare and the Rule of Reason," *Antitrust Bulletin* 25 (1980): 275–95, reprinted in Himmelberg, ed., *Business and Government*, 1–21; Winerman, "Origins of the FTC," 28–29.
34. Taft, *Anti-Trust Act*, 241.
35. Taft, Third Annual Message, December 5, 1911, in *Presidential Messages*, 166.
36. Taft, Third Annual Message, December 5, 1911, in *Presidential Messages*, 166.
37. Taft, *Anti-Trust Act*, 179.
38. Sklar, *Corporate Reconstruction*, 375.
39. Taft, *Anti-Trust Act*, 239, 240, 241 (quotation).
40. Fligstein, *Transformation of Corporate Control*, 98.
41. Lurie, *Taft*, 82–83.
42. Anderson, *Taft*, 43.
43. Kurt Hohenstein, *Coining Corruption: The Making of the American Campaign Finance System* (DeKalb: Northern Illinois University Press, 2007), 62–74, 81; Richard L. McCormick, "The Discovery That Business Corrupts Politics: A Reappraisal of the Origins of Progressivism," *American Historical Review* 86 (1981): 265–70.
44. Quoted in Anderson, *Taft*, 44.
45. Hohenstein, *Coining Corruption*, 74–81; Anthony Corrado et al., *Campaign Finance Reform: A Sourcebook* (Washington, DC: Brookings Institution Press, 1997), 27–29, 37–46.

46. On an inheritance tax, see Taft, *Popular Government,* 100. On a federal incorporation tax, see Gould, *Taft Presidency,* 98; Urofsky, "Proposed Federal Incorporation," 180–83; Winerman, "Origins of the FTC," 29–30.
47. On the significance of tax reform, see Buenker, "Urban Liberalism," 192–93; Mehrotra, "American Economic Development," 25–26; and Pettengill, "History of a Prophecy," who compares the significance of tax reform to the significance of the atom bomb in foreign policy (475). For details on the 1913 tax law implementing the amendment, see Blakey, "New Income Tax," and Pollack, "Origins of the Modern Income Tax," 324–28.
48. For example, see Taft, *President and His Powers,* 103–4.
49. For general background on the conservation movement in the Progressive era, see J. Leonard Bates, "Fulfilling American Democracy: The Conservation Movement, 1907 to 1921," *Mississippi Valley Historical Review* 44 (1957): 29–57; Char Miller, "The Greening of Gifford Pinchot," *Environmental History Review* 16 (1992): 1–20; and James Penick Jr., *Progressive Politics and Conservation: The Ballinger-Pinchot Affair* (Chicago: University of Chicago Press, 1968). For discussion of the complicated historiography of the movement, see Rickey L. Hendricks, "The Conservation Movement: A Critique of Historical Sources," *History Teacher* 16 (1982): 77–104, and Lawrence Rakestraw, "Conservation Historiography: An Assessment," *Pacific Historical Review* 41 (1972): 271–88.
50. Taft, speech to the National Conservation Congress, St. Paul, MN, September 5, 1910, appearing as First Appendix to Second Annual Message, September 5, 1911, in *Presidential Messages,* 78–100. David H. Burton dates the speech as 1911, but James Penick Jr. and other sources list 1910. See Penick, *Progressive Politics and Conservation,* 171–72, and William Howard Taft, "Conservation of the Soil," address to the National Conservation Congress at Kansas City, MO, September 1911, digital image, Library of Congress, Washington, DC, https://www.loc.gov/item/ca12000666/.
51. Taft, First Appendix to Second Annual Message, September 5, 1911, in *Presidential Messages,* 78–79. See also the federal role explained in Taft, *Popular Government,* 95–98.
52. See, for example, Donald J. Pisani, "Conflict over Conservation: The Reclamation Service and the Tahoe Contract," *Western Historical Quarterly* 10 (1979): 167–90; James Penick Jr., "The Age of the Bureaucrat: Another View of the Ballinger-Pinchot Controversy," *Forest History Newsletter* 7 (1963): 15–21; James Penick Jr., "Louis Russell Glavis: A Postscript to the Ballinger-Pinchot Controversy," *Pacific Northwest Quarterly* 55 (1964): 67–75; Elmo R. Richardson, "Conservation as a Political Issue: The Western Progressives' Dilemma, 1909–1912," *Pacific Northwest Quarterly* 49 (1958): 49–54; Elmo R. Richardson, "The Struggle for the Valley: California's Hetch Hetchy Controversy, 1905–1913," *California Historical Society Quarterly* 38 (1959): 249–58; Kendrick A. Clements, "Politics and the Park: San Francisco's Fight for Hetch Hetchy, 1908–1913," *Pacific Historical Review* 48 (1979): 185–215; and Kendrick A. Clements, "Engineers and Conservationists in the Progressive Era," *California History* 58 (1979–80): 282–303. On water power

regulation, see Charles K. McFarland, "The Federal Government and Water Power, 1901–1913: A Legislative Study in the Nascence of Regulation," *Land Economics* 42 (1966): 441–52. On wetlands drainage, see Anthony E. Carlson, "The Other Kind of Reclamation: Wetlands Drainage and National Water Policy, 1902–1912," *Agricultural History* 84 (2010): 451–78. George A. Gonzalez emphasizes elite theory as an explanation of the era's policies. Gonzalez, "The Conservation Policy Network, 1890–1910: The Development and Implementation of 'Practical' Forestry," *Polity* 31 (1998): 269–99. Cf. the response in Clements, "Engineers and Conservationists," 298, using Hetch Hetchy as the vehicle. On the expertise in this field that had developed in the later part of the nineteenth century, see Pisani, "Conflict over Conservation," 170; McFarland, "Federal Government and Water Power"; Clements, "Engineers and Conservationists"; Edwin Layton, "Frederick Haynes Newell and the Revolt of the Engineers," *Midcontinent American Studies Journal* 3 (1962): 17–26; and Penick, "Age of the Bureaucrat," 18–19. William J. Novak offers a similar appeal to recognizing complexity in issue areas and the state in "The Myth of the 'Weak' American State," *American Historical Review* 113 (2008): 769–70.

53. Taft, First Appendix to Second Annual Message, September 5, 1911, in *Presidential Messages*, 92–93.
54. Taft, First Appendix to Second Annual Message, September 5, 1911, in *Presidential Messages*, 98–99.
55. Taft, First Appendix to Second Annual Message, September 5, 1911, in *Presidential Messages*, 99.
56. Taft, First Appendix to Second Annual Message, September 5, 1911, in *Presidential Messages*, 100. See also Penick, *Progressive Politics and Conservation*, 57ff, 171–72.
57. Taft, First Appendix to Second Annual Message, September 5, 1911, in *Presidential Messages*, 100. See also Taft, Special Message, July 26, 1911, in *Presidential Messages*, 126–47.
58. See, for example, Milkis, *Theodore Roosevelt*, 29–30, and Arnold, *Remaking the Presidency*, 119–31. For reviews of the Ballinger-Pinchot affair, see Coletta, *Presidency of William Howard Taft*, 77–100, 258–59; Marc Reisner, *Cadillac Desert: The American West and Its Disappearing Water* (New York: Penguin, 1993), 81–84; and Penick, *Progressive Politics and Conservation*, esp. 122, 176, 195–96.
59. Penick, *Progressive Politics and Conservation*, xiii, 30, 52–53, 56–59, 121–22, 148, 185–96. See also Anderson, *Taft*, 72–78; Gould, *Taft Presidency*, 65–78; David H. Burton, *William Howard Taft: In the Public Service* (Malabar, FL: Krieger, 1986), 66–71; and David H. Burton, "The Learned Presidency: Roosevelt, Taft, Wilson," *Presidential Studies Quarterly* 15 (1985): 491–92.
60. Gould, *Taft Presidency*, 66–68.
61. Arnold, *Remaking the Presidency*, 120. See also Morris, *Theodore Rex*, 485–87.
62. Quoted in Bates, "Fulfilling American Democracy," 45; Richardson, "Conservation as a Political Issue," 50.

63. See Penick, "Age of the Bureaucrat," especially the discussion of "Garfield Currency," 20n21.
64. Lurie, *Taft*, 108–17, 136–37, 197; Arnold, *Remaking the Presidency*, 120; Bates, "Fulfilling American Democracy," 42, 44, 45; Pisani, "Conflict over Conservation"; John T. Ganoe, "Some Constitutional and Political Aspects of the Ballinger-Pinchot Controversy," *Pacific Historical Review* 3 (1934): 323–33; Alan B. Gould, "'Trouble Portfolio' to Constructive Conservation: Secretary of the Interior Walter L. Fisher, 1911–1913," *Forest History Newsletter* 16 (1973): 6.
65. Arnold, *Remaking the Presidency*, 117–20; Burton, *Taft: In the Public Service*, 68–69; Penick, *Progressive Politics and Conservation*, 10–11, 44–46, 59ff, 76, 94. On Ballinger's reform background and on the removal of Garfield in favor of a westerner, see Arnold, *Remaking the Presidency*, 117–18, and Coletta, *Presidency of William Howard Taft*, 82–84.
66. Diane T. Putney, "Robert Grosvenor Valentine (1909–12)," in *The Commissioners of Indian Affairs, 1824–1977*, ed. Robert M. Kvasnicka and Herman J. Viola (Lincoln: University of Nebraska Press, 1979), 236–37.
67. For summaries and discussion of the Ballinger-Pinchot controversy, see Ganoe, "Some Constitutional and Political Aspects"; Bates, "Fulfilling American Democracy," 44–45; Penick, "Age of the Bureaucrat"; Gould, "'Trouble Portfolio,'" 4–5; Pisani, "Conflict over Conservation," 181n36. Bates, "Fulfilling American Democracy," offers excellent background on Pinchot and his early career (33–34). See also Miller, "Greening," and Gonzalez, "Conservation Policy Network."
68. Melody Webb Grauman, "Kennecott: Alaskan Origins of a Copper Empire, 1900–1938," *Western Historical Quarterly* 9 (1978): 202–3; Duffy, *Taft*, 246–51; Penick, *Progressive Politics and Conservation*, 137, 172–73.
69. Taft did not help himself by clumsily handling the disclosure of a backdated report during the investigation. See Coletta, *Presidency of William Howard Taft*, 96–97, and Penick, *Progressive Politics and Conservation*, 158–64.
70. For discussion of Glavis's problems after this event—ethical, legal, and otherwise—see Penick, "Louis Russell Glavis."
71. Quoted in Duffy, *Taft*, 249.
72. Gould, *Taft Presidency*, 66–68.
73. Penick, "Age of the Bureaucrat," 16, 21. See also Gonzalez, "Conservation Policy Network."
74. Penick, "Age of the Bureaucrat," 19, 21; Ganoe, "Some Constitutional and Political Aspects."
75. Penick, "Age of the Bureaucrat," 16.
76. Richardson, "Struggle for the Valley," esp. 253–54; Ballard, "The Administrative Theory of William Howard Taft," 68–69; Clements, "Politics and the Park," esp. 212–13; Clements, "Engineers and Conservationists," esp. 299; Gould, "'Trouble Portfolio,'" 10–12.
77. Harold L. Ickes, *Not Guilty: An Official Inquiry into the Charges Made by Glavis and Pinchot against Richard A. Ballinger, Secretary of the Interior, 1909–1911* (Washington, DC: U.S. Government Printing Office, 1940). See also Gould,

Taft Presidency, 69; John F. Kennedy, *Profiles in Courage* (1956; reprint New York: Harper, 2006), 195; Penick, "Louis Russell Glavis," 75; Richard Polenberg, "The Great Conservation Contest," *Forest History Newsletter* 10 (1967): 22–23; and Ganoe, "Some Constitutional and Political Aspects," 329, 333.

78. Quoted in Anderson, *Taft,* 76.
79. Gould, "'Trouble Portfolio.'" Penick writes that reforms at the Reclamation Service under Taft and Wilson followed the course that Ballinger had charted. Penick, "Age of the Bureaucrat," 20–21. See also the discussion in Bates, "Fulfilling American Democracy," 39–42.
80. Lurie, *Taft,* 114; see also 108–17. Cf. Robert E. Ficken, "Gifford Pinchot Men: Pacific Northwest Lumbermen and the Conservation Movement, 1902–1910," *Western Historical Quarterly* 13 (1982): 165–78, reprinted in Robert F. Himmelberg, ed., *Business and Government in America since 1870,* vol. 3, *Growth of the Regulatory State, 1900–1917* (New York: Garland, 1994), 98–100. See also Penick, *Progressive Politics and Conservation,* 33–40, 182–96, and Carl Sferrazza Anthony, *Nellie Taft: The Unconventional First Lady of the Ragtime Era* (New York: William Morrow, 2005), 353.
81. Taft, *The United States and Peace,* 173–82; Taft, *Popular Government,* 154–59.
82. Taft, Inaugural Address, March 4, 1909, in *Fellow Citizens: The Penguin Book of U.S. Presidential Inaugural Addresses,* ed. Robert V. Remini and Terry Golway (New York: Penguin, 2008), 273; Taft, *The United States and Peace,* 169. Generally, see E. James Hindman, "The General Arbitration Treaties of William Howard Taft," *Historian* 36 (1973): 52–65, and John P. Campbell, "Taft, Roosevelt, and the Arbitration Treaties of 1911," *Journal of American History* 53 (1966): 279–98.
83. Campbell, "Taft, Roosevelt," 283; Hindman, "General Arbitration Treaties."
84. Anderson, *Taft,* 275–83, 281 (quotation); Campbell, "Taft, Roosevelt," 280–91.
85. Anderson, *Taft,* 276.
86. See, for example, Gould, *Taft Presidency,* 160–61. See also Campbell, "Taft, Roosevelt," 295–97.
87. Anderson, *Taft,* 276.
88. Taft, *Popular Government,* 157, 159; Taft, *The United States and Peace,* 171; Anderson, *Taft,* 281; Walter E. Leuchtenburg, "Progressivism and Imperialism: The Progressive Movement and American Foreign Policy, 1898–1916," *Mississippi Valley Historical Review* 39 (1952): 491–92.
89. Taft, *The United States and Peace,* 176–77; see also 180.
90. Duffy, *Taft,* 305.
91. Anderson, *Taft,* 278.
92. Quoted in Anderson, *Taft,* 281.
93. Anderson, *Taft,* 282; Taft, *The United States and Peace,* 170; Taft, *President and His Powers,* 82–84.
94. See Anderson, *Taft,* 282.
95. See Taft, *Popular Government,* 157–59; Anderson, *Taft,* 282; and David H. Burton, *William Howard Taft: Confident Peacemaker* (Philadelphia: St. Joseph's University Press, 2004), 80–82.

96. Quoted in Duffy, *Taft*, 270. See also Taft, *The United States and Peace*, 180, 197–200; Taft, *President and His Powers*, 83; Taft, Second Annual Message, December 6, 1910, in *Presidential Messages*, 7–8; Taft, Special Message, January 8, 1913, in *Presidential Messages*, 353–55.
97. Quoted in Helen Herron Taft, *Recollections of Full Years* (New York: Dodd, Mead, 1914), 394–95.
98. Quoted in Lurie, *Taft*, 167, 175; see also 172.
99. Quoted in Anderson, *Taft*, 73.

Conclusion

1. See, for example, Elena Kagan, "Presidential Administration," *Harvard Law Review* 114 (2000–2001): 2253–80.
2. Woodrow Wilson, *Congressional Government: A Study in American Politics* (1885; reprint New York: Meridian, 1960), esp. 173–92.
3. Kagan, "Presidential Administration," 2255.
4. Sidney M. Milkis, "The Presidency and American Political Development: The Advent—and Illusion—of an Executive-Centered Democracy," in *The Oxford Handbook of American Political Development*, ed. Richard M. Valelly et al. (New York: Oxford University Press, 2016), 287.
5. Stephen Skowronek, *Building a New American State: The Expansion of National Administrative Capacities, 1877–1920* (Cambridge: Cambridge University Press, 1982); Daniel P. Carpenter, *The Forging of Bureaucratic Autonomy: Reputations, Networks, and Policy Innovation in Executive Agencies, 1862–1928* (Princeton, NJ: Princeton University Press, 2001); Richard Franklin Bensel, *Yankee Leviathan: The Origins of Central State Authority in America, 1859–1877* (Cambridge: Cambridge University Press, 1990).
6. See, for example, Max M. Edling and Peter J. Kastor, eds., *Washington's Government: Charting the Origins of the Federal Administration* (Charlottesville: University of Virginia Press, 2021), and Jerry L. Mashaw, *Creating the Administrative Constitution: The Lost One Hundred Years of American Administrative Law* (New Haven, CT: Yale University Press, 2012).
7. See, for example, Terry M. Moe and William G. Howell, "The Presidential Power of Unilateral Action," *Journal of Law, Economics, & Organization* 15 (1999): 161–65; George C. Edwards III and Stephen J. Wayne, *Presidential Leadership: Politics and Policy Making*, 7th ed. (Belmont, CA: Thomson Wadsworth, 2006), chap. 14, esp. 485–86; and Erin Peterson, "Presidential Power Surges," *Harvard Law Today*, July 17, 2019, https://hls.harvard.edu/today/presidential-power-surges/.
8. Moe and Howell, "The Presidential Power of Unilateral Action," 155ff. On the state and war, see William J. Novak, "The Myth of the 'Weak' American State," *American Historical Review* 113 (2008): 752–72; William J. Novak, "Long Live the Myth of the Weak State? A Response to Adams, Gerstle, and Witt," *American Historical Review* 115 (2010): 798–99.

9. See, for example, Edward G. Carmines and Matthew Fowler, "The Temptation of Executive Authority: How Increased Polarization and the Decline in Legislative Capacity Have Contributed to the Expansion of Presidential Power," *Indiana Journal of Global Legal Studies* 24 (2017): 369–98, and Sidney M. Milkis and Michael Nelson, *The American Presidency: Origins and Development, 1776-2018*, 8th ed. (Washington, DC: CQ Press, 2019), 563, 573, 589. See also Fang-Yi Chiou and Lawrence S. Rothenberg, *The Enigma of Presidential Power: Parties, Policies and Strategic Uses of Unilateral Action* (Cambridge: Cambridge University Press, 2017), and Fang-Yi Chiou and Lawrence S. Rothenberg, "Presidential Unilateral Action: Partisan Influence and Presidential Power," *Public Choice* 167 (2016): 145–71.
10. Moe and Howell, "Unilateral Action and Presidential Power," 855.
11. William J. Novak, *The People's Welfare: Law and Regulation in Nineteenth-Century America* (Chapel Hill: University of North Carolina Press, 1996).
12. Novak, "The Myth of the 'Weak' American State"; William J. Novak, "A State of Legislatures," *Polity* 40 (2008): 344; Stephen Sawyer and William J. Novak, "Emancipation and the Creation of Modern Liberal States in America and France," *Journal of the Civil War Era* 3 (2013): 467–500. On the persistence of the idea of the "weak" state, see Novak, "Long Live the Myth of the Weak State?" 798–99.
13. For example, see Gregory Ablavsky's discussion of land claim boards in *Federal Ground: Governing Property and Violence in the First U.S. Territories* (New York: Oxford University Press, 2021), 97, 101, 158, 232–33.
14. *Johnson and Graham's Lessee v. McIntosh*, 21 U.S. 543 (1823); "An Act for the Government and Regulation of Seamen in the Merchants Service," July 20, 1790, U.S. Statutes at Large, 351st Congress, 2nd sess., 131–35, https://memory.loc.gov/ll/llsl/001/0200/02550131.tif; "An Act for the Relief of Sick and Disabled Seamen," July 16, 1798, U.S. Statutes at Large, 5th Congress, 2nd sess., 605–6, https://memory.loc.gov/ll/llsl/001/0700/07290605.tif. On Trade and Intercourse Acts, see, for example, "An Act to Regulate Trade and Intercourse with the Indian Tribes," July 22, 1790, U.S. Statutes at Large, 1st Congress, 2nd sess., 137–38, https://memory.loc.gov/cgi-bin/ampage?collId=llsl&fileName=001/llsl001.db&recNum=260; "An act to Regulate Trade and Intercourse with the Indian Tribes, and to Preserve Peace on the Frontiers," March 30, 1802, U.S. Statutes at Large, 7th Congress, 1st sess., 139–46, https://memory.loc.gov/ll/llsl/002/0100/01770139.tif; and "An Act to Regulate Trade and Intercourse with the Indian Tribes, and to Preserve Peace on the Frontiers," June 30, 1834, U.S. Statutes at Large, 23rd Congress, 1st sess., 729–35, https://memory.loc.gov/ll/llsl/004/0700/07770729.tif.
15. Novak, *People's Welfare*, 245, 245–46, 247.
16. Novak, *People's Welfare*, 240, 241, 244–45 (quotations), 241–48.
17. For example, see Ablavsky, *Federal Ground*.
18. Robert J. Kaczorowski, *The Politics of Judicial Interpretation: The Federal Courts, Department of Justice, and Civil Rights, 1866-1876* (New York: Fordham

University Press, 2005); Robert G. McCloskey, *The American Supreme Court*, 6th ed., revised by Sanford Levinson (Chicago: University of Chicago Press, 2016).

19. William Howard Taft, Special Message, February 20, 1912, in in *The Collected Works of William Howard Taft*, vol. 4, *Presidential Messages to Congress*, ed. David H. Burton (Athens: University of Ohio Press, 2002), 251–52 (hereafter *Presidential Messages*); Jonathan Lurie, *William Howard Taft: The Travails of a Progressive Conservative* (Cambridge: Cambridge University Press, 2012), 169. The measure passed the Senate but stalled in the House.

20. Quoted in Roy G. Blakey and Gladys C. Blakey, *The Federal Income Tax* (London: Longman, Green, 1940), 54.

21. Taft, Second Annual Message, December 6, 1910, in *Presidential Messages*, 25–26. See also Taft, Third Annual Message, December 5, 1911, in *Presidential Messages*, 159–72. Members of the House recognized the collection and dissemination of data as helping protect stockholders' interests. See Blakey and Blakey, *Federal Income Tax*, 46, 51–52; for precise provisions, see 53–54.

22. Blakey and Blakey, *Federal Income Tax*, 54–55.

23. Marc Winerman, "The Origins of the FTC: Concentration, Cooperation, Control, and Competition," *Antitrust Law Journal* 71 (2003): 1–97; James Penick Jr., *Progressive Politics and Conservation: The Ballinger-Pinchot Affair* (Chicago: University of Chicago Press, 1968), 60, 122, 176, 190, 195; J. Leonard Bates, "Fulfilling American Democracy: The Conservation Movement, 1907 to 1921," *Mississippi Valley Historical Review* 44 (1957): 39–42; James Penick Jr., "The Age of the Bureaucrat: Another View of the Ballinger-Pinchot Controversy," *Forest History Newsletter* 7 (1963): 16–17; Edmund Morris, *Theodore Rex* (New York: Random House, 2001), 422–23; Paolo E. Coletta, *The Presidency of William Howard Taft* (Lawrence: University Press of Kansas, 1973), 77–100; Donald J. Pisani, "Conflict over Conservation: The Reclamation Service and the Tahoe Contract," *Western Historical Quarterly* 10 (1979): 177–81; John T. Ganoe, "Some Constitutional and Political Aspects of the Ballinger-Pinchot Controversy," *Pacific Historical Review* 3 (1934): 324–30; Alan B. Gould, "'Trouble Portfolio' to Constructive Conservation: Secretary of the Interior Walter L. Fisher, 1911–1913," *Forest History Newsletter* 16 (1973): 4–12; Kendrick A. Clements, "Engineers and Conservationists in the Progressive Era," *California History* 58 (1979–1980): 291–97.

24. See also Sawyer and Novak, "Emancipation and the Creation of Modern Liberal States," 472–73.

25. Cf. Nathan Miller, *Star-Spangled Men: America's Ten Worst Presidents* (New York: Touchstone, 1999), 107–8; Kaczorowski, *Politics of Judicial Interpretation*, xxii, 89, 91; William Gillette, *Retreat from Reconstruction, 1869–1879* (Baton Rouge: Louisiana State University Press, 1979), 150–65, 259–73, 294–95, 301–2; Jay Tolson, "The 10 Worst Presidents," CBS News, February 20, 2007, https://www.cbsnews.com/news/the-10-worst-presidents/; "2022 Survey of U.S. Presidents: Presidents Rank Over Time," Siena College Research Institute, June 2022, https://scri.siena.edu/wp-content/uploads/2022/06/PDF-Ranking

-FINAL-REAL.pdf; Ari Hoogenboom, *The Presidency of Rutherford B. Hayes* (Lawrence: University Press of Kansas, 1988), 59; Gregory P. Downs, *After Appomattox: Military Occupation and the Ends of War* (Cambridge, MA: Harvard University Press, 2015), esp. 158, 250–53; Jean Edward Smith, *Grant* (New York: Touchstone, 2001), 18; Joan Waugh, *U.S. Grant: American Hero, American Myth* (Chapel Hill: University of North Carolina Press, 2009); Ron Chernow, *Grant* (New York: Penguin, 2017), inside flap.

Bibliographical Essay

1. For a recent review of scholarship and trends, see Stephen Skowronek, "The Unsettled State of Presidential History," in *Recapturing the Oval Office: New Historical Approaches to the American Presidency*, ed. Brian Balogh and Bruce J. Shulman (Ithaca, NY: Cornell University Press, 2015), 13–33.
2. Michael A. Genovese, *A Presidential Nation: Causes, Consequences, and Cures* (Boulder: Westview Press, 2013), 31. See also, for example, Sidney M. Milkis, "Presidents, Refoundings, and the 'Living Constitution,'" in *The Presidency: Facing Constitutional Crossroads*, ed. Michael Nelson and Barbara A. Perry (Charlottesville: University of Virginia Press, 2021), 200–226; Saikrishna Bangalore Prakash, "The Living Presidency: Always at a Crossroads," in Nelson and Perry, eds., *The Presidency*, 7–27.
3. Cass R. Sunstein, "An Eighteenth Century Presidency in a Twenty-First Century World," *Arkansas Law Review* 48 (1995): 3, 5, 19.
4. Kenneth R. Mayer, *With the Stroke of a Pen: Executive Orders and Presidential Power* (Princeton, NJ: Princeton University Press, 2001), 113. See also Peri E. Arnold, *Making the Managerial Presidency: Comprehensive Reorganization Planning, 1905–1996*, 2nd ed. (Lawrence: University Press of Kansas, 1998), 10–11.
5. Arnold, *Making the Managerial Presidency*, 7, vii, xiii. See also Peri E. Arnold, *Remaking the Presidency: Roosevelt, Taft, and Wilson, 1901–1916* (Lawrence: University Press of Kansas, 2009), 10–17.
6. Peri E. Arnold, "Effecting a Progressive Presidency: Roosevelt, Taft, and the Pursuit of Strategic Resources," *Studies in American Political Development* 17 (2003): 70, 72. See also Daniel P. Carpenter, *The Forging of Bureaucratic Autonomy: Reputations, Networks, and Policy Innovation in Executive Agencies, 1862–1928* (Princeton, NJ: Princeton University Press, 2001).
7. Arnold, "Effecting a Progressive Presidency," 62.
8. Arnold, "Effecting a Progressive Presidency," 72.
9. Hampton L. Carson, "Andrew Athinson Humphreys, Brigadier-General U.S. Army, Brevet Major-General U.S. Army, Chief of Engineers," *Proceedings of the American Philosophical Society* 22 (1885): 50, 63–68.
10. Arnold, "Effecting a Progressive Presidency," 71. Cf. William H. Goetzmann, *Exploration and Empire: The Explorer and the Scientist in the Winning of the American West* (Austin: Texas State Historical Association, 2000), chaps. 14–15. The Corps of Topographical Engineers dates back to 1838, and its split into a

separate unit in the War Department dates to 1831. See, in general, William H. Goetzmann, *Army Exploration in the American West, 1803–1863* (Lincoln: University of Nebraska Press, 1959).

11. Albert Lepawsky, "Water Resources and American Federalism," *American Political Science Review* 44 (1950): 631–49; Todd Shallat, "Water and Bureaucracy: Origins of the Federal Responsibility for Water Resources, 1787–1838," *Natural Resources Journal* 32 (1992): 23–24.
12. Arnold, "Effecting a Progressive Presidency," 63.
13. Mayer, *With the Stroke of a Pen*, 24.
14. Richard W. Waterman, "The Administrative Presidency, Unilateral Power, and the Unitary Executive Theory," *Presidential Studies Quarterly* 39 (2009): 5.
15. Lewis L. Gould, *The Modern American Presidency* (Lawrence: University Press of Kansas, 2003), xii.
16. Arnold, *Making the Managerial Presidency*, 7; see also 9–10; Arnold, "Effecting a Progressive Presidency," 63; Morton Keller, *America's Three Regimes: A New Political History* (New York: Oxford University Press, 2007). Lewis L. Gould makes numbers and formal positions like a chief of staff central elements in defining the modern president. Gould, *Modern American Presidency*, xi–xii.
17. Paul C. Light, *The True Size of Government* (Washington, DC: Brookings Institution Press, 1999).
18. Leonard D. White, *The Jeffersonians: A Study in Administrative History, 1801–1829* (New York: Free Press, 1951), 498n4. For a review essay focused on Leonard White's administrative histories, see Alisdair Roberts, "Review: The Path Not Taken: Leonard White and the Macrodynamics of Administrative Development," *Public Administration Review* 69 (2009): 764–75.
19. Keller, *America's Three Regimes*, 4–5.
20. Arnold, *Making the Managerial Presidency*, vii, xiv, vii; other such references appear throughout the book. Administrative reorganizations happened throughout the nineteenth century, including efforts focused on Indian Office leadership (1824), the creation of what would become the Topographical Engineers (1831), and so on. See David H. DeJong, *Paternalism to Partnership: The Administration of Indian Affairs, 1786–2021* (Lincoln: University of Nebraska Press, 2022); Henry Barrett Learned, "The Establishment of the Secretaryship of the Interior," *American Historical Review* 16 (1911): esp. 760–62; Robert G. Angevine, "Individuals, Organizations, and Engineering: U.S. Army Officers and the American Railroads, 1827–1838," *Technology and Culture* 42 (2001): 293–94, 294n3, 299–307, on War Department reorganizations between 1818 and 1825. Angevine writes, "The rise of system and uniformity as organizing principles within the army paralleled the growth of modern management" (293–94; see also 294n3). Calhoun created the Office of Indian Affairs in the War Department in 1824, eight years before Congress authorized a commissioner of Indian affairs and twenty-five years before the office was moved to the new Interior Department and renamed the Bureau of Indian Affairs. Christine Bolt, *American Indian Policy and American Reform: Case*

Studies of the Campaign to Assimilate the American Indians (London: Allen and Unwin, 1987), 54–55. Some reorganizations were pursued over the course of years, despite presidential support. John Quincy Adams recommended an additional executive department in his First Annual Message, to split State and what would eventually become Interior, separating foreign affairs and domestic policy. Adams followed President Madison's recommendation here, as did Andrew Jackson when he became president, and it is worth noting that both Madison and Adams served as secretary of state prior to becoming president. The House appointed a special committee to examine Adams's request, and Learned speculated that a bill was probably in the works in January 1826, but nothing came of the matter during Adams's presidency.

21. Jerry L. Mashaw, *Creating the Administrative Constitution: The Lost One Hundred Years of American Administrative Law* (New Haven, CT: Yale University Press, 2012); Max M. Edling, *A Hercules in the Cradle: War, Money, and the American State, 1783–1867* (Chicago: University of Chicago Press, 2014); Max M. Edling and Peter J. Kastor, eds., *Washington's Government: Charting the Origins of the Federal Administration* (Charlottesville: University of Virginia Press, 2021).
22. Terry M. Moe and William G. Howell, "Unilateral Action and Presidential Power: A Theory," *Presidential Studies Quarterly* 29 (December 1999): 851. See also Terry M. Moe and William G. Howell, "The Presidential Power of Unilateral Action," *Journal of Law, Economics, & Organization* 15 (1999), 176.
23. Moe and Howell, "The Presidential Power of Unilateral Action," 133. See also Moe and Howell, "Unilateral Action and Presidential Power," 851.
24. Fang-Yi Chiou and Lawrence S. Rothenberg, *The Enigma of Presidential Power: Parties, Policies and Strategic Uses of Unilateral Action* (Cambridge: Cambridge University Press, 2017), 6.
25. Mayer, *With the Stroke of a Pen*, 4.
26. Phillip J. Cooper, *By Order of the President: The Use & Abuse of Executive Direct Action* (Lawrence: University Press of Kansas, 2002), 16.
27. For example, see Raymond T. Williams, "Unilateral Politics in the Traditional Era: Significant Executive Orders and Proclamations, 1861–1944," *Presidential Studies Quarterly* 50 (2020): 147–48.
28. Mayer, *With the Stroke of a Pen*, 51, 75.
29. Mayer, *With the Stroke of a Pen*, 10.
30. Cooper, *By Order of the President*, 17; Mayer, *With the Stroke of a Pen*, 66.
31. Mayer, *With the Stroke of a Pen*, 7.
32. See *Executive Orders Relating to Indian Reservations from May 14, 1855 to July 1, 1912* (Washington, DC: US Government Printing Office, 1932), 43–44; Ulysses S. Grant, *The Papers of Ulysses S. Grant*, ed. John Y. Simon et al. (Carbondale: Southern Illinois University Press, 1967–2012), 21:201–2.
33. Cooper, *By Order of the President*, 13–14.
34. See J P Leary, *The Story of Act 31: How Native History Came to Wisconsin Classrooms* (Madison: Wisconsin Historical Society Press, 2018); on Taylor's

order, see 10–19; *Minnesota v. Mille Lacs Band of Chippewa Indians,* 119 S.Ct. 1187 143 L. Ed. 2d 270.
35. See Mayer, *With the Stroke of a Pen,* 85 (quotation), 29–31, 33, 85ff.
36. See Williams, "Unilateral Politics," 152–53.
37. David E. Wilkins, *American Indian Politics and the American Political System* (Lanham, MD: Rowman and Littlefield, 2002), 84–85.
38. Cooper, *By Order of the President,* 201, 117, 119.
39. Cooper, *By Order of the President,* 121.
40. Williams, "Unilateral Politics," 153.
41. Cooper, *By Order of the President,* 37.
42. Mayer, *With the Stroke of a Pen,* 76–79.
43. Cf. Jeffrey K. Tulis, *The Rhetorical Presidency* (Princeton, NJ: Princeton University Press, 1987), 52. Tulis misrepresented Lincoln's Emancipation Proclamation, suggesting that "he does not justify his action in the proclamation. . . . Lincoln's example represents the pure case of the proclamation as command." In fact, the preliminary proclamation (1862) and the final implementing proclamation (1863) rely on an argument based explicitly in military necessity, congressional acts, and justice. See Tulis, *Rhetorical Presidency,* 52.
44. Jeremy D. Bailey and Brandon Rottinghaus, "The Development of Unilateral Power and the Problem of the Power to Warn: Washington through McKinley," *Presidential Studies Quarterly* 43 (2013): 189–91, 190–91 (quotation). See also Ryan Lee Teten, *The Evolutionary Rhetorical Presidency: Tracing the Changes in Presidential Address and Power* (New York: Peter Lang, 2011).
45. Graham G. Dodds, *Take Up Your Pen: Unilateral Presidential Directives in American Politics* (Philadelphia: University of Pennsylvania Press, 2013), chaps. 1, 4, pp. 119 (quotation). On proclamations and Indian lands generally, though, see Dodds, *Take Up Your Pen,* 101–3. On Washington and proclamations related to Creek treaties, see Dodds, *Take Up Your Pen,* 101. On Washington's direct engagement in Indian affairs and management of the executive branch, see, for example, *Writings of George Washington,* ed. John C. Fitzpatrick (Washington, DC: U.S. Government Printing Office, 1931–44), 34:306, 308, 309, 319, 366. For a very usable framework for study of executive actions, see Cooper, *By Order of the President,* chaps. 2, 7, 8, pp. 137–42.
46. Sunstein, "An Eighteenth Century Presidency," 10–11. See also, for example, Prakash, "Living Presidency," 13.
47. Prakash, "Living Presidency," 12.
48. Abbot Smith, "Mr. Madison's War: An Unsuccessful Experiment in the Conduct of National Policy," *Political Science Quarterly* 57 (1942): 232; David Gray Adler, "The Constitution and Presidential Warmaking: The Enduring Debate," *Political Science Quarterly* 103 (1988): 17. On St. Clair's defeat, see, for example, Colin G. Calloway, *The Victory with No Name: The Native American Defeat of the First American Army* (New York: Oxford University Press, 2015).
49. Adler, "Constitution and Presidential Warmaking," 21–22.

50. See, for example, Adler, "Constitution and Presidential Warmaking," esp. 17, 26–27, 35–36; Simeon E. Baldwin, "The Share of the President of the United States in a Declaration of War," *American Journal of International Law* 12 (1918): 2–3; Smith, "Mr. Madison's War," 232; and Milkis, "Presidents, Refoundings, and the 'Living Constitution,'" 206. See also Daniel J. Tichenor, "Historical Set Points and the Development of U.S. Presidential Emergency Power," *Perspectives on Politics* 11 (2013): 769–88, for an analysis of the ahistorical nature of studies of the president's emergency powers.
51. William D. Adler, "'Generalissimo of the Nation': War Making and the Presidency in the Early Republic," *Presidential Studies Quarterly* 43 (2013): 413; Robert J. Delahunty and John Yoo, "Making War," *Cornell Law Review* 93 (2007): 123. See also Adler, "Constitution and Presidential Warmaking," and Smith, "Mr. Madison's War."
52. Arthur M. Schlesinger Jr., *The Imperial Presidency* (New York: Popular Library, 1974), 61.
53. Norman A. Graebner, "The President as Commander in Chief: A Study in Power," *Journal of Military History* 57 (1993): 116.
54. Graebner, "President as Commander in Chief," 117.
55. Terry L. Anderson, *Sovereign Nations or Reservations? An Economic History of American Indians* (San Francisco: Pacific Research Institute for Public Policy, 1995), 70.
56. Ira Katznelson, "Flexible Capacity: The Military and Early American State-building," in *Shaped by War and Trade: International Influences on American Political Development*, ed. Ira Katznelson and Martin Shefter (Princeton, NJ: Princeton University Press, 2002), 91–93, 98–99. See also Harry M. Ward, *The Department of War, 1781–1795* (Pittsburgh: University of Pittsburgh Press, 1962); Francis Paul Prucha, *The Sword of the Republic: The United States Army on the Frontier, 1783–1846* (Bloomington: University of Indiana Press, 1977); Mark R. Wilson, *The Business of Civil War: Military Mobilization and the State, 1861–1865* (Baltimore: Johns Hopkins University Press, 2006); and Edling, *A Hercules in the Cradle*.
57. Graebner, "President as Commander in Chief," 117.
58. Moe and Howell, "The Presidential Power of Unilateral Action," 164 (table 1); Francis Paul Prucha, *American Indian Treaties: The History of a Political Anomaly* (Berkeley: University of California Press, 1997), appendix B.
59. See, for example, Delahunty and Yoo, "Making War"; John C. Yoo, "War and Constitutional Text," *University of Chicago Law Review* 69 (2002): 1639–84; Adler, "'Generalissimo of the Nation'"; Saikrishna Bangalore Prakash, "The Separation and Overlap of War and Military Powers," *Texas Law Review* 87 (2008): 314–15, 322–24, 330, 334–40; Saikrishna Prakash, "A Two-Front War," *Cornell Law Review* 93 (2007): 204, 213–17; and Edling and Kastor, eds., *Washington's Government*.
60. Mayer, *With the Stroke of a Pen*, 20. See also Sunstein, "An Eighteenth Century Presidency," 8.

61. George C. Edwards III and Stephen J. Wayne, *Presidential Leadership: Politics and Policy Making*, 7th ed. (Belmont: Thomson Wadsworth, 2006), 410. See also Thomas E. Patterson, *We the People: An Introduction to American Government*, 14th ed. (New York: McGraw-Hill, 2022), 347.
62. Stephen J. Rockwell, "Indian Affairs and the Relentless American State," in Edling and Kastor, eds., *Washington's Government*, 134–70. See also David K. Nichols, *The Myth of the Modern Presidency* (University Park: Pennsylvania State University Press, 1994).
63. Jeffrey E. Cohen, *The President's Legislative Policy Agenda, 1789–2002* (Cambridge: Cambridge University Press, 2012), 14–18, 154, 30; see also 53, 97–139.
64. Tulis, *Rhetorical Presidency*; Jeffrey K. Tulis, "The Two Constitutional Presidencies," in *The Presidency and the Political System*, 11th ed., ed. Michael Nelson (Thousand Oaks, CA: CQ Press, 2018), 1–33.
65. Tulis, *Rhetorical Presidency*, 4, 5.
66. See, for example, Barbara A. Perry and Stefanie Georgakis Abbott, "The Personal Presidency at a Constitutional Crossroads," in Nelson and Perry, eds., *The Presidency*, 137–53; Daphna Renan, "The President's Two Bodies," *Columbia Law Review* 120 (2020): 1148; David A. Crockett, "*The Rhetorical Presidency*: Still Standing Tall," *Presidential Studies Quarterly* 39 (2009): 932–40; Michael Nelson, ed., *The Evolving Presidency: Landmark Documents*, 6th ed. (Thousand Oaks, CA: Sage, 2019), 44; Edwards and Wayne, *Presidential Leadership*, 9–10, 154–92; and Patterson, *We the People*, 348, 358–60.
67. Ryan L. Teten, "Evolution of the Modern Rhetorical Presidency: Presidential Presentation and Development of the State of the Union Address," *Presidential Studies Quarterly* 33 (2003): 334; see also 336.
68. Michael Nelson, "Crossroads of the (c)onstitutional Presidency: How Ten Extraconstitutional Landmarks Shaped the Office," in Nelson and Perry, eds., *The Presidency*, 38.
69. Nelson, "Crossroads of the (c)onstitutional Presidency," 31. See also George Washington, First Inaugural Address, April 30, 1789, in *Fellow Citizens: The Penguin Book of U.S. Presidential Inaugural Addresses*, ed. Robert V. Remini and Terry Golway (New York: Penguin, 2008), 4–7; Thomas Jefferson, Second Inaugural Address, March 4, 1805, in Remini and Golway, eds., *Fellow Citizens*, 30–34; Milkis, "Presidents, Refoundings, and the 'Living Constitution,'" 208–9; and Adams, Inaugural Address, March 4, 1825, in Remini and Golway, eds., *Fellow Citizens*, 73–80.
70. Teten, "Evolution of the Modern Rhetorical Presidency," 337, 341.
71. Tulis, *Rhetorical Presidency*. See also Teten, "Evolution of the Modern Rhetorical Presidency."
72. Ryan Lee Teten, "'We the People': The 'Modern' Rhetorical Popular Address of the Presidents during the Founding Period," *Political Research Quarterly* 60 (2007): 669–82; Ryan Lee Teten, "The Evolution of the Rhetorical Presidency and Getting Past the Traditional/Modern Divide," *Presidential Studies Quarterly* 38 (2008): 308–14; Teten, *Evolutionary Rhetorical Presidency*.

73. Mel Laracey, *Presidents and the People: The Partisan Story of Going Public* (College Station: Texas A&M University Press, 2002); Jennifer Rose Hopper, "Reexamining the Nineteenth-Century Presidency and Partisan Press: The Case of President Grant and the Whiskey Ring Scandal," *Social Science History* 42 (2018): 109–33; David Zarefsky, "Presidential Rhetoric and the Power of Definition," *Presidential Studies Quarterly* 34 (2004): 607–19; David Zarefsky, "Lincoln's 1862 Annual Message: A Paradigm of Rhetorical Leadership," *Rhetoric and Public Affairs* 3 (2000): 5–14; Daphna Renan, "Presidential Norms and Article II," *Harvard Law Review* 131 (2018): 2231–33; Samuel Kernell, *Going Public: New Strategies of Presidential Leadership*, 2nd ed. (Washington, DC: CQ Press, 1993).

74. Tulis, *Rhetorical Presidency*, 5.

75. Abraham Lincoln, Speech at Pittsburgh, Pennsylvania, February 15, 1861, in *The Collected Works of Abraham Lincoln*, vol. 4, ed. Roy P. Basler (New Brunswick, NJ: Rutgers University Press, 1953), 210–15. This is the same source cited by Tulis.

76. Lincoln, Speech at Pittsburgh, Pennsylvania, February 15, 1861, in Basler, ed., *Collected Works*, 213.

77. Tulis, *Rhetorical Presidency*, 5–6.

78. Rockwell, "Indian Affairs and the Relentless American State."

79. Laracey, *Presidents and the People*; Kernell, *Going Public*. See also the discussion in Crockett, "*The Rhetorical Presidency*: Still Standing Tall," 934–37.

80. Tulis, *Rhetorical Presidency*, 55. See also Arnold, "Effecting a Progressive Presidency," 66.

81. George Washington, First Annual Message, January 8, 1790, American Presidency Project, https://www.presidency.ucsb.edu/documents/first-annual-address-congress-0; Washington, Third Annual Message, October 25, 1791, American Presidency Project, https://www.presidency.ucsb.edu/documents/third-annual-address-congress-0; Washington to John Jay, November 1, 1794, in Fitzpatrick, ed., *Writings*, 34:18; Washington to Alexander Hamilton, October 29, 1795, in Fitzpatrick, ed., *Writings*, 34:351–52; Rockwell, "Indian Affairs and the Relentless American State"; Frank T. Reuter, *Trials and Triumphs: George Washington's Foreign Policy* (Fort Worth: Texas Christian University Press, 1983), 172–73, 199.

For his communication with individuals and organizations, see, for example, many of Washington's letters reprinted in Fitzpatrick, ed., *Writings*, vol. 34, such as Washington to the secretary of state Edmund Randolph, October 16, 1794 (2–3); to John Jay, November 1, 1794 (15–19); to the towns of East Hampton, Southampton, etc., September 7, 1795 (301); to William Falkener, September 14, 1795 (303); to Jesse Sanders, September 30, 1795 (320); to the citizens of Frederick County, Virginia, December 16, 1795 (395–96); communications contained in *The Papers of George Washington*, Presidential Series, ed. W. W. Abbot et. al. (Charlottesville: University Press of Virginia, 1987–), such as Washington to the Delaware Society for Promoting Domestic

Manufacturers, April 19–20, 1789, 2:78–79; Washington to the Judges of the Pennsylvania Supreme Court, April 20, 1789, 2:84–85; Washington to the President and Faculty of the University of Pennsylvania, April 20, 1789, 2:86–87; Washington to the German Lutherans of Pennsylvania, April 1789, 2:179–80; and Laracey, *Presidents and the People*.

82. On southern tours by Washington and Monroe, see E. Merton Coulter, "Presidential Visits to Georgia during Ante-Bellum Times," *Georgia Historical Quarterly* 55 (1971): 329–64. Coulter mentioned Monroe's discussing defense policy at a stop in Georgia (338).
83. Crockett, "*The Rhetorical Presidency*: Still Standing Tall," 935, 937.
84. Roger B. Porter, "Presidential Power and Public Policy," in Nelson, ed., *Presidency and the Political System*, 516.
85. Teten, "'We the People'"; Teten, "Evolution of the Modern Rhetorical Presidency."
86. Laracey, *Presidents and the People*, 12, 6. Laracey excludes George Washington, John Quincy Adams, and Ulysses S. Grant from his tally of presidents who went public; see *Presidents and the People*, 141 (table 2) and chap. 6 generally, as well as 12, 15, 66, 120–21, 143.

INDEX

Act for the Government and Regulation of Seamen in the Merchants Service (1790), 216
Act for the Relief of Sick and Disabled Seamen (1798), 216
Adams-Onis Treaty (1819). *See* Transcontinental Treaty
Adams, Charles Francis, 35, 115–16
Adams, John, 16, 38, 44, 86
Adams, John Quincy: as abolitionist, 74; administrative leadership, 35–36, 45–47, 52, 56–62, 76–78, 81–84; and administrative reorganization, 19, 56–57; 58, 78, 229; and Amelia Island, 18, 59; and *Amistad*, 21–23, 24, 78; and annual messages, 54, 57, 60, 62, 78, 84–85, 88–91, 243; appointments, use of, 10, 45–46, 54–55, 57–58, 59, 77, 80, 80–83; and Asia, 17, 18; and assassins, 35; attitudes toward Indigenous peoples, 59–60, 65, 67, 68, 69, 69–70; and bankruptcy legislation, 42, 44; and census (1820), 19; and Samuel Chase, impeachment of, 15–16, 58; and Cherokee constitution, 50–51; and Cherokees in Arkansas, 51–52, 53–54; and China, 18; and coastal defense, 56; collaboration, 63; compared with Grant, 26, 28, 92, 109, 122, 123, 127, 147–48; compared with Taft, 155, 178, 183; confidence in own accomplishments, 36, 37, 42, and Congress, 40–41, 42, 43, 44–45, 45–46, 47–52, 53–55, 57–58, 58–62, 66–67, 70, 71–72, 73, 75, 76, 78–80, 84–91, 215, 228, 239–40, 242–43; in Congress, 6, 13, 14–15, 19–21, 24, 59, 74, 78, 214; and conservation, 17, 61–62 ; and Constitution, 20, 38, 39, 50, 59, 60, 62, 64, 65–66, 69–72, 73, 74–75, 76, 79–80, 82, 83–84, 84–91; and continuity in office, 56–57, 81–83; and courts, 15, 16, 19, 22, 58, 215; and Creeks, 35, 50, 56, 60, 63, 64–73, 213, 237; and Creek Agency, 60; delegates authority, 48, 57–58, 77–84; as diplomat, 10, 13, 14, 16–19, 23, 47–52, 73; and diplomacy, 73, 78–80, 81; and domestic affairs, 38–47; and education, 19–20, 38, 42, 44–45, 47, 60, 88, 263n77; effectiveness as president, 36–38; and embargo, 15, 23; and executive action, 7, 9–10, 12, 43, 58, 59–62, 64–73, 74, 76–84, 91, 92; and First Amendment, 20–21; and fisheries agreements, 17–18, 226, 232; and Florida, 17, 18, 19, 35, 40, 49, 50, 56, 59, 60, 61–62, 87, 214; and Florida live oak farm, 61–62; and Force Bill (1833), 59; and foreign affairs, 52–56; and gag rule, 13, 14, 20–21, 23, 24; and Gallatin Report, 39, 42; and Georgia-Creek conflict, 50, 63, 64–73, 91, 213, 237; and government, role of, 38, 39, 84–91; and hidden-hand presidency, 10, 74–84, 91, 244; Inaugural Address, 84–88, 240, 243; and independent judiciary, 15–16, 58; and Indian affairs, 10, 40–41, 47–52, 55–56, 58, 59–60, 64–73, 78, 90; and Indian removal, 52, 65; and interbranch collaboration, 58; and internal improvements, 10, 15, 35, 36, 37–44, 47, 58, 63, 80–84, 84–91, 216, 218, 221, 239, 240, 242, 244; and Latin America, 18, 54, 203; leadership, 6, 9–10, 34, 40–41, 45, 51–52, 54–55, 57–62, 63–91; legacy, 220–21; legislative initiatives, 6, 8–9, 9–10, 36, 37, 40, 42–43, 44, 59–60, 61–62, 63, 72, 73, 84–91; and Louisiana Purchase, 6, 15–16, 18–19, 23, 214; and John McLean, 58, 81–83, 221; and metric system, 19, 163; and Mexican War, 24; and military, 35, 40, 42, 53, 56, 59, 66, 68–73, 86, 89; as minister to Great Britain, 16–17; as minister to Prussia, 16; as minister to Russia, 16; and Monroe Doctrine, 6, 18, 54, 214;

319

320 INDEX

Adams, John Quincy (*continued*)
and moral suasion, 84–91; and national supremacy, 10, 47–48, 49, 52, 64–73, 83, 91, 218, 244; as nationalist, 15, 52; and naval academy, 19, 37, 42, 78, 89; and naval observatory, 37; and Navy, U.S., 57, 58, 60, 61–62, 78–80, 87, 90; and Negro Seamen's Acts, 19; and news media, 46, 59, 66, 265n106; and nudity, 46, 261n51; and Pacific Expedition, 35, 43–44, 60, 61, 213, 228, 233, 244; and Panama Congress, 54–55, 59, 80, 221; and pardons, use of, 49, 59; pardons Winnebago leaders, 49, 59; and piracy, 79, 80; and pirates, 18, 78, 79; and Peter Porter, 42, 50, 59–60; and postal network, 39, 41, 58, 77, 80–84, 90; as procedurist, 6, 7, 9–10, 13, 14–25, 33–34, 35–36, 37–38, 44, 45–47, 48, 50, 51–52, 52–53, 54, 56, 57, 63–64, 67, 68, 69–72, 74, 79–80, 81–82, 83–84, 84, 88, 89–91, 220–22; and proclamations, use of, 7, 46–47, 60, 66; and public communication, 8–10, 39, 62, 66, 72, 74, 75, 76, 78, 84–91, 244; and public opinion, 62; and public reputation of the president, 44–45, 46–47, 54–55; and religious freedom, 54; Report on Weights and Measures, 19, 161, 163; and right of petition, 20–21, 23; and rights of neutrals, 16, 79–80; and role of government under the Constitution, 84–91; and scientific research, 19–20, 37, 42–43, 58, 87, 88–89, 90 (*see also specific projects*); and secrecy, 59; as secretary of state, 14, 17–19, 59, 78–79; and Seneca treaty, 49–50, 111; sense of humor, 21, 22; and slavery, 10, 18, 20–24, 37–38, 53, 55, 58, 59, 60, 63, 74–84, 87, 91, 214; and Smithsonian, 19–20, 58; and social policy programs, 35, 36–38, 42–43, 44, 47–48, 52–54, 55–56, 80, 84–91 (*see also specific programs*); as "strong" president, 12, 18, 220; and subscriptions, 46–47; supports presidential power, 16, 18; and Supreme Court, U.S., 21–23, 78–79, 82–83; as synthesist, 18; takes the long view, 20–21, 37, 74, 80–84, 87–91; and Texas, 17, 24; and trade, 16, 17–18, 36, 38, 39, 44, 47–49, 52–53, 56, 84, 90; and Transcontinental Treaty (1819), 17, 18–19, 22; and treaties, 14, 15, 16–19, 21–23, 35, 36, 40–41, 47–56, 59–60, 64–73, 78, 86, 244; and Treaty of Ghent, 16, 22; as US Senator, 14–16; values discretionary authority, 57–58; and warmaking authority, 59; and West Point, administration of, 46–47

Addams, Jane, 163

Addyston Pipe & Steel Co. v. United States, 29, 191

administration, public, 1, 2–4, 25, 30, 36, 45, 47, 52, 57, 81, 82, 83, 95, 105, 109, 113, 114, 124, 126, 131, 140, 141, 144, 146, 152, 160, 165, 168, 173, 178, 196, 199, 200, 210, 211, 212, 222, 224–30, 235–36, 245. *See also specific departments and programs*

administrative reform, 6, 138, 145, 173, 183, 229, 230. *See also* administrative reorganization; *and specific programs and departments*

administrative reorganization, 19, 33, 56–57, 58, 78, 131–32, 138, 139–46, 160–68, 191, 217, 229, 311n20. *See also* administrative reform; *and specific programs and departments*

administrative state, 1–5, 47, 74, 76–78, 86, 90–91, 92, 109–23, 124–53, 157, 160–68, 210–11, 222, 224–30, 234. *See also specific policies*

administrators, public, 1, 37, 40, 42, 57, 61, 64, 91, 102, 112, 114, 140, 144, 155, 184, 200, 201, 202, 211, 226, 227, 230. *See also specific individuals*

Africa, 21, 23, 75, 78–79

African Colonization Society, 80

Agricultural Bureau, U.S., 94

Akerman, Amos, 110, 111, 113–14, 126, 128, 132

Alabama, 42, 64, 66

Alabama claims, 95, 111, 115–19, 120–21, 279n98

Alaska, 102–3, 200, 226; administration of, 112

alcohol, regulation of, 3, 219. *See also* liquor

INDEX   321

Aldrich, Nelson, 187
allotment, 145, 150, 151, 165, 166
American Presidency Project, 102, 103, 232
American System, 39
Amistad (ship), 21–23, 24, 78
ammunition, regulation of, 103, 147
Anderson, Richard Clough, 68
Anglo-American Commercial Convention (1815), 16, 53
Antelope (ship), 78
Anthony, Susan B., 102
Anti-Assessment Act (1872), 105, 275n50
Anti-Bigamy Act (1962), 104
antitrust, 11, 29, 33, 185, 189–92, 193–94, 219, 219–20. *See also* Sherman Antitrust Act
Appomattox, Virginia, 26, 111
Arapahoes, 140
arbitration, 174, 178, 202–5; agreements, 159, 202–5; treaties, 11, 16, 28, 115–16, 168, 183–84, 202–5
Argentina, 174–75
Arizona, 152, 158, 172, 179–81, 213
Arkansas, 26, 35, 40, 49, 50, 51–52, 56, 97, 103, 129
armories, 3
Army Reserve, U.S., 167
Army, U.S., 24, 25, 28, 31, 37, 39, 41, 42, 43, 53, 59, 64, 69, 72, 110, 112, 140, 146–49, 159, 179, 226, 236
Arnell Act (1872), 105
assimilation, of Indigenous peoples, 70, 145, 165, 166
Asia, 17, 18, 28, 31–32, 167, 173–74, 183
Astor, John Jacob, 18
Atkinson, Henry, 49
attorney general, U.S., 35, 103, 113–14, 126, 132, 149, 163–64, 170, 178; conflicts of interest, 35, 256n1. *See also specific attorneys general*
Austria, 53

Babcock, Orville, 120
Bagwell, John, 135
Ballinger, Richard, 167, 195, 198–202, 226, 306n79

Baltimore & Ohio Railroad, 37, 41
bank holiday (1933), 101
Bank of the United States, 5, 45
bankruptcy legislation, 42, 44, 95
Barbour, James, 40, 41, 51–52, 66, 67–68, 69–70, 71, 82
Bassett, Ebenezer Don Carlos, 107
Baxter, Elisha, 129
Belknap, Walter, 106, 107
Bensel, Richard Franklin, 211
Benton, Thomas Hart, 52
Bernard Board, 40, 211
Bernard, Simon, 40, 56
Berrien, John, 251n34
big government, 1, 4, 77–78, 84, 85, 211; and Jacksonian Democrats, 36–37, 39
Black Hills, 95, 147–48, 213, 244
Blackfeet, 151
Board of Engineers of Internal Improvements, 40
Board of Indian Commissioners, 102, 114, 140–43, 145, 150, 211
boards and commissions, 21, 141, 155, 211, 235. *See also specific boards and commissions*
Bosque Redondo, 140
Botanic Garden, U.S., 37
Boutwell, George, 100, 109–10, 114
Bradley, Joseph P., 103–4, 126
Brazil, 55, 120, 175
Bristow, Benjamin, 111, 114, 126, 132
Brooks-Baxter war, 129
Buckner, Simon Bolivar, 26
Budget and Accounting Act (1921), 160, 162–63
buffalo, protection of, 146–47, 151, 226
Buffalo Creek Reservation, 49
Building a New American State (Skowronek), 211
Bunker Hill Monument, 75
Bureau of Corporations, 190
Bureau of Indian Affairs. *See* Indian Office
Bureau of Navigation, 112
bureaucratic autonomy, 61–62, 131, 142
Butler, David, 126
Butt, Archie, 188

cables, international communications, 94, 95
Calhoun, John C., 50, 51–52, 81
California, 27, 112, 139, 152, 232, 233
campaign finance regulation, 10, 11, 95, 168, 172, 183–84, 185, 192–94, 195, 218, 220, 275n50
Canada, 17, 18, 103, 122, 173, 176–77, 181
cannibals, 22
Carpenter, Daniel P., 211
Carpenter, L. Cass, 128
Carson, Kit, 140
Cass, Lewis, 52
Cass-Clark report, 229
census, U.S., 95; 1820, 19; 1870, 94, 102, 226; proposed census of 1875, 97
Centennial Exhibition (1876), 95, 102
Century of Dishonor, A (Jackson), 153
Chance, Merritt, 160–61
Chandler, Zachariah, 96, 114
Chase, Samuel, 15–16, 58
Cherokee Nation, 51, 64, 65, 68, 149
Cherokees, 35, 49, 50, 50–51, 51–52, 53–54, 65, 111, 149
Chesapeake & Ohio Canal, 35, 37, 39, 41, 256n1
Cheyennes, 49, 140
Chicago Tribune, 105
chickens, 163
Chief Joseph, 152
Child, Lydia Marie, 153
children, 19, 21, 75, 118, 137, 163, 164–67, 196
Children's Bureau, U.S., 163–64, 167
Chile, 175
Chin-Ai Railway project, 174
China, 18, 95, 122, 173–74, 177, 181; currency loan to, 174
Chinese slaves, 94
Chippewa, 53, 232
Chiricahua, 151
Choctaw, 35
Choctaw Academy, 263n77
Choctaw Nation, 53
Christian Commission, U.S., 141
cities, planning of, 38
civil rights, 6, 109, 110, 114, 125–26, 131, 132, 133–36, 137, 138, 153–54, 163, 218, 225, 229, 239

Civil Rights Act (1875), 125, 131, 136
Civil Rights Bill (1875), 110, 137
Civil Rights Cases, 136
civil service, 10, 102, 105, 108, 109, 162, 167, 232; in Philippines, 29–31
Civil Service Commission, 105
Civil War amendments, 10, 11–12, 104, 110, 126, 127, 130, 133–36, 155, 216–17, 218
Civilization Fund (1819), 141
civilization programs, 31, 60, 141, 144–45, 150
claims, involving U.S., 17, 23, 33, 47, 53, 54, 55–56, 73, 95, 96, 116, 117, 121–22, 149, 165, 166, 174. See also Alabama claims
Clark, Champ, 176
Clark, David, 276n52
Clay, Henry, 16, 39, 46, 58, 69–70, 82, 264n84, 268n24
Cleveland, Frederick, 160
Coast Survey, U.S., 112
coastal defense, 3, 56, 192, 211. See also Bernard Board
Cobb, Thomas, 70
Cohen, Jeffrey, 2
Coke, Richard, 129
Cold War, 212–13
Colfax Massacre, 135, 136
Colombia, 55, 95
Colton, George, 171
commerce clause, 29, 224–25
Commerce Court, U.S., 158–59, 169–70, 172, 295n66
Commission on Economy and Efficiency, 160–63, 163
commissions and boards, 21, 141, 155, 211, 235. See also specific commissions and boards
Congress, 6, 13, 14, 15, 19, 20, 21, 22, 23–24, 37, 51, 68, 71, 75, 76, 77, 110, 125, 126, 136, 137, 168, 199. See also president and Congress
Congressional Government (Wilson), 210
Connecticut River, 39, 42
conservation, 11, 17, 61–62, 159, 167, 168, 169, 172, 183–84, 194–202, 203, 207, 219, 220, 226–27. See also Florida, live oak farm; forests; land policy; seals; *and specific legislation*

Constitution, U.S., 4–5, 39, 50, 59, 60, 62, 64, 65–66, 69–72, 74–75, 76, 79–80, 82, 83–84, 84–91, 101, 102, 130, 133–34, 135, 137, 155, 156–60, 162–63, 167–68, 172, 178, 179–81, 185–89, 195, 203–4, 206–7, 209, 210, 215–20, 220, 224, 229, 237–38, 240, 242, 243–44; and presidency, 150–56, 162–63. *See also individual presidents*
copyright and patents, 89
corporate consolidation, 184–85, 191–92, 192–93
corporation tax, 11, 185–89, 193–94, 218
corporations, regulation of, 184–92, 193–94, 207, 219
Corps of Topographical Engineers, U.S., 43–44, 48–49, 226, 310n10
Court of Claims, U.S., 166
courts, 3, 10, 15, 16, 19, 22, 29, 32, 33, 51, 58, 86, 87, 104, 109, 111, 126, 129, 130–36, 137, 147, 149, 151, 156, 167, 168, 172, 186, 189, 192, 194, 206, 209, 213, 215, 216–20, 233
Cox, Jacob, 114, 142, 285n54
Crawford, William, 57
Creeks, 35, 56, 60, 64–73
Creek Agency, 60, 178
Creek-Georgia conflict, 50, 64–73, 213, 237
Creek Nation, 63, 64–73, 213, 237
Creswell, John 110
criminal justice, 3, 47, 49, 56, 152, 212, 215, 229
Cuba, 10, 21, 23, 28, 32, 55, 95, 96, 115, 116–19, 120, 121, 123, 159, 179, 243
Curtis, George William, 105
Custer's defeat, 213
customs duties, 3, 17, 211
Customs Service, U.S., 212

Dakotas, 140
Dakotas (region), 212
Dana, Francis, 74
Davis, E. J., 129
Declaration of Independence, 22, 39, 75, 85
defense, 3, 36, 37, 38, 41, 42, 52–56, 85, 87, 89, 92, 99, 122, 192, 211
Delano, Columbus, 112, 114
Delaware Bay, 41
Denmark, 53, 55
Dent, Julia, 24

Department of Agriculture, 104–5. *See also* Agricultural Bureau
Department of Interior, 112, 114, 142, 144, 146, 147, 149, 150, 161, 165, 198–202
Department of Justice: 10, 95, 110, 113–14, 126, 129, 131–33, 134, 138, 143, 161, 191, 216, 229; and politics, 95, 131–32, 133; professionalization, 131–32; compared with Board of Indian Commissioners, 143
Department of Justice Act, 131
Department of State, 19, 56–57, 77, 95, 111, 115–16, 167, 179, 229; reform of, 111, 167
Department of War, 40, 41, 57, 76, 77, 94, 113, 144, 146, 147–48, 160–61, 167, 171, 212, 229
Desert Land Act (1872), 105, 226
Diaz, Porfirio, 180–81
diplomacy, 1, 3, 10, 16–19, 23, 47–52, 54–55, 73, 80–81, 90, 109, 138, 173–81, 211, 213, 222, 223, 236–38, 239, 242
disaster relief, 2, 107–9, 138, 159, 166, 228, 244
discretionary authority, 3, 15, 41, 58, 72, 109, 110, 128, 142, 157, 172, 178, 201
Dodds, Graham C., 2
dollar diplomacy, 173, 174–76, 177, 178–79, 181
Dolliver, Jonathan, 200
Dominican Republic, 115, 119–21, 122, 123, 137, 159
Douglas, Arizona, 179–80
dry docks, 42
Dumas, Anna, 106
Dunn, Oscar J., 106

Eads, James, 103
economic policy, 2, 3, 6, 39, 44, 49, 52, 56, 65, 81, 84, 90, 100, 119, 125, 151, 173, 195, 207
economic regulation, 3, 6, 15, 84, 155, 184, 185, 192, 216; *see also* regulation, federal; regulation, state; *and specific industries and sectors*
Ecuador, 175
education, 2, 6, 19–20, 31, 38, 39, 42, 44–45, 47, 54, 60, 80, 88, 96, 99, 110, 125, 127, 137, 141, 144, 145, 154, 164–65, 233, 239, 263n77, 273n13; in Philippines, 30–31, 254n69

324   INDEX

Eisenhower, Dwight, 64, 77
election of 1800, 38
election of 1828, 35, 36, 37, 41, 50, 70, 81, 82, 132
election of 1840, 21
election of 1868, 133
election of 1872, 100, 132, 133
election of 1876, 96, 103, 108
election of 1904, 132
election of 1908, 170, 193
election of 1912, 166, 180, 205–6, 213
Emancipation Proclamation, 75, 231, 313n43
Embargo Act (1807), 2, 3, 15, 16, 23, 39
Enforcement Act (1870), 130, 135
Enforcement Act (1871), 103, 130
enforcement acts, 110, 133–36
Entomological Commission, U.S., 108, 113, 132
entomologists, 107–8, 109
equal rights, 85, 99, 109–10
equality, 75, 85, 114, 125–126, 131, 138, 164, 166, 216, 221
Estrada, Juan, 175
ethnic cleansing, 65
executive action. See president and executive action
executive order reservations, 151–53, 166, 233, 238
executive orders. See president and executive orders
executive privilege, 214
expertise, in government, 1, 3–4, 28, 30, 40, 42, 58, 61, 62, 104–5, 107–8, 109, 110–12, 116, 131–32, 143, 150, 155, 158, 160–61, 161–62, 165–67, 168, 170, 171, 180, 181, 187, 201, 211, 214, 226–27

fake news, 25–26
Federal Corrupt Practices Act (1925), 193
Federal Reserve system, 172, 193
federalism, 29, 40–41, 51–52, 73, 134, 195
Federalist Papers no. 10, 172
Fernald, H. T., 108
Fifteenth Amendment, 104, 109–10, 125, 126–27, 129, 135, 136, 217
Fifth Amendment, 218–19
filibusters, 95, 118, 121

First Amendment, 20–21
fiscal policy, 138
Fish, Hamilton, 96, 110–11, 115–19, 121, 122, 123, 128, 279n98
Fisher, Walter L., 195, 201, 202
fisheries, 17–18, 122, 226
Fisk, Jay, 100
Flipper, Henry O., 106
Florida, 17, 18, 19, 35, 40, 49, 50, 56, 59, 60, 87, 214, 256n1; live oak farm, 61–62, 226, 232
Force Bill (1833), 59
Forest Service, U.S., 159, 195, 198–202
forests, 30, 61–62, 95, 104–5, 165–66, 169, 196, 198–202, 227; Pawnee timber resources, 152
Forging of Bureaucratic Autonomy, The (Carpenter), 211
Fort Knox (Maine), 56
Fort McHenry, 56
Fort Sumter, 25, 56
forts and fortifications, 3, 35, 53, 56, 87
Forward, Oliver, 49–50
Fourteenth Amendment, 103, 125–26, 130, 135, 136, 216, 217
Fourth Amendment, 219
France, 15, 48, 53, 55, 103, 110, 174, 204–5, 236
Franco-Prussian Conflict, 103, 110, 119
Freedman's Commission, 211
Freedmen's Bank, 164
Freedmen's Bureau, 25, 106, 133, 137, 141, 226, 254n69
Freeman, The, 164
fur trade, 3, 38, 47, 49, 84, 155, 212

gag rule, 13, 14, 20–21, 23, 24
Gaines, Edward P., 59, 66, 67, 68, 261n54
Galena, Illinois, 24, 59
Gallatin, Albert 16, 39, 53
Gallatin Report, 39, 42, 260n33
Galveston, Texas, 18
Garfield, James R., 157, 199–200
gender equity, 92, 105, 106, 107, 155, 166
General Dam Act (1910), 172
General Land Office, 40, 76, 104–5, 165, 200
General Mining Act (1872), 105

INDEX   325

General Survey Act (1824), 40, 41
General Technical Service, Office of, 161
Geological Survey, U.S., 104–5, 107–8, 113, 227
Georgia, 50, 56, 64–73, 91, 94, 126, 128, 129, 148, 213, 237; 1802 land cession, 66, 70–71; and Black state representatives, 94, 126, 129. *See also* Georgia-Creek conflict
Georgia Patriot, 66
Georgia-Creek conflict, 50, 63, 64–73, 91, 213, 237
Germany, 174
Gettysburg, battle of, 26
Gibbons v. Ogden, 251n34
Gila River Reservation, 165
Glavis, Louis, 200
Goingsnake affair, 149
gold, 94, 100; in Indian country, 64–65, 95, 147–48
Gould, Jay, 100
Government Publishing Office, U.S., 161
Grant, Ulysses S.: and administrative leadership, 6, 8–9, 10–11, 12, 25, 92–93, 93–96, 99, 102, 109, 109–14, 115, 116, 117, 123, 124, 125, 126, 127, 128, 131, 132–33, 137–38, 139, 140, 141–42, 144, 145–46, 147–49, 150, 154; and administrative reorganization, 6, 131–32, 138, 139–46; and *Alabama* claims, 95, 111, 115–119, 120–121; annual messages, 93–99, 101, 104, 105, 111, 116, 118–19, 120, 122, 131, 144, 148, 153, 243; appointments, use of, 103–4, 106–7, 109–14, 115–16, 120, 121, 123, 125, 126–27, 131, 134–36, 141, 143, 150, 229; at Appomattox, 26, 111; and attorney general, 103, 113–14, 126, 132, 149; and Black Hills, 95, 147–48, 213, 244; and Board of Indian Commissioners, 102, 140–43, 145, 150; and buffalo, 146–47, 151, 226; in business, 24, 25, 28, 34; and campaign finance regulation, 10, 95; and census, 94, 95, 97; and Centennial Exhibition, 95, 102; and Chinese immigrants, 94; and civil rights, 6, 109, 125–26, 131, 132, 133–36, 137, 153–54; and civil service, 10, 102, 105, 108, 109, 162; and Civil War amendments, 10, 104, 126, 127, 130, 133, 133–36, 216, 218; compared with John Quincy Adams, 26, 28, 92, 109, 122, 123, 127, 147–48; compared with William Howard Taft, 127, 138; and Congress, 6, 93–99, 100–102, 102, 103, 104, 104–5, 107–8, 112, 115–16, 117–19, 119–21, 122, 123, 125, 126–27, 129–33, 137, 139, 141–44, 144–54, 215; and Constitution, 101, 102, 130, 134; and courts, federal, 10, 104, 109, 111, 126, 129, 130–36, 137, 147, 149, 215; and Cuba, 10, 28, 95, 96, 115, 116–19, 120, 121, 123, 243; delegates authority, 109–14, 115, 116, 122, 128; and Department of Justice 10, 95, 110, 113–14, 126, 129, 131–33; and diplomacy, 10, 109, 138; and discretionary authority, 109, 110, 128, 142; and domestic affairs, 99–109; and economic policy, 100, 119, 125; and education, 6, 96, 99, 125, 127, 141, 144, 145, 154; and equal rights, 99; and equality, 125–26, 131, 221; and executive action, 6–7, 10, 92, 93, 95, 105–9, 117–19, 121, 123, 124, 126–29, 131, 144–54; and executive order reservations, 151–53; and executive orders, 7, 102–3, 109, 125, 131, 142, 147–49, 151–53, 213, 235; and federal liquor taxes, 104, 109; and federal workers' pay, 103; and Fifteenth Amendment, 104, 125, 126–27, 129, 135; and filibusters, 95, 118, 121; firefighters, speech to, 98–99, 243; and Fourteenth Amendment, 103, 125–26; and Freedmen's Bureau, 25; and "Goingsnake" affair, 149; and gold, 94, 100; and gold in Black Hills, 95, 147–48; and habeas corpus, 103, 105, 131; and Hawaiʻi, 95, 103, 122; and health care, 112; Inaugural Address, First, 101, 125, 126, 141, 144; Inaugural Address, Second, 101, 125, 131, 144–45; and Indian affairs, 95, 99, 111, 124, 125, 139–154; and Indian Office, 111–12, 140–43; and inflation bill, 100–102, 109, 123, 192, 243; and international affairs, 114–22; and international law, 117–19; and interoceanic canal, 95, 112; and Jews, 102, 121; and Korea, 10, 95, 122, 211, 237; and Ku Klux Klan, 95, 105,

Grant, Ulysses S. (*continued*)
111, 128, 129, 130–31, 132, 133, 134, 136; leadership, 6, 10, 92–93, 93–99, 99–100, 100–102, 109–14, 114–15, 117–21, 122, 123, 128, 130–31, 140–43, 146–49, 149–50, 153–54; legacy, controversial, 26, 28, 114, 123, 128–29, 144, 145, 153–54, 195, 221; legislative initiatives, 8, 10, 92, 93–99, 100–101, 104, 104–5, 108, 130–31, 149; and line-item veto, 95, 102; and Belva Lockwood, 107, 109; and locusts, 10, 95, 107–8, 109, 244; mercurial, 92, 99–100, 100–102, 106–7, 109, 114, 120, 123, 145–46, 146–47, 147–48, 151–52, 153–54; in Mexico, 24, 25, 27, 99; and military, 10, 92, 95, 102, 106–7, 107–9, 112, 114, 116, 122, 124, 125, 127–29, 129–33, 138, 143–44, 145–46, 146–49, 151, 152; military service of, 24, 25–26, 27–28, 34, 99, 102; and monetary policy, 100–102, 109, 243; and moral suasion, 97–98, 119–20, 124, 131, 136, 145, 153–4; and national university, 97; and news media: critical of Confederate, 25–26; and Pacific railroad surveys, 24, 139; and pardons, use of, 102, 149; and Ely Parker: 110, 111–12, 113, 114, 141–44, 145, 146, 226, 229; and peace, 10, 26, 97, 99, 112, 115, 117, 125–26, 127, 129–32, 136, 140, 144, 145, 146, 153–54; Peace Policy of, 124, 140–45, 146, 149, 151, 153, 254n69; political shrewdness, 26–27; as principled innovator, 6, 7, 10, 24–28, 33–34, 92–93, 102, 106–7, 107–8, 109, 114, 119–20, 122, 123, 124, 125, 126, 128, 129, 130–31, 136, 140–41, 143, 144, 145–49, 153–54, 221; and proclamations, 7, 103, 109, 116, 125, 129, 131, 234; and public communication, 7, 93–99, 100–102, 102–103, 104, 105, 116, 117, 117–119, 119–121, 122, 125, 126, 127, 130–31, 136, 139, 141–42, 144, 144–45, 147–49, 153, 244; and race, 96, 97–98, 106–7, 109–10, 123, 125–26, 134, 153; and Reconstruction, 10, 124, 125–39, 140, 213; and right to vote, 125, 126–27, 132, 135; and Santo Domingo, annexation of, 115, 119–21, 122, 123, 137; and scandal frames, 113–14, 120, 133; sense of humor, 24; and signing statements, 7, 102, 234; and slavery, attitude toward, 24–25; and steam boilers, 112; as "strong" president, 12, 220; and Supreme Court, 94, 103–4, 125, 126, 133–36, 137, 154; and Ten Years' War, 115, 117–19, 243; and Tenure of Office Act, 13, 27–28, 34, 94, 102; and Timber Culture Act (1873), 104–5, 226; and transfer issue, 145–46; and treaties, 26, 115–16, 120–21, 121–23, 147–48, 149–53, 213; values, sense of, 92, 101, 109; and veto, use of, 7, 98, 100–102, 102, 109, 123, 147, 243 (*see also* inflation bill); at Vicksburg, 26; and *Virginius*, 115, 116–19, 122, 243; and voting rights, 110, 127, 128; and Washington, DC, 97, 98–99; and weather, 112–113; on West Coast, 24, 25; and West Point, 10, 24, 106, 109, 123, 166; youth, 24

Great Britain, 15, 16, 17, 18, 23, 48, 49, 53, 78, 79, 80, 95, 96, 115–16, 116–17, 121, 122, 170, 174–75, 177–78, 203, 204–5, 236

Great Sioux Reservation, 147

Greeley, Horace, 98

Guatemala, 175

Gulf Crisis, 212–13

habeas corpus, 30, 103, 105, 131

Habersham, Richard, 69, 268n24

Hague, The, 203, 204

Haiti, 80, 175

Hallowell, Benjamin, 141

Hamburg Massacre (South Carolina), 135

Hamilton, Alexander, 3, 226

Hanseatic League, 53

Harding, William, 32, 33

Harlan, John Marshall, 135

Harriman, E. H., 160, 174

Harrison, Benjamin, 29

Hawai'i, 95, 103, 122

Hay, John, 203

Henderson, Archibald, 45–47

Hepburn v. Griswold, 103–4

Hetch Hetchy Dam, 201

hidden-hand presidency, 10, 74–84, 91, 244

Hidden-Hand Presidency, The (Greenstein), 10, 77–78, 83, 84, 85

Hine, Charles, 160

Hoar, E. Rockwood, 111, 120, 131
Homestead Act (1862), 104
Honduras, 175–76
Hoopa Valley Reservation, 152
Howard, O. O., 106, 226, 254n69, 276n52, 290n120
Hukuang loan, 174
Humphreys, Andrew, 226
Humphreys, Joshua, 61, 226
Humphreys, Samuel, 226

Ickes, Harold, 201
Idaho, 152
Ide, Henry Clay, 30
Illinois, 59, 139
immigrants, 166–67, 170–71; Chinese, 94, 110
immigration, 95, 163, 166–67, 205, 213
imperial presidency, 8
income tax, personal, 11, 185–89, 193–94, 218
incorporation tax, federal, 193
indemnification programs, 2, 39, 47, 90, 149
Indian affairs, 1, 4, 5, 6, 10, 11, 40–41, 47–52, 55, 58, 59–60, 64–73, 78, 90, 92, 95, 99, 109, 110, 111–13, 123, 124, 125, 138, 139–54, 163, 165–66, 211, 212, 213, 216, 222, 225, 226, 229, 233, 235, 237, 238, 239, 242. *See also specific presidents, administrative leaders and departments, policy initiatives, Native nations, Native leaders, Indigenous peoples*
Indian Claims Commission, 166
Indian health, 165–66
Indian Office, 56, 76, 111–12, 112, 113, 141, 142, 143, 144, 149, 152, 163, 164, 165, 199, 229
Indian removal, 3, 37, 39, 41, 49–50, 50–51, 52, 60, 64, 65, 69, 111, 139, 140, 165, 228, 229
Indian Removal Act (1930), 73, 139
Indian rings, 140, 143
Indian Trade and Intercourse Acts (1790–1834), 15, 47, 216
Indiana, 35, 40–41, 139
inequality, 184–85, 189–92, 213
inflation bill, 100–102, 109, 123, 192, 243

infrastructure, 175, 216, 219, 222, 235. *See also internal improvements*
inheritance tax, 186, 193
insects, 107–8, 109
internal improvements, 1, 3, 10, 15, 24, 30, 35, 36, 37–44, 48–49, 56, 58, 63, 80, 81–84, 84–91, 92, 95, 97, 98–99, 216, 218, 225, 235, 239, 240, 242, 244; and politics, 40–42; popularity of, 41–42; Democratic support for, 36–37, 41, 81, 257n8; vs. slavery, 80–84; and presidential rhetoric, 84–91. *See also specific projects*
International Criminal Court, 207
International Harvester, 190
international law, 117–19
interoceanic canal, 95, 112
Interoceanic Commission, 112
Interstate Commerce Commission, 169–70, 172, 210
Ireland, 121
isthmian canal exploration, 112, 226

J. P. Morgan Co., 190
Jackson administration, 41, 61–62, 65, 139, 224, 236
Jackson, Andrew, 5, 17, 18, 36, 37, 39, 43, 49, 50, 51, 53, 56, 59, 61, 64, 65, 68, 70, 73, 81, 82, 86, 111, 132, 139, 156, 158, 214, 229; support for internal improvements, 36–37, 39, 41, 81, 257n8; in Florida, 17, 18
Jackson, Helen Hunt, 153
Japan, 31, 95, 122, 174
Jeanes Fund, 164
Jeanes, Anna, 164
Jefferson administration, 15, 89
Jefferson Barracks, 24
Jefferson, Thomas, 2, 3, 15, 38, 39, 44, 156, 231, 240
Jewell, Marshall, 110
Johnson v. McIntosh, 216
Johnson, Andrew, 6, 27–28, 103, 111, 127, 130, 133, 137, 138, 214
Johnson, William, 251n34
Jones, John B., 149
judges, 32, 33, 104, 133–34, 158, 172, 185, 192, 209, 216–20

328   INDEX

Judges Bill (1925), 33
Judicial Conferences Act (1922), 33
judicial independence, 15–16, 58, 158, 168, 172, 186, 188–89, 191–92, 213
judicial recall, 158, 172, 185
judicial reform, 29, 32–33, 95
judiciary. *See* courts

Kagan, Elena, 210
Kelley, Florence, 163
Kellogg, William, 129
Kelly, Fanny, 149
Kentucky, 111, 129, 133, 135
Kickapoo, 232
King, Rufus, 80
Knox, Henry, 3, 226
Knox, Philander, 167, 175
Korea, 10, 95, 122, 174, 211, 237
Ku Klux Klan, 95, 105, 111, 128, 129, 130–31, 132, 133, 134, 136
Ku Klux Klan Act (1871), 130, 131, 136
Kuhn, J. L., 45–46
Kumeyaay, 151, 232

Lamar, Joseph, 167
land grant claims, 17
land grants, Spanish, 17, 56, 62, 212
Land Ordinance of 1785, 80
land policy, 1, 2, 3, 5, 6, 10, 11, 14, 15, 17, 24, 37, 38, 39, 40, 41–42, 45, 47–48, 49, 51–52, 53, 55, 60, 61–62, 62, 64–69, 80, 84, 90, 94, 104, 105, 144, 145, 150–54, 165–66, 169, 194–98, 199, 200–202, 211, 211–12, 216, 219, 222, 225, 226–27, 229, 232, 233, 235. *See also* conservation, Desert Land Act (1872), Homestead Act (1862), Indian affairs, treaties, Weeks Act (1911)
land surveys, 228; conflicts over, 51–52
land title commissions, 39
land titles, 39, 62, 211, 212. *See also* land grant claims; land grants, Spanish
Laracey, Mel, 2
Lathrop, Julia, 163–64, 166–67
Latin America, 18, 54, 167, 173, 174–76, 203
Lawrence, Charles L., 121
League of Nations, 28, 32
League to Enforce Peace, 205

Lee, Robert E., 26, 226
Legal Tender Act (1862), 103–4
Lewis and Clark expedition, 37, 43
Lewis, William Henry, 164, 166
Liberia, 107
Library of Congress, 14–15
lighthouses, 42
Lincoln administration, 224
Lincoln Memorial Commission, 32
Lincoln, Abraham, 6, 27, 75, 98, 156, 214, 231, 241–43, 313n43
line-item veto, 95, 102
liquor: federal taxes, 104, 109; regulation of, 166. *See also* alcohol
Little Rock, Arkansas, 64
Lockwood, Belva, 107, 109
locusts, 10, 95, 107–8, 166, 244
Logan, John, 98
Long Walk of the Navajo, 140
Louisiana, 15, 17, 26, 97, 103, 106, 131, 135, 136
Louisiana Purchase, 5, 6, 15, 17, 18–19, 23, 39, 212, 214, 231, 232, 240
Louisiana Territory, 15
Lovely's Purchase, 51–52
Lurton, Horace, 167

Macomb, Alexander, 59
Madison, James, 172
Maine, 56
Major League Baseball, 29, 33
Makah, 152
Mandans, 49
Mann-Elkins Act (1910), 158–59, 169–70, 172
marines, U.S., 32, 122, 175
Maryland, 41, 164
Massachusetts, 14, 42, 56
Maury, Matthew, 43
McClellan, George, 24, 25
McHenry, James, 61
McIntosh, William, 66
McKean, James B., 104
McKenney, Thomas, 3, 50, 51–52, 226
McKinley, William 29, 214
McLean, John, 58, 81–83, 199, 221, 226, 271n71, 271n73
Medill, Joseph, 105

INDEX   329

Menominee, 53
Mescalero Apache, 152, 165
metric system, 19, 163
Mexican War, 24, 99, 203
Mexico, 11, 17, 24, 27, 53, 54, 55, 173, 175, 177, 178–81, 214
Michigan, 35, 40, 139
military, policy and deployment of, 3, 10, 13, 30, 35, 40, 41, 49, 53, 59, 66, 68–73, 76, 86, 90, 92, 95, 102, 107–9, 112, 114, 116, 122, 125, 127–29, 129–33, 138, 143–44, 145–46, 146–49, 151, 152, 175, 179–81, 228, 229, 235, 236–38, 242; drawdown in South after Civil War, 124, 129–33, 134
military roads, 40, 42
mining, regulation of, 3, 24, 30, 53, 59, 105, 147, 148
Minnesota, 27, 140, 166, 195
Mission Indians, California, 152
Mississippi, 35, 42, 103, 129, 131
Mississippi River, 26, 42, 53, 60, 86, 108, 139, 213
Missouri, 48
Missouri River, 49
Modoc War, 149
money issue, 41, 94, 100–102, 142
Monroe administration, 17, 18, 56–57, 66, 87
Monroe Doctrine, 6, 18, 54, 119, 119–20, 176, 203, 205, 214
Monroe, James, 17, 18, 19, 40, 51, 57, 58, 61, 82, 86, 87, 243
Montauk Point, 21
moral suasion. *See* president and moral suasion; *and individual presidents*
Mormons, 95, 104
Moses, Bernard, 30
Motley, Charles Lothrop, 115, 120
mummies, 29
Myer, Albert, 112
Myers v. U. S., 158
Myth of the Modern Presidency, The (Nichols), 4–5, 12

Nashville Republican, 68
nation building, 29–31, 214
National Conservation Congress, 195–98
National Road, 37, 38, 39–40, 44, 88, 228

national supremacy, 10, 64, 83, 99, 218, 244, 251n34; in Indian affairs, 47–48, 49, 52, 64–73, 91
national university, 19, 39, 42, 44, 89, 97
National University Law School, 107
National War Labor Board, 32
Navajo (Dine), 140, 165
Navajo Nation National Monument, 166
Navajo Reservation, 152
naval academy, 19, 37, 42, 78, 89
naval observatory, 37
Naval-Timber Purchase Act (1799), 61
Naval-Timber Reserve Act (1817), 61
Navy, U.S., 60, 61–62, 75, 78–80, 87, 90, 112, 122, 161, 196, 226, 237; reorganization of, 57, 58, 78, 167
Nebraska, 126, 148
Negro Seamen's Acts, 19
Netherlands, 53, 55
Neutrality Proclamation, 212, 231, 236
Nevada, 126
New Deal, 2, 9, 77, 165, 220, 231, 245
New London, Connecticut, 21
New Mexico, 48
New Orleans, 17, 39, 129
New York (state), 35, 49–50, 53, 76, 139
New York Times, 203, 233
Newell, Frederick, 226
Nez Perce, 152
Nicaragua, 95, 175–76, 181
Nicaragua claims commission, 175
Nixon administration, 227
North American Free Trade Agreement (NAFTA), 176, 203
North Carolina, 104, 129, 131, 133
Northern Securities v. U.S., 191
Novak, William J., 211, 215–20
nudity, 46, 261n51

O'Fallon, Benjamin, 49
Obama, Barack, 213
Office of Indian Affairs. *See* Indian Office
Ogden Land Company, 49–50, 111
Oglalas, 49
Ohio, 24, 27, 28, 139
Ohio River, 42
Ojibwe, 232–33
Omahas, 49

330   INDEX

Onis, Luis de, 17, 18–19, 22, 58
Ord, Edward O. C., 107
Oregon, 17
Oregon Trail, 139
Otos, 49
Owen, David Dale, 37

Pacific Expedition, 35, 37, 43–44, 60, 61, 213, 228, 233, 244
Pacific railroad surveys, 3, 24, 139
Packard, A. S., Jr., 107–8
Palma, Estrada, 32
Panama, 31, 80, 159
Panama Canal, 28, 31, 173; tolls, 177–78, 181, 298n106
Panama Congress, 54–55, 59, 68, 80, 221
Panic of 1873, 100
papacy, 46
Paraguay, 95
pardons. *See* presidential pardons
Parker, Ely S., 110, 111–12, 113, 114, 141–43, 144, 145, 146, 164, 226, 229
Patent Office, U.S., 19, 226
patronage, 57, 81–83, 110, 120, 131, 143, 164, 167, 168, 225
Pawnees, 49, 152; timber resources, 152
Payne-Aldrich tariff, 169, 186–89, 234–35
peace, 10, 16, 26, 28–29, 38, 49, 53, 55–56, 70, 73, 85, 86, 97, 99, 112, 115, 117, 125–26, 127, 129–32, 136, 140, 145, 146, 153–54, 168, 175, 176, 181, 182, 195, 202–5, 207. *See also* Peace Policy
Peace Policy, 124, 140–45, 146, 149, 151, 153, 254n69
Pemberton, John, 26
Pennsylvania coal strike (1902), 157
People's Welfare, The (Novak), 11–12, 84, 215–20
Persia, 177
Peru, 95, 175
petitions, 4, 20–21, 152, 172
Philippines, 28, 29–31, 171, 177, 185, 212, 254n69
Pierce, Franklin, 102, 151
Pierrepont, Edwards, 135
piers, 40
Pinchot, Gifford, 159, 195, 198–202, 226
Pinckney's Treaty (1795), 22

piracy, 18, 21, 78, 79, 80, 237
Plessy v. Ferguson, 135
Poinsett, Joel R., 262n54
Poland, 74
Poland Act (1874), 104
Polk, James K., 24, 156
Pollock v. Farmer's Loan Company, 186
Poncas, 49
Porter, Peter, 42, 50, 59–60, 262n54
Postal Service, U.S., 1–2, 3, 39, 41, 76, 77, 81–83, 90, 106, 109, 110, 160–61, 168, 170–71, 225, 226, 228; vs. slavery, 80–84; and telegraph system, 95, 110, 112, 169; postal savings banks, 166, 168, 170–71, 172, 296n71
Potawatomi, 40, 232
Powell, John Wesley, 113
presidency, development of, 1–2, 4, 7–8, 11–12, 89, 159; non-development of, 209–22, 223–45
presidency, traditional-modern dichotomy: explored, 1–8, 156–60, 209–22, 223–45; and the state, 210–15; and rise of administrative state, 210–11; and U.S. on the world stage, 211–12; and severity of crises, 212–13; and partisanship and gridlock, 213
president and administrative leadership, 1, 4, 6–7, 8, 8–12, 40–41, 56–62, 81–83, 92–93, 109–14, 125, 131, 139, 148, 156–57, 160, 160–68, 181, 209, 210, 212, 223–24, 224–30, 239. *See also specific issues and presidents*
president, annual messages and, 54, 57, 60, 62, 78, 84–85, 88–91, 93–98, 101, 104, 105, 111, 116, 118–19, 120, 122, 131, 144, 148, 153, 161, 171, 180–81, 187, 188, 191, 192, 219, 239, 241–42, 243. *See also specific issues, messages, and presidents*
president and appointments, use of: 10, 27–28, 45–46, 54–55, 57–58, 59, 77, 80–83, 103–4, 106–7, 109–14, 115–16, 120, 121, 123, 125, 126–27, 131, 134–36, 141, 143, 150, 161, 163–65, 166–67, 167–68, 170, 171, 181, 191, 192, 198–202, 229. *See also specific presidents*
president and Congress, 1–2, 3, 3–4, 6, 7, 9, 10–11, 15, 23–24, 27–28, 33, 35, 40–45,

INDEX   331

45–46, 47–48, 49–50, 51–52, 53–55, 56, 57–58, 58–62, 65, 66–67, 68, 70, 71–72, 73, 75, 78–80, 83, 84–91, 92–93, 93–99, 100–102, 102, 103, 104–5, 107–8, 112, 114, 115–16, 117, 117–19, 119–21, 122, 123, 125, 126–27, 129–33, 133–34, 137, 139, 141–44, 144–54, 156–60, 160–63, 165–66, 167, 169–72, 175, 176, 177–81, 182, 183–84, 184–94, 196–98, 200–202, 203–5, 206, 210–11, 213, 214, 215, 216, 218, 220, 228, 235–36, 236–38, 238–41, 242–43. *See also specific issues and presidents*

president and diplomacy, 1, 10, 47–54, 55, 73, 78–80, 92, 109, 174, 175, 177, 178, 181, 211, 212–13, 222, 223–24, 236–38, 242. *See also specific presidents*

president and executive action, 1, 5–9, 10, 12, 43, 47, 58, 59, 61–62, 64–73, 74, 76–84, 91, 92, 93, 95, 102–4, 105–9, 117–19, 121, 123, 124, 126–29, 131, 136–39, 144–54, 155–60, 163–68, 171, 173, 174, 177–81, 195, 196, 198–202, 209–15, 219, 220–22, 223–24, 230–38, 239, 244–45. *See also specific applications and incidents*

president and executive orders: 1, 5–6, 7, 9, 61, 102–3, 109, 125, 131, 142, 147–49, 150–53, 159, 162, 166, 167, 179, 181, 196, 201, 213–14, 223, 224, 230–39. *See also* executive order reservations; *and individual presidents*

president and inaugural addresses, 84–88, 101, 125, 126, 141, 144–45, 187, 203, 240, 243. *See also specific addresses and presidents*

president, legislative initiatives and: 1, 4, 6, 8, 8–12, 36, 37, 40, 42–43, 59–60, 61–62, 63, 72, 73, 77, 84–91, 92–93, 93–99, 100–101, 104, 104–5, 108, 130–31, 149, 158, 166, 168–72, 178, 181, 184–94, 195–98, 209, 210, 218–19, 223–24, 238–41, 242–43, 244. *See also specific policies and presidents*

president and moral suasion, 8, 84–91, 97–98, 119–20, 124, 131, 136, 145, 153–54, 218–19, 223, 242–43, 273n13. *See also specific presidents*

president and proclamations: 1, 5, 7, 46–47, 60, 66, 75, 103, 109, 116, 125, 129, 131, 166, 212, 214, 223, 230–31, 234–36, 238, 313n43. *See also specific presidents*

president and public communication: 1, 4, 5, 7, 8, 8–12, 39, 62, 66, 72, 74, 75, 76, 78, 84–91, 93–102, 102–3, 104, 105, 116, 117–19, 119–21, 122, 124, 125, 126, 127, 130–31, 136, 139, 141–42, 144–45, 147–49, 153, 156, 158, 160, 161, 167, 169, 170, 171, 177, 179–81, 185, 186–88, 189, 191–92, 194, 195–98, 203–5, 209, 210, 213–14, 219, 223–24, 235, 240–45. *See also specific addresses, issues, presidents, and speeches*

president and signing statements, 7, 102, 223, 230, 234–36. *See also specific policies and presidents*

president and veto, 7, 27, 98, 100–102, 102, 109, 123, 147, 158–59, 166, 172, 181, 192, 213, 243. *See also specific policies and presidents*

presidential behavior, predicting, 33–34. *See also* principled innovator; procedurist; synthesist; *and specific presidents*

presidential budgeting, 11, 158, 159, 160–63, 167, 168, 181, 183, 193, 195, 203, 213, 228

presidential pardons, 49, 59, 102, 149, 238. *See also specific presidents*

principled innovator, 6, 7, 10, 14, 24–28, 34, 92–93, 102, 106–7, 107–8, 109, 114, 119–20, 122, 123, 124, 136, 159, 183, 195, 197–98, 203–4, 221–22. *See also* Grant, Ulysses S., as principled innovator

procedurist, 9–10, 13, 14, 15–16, 16, 19–25, 33–34, 35–36, 37–38, 44, 45–47, 48, 51–52, 52–53, 54, 56, 57, 63–64, 67, 68, 69–72, 74, 79–80, 81–82, 83–84, 84, 88, 89–91, 159, 199, 220–22. *See also* Adams, John Quincy, as procedurist

proclamations. *See* president and proclamations

Proctor, Zeke, 149

property rights, 23, 25, 33, 75, 159, 185, 189, 195, 215, 216, 218, 219

prostitutes, 104

Prussia, 16, 53, 103, 110

public credit, 100–102

Public Credit Act (1869), 100, 104
public debt, 42, 45, 87, 120, 172, 279n98
public health, 3, 38, 39, 84, 90, 112, 113, 165–66, 168, 169, 195, 215, 216, 219, 239
Public Health Service, U.S., 165
Publicity Act (1910), 193
Puerto Rico, 120, 121, 212; governance reform in, 168, 171

Quinault, 152

race, 31, 92, 96, 97–98, 106–7, 109–10, 123, 125–26, 134, 153, 155, 164–65, 166, 222
Reagan administration, 234
Reagan era, 213
Reclamation Service, U.S., 201, 306n79
Reconstruction, 10, 27, 96, 98, 124, 125–39, 140, 213, 216, 244
Red Cloud Agency, 108
Red Jacket, 49–50
Reese v. U.S., 135
regulation, federal, 2–6, 11, 15, 19, 24, 33, 40, 47, 49, 84, 89, 90, 97, 105, 110, 155, 169, 170, 172, 178, 183–84, 184–92, 192–94, 196–97, 203, 210, 212, 213, 215–20, 242. *See also* ammunition; campaign finance; conservation; corporations; criminal justice; economic regulation; fisheries; forests; fur trade; land; liquor; mining; roads; shipping; slavery; steamboat boilers; treaties; weapons
regulation, state, 33
religion, promotion of by government, 3, 141, 165, 228
removal of white squatters from Native land, 53, 71, 72, 147, 148, 152, 212, 268n39
Report on Weights and Measures, 19, 161, 163
reservations, 65, 140, 143–44, 149–53, 154, 165, 166, 228, 233, 238. *See also* executive order reservations; *and specific reservations*
Rhetorical Presidency, The (Tulis), 99, 273n19
right of petition, 20–21, 23
right to assemble, 135
right to bear arms, 135

right to vote, 110, 125, 126–27, 130, 132, 135
rights of neutrals, 16, 79–80, 115–19
Riley, C. V., 107–8
Rivers and Harbors Act (1876), 102, 278n85
Rogowski, Jon C., 1–2, 83
Romania, 121
Roosevelt, Franklin D., 101, 138, 164–65, 232, 234
Roosevelt, Theodore, 6, 8, 28, 29, 31, 36, 132, 156, 157, 159, 165–66, 167, 168, 169, 172, 175, 180, 184, 185, 186, 190, 193, 194, 194–95, 196, 197, 198, 198–202, 203–4, 206, 214, 219, 220, 223, 226, 227, 229, 232, 234, 235, 245; compared to Adams, 219
Root, Elihu, 175, 187, 204
rule of law, 23, 29, 64, 132, 133, 155, 157, 168, 189–92, 198–202, 205, 217
Rush, Richard, 35, 40, 43, 45
Russia, 16, 31–32, 55, 121, 122, 173, 174, 177

Sac and Fox, 53
Sand Creek Massacre, 140
Santo Domingo (Cuba), 116
Santo Domingo (Dominican Republic). *See* Dominican Republic
Santa Fe Trail, 48, 139
scandal frames, 113–14, 120, 133, 140
Schenck, Robert, 115
Schoolcraft, Henry, 37
scientific exploration and research, 3, 19–20, 37, 42–43, 58, 76, 87, 88–89, 90, 112, 113, 239. *See also specific initiatives*
Scott, Winfield, 59, 261n54
seals, 17, 94, 226
Second Philippines Commission (Taft Commission), 29–31, 161
Second Seminole War, 49, 236
Seminoles, 60, 236
Seneca, 35, 49–50, 111
Senecas, 111
Seward, Henry, 112
Shepherd, Alexander, 98
Sheridan, Phil, 136, 146, 148
Sherman Anti-Trust Act, 29, 167, 190–92. *See also* antitrust
Sherman, William Tecumseh, 110, 146, 147

shippers and shipping, 3, 15, 21, 23, 35, 43, 47, 52–53, 55, 58, 79, 94, 174–75, 177–78, 181
Shuster, William Morgan, 177
Signal Corps, U.S., 108, 112–13, 132
Sioux, 151, 236
Sixteenth Amendment, 185–89
Skowronek, Stephen, 4, 211
Slaughterhouse Cases, 134
slave trade, 3, 21–23, 65, 76, 78–80, 83, 237
Slave Trade Convention, 80
slavery, 1, 2, 10, 18, 20–21, 21–23, 24–25, 37–38, 39, 53, 55, 58, 63, 64–65, 74–84, 87, 91, 92, 110, 118, 120, 121, 123, 214, 228, 229, 235, 237, 244, 270n68; federal efforts to end, 75; lack of popular consensus on, 76; as piracy, 79, 80; state measures to end, 75, 76; and treaties, 75. *See also* Adams, John Quincy, and slavery; Grant, Ulysses S., and slavery
Smith, Edward P., 114
Smith, James Webster, 106, 109, 166, 276n52
Smithson bequest, 19–20, 58
Smithson, James, 19–20
Smithsonian Institution, 19–20, 105
social policy and programs, federal, 1, 2–3, 4, 11, 35, 36, 38, 42–43, 44, 47–48, 52–54, 55–56, 80, 84, 87, 90–91, 92, 95, 96, 104, 107–8, 109, 112, 125, 126, 133, 138–39, 141–44, 144–45, 146–47, 149, 150–51, 155, 163–64, 165–67, 168–72, 181, 216, 217, 222. *See also specific programs*
South Carolina, 19, 103, 129, 131, 133, 135, 251n34
Southard, Samuel, 35, 45, 58, 60, 61–62, 78
Spain, 15, 17, 18, 21–23, 48, 59, 95, 96, 116–19, 121
Spanish-American War, 203, 234
Standard Oil, 190, 191
Standard Oil v. U.S., 191
Stanton, Edwin, 27–8, 102, 111
state, American: development of, 1–12, 13–14, 51–52, 54, 83, 84–91, 105, 113, 138–39, 209–22; literature on, 2–5, 10–12, 210–16, 223; scope and maturity of, 19, 23–24, 33–34, 35–36, 38, 47, 62, 63–64, 65, 71, 74, 77–78, 92–99, 109, 124, 129, 137–38, 147, 153–54, 155, 195; continuity after Civil War, 8, 93, 105, 124, 138–39, 139, 150, 151, 155, 209–15; redirected after Civil War, 10, 92, 124, 125, 138–39, 150–52; adapting, 92, 93, 124, 150, 155, 181–88; goals change, 209, 215–20; as protector of individual and group rights, 8, 10–12, 124, 133–36, 137, 138, 155, 169, 194, 202, 206, 209, 215–20; of courts and parties, 3, 93, 137, 139, 229. *See also* administrative state; big government; *and specific state functions*
steamboat boilers, 2, 3, 155
St. Clair, Arthur, 229, 236, 237
St. Louis, Missouri, 24, 39–40
Stoddert, Benjamin, 61
Story, Joseph, 23
Stowe, Harriet Beecher, 153
Straus, Oscar, 177
Strauss Amendment (Maryland), 164
"strong" president/leader, 8, 12, 18, 59, 139, 159, 180, 194, 220, 224, 236
Strong, William, 103–4, 126
Stuart, George, 285n54
Sumner, Charles, 115, 120, 131
Supreme Court, U.S., 13, 15, 21–23, 28, 29, 32–33, 78–79, 82–83, 94, 103–4, 107, 125, 126, 133–36, 137, 154, 158, 167–68, 182, 186, 187–88, 188–89, 191–92, 201, 216, 217, 218, 219, 233
Surgeon General's Office, 113
Sweden, 55
synthesist, 7, 10–11, 13, 28–33, 33–34, 127, 155, 159, 160–63, 168, 169–70, 170–71, 172, 176–77, 177–78, 182, 183, 185, 186–87, 191–92, 193, 193–94, 194–95, 197, 198–99, 202, 204–7, 217, 219, 221–22. *See also* Taft, William Howard, as synthesist

Taft, Alphonso, 110
Taft, Nellie, 31
Taft, William Howard: administrative leadership of, 6, 8, 10–11, 12, 28, 29–31, 31–33, 158, 160–68, 171, 173, 181, 183, 185, 190, 194–202, 206–7; and administrative process and law, relationship of, 165–66, 194–202, 206–7; and administrative reorganization, 6, 160–68, 183;

Taft, William Howard (*continued*)
and administrative state, 160–68; and annual messages, 161, 171, 180–81, 187, 188, 191, 192, 219; and antitrust, 11, 29, 33, 185, 189–92, 193–94, 219 (*see also* Sherman Antitrust Act); appointments, use of, 30, 33, 161, 163–65, 166–68, 170, 171, 181, 191, 192, 198–202; and arbitration, 174, 178, 202–5; and arbitration agreements, 11, 159, 202–5; and arbitration treaties, 11, 28, 168, 183–84, 202–5; and Asia, 28, 31–32, 167, 173–74, 183; and automobiles, 33, 168; as balancer of government power with group and individual rights, 11–12, 29, 155, 157, 169, 217, 218–20; and budgeting, national, 11, 158, 159, 160–63, 168, 181, 183, 193, 195, 203, 213, 228; and campaign finance regulation, 11, 168, 172, 183–84, 185, 192–94, 195, 218, 220; and Canada, 173, 176–77, 181; as chief justice, U.S. Supreme Court, 13, 29, 32–33, 158, 217; and Children's Bureau, 163–64, 167; and civil service, 29–31, 167; collaborative, 29–31, 31–33, 161, 166–67, 168, 182, 194, 205, 206–7; and Commerce Court, 158–59, 169–70, 172; compared with John Quincy Adams, 155, 178, 183; compared with Grant, 155, 156, 192; and Congress, 6, 10–11, 156–60, 160–63, 165, 167, 169–72, 175, 176, 177–78, 178–81, 182, 183–84, 184–94, 196–98, 200–202, 203–5, 206, 215; and conservation, 11, 159, 167, 168, 169, 172, 183–84, 194–202, 203, 207, 219, 220 (*see also* National Conservation Congress); and Constitution, 155, 156–60, 162–63, 167–68, 172, 178, 179–81, 185–89, 195, 202, 203–4, 206–7; and corporation tax, 11, 185–89, 193–94, 218; and courts, federal, 29, 32–33, 167–68, 172, 186, 189, 192, 194, 206, 215; and Cuba, 28, 32, 159, 179; and delegated authority, 211; and diplomacy, 173–81; and dollar diplomacy, 173, 174–76, 177, 178–79, 181; and domestic affairs, 168–72; early career, 28; and education, 29–31, 164–65; and executive officers, dismissal of, 158; and executive orders, 7, 159, 162, 166, 167, 179, 181, 196, 201; and executive order reservations, 166; and executive powers, 33; and Federal Reserve system, 172, 193; and foreign policy, 159, 173–81; and forests, 30, 169, 196, 198–202; and Friars' lands, 255n74; and health care, 30, 165–66, 168, 169, 195; and immigration, 163, 166–67, 170–71; and imperialism, 31, 176; inaugural address, 187, 203; and income tax, 11, 185–89, 193–94, 218; and incorporation tax, federal, 193; and Indian affairs, 163, 165–66; and Indian health, 165–66; and Indian Office/BIA, 165–66; and inequality, 184–85, 189–92, 213; and inheritance tax, 186, 193; and Interior Department, 165, 198–202; and international affairs, 159, 173–81; and Jews, 173, 177; as judge, 28, 29, 34, 185; as judge, federal, 13, 28, 29, 189, 191, 217, 218; and Judges Bill (1925), 33; and judicial independence, 32–33, 158, 168, 172, 186, 188–89, 191–92, 213; and judicial recall, 158, 172, 185; and Latin America, 167, 173, 174–76, 203; leadership, 6, 29–31, 31–33, 155–56, 160–63, 168–72, 173–81, 185–89, 191–92, 192–94, 194–98, 198–202, 205–7, 218, 254n68; legacy, 221–22; legislative initiatives, 10–11, 158, 166, 168–72, 178, 181, 184–94, 195–98, 209, 218–19; and Lincoln Memorial Commission, 32; and Mann-Elkins Act (1910), 158–59, 169–70, 172; and Mexico, 11, 173, 175, 178–81, 214; and military, 29–31, 32, 159, 175, 179–81; and nation building, 29–31, 214; and National Conservation Congress, 195–98; and National War Labor Board, 32; and Nicaragua claims commission, 175; and "nineteenth-century presidency," 156–57, 159; overlooked, 6, 10–11, 159, 194; and Panama Canal, 28, 31, 173, 177–78, 181; and patronage, 164, 167, 168; and Payne-Aldrich tariff, 169, 186–89, 234–35; and peace, 28–29, 168, 175, 176, 181, 182, 202–5, 207; and

INDEX 335

Philippines, 13, 28, 29–31, 171, 177, 185; and postal savings banks, 166, 168, 170–71, 172; and U.S. Postal Service, 30; post-presidency, 32–33; presidency, views on, 155, 156–60, 160–63, 172, 179–81, 198–202; and proclamations, 7, 166, 234–35; as "progressive conservative," 29, 168, 184–85, 198; and progressive reform, 6, 184–94; and property rights, 33, 159, 185, 189, 195; and public communication, 7, 8–9, 156, 160, 161, 167, 169, 170, 171, 177, 179–81, 186–88, 189, 191–92, 194, 195–98, 203–5, 219; and Puerto Rico, governance reform, 168, 171; and race, 31, 164–65, 166–67; and religious minorities, 166–67; and Republicans, 168, 176, 180–81, 186–88, 206, 213; and Theodore Roosevelt, 6, 8, 28, 29, 31, 156, 157, 159, 167, 168, 169, 172, 175, 180, 184, 185, 186, 190, 193, 194, 194–95, 196, 197, 198, 198–202, 203–4, 206; sees Roosevelt as lawless, dangerous, 157, 206; and rule of law, 29, 155, 157, 168, 189–92, 198–202, 205; and Russia, 31–32, 173, 174, 177; and Second Philippines Commission (Taft Commission), 29–31, 161; as secretary of war, 28, 31–32, 159, 185; sense of humor, 33, 182; and Sherman Antitrust Act, 29, 167, 190–92 (see also antitrust); as solicitor general, 28, 29, 34, 189; as "strong" president, 159, 220; and Supreme Court, 29, 32–33, 158, 167–68, 182, 186, 187–88, 188–89, 191–92, 201; and Supreme Court building, 33; as synthesist, 7, 10–11, 13, 28–33, 33–34, 127, 155, 159, 160–63, 168, 169–70, 170–71, 172, 176–77, 177–78, 182, 183, 185, 186–87, 191–92, 193, 193–94, 194–95, 197, 198–99, 202, 204–7, 217, 219, 221–22; Taft Commission, see Second Philippines Commission; Taft myth, 155–56, 156–60; takes long-term view, 30, 127, 162–63, 166–67, 173, 176–77, 177, 182, 183–84, 191–92, 193–94, 195, 197–98, 203, 205; and taxation, 11, 183–84, 184–89, 193–94, 195, 203, 218–20 (see also specific taxes); trade, 173, 174–76, 176–77, 177; and treaties, 166, 176–77, 177–78 (see also arbitration, treaties); and treaty-making authority, 159; and veto, use of, 7, 158–59, 166, 172, 181, 213; against Arizona statehood, 158, 172, 213; and voting rights, 33, 164; and warmaking authority, 159, 179–81; and Weeks Act (1911), 169; and worker protections, 168, 169; and workers' compensation, 169, 218–19; and Yale Law School, 28, 32; and Yale University, 28, 32
Tappan, Lewis, 21
Tariff Board, 186–87, 188, 300n10
tariffs, 3, 59, 94, 168–69, 186, 188–89, 213, 229, 241. See also Payne-Aldrich tariff
taxes, 3, 11, 15, 30, 89, 94, 183–84, 184–89, 193–94, 195, 203, 218–20. See also specific laws and taxes
Taylor, Zachary, 232–33; 1850 executive order, 232–34
Telecommunications Act (1934), 169
telegraph lines, 108, 112
Ten Years' War, 115, 117–19, 243
Tenure of Office Act, 13, 27–28, 34, 94, 102, 131
territories, U.S., 3, 15, 50–51, 80, 148, 212. See also specific territories
Terry, Alfred, 148
Texas, 17, 24, 25, 26, 108, 129, 179–81
Thirteenth Amendment, 217
Thomas, Cyrus, 107–8
Thompson, David, 175
Thornton, William, 226
Timber Culture Act (1873), 104–5, 226
Timber Trespass Act (1827), 62
Totten, Joseph, 40, 226
trade, 3, 15, 38, 39, 44, 47–49, 52–53, 56, 84, 90, 94, 112, 119–20, 121–22, 173, 176–77, 203. See also specific trade participants and sectors
traders, licensing of, 47, 49
trading house system, government (factory system), 3, 47
Trail of Tears, 65
Transcontinental Treaty (1819), 17, 18–19, 22

transfer issue, 145–46; as administrative reform, 146
Treasury Department, 57, 94, 110, 111, 143, 160, 161, 212
treaties, 3, 14, 15, 16–19, 20, 21–23, 26, 35, 36, 40–41, 47–56, 59–60, 64–73, 75, 78, 86, 110–11, 115–16, 120–21, 121–23, 139–40, 147–48, 149–53, 155, 159, 166, 176–77, 177–78, 212, 213, 232–33, 237–38, 244; end of treaty-making with Native nations (1871), 73, 149–53. *See also* international arbitration treaties; *and specific treaties*
Treaty of Buffalo Creek, 111
Treaty of Council Bluffs (1825), 48
Treaty of Doak's Stand (1820), 53
Treaty of Fort Laramie (1868), 147
Treaty of Fort Mitchell (1827), 73
Treaty of Ghent, 16, 22, 53
Treaty of Indian Springs (1825), 66, 67, 68, 68–69
Treaty of Prairie du Chien (1825), 53
Treaty of Washington (1826), 68
Treaty of Washington (1871), 115–16, 122, 202
Treaty with Osage and Kansa (1825), 48
Troup, William, 66, 67–68, 68–69, 73
"true size" of government, 228
Trump, Donald, 213
Turkey, 53, 177
Turner, James Milton, 107
Tweed, Boss, 121
Tyler, John, 75

United Nations, 203, 207
U.S. Steel, 190
U.S. v. American Tobacco Company, 191
U.S. v. Blyew, 134
U.S. v. Cruikshank, 135, 136
U.S. v. Harris, 136
U.S. v. Trans-Missouri Freight, 191
U.S. v. Zeke Proctor, 149
U.S.-Dakota War (1862), 140
Utah, 95, 104

vaccinations, 3, 38, 39, 165
Valentine, Robert G., 165–66, 200
Van Buren administration, 21–23

Van Buren, Martin, 21–22, 37, 43, 50, 51, 111
veterans, pensions and benefits, 2, 38, 43, 44, 95, 96, 155, 236
Vicksburg, Mississippi, 26, 129
Vinton, John, 268n39
Virginia, 268n39
Virginius (ship), 115, 116–19, 122, 243
voting rights, 33, 110, 127, 128, 164

Waite, Morrison, 135
Walker, Francis, 226
War of 1812, 16, 18, 203, 213
Washburne, Elihu, 110, 114
Washington (state), 27
Washington administration, 48, 209, 226, 238
Washington, DC, 16, 39–40, 52, 53, 69, 97, 98–99, 161, 228, 243
Washington, George, 7, 52, 64, 72, 75–76, 89, 98, 156, 214, 229, 231, 236, 237, 239, 240, 242, 243
Washington-New Orleans Road, 39
weapons, regulation of, 3, 102–3, 147
weather, 112–113
Weather Bureau, U.S., 278n88
Weeks Act (1911), 169
Wells, G. Wiley, 131
Welsh, William, 142
West India Squadron, 78
West Point, 10, 24, 37, 39, 46, 47–48, 89, 106, 109, 123, 166
Western Union, 110
Whiskey Rebellion, 64, 68
Whiskey Ring scandal, 104
white rifle clubs, 103, 129
White, Edward, 191
White, Hugh L., 54
Wickersham, George, 163, 167, 187–88, 190, 300n14
Wilkes, Charles, 37
Willard, Emma, 44–45
Williams, George, 114, 135
Wilson, Henry, 110
Wilson, Henry Lane, 175, 180
Wilson administration, 201, 241
Wilson, Woodrow, 158, 172, 190, 194, 206, 210, 220, 227, 245, 298n106

Winnebago 35, 49, 53, 59
Wirt, William, 251n34, 256n1, 265n101
Wisconsin, 53, 59, 232–33
women: employment in government, 31; equality of, 107; equal pay, 105; suffrage, 32, 102, 166
Worcester, Dean Conant, 30
workers' compensation, 169, 218–19

World Trade Organization (WTO), 203
Wright, Luke Edward, 30

Yale Law School, 28, 32
Yale University, 28, 32
Yankee Leviathan (Bensel), 211
Yellowstone Park Act (1872), 105, 226–27
Young King, 50

Miller Center Studies on the Presidency

Mourning the Presidents: Loss and Legacy in American Culture
Lindsay M. Chervinsky and Matthew R. Costello, editors

The Peaceful Transfer of Power: An Oral History of America's Presidential Transitions
David Marchick and Alexander Tippett, with A. J. Wilson

Averting Doomsday: Arms Control during the Nixon Presidency
Patrick J. Garrity and Erin R. Mahan

The Presidency: Facing Constitutional Crossroads
Michael Nelson and Barbara A. Perry, editors

Trump: The First Two Years
Michael Nelson

Broken Government: Bridging the Partisan Divide
William J. Antholis and Larry J. Sabato, editors

Race: The American Cauldron
Douglas A. Blackmon, editor

Communication: Getting the Message Across
Nicole Hemmer, editor

American Dreams: Opportunity and Upward Mobility
Guian McKee and Cristina Lopez-Gottardi Chao, editors

Immigration: Struggling over Borders
Sidney M. Milkis and David Leblang, editors

Crucible: The President's First Year
Michael Nelson, Jeffrey L. Chidester, and Stefanie Georgakis Abbott, editors

The Dangerous First Year: National Security at the Start of a New Presidency
William I. Hitchcock and Melvyn P. Leffler, editors

The War Bells Have Rung: The LBJ Tapes and the Americanization of the Vietnam War
George C. Herring

www.ingramcontent.com/pod-product-compliance
Lightning Source LLC
Chambersburg PA
CBHW021149230426
43667CB00006B/315